The Unmaking of a Mayor

The Unmaking
of a Mayor

William F. Buckley, Jr.

ARLINGTON HOUSE·PUBLISHERS
NEW ROCHELLE, NEW YORK

First published in 1966 by The Viking Press, Inc.
625 Madison Avenue, New York, N.Y. 10022

Published simultaneously in Canada by
The Macmillan Company of Canada Limited

Library of Congress catalog card number: 66-20339
Printed in U.S.A.

Grateful acknowledgment is made to Atheneum Publishers for permission
to quote from *The Making of the President, 1964* by Theodore H. White,
Copyright © 1965 by Theodore H. White, and to The M.I.T. Press for
permission to quote from *Beyond the Melting Pot* by Nathan Glazer and
Daniel P. Moynihan, Copyright © 1963 by The Massachusetts Institute
of Technology and the President and Fellows of Harvard College.

Second printing February 1967
Reprinted 1977

Library of Congress Cataloging in Publication Data

Buckley, William Frank, 1925–
    The unmaking of a mayor.

    Reprint of the 1967 issue of the ed. published by Viking
Press, New York.
    Includes bibliographical references and index.
    1. New York (City)—Politics and government—1951–
2. Lindsay, John Vilet.   I. Title.
[F128.52.B8 1977]   329'.023'747104   77–3295
ISBN 0–87000–391–7

Acknowledgments

I wish to thank, for their incalculable aid in helping to prepare the manuscript and arrange the material, and for their indomitable patience and amiability, Agatha Schmidt and David Stuhr. I am also grateful to my old friend Alan Williams of Viking for making such shrewd and helpful suggestions. To Mrs. Mabel Wood, my colleague and friend of long standing, for proofreading the galleys. And to James Buckley, Harry Elmlark, Neal Freeman, Marvin Liebman, and Carl Wohlenberg, for taking the time from their busy schedules to read the book in manuscript. I scarcely need to say that if I had taken all their suggestions, this would have been a better book.

—W. F. B., JR.

NEW YORK CITY, MAY 1, 1966

Contents

Illustrations following page 150.

The Unmaking of a Mayor

Prologue

(A self-interview, delivered before the
National Press Club, Washington, D.C., August 4, 1965)

Q. Mr. Buckley, why are you running for Mayor of New York?

A. Because nobody else is who matters.

Q. What do you mean, "who matters"?

A. Who matters to New York. New York is a city in crisis, and all the candidates agree it is a city in crisis. But no other candidate proposes to do anything about that crisis.

Q. What is it that distinguishes you from these other candidates? Why should only great big brave you consent to run on a program that would really liberate New York, while the other candidates do not?

A. Because the other candidates feel they cannot cope with the legacy of New York politics. That legacy requires the satisfaction of voting blocs, with special attention given to the voting bloc or blocs most fractious at any given election period. But to satisfy voting blocs increasingly requires dissatisfying the constituent members of those same voting blocs in their private capacities. However, since it is more dangerous to dissatisfy organized blocs of voters than individual voters—even if they happen to be members of voting blocs—political candidates in New York address their appeals to the bloc rather than to the individual.

Q. Would you mind being specific?

A. As far as New York politicians are concerned, a New Yorker is an Irishman, an Italian, or a Negro; he is a union member or a white collar worker; a welfare recipient or a city employee; a Catholic or a Protestant or a Jew; a taxi driver or a taxi owner; a merchant or a policeman. The problem is to weigh the voting strength of all the categories and formulate a program that least dissatisfies the least crowded and least powerful categories: and

3

the victory is supposed to go to the most successful bloc Bentha-
mite in the race.

Q. What's the matter with that?

A. What is the matter with it is that New York is reaching the point
where it faces the marginal disutility of bloc satisfaction. The race
to satisfy the bloc finally ends in dissatisfying even the individual
members of that same bloc. If, for instance, you give taxi owners
the right to limit the number of taxis available in the city, people
who need taxis to get from where they are to where they want to
go can't find taxis when they most want them. If you allow truck
drivers to double-park because it is convenient to them and to the
merchants whose goods they are unloading, traffic is snarled and
taxi drivers can't move fast enough to make a decent living. When
the traffic is snarled, people stay away from the city and the merchants lose money. If the merchants lose money they want to
automate in order to save costs. If the unions don't let them automate they leave the city. When they leave the city there are fewer
people to pay taxes to city officials and to the unemployed. (The
unemployed aren't allowed to drive taxis because the taxi owners
share a monopoly.) Taxes have to go up because there are fewer
people to pay taxes. The unemployed grow restless, and breed
children and crime. The children drop out of school because there
isn't anyone at home to tell them to go to school. Some of the
children who go to school make school life intolerable for other
children in school, and they leave and go to private schools. The
teachers are told they mustn't discourage the schoolchildren or
they will leave the schools and commit crime and unemployment.
The unions don't want the unemployed hired because they will
work for less money, or because they are Negroes and Puerto
Ricans and obviously can't lay bricks or wire buildings like white
people can, so they are supposed to go off somewhere and just
live, and stay out of the way. But they can't live except in houses,
and houses are built by plumbers and electricians who get eight,
ten, twelve dollars an hour, which means that people can't afford
to buy houses, or rent apartments, at rates the city can afford to
pay its unemployed, so the federal government has to build
housing projects. But there aren't enough housing projects, so
there is overcrowding, and family life disintegrates. Some people
turn to crime, others to ideology. You can't walk from one end of
New York to another without standing a good chance of losing
your wallet, your maidenhead, or your life; or without being told
that white people are bigoted, that Negroes are shiftless, that free
enterprise is the enemy of the working class, that Norman Thomas

has betrayed socialism, and that the only thing that will save New York is for the whole of the United States to become like New York.

Q. What would you do, if you became Mayor of New York?

A. I would treat people as individuals. By depriving the voting blocs of their corporate advantages, I would liberate individual members of those voting blocs.

Q. What would the individual stand to gain, if you were Mayor of New York?

A. (1) The security of life and limb; (2) an opportunity to find gainful employment without the artificial hindrances now imposed by monopoly labor unions and certain minimum wage laws; (3) the hope of finding decent living quarters without paying profits to land speculators or oligopolistic construction companies; (4) the opportunity to be educated without weekly litmus tests administered by an Interracial Commissioner to determine whether the composite color of every school is exactly the right shade of brown; and (5) the internal composure that comes from knowing that there are rational limits to politics, and that one tends to be better off where government is devoted to dismantling, rather than establishing, artificial privileges of the kind New York has been establishing for years, following the lead of Washington, D.C.

Q. What does Washington, D.C., have to do with this?

A. Many of the reforms that New York needs New York cannot effect unless Washington grants it the authority to proceed. For instance, New York can't guarantee newspaper service or shipping service to New Yorkers unless national legislation is passed which would permit the prosecution of union monopoly practices in restraint of trade. New York can't finance its own reforms so long as the money it needs to effect them drains down to Washington to be spent in watering the *caliche* country surrounding the Pedernales River. New York can't do anything about the structural unemployment problem unless the minimum wage laws are eased— that kind of thing.

Q. Why didn't you run in the Republican primary?

A. Why didn't Martin Luther King run for Governor of Alabama?

Q. For one thing, he isn't a resident of Alabama.

A. That could be arranged.

Q. Are you comparing yourself with Martin Luther King?

A. No.

Q. Why haven't you availed yourself of the two-party system in New York and fought your fight with John Lindsay in the primaries?

A. Because if I had entered the Republican primary and lost to John Lindsay I'd have felt obliged to support him in the election. Party loyalty demands that sort of thing. Since I could not in good conscience have endorsed Mr. Lindsay, I could not in good conscience have accepted the implicit discipline of a Primary contest. To avoid this dilemma, I am running as a Republican but on the Conservative ticket, whose platform is wholly congruent with the Republican National Platform of 1964.

Q. If the Republican Party in New York City is oriented toward Democratic principles, then isn't that because New York Republicans wish it to be so, and don't New York Republicans have the right to shape the character of their own Party?

A. (1) John Lindsay got 135,000 votes in New York in 1964, having repudiated the national candidacy of Barry Goldwater. (2) Barry Goldwater, in 1964, got 800,000 votes in New York City. Granted that Lindsay ran only in a single Congressional District. But grant, also, that he won a lot of Democratic votes. If there are 800,000 people in New York City willing to vote for Barry Goldwater, you have to assume that the Republican Party, understood as a party reflecting an alternative view of government to that of the Democratic Party, isn't dead in New York. The question, then, is whether the Republican Party should have tried, by evangelizing the Republican faith, to double that 800,000 votes, sufficient to win an election, or do as John Lindsay is doing, which is to unsex the Republican Party and flit off with the Democratic majority—which effort would ultimately convince the voters that the Republican Party, as commonly understood, offers no genuine alternative.

Q. Isn't John Lindsay engaged in revitalizing the Republican Party?

A. No, he is engaged in devitalizing the Republican Party. A party thrives on its distinctiveness. John Lindsay's decision, made years ago, to bestow himself upon the nation as a Republican rather than as a Democrat was clearly based on personal convenience rather than on a respect for the two-party system, let alone a respect for the Republican alternative. The two-party system, if it is meaningful, presupposes an adversary relationship between the parties. John Lindsay's voting record, and his general political pronouncements, put him left of the center of the Democratic Party. As such he is an embarrassment to the two-party system.

Q. Does the Conservative Party's position in New York bear on the struggle for power within the Republican National Committee?

A. It appears to me obvious that it does. Mr. Bliss, understandably hungry for any victory by anyone who, off the record, concedes a formal affiliation with the Republican Party, has shown enthusiasm for Mr. Lindsay's campaign. That enthusiasm is not shared by an important wing of the Party, probably the dominant wing of the Party, some of whose spokesmen have directly encouraged me to run for office and thereby uphold nationally authorized Republican principles.

Q. Granted John Lindsay is running for Mayor of New York alongside a Democrat and a Liberal. He has said that the problems of New York require a fusion approach. What do you think of that?

A. It is a relief when John Lindsay rises from banality, if only to arrive at fatuity. In this case—it was on *Meet the Press,* I remember—he rose to the occasion. If Gracie Mansion ought to be above factionalism, why not also the White House? And anyway, fusion in behalf of what? ·Who can predict what would be the differences, in the life of New York, if Lindsay were to become Mayor, or Mr. Screvane, or Beame, or O'Dwyer, or Ryan? By soliciting the endorsement of the Liberal Party and the companionship of Milton Mollen, Mr. Lindsay has promised New York only a single thing: that, if elected, not the most sensitive seismograph in the country will detect the slightest interruption in the disintegration of New York City.

Q. Are you saying it makes no difference whether Lindsay or a Democrat wins in New York?

A. I am saying it makes no difference to New Yorkers at large. It makes a lot of difference to John Lindsay, and his entourage, and to Mr. Screvane, or Mr. Beame, and theirs. And it makes a lot of difference to people outside New York, both Democrats and Republicans.

Q. Oh?

A. Democrats around the country, if we are to believe Democratic dogma, believe in the two-party system. The two-party system would be damaged by the election to a very prominent position of an ambitious gentleman whose policies are left-Democratic but whose affiliation is Republican. As far as Republicans are concerned, out over the country, they may very well not care at all what kind of government New York gets. But they should care very much if a Republican running in New York, who refused to support the Republican presidential candidate, now gladly supports New York socialists and is supported by them, hoping to graduate into eminence in the national Republican Party. There was weeping and gnashing of teeth only a year ago among the Democrats when George Wallace piled up huge votes in Democratic primaries in Wisconsin, Indiana, and Maryland. Shouldn't Republicans also worry about interlopers?

Q. Then you believe that your primary duty is to beat Lindsay?

A. Stop putting words into my mouth. My primary ambition is to breathe a little hope into New York, for the benefit of those who want to escape some of the dilemmas group politics has imposed on us. And to breed a little fear in the political nabobs who believe they can fool all the people all the time.

Q. What does Barry Goldwater think of all this?

A. Ask him. But I can tell you what it is reasonable that he should think. It is reasonable that he should think it time that responsible elements in New York City organize to liberate New York from the one-party system.

Q. Have you heard from Senator Goldwater directly?

A. Yes.

Q. What did he say?

A. He said watch out for prying reporters.

I.

A Preliminary Experience

I suppose a controversialist reaches the point, or goes mad, where he simply ignores criticism that is genuinely unjust. I have learned, but incompletely. Give the benefit of every doubt to the critic; but what do you do—*should* you do?—*can* you do?—when there aren't any doubts that he is factually incorrect? The orderly stages of re-dress are (a) a letter to the misrepresenter; (b) a letter (where relevant) to his editor; and (c) a lawsuit. Almost immediately after my first book (about Yale) was published, circumstances forced me to meditate on the textbook recourses. In those days I felt a fierce indignation whenever I ran across what I deemed not merely unfair criticism but positively indefensible criticism—*i.e.*, of the kind that misstated the facts, or that gratuitously advanced nonexistent motives. (I knew less than I do now about perspectives of controversy.) In the first category I remember an exchange in the *Atlantic* with McGeorge Bundy, who flatly misstated (no doubt innocently) a set of facts integral to my analysis concerning which it happened that I was, very simply, correct. We slugged out an exchange in the *Atlantic*, from which I came to know, for the first time, how horribly incon-clusive such exchanges are and learned something about the necessity of being fatalistic (some would say cynical)[1] about the chances of

---

1. I remember, as a very young (nineteen) second lieutenant in the army, being approached for advice by a private in his early thirties who told me his wife was in Reno suing him for divorce, which he was quite prepared to give her, but that he wondered whether her affidavit, to which he had been asked to acquiesce, charging him with afflicting extreme mental cruelty upon her, wouldn't forever stigmatize him—unfairly, inasmuch as it simply wasn't true. I counseled him, from the depths of my experience, never ever to yield, not under any circum-stances to sign any such waiver. That evening I mentioned the episode to my uncle, a retired lawyer of bellicose personal rectitude, who gently informed me that my advice had been mistaken, that the adversary rhetoric of divorce pro-

9

historical justification. For one thing, one is not history, and history doesn't care very much about one. For another, history is highly tendentious. For another, it is simply more than one can as a practical matter hope to do, to retain the interest, or to capture the attention, of the truth-minded concerning the rectification of factual inaccuracies which do not bear on the movements of the sun or the planets. I was greatly intrigued, when I first saw Simone Weil's essay *The Need for Roots*, by her fervent, ingenuous statement that the service of the truth is everything—so much so, she said, that she would support a universal law to punish historical libel, such a law as would, for instance, have had the effect of putting Etienne Gilson in jail for writing that there had been no substantial opposition in Attica to the institution of slavery—*how could he know?* she asked indignantly.

Nobody—happy days—is going to put Etienne Gilson in jail for deductive slanders against the Greeks; to say nothing of McGeorge Bundy for explicit slanders against me. What to do—assuming one cares? Mr. George Sokolsky, the late and volatile columnist, told me on one occasion that in 1935, after a series of psychologically ruinous encounters with his critics, he instructed his secretary never ever again to permit him to see a single newspaper, magazine, or letter which contained material in it unreasonably critical of himself. Sometimes, he chuckled, his directive resulted in a deskload of correspondence that looked like a pile of those indiscreet letters written by GIs to their sweethearts during the Second War, with gaping holes cut out by the censor's scissors. But the arrangement secured Sokolsky's serenity, and that is worth something, one supposes.

Indeed, I see Mr. Sokolsky's point. However, pending the day when I adopt his recourse, I find it continuingly relevant, in a book on contemporary politics, to attempt to controvert controvertible misrepresentations, not so much because I hunger after retroactive vindications (though they are always satisfying) but because it is generally interesting, or ought to be, to know the extent to which that kind of thing does in fact go on in matters in which the public is concerned, and especially interesting to inquire (a) what is the current appetite for pursuing the facts in a controversy; (b) whether that appetite is stimulated by pressures that are inner- or other-directed; or, if a little of both, in what balance; (c) what kinds of pressure are routinely brought to effect clarification; and whether they tend to be efficacious or not; and (d) what is the fallout of a

---

ceedings meant nothing, absolutely nothing at all. I was shattered, and only wish that, in my disillusion, I had, while I was at it, asked him about the adversary language of nonmarital polemics.

lackadaisical concern for the truth on the morale and the potency of the general will and on the practice of democracy.

I had an experience a couple of months before the beginning of the New York campaign from which I learned a great deal and should have learned a great deal more. I learned at first hand something about how politicians react to certain kinds of provocations; something about the inflammatory leverage of even a single newspaper; and a great deal about the general journalistic indifference that immediately descends on the discovery that, after all, there wasn't any scandal there at all, and never mind the incidental victims of the flurry.

Once a year, in New York City, Catholic policemen gather, under the auspices of the Holy Name Society, at a Communion breakfast. The affair habitually brings together more policemen than any other occasion of the year—about 6000 of them (roughly a quarter of the total force). I was invited to address the policemen at the breakfast of 1965.

The next day all hell broke loose. Newsworthy New Yorkers were suddenly demanding that Mayor Wagner, who had been present at the breakfast, rebuke the police force—"for cheering Buckley on Sunday" (I quote Roy Wilkins)—and that the Police Commissioner, Michael Murphy, resign—"for permitting a rabble-rousing right-wing extremist . . . to address the breakfast" (I. D. Robbins, president of the City Club, and a candidate for anybody's nomination for Mayor).

There had been three reporters at the affair, one of whom, representing the New York *Herald Tribune*, decided to play up my address as a major story. *The New York Times'* reporter was also there, and he filed a substantial, though by no means sensational, report which, reduced, occupied a routine paragraph or two in the early-bird City Edition. The night editor of the *Times*, spotting the sensational spread in the rival *Tribune*, was alarmed at the prospect of missing a big story and thereupon escalated the original version for the later and definitive editions of the *Times*, leaning in part on the notes that had been left by the *Times* reporter (who had left the building and was unavailable), in part on the *Tribune* account. The *Times* headline: "BUCKLEY PRAISES POLICE OF SELMA/HAILED BY 5,600 POLICE HERE AS HE CITES 'RESTRAINT.' " The stories, appearing on Monday morning (April 6), created a first-rate uproar, and members of the political celebrity register lined up to record their denunciations. In the afternoon a *Times* reporter called me for a statement. I wrote out and telephoned back one hundred and fifty words, of which the *Times* published, the next morning, about one hundred, omitting two passages I would not myself have omitted if I had been invited to edit my own statement.[2]

To my astonishment, by Tuesday morning the uproar, far from abating, increased. "PROTESTS POUR IN ON BUCKLEY SPEECH" (New York *World-Telegram*). ". . . The protests continued to pour in today —from the NAACP, CORE and a State Supreme Court Justice—deploring the inaction of Mayor Wagner and Police Commissioner Murphy in the face of William Buckley's blast at civil rights demonstrators before an audience of 6,000 City policemen" (New York *Post*). ". . . Large disquieting issues are stirred by the ovation some 6,000 New York policemen accorded a defense of the Selma police force—and an attack on Martin Luther King—delivered by William Buckley, Jr., the noted thunderer of right-wing extremism. . . . The ordeals of police service in these times in no way justify the salvos of applause that greeted the impassioned apologia for the Selma possemen recited by Buckley [in his] spirited whitewash of Southern police terrorism" (New York *Post,* editorial).

Could it be that my talk had been recorded? I telephoned the good monsignor in charge of the breakfast, and indeed a tape existed; and the press assembled at noon to hear it. The paramount question, curiously, was less what I had said, than how the audience had responded. Was the *Tribune* correct in reporting that the police had laughed—and applauded—when I alluded to the death of Mrs. Viola Liuzzo, the Detroit housewife who, one month earlier, had gone to Selma to join the demonstrators—and got killed. The roomful of reporters listened intently to the tape as it unwound. And then, a paragraph or two before the critical moment, the tape suddenly and mysteriously stopped. Neal Freeman, of the staff of *National Review*, bent over the recorder to find that the tape, having first stuck in the external pressure pads, was twined all over the entrails of the machine. We waited nervously while he fiddled with it. I could not escape the growing sense of skepticism in the crowded room. Had the critical few feet of tape—recording the policemen's misbehavior in response to my own—been intentionally wiped out? Five, ten minutes went by while Freeman—and I—sweated. Finally a technician with

2. The statement I wrote was as follows. The italicized passages were omitted: "I am shocked in turn at the ease with which a routine job of misrepresentation by the press of a public speech can cause distinguished public figures to believe the unbelievable, namely that *at a Communion Breakfast sponsored by the Holy Name Society of the Catholic Church,* bigotry was applauded. *I did not on the occasion in question breathe a word of prejudice against any people.* I spoke sympathetically of the plight of the Negroes in the South. I deplored the violence in the South and the attitude of lackadaisical white Southerners towards it. I did criticize the general tendency of some of the noisiest elements in our public life to jump to false and contumacious conclusions about policemen. *The trigger-willingness, shown today, to impute to the police a sympathy with bigotry is exactly the kind of thing I had in mind.*"

one of the television crews volunteered his services. In a few minutes, the tape was going again. Sure enough, a half-minute or so of the speech had been—irretrievably—destroyed. But it was before the critical passage. The voice resumed:

. . . Mrs. Liuzzo of Detroit went down to Alabama to protest conditions there [I was saying], conditions of injustice to Negroes and a general, lawless disregard of their rights and honor. It was generally conceded—most specifically conceded by the Governor of Alabama—that anyone arriving in Alabama to protest the existing order under the glare of national klieg lights, precisely needed protection against the almost certain recourse to violence of the unrestrained members of almost every society, who are disposed to go to criminal lengths to express their resentment. That, after all, is why the President mobilized the National Guard of Alabama—at the Governor's urging. So the lady drove down a stretch of lonely road in the dead of night, ignoring the protection that had been given her, sharing the front seat with a young Negro identified with the protesting movement; and got killed. [*Pause, and, from the audience, a dead silence.*] Why, one wonders, was this a story that occupied the front pages from one end of the country to another, if newspapers are concerned with the unusual, the unexpected? Didn't the killing merely confirm precisely what everyone has been saying about certain elements of the South? About the intensity of its feelings? About the disposition of some of its members to resort to violence in order to maintain the status quo? Who could have been surprised by this ghastly episode? Not Governor Wallace—who had precisely called on the Federal Government to provide protection for the demonstrators. Not, surely, *The New York Times,* which has told us for years that in the South lawlessness is practiced.

There was, again, not a sound from the audience, as I went on to state my thesis.[3] ("Laughter and more applause"—Tuesday's New York *Post* had already reached the stands—"greeted Buckley's query, 'Didn't the killing confirm what some elements in the South said would happen?'" And, again the New York *Post*: "The cheers were even louder when Buckley criticized Mrs. Viola Gregg Liuzzo, the slain Detroit mother of five, for going to the march on Montgomery. . . .")

And, on the matter of my alleged praise of the "restraint" of the Selma police, again the tape rolled on:

3. The point I was trying to make, concerning which a reference to the treatment by the press of Mrs. Liuzzo's murder (in contrast with its treatment of another category of crimes) was relevant, is irrelevant to this narrative. But for the convenience of those who wonder about the context of the controversial remarks, the entire (short) address is reprinted in Appendix A to this book, together with indications of audience reaction.

Four weeks ago at Selma, Alabama, the conscience of the world was aroused at the sight of policemen swinging their sticks with purpose on the bodies of demonstrators who had set out to march to Montgomery, Alabama. The television cameras did not show— how indeed could they have done so?—the most dramatic part of the sequence. Dr. King and the demonstrators had crossed the bridge and there the policemen, acting under orders—whether ill-advised or not is most precisely not the business of policemen, who are not lawmakers or governors but agents of the lawmakers and governors—there the policemen informed them that they might not proceed. The next thing the American viewer saw was a flurry of night sticks and the pursuit of the screaming demonstrators back across the bridge into the streets of Selma. What the viewer did not see was a period of time, twenty long minutes, 1200 seconds,[4] freighted with tension, when the two camps stood facing each other, between the moment the sheriff told the demonstrators to return, which order the demonstrators refused by standing there in defiance of it, until the moment when the human cordite was touched—who threw the lighted match? We do not know—and the policemen moved, excitedly, humanly, forward: excessively, yes, and their excesses on that day have been rightly criticized, but were ever the excesses criticized of those who provoked them beyond the endurance that we tend to think of as human?

Again, the tape registered a dead silence from the audience. ("He said the demonstrators 'refused the order' not to march in defiance. And the cameras showed only the beatings, 'nothing of policemen's restraint' in the face of orders defied. The Hilton's Grand Ballroom rocked with applause, as Mr. Buckley smiled out at the crowd," reported the *Tribune*, April 5).

A week or two later Mr. John Leo, an associate editor of *Commonweal*, undertook, in the context, I hasten to say, of his own emphatic disapproval of my speech, a close textual analysis of the original report in the *Tribune*:

> Mr. Buckley's recent speech to Catholic policemen in New York City, dealing with police comportment in and around Selma, was objectionable enough on its face. But the reporter who spread the word [in] the *Tribune* was not content with his minor role in this little ritual. He apparently thought it was up to him to make a blood sacrifice of Mr. Buckley. According to good form, this is usually performed later by indignant editorial writers.
>
> In his *Tribune* story, [the reporter] offered 26 quotes from the

4. Although it never became a part of the controversy, I was factually incorrect here. I myself subsequently ascertained that the "twenty minutes" I had been told about by someone who misinterpreted a television comment on the day of the riots was more like three or four minutes.

Buckley speech, most of them quite short. Nineteen of them were misquotations. Of the seven he got right, at least two were used unfairly. The ones he got absolutely straight, and used fairly (here presented in their entirety) were "10 days later," "acting under orders," "they might not proceed," "you must stand mutely," and "the Governor of Alabama." Lest the reader think [the reporter] is particularly astute in handling quotes of four words or less, it should be pointed out that he flubbed six in this category.

Partial quotes, or quotes of less than a sentence, are themselves a debatable journalistic practice. Most papers use them sparingly; *The New York Times* won't allow them at all. But it is safe to say that someone who offers us a whole story full of partial quotes is an amateur. Someone who gets four-fifths of them wrong is more than an amateur. He is a menace.

For instance, Mr. Buckley did not defend the actions of the police in Selma. In a phrase unreported by the *Tribune* he said clearly that they were guilty of excesses. All he asked was whether we are sure that some of the fury of the Selma police might not have been due to provocation under pressure. My own sympathy for Alabama law enforcement is not high, but Mr. Buckley's question is worth considering. A friend of mine who was on the scene told of one excited Negro who kept dancing within inches of a policeman and taunting him to try clubbing him over the head.

I think Mr. Buckley's speech, on the whole, was quite objectionable, both in thought and rhetoric. But there is no doubt that he has been treated rather shabbily, first by being subjected to a Pavlovian liberal response on the part of New York papers and pressure groups, few of which seem to have troubled themselves to discover what he actually said, and secondly, by the disinclination of the *Tribune* to apologize for a wretched story⁵ (*The National Catholic Reporter*, May 12, 1965).

I expected remedial action at three levels. First from the press. Second from public figures who had been misled by the press. Thirdly, from Mayor Wagner, whose protracted silence dumfounded me.

1. *The Press*

The New York Times' story the next day devoted not a single word to the discrepancies between the tape and the *Tribune's*—and its own —original stories.

5. As a matter of record, I should note that the vilification that continued to come in from all corners of the country, based on the *Tribune's* story and subsequent aggrandizements on the theme, prompted me, finally, to file a lawsuit for libel. The *Tribune* thereupon agreed (July 7) to reprint Leo's article preceded by what amounted to the publisher's apology ("The *Herald Tribune* regrets that erroneous conclusions arose from the report . . .."). It was reassuring to ascertain that right, plus a good lawyer, can sometimes stimulate the dormant conscience.

The *Tribune* went this far in its story: "The tape recordings did not register any applause at a point where Mr. Buckley spoke of restraint by Selma police before they charged into the crowd of civil-rights people. However, [the] *Tribune* reporter who wrote the story said there was applause in the vicinity of his table in front of the dais that apparently was not picked up by the microphone." This is the same applause that, the reporter in question had written, "rocked the Hilton's Grand Ballroom."

2. *The Public Figures*

I sent a telegram to James Wechsler, chief editorial writer for the New York *Post*. I was especially cross with him because, I reasoned, he was both a professional newspaperman and an acquaintance, and should therefore have approached the *Tribune* story with skepticism: "I ASSUME YOU WILL APOLOGIZE IN TOMORROW'S EDITIONS."

To which he replied in an editorial (April 8) entitled "We Herewith Extend a Non-Apology": "William F. Buckley, Jr., has addressed an imperious telegram . . . demanding an apology. His eagerness to keep his name in the papers is understandable. [Note the implicit premise: rather than that one's name should reappear in a newspaper, one should acquiesce in a published distortion of one's views.] . . . There will of course be no apology here. . . . [Our] editorial was seemingly [*sic*] inaccurate only in stating that the police specifically applauded Buckley's defense [*sic*] of the possemen in Selma. The tape does not confirm that. But the laughter and applause scattered throughout the speech and the ovation at the end surely confirm the sympathy of the audience with the doctrine [*sic*] Buckley was expounding."

To Roy Wilkins, executive director of the National Association for the Advancement of Colored People, I wired: "I trust you will publicly withdraw your criticisms of the Mayor and of myself.after reading my speech, which is on its way to you by messenger. If there is a sentence in it with which you disagree, I should be greatly surprised. I believe you yourself if you had been present would have applauded my remarks."

Eight days later I had no direct reply; so I wrote again:

April 14, 1965

Dear Mr. Wilkins:

I have not had an acknowledgment of my telegram to you, sent on the 6th of April, asking you to read my speech and then reconsider your criticisms of it. However, last Sunday's *New York Times* quotes "a spokesman for Roy Wilkins" as saying that you have read the speech and nevertheless do not withdraw your charges. Would you be so good as (a) to confirm whether or not this statement is true; and (b) if it is, would you be so kind as to indicate what passages in the speech justified the criticisms you made public?

Mr. Wilkins finally responded:

April 19, 1965

Dear Mr. Buckley:

It was thoughtful of you to send me a full copy of your speech of April 4, 1965, to the Holy Name Society breakfast of the New York Police Department and I appreciated having the complete text before me. Only a murderous schedule which left me free only over the Easter weekend has delayed my written thanks until this late date.

I am afraid that from my particular point of vantage and of special interest I see more cause for alarm in the complete text than I could possibly see in the disputed frequency and exact location of the applause which greeted portions of the speech.

Enclosed is a reproduction of a column of comment I wrote for the New York *Amsterdam News* hard on deadline time. This fact plus the format of the column and its word limit precluded a full analysis.

I have never been one to discount your talents in putting an idea on paper and in employing, in the majority of cases, precisely the language required to evoke the response you seek, despite my disagreement with many of your theses.

In the Holy Name speech you were near your conservative best, and as excellent, ironically (to you), as is the Rev. Dr. Martin Luther King, Jr., in some of his expositions.

The underlying theme that the wrong-doers are now top-dog and the defenders of law and order are forced to defend themselves, their faith and their deeds, while a popular one bolstered by many an appeal to unthinking emotion, is not tenable. Equating silent, orderly immobility, rooted in the certainty of the validity of the right of protest, with active anti-social acts such as robbery, assault and overt disorderly conduct is no service to the problem facing the Negro minority, the police and the nation.

This reasoning and its accompanying oratory serve the cause, not of conservatism, but of repression and retrogression. It is yet another stand of the Haves against the increasingly frequent and increasingly diversified sallies of the Have Nots. When the latter are of a different color the exhortations against change are even more effective than exhortations against dat ole debbil Communism.

Thank you again for sending me the text.

Very sincerely yours,
Roy Wilkins
Executive Director

All very interesting. But here is what Roy Wilkins had been quoted in the press as telegraphing Mr. Wagner: "approval . . . by New York City police of speech by William F. Buckley, Jr., who condemned peaceful demonstrators and praised the tear gas and club attacks on them by Selma police demands rebuke by you" (*Tribune*, April 6).

Jackie Robinson, the former baseball player and now banker and polemicist-about-town, had been quoted by the newspapers as saying: ". . . the Mayor's failure to respond to the attack on the civil rights movement constitutes a tremendous injustice to what is going on. . . . [The Mayor should] launch an immediate inquiry into the number of policemen in New York who belong to the John Birch Society" (*World-Telegram*, April 5). It was especially piquant, under the circumstances, to receive from him, hard on the heels of his statement, a telegraphed invitation to appear on his new television program:

> Dear Sir:
> Your statements before the Holy Name Society as reported in today's New York *Herald Tribune* upholding the gestapo-like troops of little Governor Wallace are not surprising considering the kind of philosophy that you have constantly projected. It's my belief that this philosophy poses a distinct threat to our democracy. On April 25 I begin a television show on the new UHF Channel 47. I challenge you to appear with me on that date to debate the position which you have taken and request that you have your representative contact my producer, Alfred Duckett, at LO 3-7154 to set up ground rules and arrangements.
>
> > Sincerely yours,
> > Jackie Robinson

I replied: "I shall not appear on your program until you have publicly apologized to me and to the police for your misrepresentations."

Whereupon, the following day from Mr. Robinson:

> If, as you claim, there are misrepresentations, are you again accusing the press of misquoting you, as you constantly said they misquoted Goldwater? You state you will not appear on my program "until I publicly apologize." As you probably very well know, this means you do not ever expect to appear on the program.

I tried, to be sure exasperatedly, one more time:

> Dear Mr. Robinson:
> Why don't you stop moralizing long enough to *read* my speech— or have it read to you—and *then* conclude whether or not I was misrepresented?

To which a reply which I leave it to the cryptographers to decipher, and reproduce here only to stress one of the points of this excursion, namely the difficulty—for reasons I shall be touching on—of persuading any living human being to rue, publicly or even privately, a misrepresentation to which he has become committed:

Dear Mr. Buckley:
I would like very much to see your position, you were as eloquent as ever in defending that position on Bary Farbus' [sic] program. I find it most difficult to change, for all I said, I expect this from William Buckley. Your attitude regarding Mrs. Liuzzo, is most disturbing. I read in it that her having a Negro on the front seat is a provocation that you understand. Your speech as I see it is cleverly written to appeal to all the prejudices that were just below the surface in the last [Goldwater] campaign. I will digest it further and give you a more detailed personal analysis later. [I still await it.] However Mr. Buckley, I find it most interesting that Mayor Wagner publicly repudiated your speech.

I felt more optimistic about getting justice from Judge Samuel F. Hofstadter of the Supreme Court of New York City.

I wired him: "I regret that the misrepresentations of a press story caused you to reach most injudicious conclusions about what I said. Far from condoning police excesses in Selma I criticized them, praising only the restraint that preceded the violence. A copy of my full text is on its way to you by messenger. I am confident that you will agree with every line in it and would yourself have applauded it[6] if you had been at the function. I believe you owe the Mayor an apology."

No answer.
I tried again on April 14, in a registered letter.
Whereupon a reply:

Dear Mr. Buckley:
This is to acknowledge your courteous letter. I thought your telegram rather peremptory and its suggestions ill-founded. In any event I could see no useful purpose in prolonging the incident, which I regarded as closed. That seems to be Commissioner Murphy's idea, too. He has not responded to *my* telegram. As one with large experience in public affairs and exchanges, you will recognize this is a not unusual course.
God's supreme gift to man is speech. Its anatomy does not lend itself to such dissection as you now suggest—after the event. Utter-

---

6. This was not merely impudence: Judge Hofstadter has often been quoted as deploring the relative concern for the criminal, rather than the victim, which was the principal focus of my talk.

ance must be heard as well as read whole: in complete context, background and occasion, and in intent and mood—not only of speaker, but audience—for it is not a unilateral episode.

My telegram, [quoted in the press] too, must be read entire, in context. Its essential thrust was protest against silence of city officials at an outbreak by public servants which, as described in the Press, betokened a grave deterioration in community relations.

Perhaps when we chance to meet some time the discussion can be carried forward if you think it helpful.

Faithfully yours,
Samuel H. Hofstadter

Judge Hofstadter's telegram to the Police Commissioner, as quoted in the New York *Post*, April 6, had said: "5600 members of the force cheered an attack on national civil rights leaders that would have done credit to the most rabid race-baiters."

3. Mayor Wagner

Wagner's behavior was a revelation. If an attempt to understand it is based on *a priori* grounds, one is absolutely baffled. Suppose he had said on Monday to the press: "Look, boys, if Buckley had said what he was reported to have said in the way he was reported to have said it—I'd have walked out of the room there and then. Why don't you go get a text of his speech, or listen to the tape recording—and stop bothering me?"

It is very hard for someone outside politics to comprehend why this simple course was not the one he took. It required an act of heroic intellectual discipline to force myself to reason *a posteriori,* from the *fact* of what he did say, on back to the presumptive political wisdom of it. I did not, in the course of the forthcoming campaign, learn anything of more striking methodological significance than that politicians' behavior should, as a general rule, be examined in that way. This is, I believe, to say something more than the truism that that which works, works. It is to ask why it is that that which works, works. The process requires, to begin with, an act of faith—in this instance, that Robert Wagner knows New York and knows politics far better than the little Platonists who, in that crowded room, fussed with the tape recorder, thinking to draw the curtain on absolute truth, and to induce universal agreement on it. Assuming the political competence of Mr. Wagner—which his record enjoins—productive reasoning begins, for the amateur, not with what he *should* have done, but with what he *did;* and what he did was subtly to underwrite the distorted newspaper accounts.

"Why?" is the next question; to which the necessary answer, barring tangential motives of unscientific bearing, is—because to do so made good politics. But why would it make for good politics to endorse the impression that (a) Mayor Wagner permitted himself to sit through a racist and brutal speech without protest, either on the spot or later in the day to the press; (b) the New York City police force is latently sympathetic with the brutality shown under stress by the Selma police force; and (c) the New York police force, or at least the Catholic—*i.e.*, Irish and Italian—members of it, are latently anti-Negro?

Consider, first, the consequences of alternative reactions. Mayor Wagner could not, while I was speaking, very well have got up and left the Ballroom—for several reasons. The first (a) is that his act would have struck the audience, unaware of anything exceptionable in the address itself, as outrageous. The Mayor would have offended not only the police but the surrounding Catholic dignitaries, clerical and nonclerical. (b) So drastic an action would have been, for Mr. Wagner, totally out of style. He is not the kind of man who is given to instant demonstrations. (c) If he had subsequently denounced the speech, he'd have run, in diluted form to be sure, something of the risk of having done (a); the police would have resented his action as an act of demagogy and disloyalty.

He avoided this risk by divulging at a news conference April 6, after great pressure had been put on him for comment, that he disagreed "fundamentally with Mr. Buckley's views," and then with an indirect disavowal of the police: "I cannot control, and should not control the off-duty reaction of any group." What did he accomplish? On one hand, he pleased those who were looking for a disavowal but, accustomed to the guarded nature of the Mayor's political rhetoric, didn't even hope for anything more categorical; on the other hand he seemed somehow to be saying to the police that he would never forsake their right to their own points of view.

But Wagner accomplished more than just this. He sustained a popular demonology. A primary obligation of a successful politician, I meditated, is to cherish and preserve all the reassuring demonologies. Now this is a tricky business, as this episode suggests: because the art, as practiced with the highest finesse, requires the preservation of a demonology but great vagueness concerning the identification of the demons. If Wagner had flatly identified the police as demons, he'd have risked too much by far, counting in not only the policemen's votes, but their admirers'. Sometimes the politician will want to directly identify the demons, in which case the accusations are direct in reference, and unmeeching in tone. Franklin Roosevelt, even while specializing in the construction of coalitions, found it useful directly and provocatively to alienate the Wall Street community, which he hobgoblinized with relish, quite correctly calculating that for every banker's vote he thereby lost, he won a hundred nonbankers'. Dwight Eisenhower rang down his thunder on a class less sharply identified, but nevertheless generally identifiable—the Washington bureaucratic jobholders, those "rascals" who needed "throwing out." And Joe McCarthy inveighed against a group numerically insignificant and one stage further removed from instant identification, the "pro-Communists and the striped-pants diplomats." Suppose that Franklin Roosevelt had announced that Wall Street was finally cleansed, and that therefore there was no longer any need to regard with suspicion the machinations of the big business community. Imagine if General Eisenhower had at some point in his campaign blurted out that, on sober reflection, he had not found enough rascals in Washington to warrant a national effort at uprooting them. Or if Senator McCarthy had announced his conclusion that the fellow travelers were of minor consequence, not worth a supererogatory persecution. The sense of deprivation by the followers of Roosevelt, Eisenhower, and McCarthy would have been acute.

Wagner knew in 1965, even as John Lindsay came to know, that there are imagined evils the dissipation of which is not merely *not* a public duty, but more nearly a public anti-duty. It would have been almost antireligious, it being the living faith of many of Mr. Wagner's followers that the police are racist, to shatter the revelation that the police had finally, *en bloc,* betrayed their anti-Negro prejudices.

It was terribly clear from the visceral reactions of such people as Jackie Robinson that thousands upon thousands of people were taking a very special, even an acute, pleasure, from believing that a sudden flash of light had exposed the lineaments of the wolf—and how especially satisfying that it had been spotted under the ironic auspices of a Communion breakfast of the Holy Name Society! "I hope you have not been leading a double life, pretending to be wicked and being really good all the time," says the character in *The Importance of Being Earnest.* "That would be hypocrisy." In due course I learned that it was emotionally necessary that Mr. Lindsay and, later, poor Mr. Beame, should denounce the conservatives as racists and rabble-rousers and hate merchants. They owed it to their public, even as the minister of religion owes it to his, to enjoin against the wiles of the devil. The devil, I happen to believe, exists. And many people believe that conservatives are basically racist and misanthropic: so never mind, the politician reasons, *whether* the devil exists, take advantage of him. If necessary, give him flesh.

It is always interesting to speculate on whether the care and feeding of hobgoblins is altogether cynical, whether the politicians come to believe their own myths. I can very well imagine Jackie Robinson at a cocktail party asking Wagner, "Why didn't you do something about that vicious, racist address?" How would Wagner—the politician—have responded? I can less easily imagine the question being raised with Wagner by, say, Roy Wilkins; or by Mr. Justice Samuel Hofstadter ("Are you nuts, Sam?" would probably have been the response). There isn't much point in speculating on Wagner's subjective evaluation of a speech the misimpression of which he intentionally ratified. He would not be the first cynic to reach high office, nor his office the highest ever occupied by a cynic, however amiable. I recall an anecdote told me by Mr. Herbert Hoover a few years ago. He began it by saying how good a friend he was of Mr. Harry Truman and how well they had got on together during the period after the Second World War, when Hoover consented to head the commission on the operations of government. Then one day, in October 1948, while Truman was campaigning feverishly for re-election, Hoover picked up the morning paper and read that the evening before, in Boston, Truman had denounced the Republican Party as desiring to reintroduce the age of Hoover, defined as the exploitation of the poor for the benefit of the greedy rich. "I vowed," Hoover told me, "never to speak to Truman again." But when, a few months after his election, Truman asked Hoover to drop in at the White House on an urgent matter, "I couldn't, of course, refuse a summons from the President of the United States. But I was determined to tell him off before we got down to business, and I did: 'Mr. President,' I said, 'the remarks you made about me in Boston were as dirty and unforgivable as any I ever heard in a lifetime of politics.' 'I couldn't agree with you more,' Truman replied affably. 'When I came to that paragraph in my speech, I *almost* didn't read it.' "

Concerning the press, I learned at first hand not only the obvious lesson, that corrections very seldom catch up with distortions, but several other things besides. One of them is that, other than on the obvious occasions, one cannot know when a news story is going to be midwived by an enterprising reporter. I had expected no coverage at all, indeed I had completed the preparation of my talk late the previous night and did not even bother to make arrangements to have it retyped and reproduced. In the unlikely event that a reporter should want a copy, we could easily go off somewhere and Xerox a copy or two direct from my own manuscript—the time would be noon Sunday, and there would be no immediate pressure from deadlines.

No reporter asked for a copy, nor, as a matter of fact, approached me in any way. It had never at that point crossed my mind to enter politics, so that it wasn't a matter of cautionary coverage that brought the press there. The Mayor and the Police Commissioner, after all, were present, and each of them spoke briefly, and just conceivably the Mayor would say something electric—this was to be a campaign year.

As it happened, the affair did turn out to be news. But *I* didn't make the news because of what I had said, nor the policemen because of how they acted: a single reporter made the news. What I said, if it had been literally transcribed in a news story, would I think have been very interesting indeed—obviously one finds one's own analyses interesting: but it would not have been news, it would have been commentary. What I said in that talk I could not myself digest into two paragraphs, so that if a reporter felt the obligation to report on my part in the affair, he'd have done what so often is done, which is merely to take one or two statements from the speech, decide that they should be those that are reproduced, and file the story.

But here a reporter had taken words not quite my own; failed to qualify them as I had qualified them; and—an infinitely adaptable resource at the disposal of any reporter who lacks either skill or conscience—there is the audience. The size, nature, and behavior of an audience are the most malleable factors in a newspaper story, and I saw them shaped time and again during the campaign. One can always produce, in self-defense, a copy of one's speech. But one cannot produce the audience—for instance to establish that it was *not* true that it was rowdy; or that it *was* true that it was rowdy; or that it was *not* true that there wasn't a single Negro in it, or the opposite; or that it wasn't composed primarily of people in their late sixties, or of children in their early teens; to ascertain whether or not someone was carrying a placard suggesting that John Lindsay was a Communist, or whether someone else was there carrying one suggesting that Buckley was a Fascist.

Audience reaction can be ascertained through a tape, but that is a pretty clumsy business. To prove that there was silence requires the use of an extra-literary dimension—the use of the ear; and such awkward and humiliating arrangements as calling in a group of witnesses, and playing back the tape. It is risky at best. For one thing a tape may not have been made; for another, newspapers simply aren't as a general rule interested in workaday historical revisionism. So that the mere process of self-defense against a press which manipulates the audience factor is at worst impossible, at best terribly clumsy. Yet consider, remaining with the present example, the impression that can be conveyed by the journalist's brush:

He said the demonstrators "refused the order" not to march in defiance. And the cameras showed only the beatings, "nothing of policemen's restraint" in the face of orders defied. The Hilton's Grand Ballroom rocked with applause, as Mr. Buckley smiled out at the crowd.

Now the exact words are not mine, nor is the emphasis the emphasis I made; but that much, at least, is correctible by the release of the text, though to be sure only effectively so depending on one's access to those who read the original misrepresentation, and that of course is virtually impossible to achieve. We have seen that by good luck a tape recorder was rolling, and the press did turn out to hear the silence that didn't rock the ballroom at this point in the address. But, finally, how could I prove that I didn't smile out at the crowd? The answer of course is that I couldn't; can't. In fact I *didn't* smile— at a professional level because at that point in my text, in heat after an elusive point, I needed to generate a fierce concentration of the kind that induces an audience to follow closely an intricate analysis. A smile would snap the mood. And, of course, because to have smiled at the moment would have been humanly, aesthetically, and emotionally unthinkable. In tense situations, unmonitored by television, a single reporter has the same power to create an image of his own choosing that a sculptor has sitting in front of a lump of clay.

A week or so after the affair, I appeared before a seminar of the Columbia School of Journalism, and in that bright company speculated on the theme that however you dot your i's or cross your t's, it may in fact be that to bring up a particular subject before a particular audience results in a dialectic whose meaning is a function of time and place. I remembered that a year ago Senator Goldwater had made his famous remark about atomic defoliation of the forests in Vietnam. The reporter had asked what is to be done in South Vietnam about the Communists' supply lines, which move under cover of the forests and the jungles. Goldwater had answered: "There have been several suggestions made. *I don't think we would use any of them.* But the defoliation of the forest by low-yield atomic weapons could well be done. When you remove the foliage you remove the cover." Headlines. New York *Herald Tribune:* "GOLDWATER'S NUCLEAR PLAN TO WIN VIET." *New York Times:* "GOLDWATER URGES NEW VIETNAM AID: WOULD USE ATOMIC WEAPONS TO CLEAR RED SUPPLY LINES." Washington *Post:* "A-ATTACK ON VIET JUNGLE PROPOSED BY GOLDWATER." Chicago *Tribune:* "GOLDWATER PROPOSES ATOMIC FIGHT IN ASIA."

I remember, at the time, calling these extraordinary misrepresentations to the attention of a reporter from *The New York Times,* who expressed himself as outraged, no doubt sincerely, that this should have happened. He went on to track down a sensationalized dispatch from the Associated Press as having been originally at fault.

Before a blue-ribbon jury composed, say, of professors from the Columbia School of Journalism (the seminar was gratifyingly impressed by the experience I related), a Goldwater who had done no more than to speculate on hypothetical means by which to denude North Vietnamese supply lines might hope to be thoroughly exonerated from responsibility for such headlines as reported on what he had allegedly recommended: and the offending reporter or reporters, the wire services, and the newspapers might be fastidiously censured on an inside page in the school's fortnightly bulletin. That kind of justification is, of course, immaterial in politics; moreover, the case might even be made that it is immaterial intellectually, on the grounds that, at least in nonacademic circumstances, political speculation is necessarily framed by the values that contemporary history composes. So that any distinction-making, however interesting or relevant *sub specie aeternitatis,* simply ought not to be attempted in addressing, for instance, six thousand policemen three weeks after the horrors of Selma, Alabama, if the purpose is to point out that the situation in Selma was *complicated.* The audience itself, with the benefit of the full context of the analysis, might very well understand. But there are reporters present, one of whom is likely to assume the position of Defender of the People's Prejudices and construct his story on the basis of a putative irreverence to the people's passions. It may very well be that constant attention needs, in politics, to be given less to the nature of what one has to say than to the nature of the audience before which one speaks it, and the surrounding order of prejudices. If the intellectuals of a community were poised to correct blatant misimpressions, that would be one thing. They aren't. Politically active people must learn this; and those who believe that distinctions are *always* worth making, the more so the more impatient the public mood as regards them, should worry a little more than they apparently do about the difficulty of making such distinctions—other than, say, in the cozy surroundings of a book, or an academic quarterly, or a seminar at Columbia.

The press, I noticed, is not greatly concerned with self-discipline. For reasons perfectly understandable in commercial terms, the press cares about the scandal, much less about subsequent developments tending to dissipate the scandal—less, in a word, about exact history, exactly understood. Exact history, it might be maintained, isn't necessarily what was said at a particular situation, but what subjects were treated, and how the speaker angled in on them, and how the audience reacted to what he said. It remains generally true, I was to find, that politicians tend to say nothing very much, as a general rule, primarily because they desire to say nothing very much. But it is also true that the cautious politician, if he desires to say something hazardous, had better come prepared with tape recorders, stenotypists, and, ideally, motion picture cameramen, trained on himself and on the audience. Even then, there is a risk: Who can be persuaded to come to the grand opening—and closing—of a cinemascopic version of what *really* did happen when the gamier story of what didn't happen is already a few days old and, in any case, ever so very much more interesting?

II.

New York, Spring 1965

1. The Declining City

The horror-stories piled up, and the word was "crisis." The *Tribune* embarked on an extensive and highly useful series identifying the constituent crises. Long exposés tumbled out, one after another, concerning the crisis in education, the crisis in housing, the crises in traffic, in crime, in air- and water-pollution, in dope traffic, in the economy, and—what was perhaps most significant—in the public morale.

They are not crises in the technical sense that the situation must improve or else the patient will die. Excepting the fiscal deficit, which presumably cannot be kited indefinitely, things could probably stumble along pretty much as before without causing New York City to close down its doors. But even discounting the irresistible urge to melodramatization during political campaigns, New York was—is— in bad shape. This was no phony missile gap of the kind a Presidential campaign had been fought over in 1960; nor, on the other hand, was it anything that had just recently afflicted New York. The crises had been around for quite a while but hadn't attracted very much public attention. Some crises are of course more modish than others, and they tend to have their day in court, as, for instance, the poverty crisis has recently had. The crisis of Cuba, as another example, was on everybody's mind for several years and was all but washed away by the sigh of relief that followed the great confrontation of October 1962, even though the net result of the showdown was merely to return Cuba to the *status quo ante*—which up until then was precisely what the crisis was all about. (Already the election of a new Mayor of New York seems to have had something of the effect of causing the crisis of New York to recede from the public consciousness.) The crisis of air pollution in New York, for instance, has occurred partly because the air is very dirty and actually dangerous to those who suffer from asthma and emphysema; but partly also because crisis-collectors discovered it, as they recently discovered the poverty crisis, and can, one gathers, be counted upon to discover crisis after crisis in the Dominican Republic, which seems to have developed as a year-round crisis resort.

There was, however, a considerable spontaneous restlessness in New York in the spring of 1965 which seemed to center on the widely held conviction that the incumbent administration had exhausted its powers of problem-solving. The question, rather surprisingly, was infrequently raised as to whether such derelictions as had crystallized could be corrected merely by electing a new Mayor. Quite possibly the aspirant mayor, in order to get himself elected, would need to make precisely those commitments to the old order which preclude the very actions needed to overcome those crises. Lincoln Steffens' aphorism is frequently quoted, that one should "*always* vote against the incumbent," the theory being that incumbents are necessarily corrupted by the exercise of power. The aphorism is refreshing, even as a little trace of anarchism is always refreshing: but the myth it stealthily subsidizes—the myth that things will improve with a change in personnel—is tricky. Because sometimes that is what happens; but on the other hand, sometimes, notoriously, that *isn't* what happens. What is sometimes most greatly needed is not a change in personnel but a change in political ideas. For instance, almost every problem in New York that doesn't have to do merely with maladministration arises out of a series of capitulations to special interests. Now it is sometimes both wise and prudent to capitulate to a special interest (*e.g.*, to avoid revolutions, or to right a grave wrong), but it should be recognized that that is what was done in order that the relationships between crisis and cause be manifest.

It is difficult for an ambitious politician to talk seriously about New York City's problems insofar as they spring from such relationships. But it shouldn't be all that difficult for critics to talk seriously about New York: which leaves one wondering why the literature of protest is so slender on the subject of those special relationships.

My own estimate is that some of New York's problems cannot be solved by politics, and that those that can would first require tweaking a few taboos by the nose. But since political taboos exist precisely for the benefit of one or another class of voters, it is unlikely that the taboos will be violated and therefore unlikely that the problems will be solved; and I expect that it is the general intuition of that dilemma that lies at the heart of the demoralization that New York's critics have so eloquently berated in article after article, book after book. "It is not the economic disorders of New York," writes Mr. Richard Whalen in his galvanizing book, *A City Destroying Itself*,[1] "that throws a shadow across an urban civilization. The truly terrible costs of New York are special and spiritual. These accrue in endless human discomfort, inconvenience, harassment, and fear which have become part of the pervasive background, like the noise and filth, but are much deadlier. For it is people who breathe life into an environment, who create and sustain a healthy city. If people are driven and their senses dulled, if they are alienated and dehumanized, the city is on the way to destroying itself." It seems to me highly unlikely that very much can be expected in the way of the people's reanimation if the people's leaders keep missing the point.

What is wrong with New York? The taxes are high, and the means of collecting them barbarous. The cost per person of operating the government of New York is $412. The comparative cost per person of operating Philadelphia is $264; of Chicago, $293.

Yet no matter how high the taxes soar, things somehow do not appear to improve. The public schools are not as good as they should be; or, at least, the children aren't as well educated as they should be. The recreation areas are drab and, worse, unsafe. Police protection is inadequate. Garbage collection is irregular and discriminatory. The surrounding rivers are dirty, the air unclean. The traffic congestion is appalling, and the facilities of the rapid transit system are inadequate. Low-cost housing is scarce, and especially scarce for Negroes and Puerto Ricans. Much of the new architecture is dispirited and graceless.

Great jeremiads can be written—and indeed have been—on each of these major deprivations which, taken together, underwrite such a categorical disillusion as Mr. Whalen's. A modern Justine *could*, in New York City, wake up in the morning in a room she shares with her unemployed husband and two children, crowd into a subway in which she is hardly able to breathe, disembark at Grand Central and take a crosstown bus which takes twenty minutes to go the ten blocks to her textile loft, work a full day and receive her paycheck from which a sizeable deduction is withdrawn in taxes and union fees, return via the same ordeal, prepare supper for her family and tune up the radio to full blast to shield the children from the gamy denunciations her next-door neighbor is hurling at her husband, walk a few blocks past hideous buildings to the neighborhood park to breathe a little fresh air, and fall into a coughing fit as the sulphur dioxide excites her latent asthma, go home, and on the way, lose her handbag

1. Richard Whalen, *A City Destroying Itself* (New York: William Morrow, 1965).

to a purse-snatcher, sit down to oversee her son's homework only to trip over the fact that he doesn't really know the alphabet even though he had his fourteenth birthday yesterday, which he spent in the company of a well-known pusher. She hauls off and smacks him, but he dodges and she bangs her head against the table. The ambulance is slow in coming and at the hospital there is no doctor in attendance. An intern finally materializes and sticks her with a shot of morphine, and she dozes off to sleep. And dreams of John Lindsay.

The statistician for the defense (Mr. Beame?) appears on the scene with a great big file. (1) Even though the population of New York did not grow at all between 1950 and 1960, 255,178 housing units were constructed during that period by private and public sources; so that, with regard to housing Justine is better off, statistically, than she was before. (2) The trains into Manhattan are sure to be crowded during the rush hours, but in the past ten years new approaches have been built into the city for automobiles, so that the city has not been derelict in providing more means of ingress; and, besides, a new tube is planned which will make things easier. (3) Yes, crosstown traffic is bad, but a new traffic commissioner who performed prodigies in Baltimore is now in charge and very soon brand-new electronically operated devices will greatly reduce the time it takes Justine to go from the subway stop to her place of employment. (4) A new building code is in force which will require thicker, more soundproof walls, which will insulate her children against contiguous obscenities. (5) A million dollars was spent last year by the city on the special question of air pollution and Consolidated Edison has spent over one hundred million dollars on a program to reduce its contribution to air pollution. Meanwhile the city has passed ordinances prohibiting the burning of fuel oil with a high sulphur content and New York State has passed laws requiring cars to carry special devices—recirculating exhausts—which will mitigate the toxification of the air. (6) The educational budget in New York City in 1950 was $240 per child. In 1964 it was $850 per child, which means, among other things, that the student-teacher ratio is now at 23 to one, an improvement over the 27 to one ratio back in 1950. (7) In 1950 there were only 19,000 policemen in New York City. Now there are 28,000. (8) Many of those policemen are especially concerned with the dope traffic, and if Justine will let me have the name of that pusher . . . (9) The hospitals are understaffed, but the public hospitals plus city subsidies to (voluntary) private hospitals are costing $176 million per year compared to $105 million in 1950.

By statistical analysis, Justine lives in an enlightened, progressive city.

In purely positivist terms, the counsel for the defense makes a good case—provided two premises are accepted. The first is that the administrative overhead of the city is not soaking up most, or at any rate too many, of the funds originally appropriated for the relief of Justine. The second is that the crisis of New York is largely a function of money.

There is no doubt that the administration of the New York government was overlarded in the spring of 1965, and in this respect Lincoln Steffens' axiom is directly to the point. Except, of course, that it seldom happens that reform government succeeds in shrinking the expenses of government after the initial period of flamboyant husbandry. It has not proved that way, however strongly economy is emphasized by the challenger, whether he is Franklin Roosevelt calling for a balanced budget, Dwight Eisenhower calling for a reduction in the bureaucracy, or Lyndon Johnson decreeing that the unused light at the White House be snuffed out. The probabilities are small that the cost of any modern government will reduce; which puts the onus on the private sector to generate additional revenues, and ends us up back with the question: Is the scarcity of public funds the major problem?

It was my contention during the campaign that the money shortage was not at the root of all evil; that although there are problems in New York, in other cities, and in the United States, which cannot be solved except by the expenditure of public money, there are problems in New York—and elsewhere—that cannot be solved through the expenditure of public money. But every one of these problems called for an approach highly unpalatable to *somebody;* and somebody, in an advanced democratic society, tends, unless he has been horribly forsaken, to be a vested interest, whose good favor is either essential to a successful political campaign or, at any rate, thought to be essential to a successful political campaign. I tried to make the point that catering to more and more private interests, under the competitive pressures of democratic elections, tends to elevate to politically preferred positions as many private interests as do not, by their elevation, alienate the more powerful private interests. And that what then happens is that—as I put it to the Washington Press Club—the marginal disutility of bloc satisfaction sets in; whereat the opportunity arises to speak directly to the apparently indulged bloc voter, and suggest an avenue for his escape, hoping to be able to make the demonstration that even by the application of strict utilitarian logic he is better off surrendering his synthetic political advantages in favor of the superior blessings that would then shower down on him.

I proceeded to do so. As it is elsewhere recorded, Mr. Lindsay won the election.

2. New York Is Not Hong Kong

If we accept such categorical indictments of New York as Richard Whalen's, quoted above, we should certainly ask why the free market hasn't asserted itself to drain the city of its population. Or ask, at least, whether we have unconsciously accepted the proposition that rather than endure emigration, urban residents will be progressively bribed to stay where they are. In the postwar years, hundreds of thousands of men, rich and poor, skilled and unskilled, fled East Berlin to go to the West, resulting finally in the erection of a Great Wall to stanch the costly and humiliating flow. It is no one's contention, of course, that New York is East Berlin; on the other hand, those who leave New York need not, in order to do so, make such sacrifices as are made by those who, leaving East Berlin, have left their families, their friends, and whatever goods they had accumulated. The United States, as we all know, is a highly transient country—an incredible twenty per cent of the population changing its address every year. To pick up and go requires, of course, that there be some place to go to. There *are* places to go to, outside New York. Places where there are more jobs, where housing is cheaper, the crime rate lower, the traffic less congested, the air cleaner, schooling better. Then, too, there are places outside New York where, by the testimony of those who have described the relative hardships, it is less miserable to be poor—where, for instance, one can, for the same amount of money, escape life in the rat-infested tenement. To what extent is the existence of spurned alternatives testimony (a) to the net desirability of living in New York, even after accounting for the special pains and annoyances of life there? To what extent (b) is New York, for mysterious ecological reasons, a kind of major dumping ground toward which the inertial forces of despair tend to propel the loose and the restless who, having come there, huddle down and will not go away, no matter what the attendant miseries of their new life, because by now they are spiritually exhausted? To what extent (c) is mobility simply a factor of wealth?

The very rich, it appears, do not feel the pressure to leave New York because except for occasional interruptions—a sneak-thief, a mugger, a murderer—they can afford to insulate themselves from the major inconveniences. To be sure, they must breathe the common air and strangle in the same traffic jams. But they do not need to use the subway, or live in crowded conditions, or use the public schools. That class of people is in absolute terms tiny, in relative terms large, because New York has a high concentration of very rich people. Mr. Richard Whalen tells us that, asking around, he came up with the figure of three thousand dollars per month after taxes (!) to finance that kind of life: a big apartment in a highly habitable area of Manhattan; private schools for the children; vacations, maybe some sort of cottage in the country.

There *is* movement from the middle class out of New York. The suburbs grew by 40 per cent during a period (1950–1960) when New York City's population diminished by 10,000. The principal complaint of middle-class emigrants from New York, by various accounts, is the public schools, which, the famous exceptions aside, are academically backward, unruly, and, increasingly, the arenas for interracial experiments which, at least over the short run, bring dislocative social and intellectual consequences. (The white population of Manhattan schools was 62 per cent in 1958; 51 per cent in 1963.) The next complaint is living space—New York, it is not widely known, actually had, in 1960, more living space per inhabitant than in 1940 (between 1941 and 1961 housing units increased by about 400,000, while the population during that period increased by less than 350,000). But by 1960 more people desired, if they could possibly afford to do so, to stretch out a little bit, and so began to flock to areas where they could do this at the same cost that would be required in New York City, or even less. And, third, there is the much-discussed dissatisfaction with the business climate. (The cost of city government rose 138 per cent between 1954 and 1965 [during the Wagner administration], while average income rose by 46 per cent.)

According to the data, over 800,000 white people left New York between 1950 and 1960, during which period the Negro and Puerto Rican population in New York increased by almost the identical figure. Of those 800,000-plus, many of the breadwinners continue to come into New York to work, and thereby, of course, contribute to New York City's revenues through taxes paid to the State of New York, a portion of which is remitted to the city, and through old-age retirement taxes, and excise taxes on whatever they purchase while in New York.

Among the lowest income groups, which arbitrarily (though not unreasonably) one might define as those families whose income is four thousand dollars per year or less,[2] the emigration is considerably less

2. The (private) New York Community Council's Budget Standard Service sets $6400 per year as the acceptable income for a family of four. The median income of New York's white population is $6600; of the nonwhite population, $4440.

than the national average—even though unemployment in New York is above the national average. In 1960, the unemployment figure among Negroes was 11 per cent; in New York, it was 14 per cent. Among the general population, 6½ per cent were unemployed. In New York (the figures differ) it was, by all accounts, higher.

One wonders about the extent to which free-market pressures continue to be culturally relevant to the distribution of human beings. I do not remember just when the principle that natural economic pressures ought to bear on the movements of the population was formally abandoned by social theorists, but somewhere along the line it seems to have been. It used to be taken for granted that if in one place there is overcrowding, unemployment, obloquy, whereas somewhere else there is room and work, and there is no barbed wire between place A and place B, there is sufficient reason for a flow of people from the one to the other locality. I remember a photograph in *Life* of Senator John Kennedy, campaigning in West Virginia in the spring of 1960 for the Democratic Presidential nomination. He was talking to a miner who, the caption revealed, had worked a cumulative total of three years out of the preceding twenty, and was now, with *Life* as his witness, receiving from the future President the pledge that he would be looked after by special legislation under the forthcoming dispensation: that he would, in effect, be paid *not* to mine coal for a living. There are any number of arguments, and I am acquainted with them—having to do with absent skills, with family ties, with other tangibles and intangibles—that make it difficult to suggest to someone that he move to another area, even if the objective is his own happiness and the general productivity. But one wonders whether it is not shortsighted of those who, in deference to the inertial logic that people should stay where they are, appear to refuse to probe the alternative that they might be better off elsewhere than in New York City, with its inhuman living conditions, its 200,000 unemployed and its 500,000 on relief. The case might be made, however paradoxical it may sound, that although New York should not positively discourage immigration, at least it should positively encourage emigration.

This isn't the moment to speculate on means by which private and public agencies might either encourage unemployed West Virginian coal-miners to retrain for jobs elsewhere, or, compassionately, discourage people from coming to New York to be poor. I touched, in the course of the campaign, on the theme that New York was thoughtlessly concerned with its size, and intended to probe the question whether an inverted kind of subsidy, to middle and big business, was, in fact, going on under our eleemosynary noses—by our encouraging, with social welfare schemes, a cheap labor market. I never got around to it, in part because of the lack of time, in part because, of course, it would not, in the hurly burly, have been publicly pondered. It is worth noting, however, that it costs the City of New York more money to sustain a great many of its *employed* workers—in schooling for their children, in free hospital care, in subsidized housing, etc.— than those workers produce; that we have going, then, a strange kind of subsidy which might be understandable if the workers were themselves the beneficiaries, but is less so when third parties who pay substantial dividends to their stockholders might be shown to be the beneficiaries. On the one hand, General Electric in New York will not pay a janitor as much money as the janitor needs in order to bring up his family; and on the other hand, the structure of taxes and social services contrives to put the janitor at the disposal of General Electric. The effect is to permit GE to underbid even the iron law of wages—by paying even less than those straitened wages which Marx predicted the capitalist community would inevitably end up paying—*i.e.*, just enough to keep the workers alive. General Electric, of course, pays heavy taxes, in about as many directions as its light bulbs throw out rays. It would require the services of a first-rate economic sleuth to figure out exactly who is subsidizing whom. But the existing economic tangle is at least one of the results of the crazy situations encouraged by impenetrable social accounting practices and by the proliferation of "free" services whose residual beneficiaries are as difficult to track down as Hetty Green's. And one of whose side effects is to encourage unnatural movements of the population; and the crisis of the cities.

I touched on the theme, as I say, early in the campaign. I was speaking in the Bronx at a Party Rally:

I have been wondering about New York City's unthinking obsession with Size. We are expected to work ourselves up into a great lather any time we learn that the population of New York City has shrunk, as the 1960 census showed it had done, rather than grown. I wonder why this should be so. If this were a compassionate reason to take pride in the growth of the city, that is one thing. But surely we are not entitled to feel that we can take pride in the growth of the city in the sense, let us say, that the Maryknollers can take pride in the growth of a mission in Latin America, or Africa. A growth in the population of New York City is hardly to be considered a growth in the parish of the evangelized.

New York should always be prepared to do emergency duty, to act as a haven for the politically oppressed; to do, subject to our raw capacity, what we can for refugees, even as we have done in the past. But there is no such stream crowding in at our gates. New York is not Hong Kong, which feels the moral burden of admitting people by the hundreds of thousands in order to save them from persecution and even death.

If, then, we cannot take any spiritual satisfaction from the number of people who live in New York City, is it for material reasons that we encourage them to come in? Is it the kind of growth that is rationally welcomed by the New York Chamber of Commerce?

Why should it be? Just as it is safe to say that people do not come to New York for the same kind of reason that they go to Lourdes, it should be safe to say that they do not come to New York because New York is an Emerald City. There are emeralds in New York, but they are very scarce; and available only to the very few who combine a happy mixture of skill and good luck. Many people come to New York because they are deluded, at least momentarily, into believing the myth of New York's munificent opportunities. And, indeed, New York's improvident policies encourage some people to stay in New York who would be better off to return from whence they came, where job opportunities are better, living conditions more spacious, and the temptations to crime and vice less alluring.

But many people stay in New York, at New York's expense, for reasons of their own which are only dimly understandable; for reasons, from New York City's point of view, which are utterly inexplicable. The half-million-plus people in New York City who are unemployed and/or on relief do not contribute anything tangible to the city's welfare. What is the point in encouraging them to stay, when they might go elsewhere, where employment opportunities are greater, the cost of living less, living conditions better? Why that false sense of civic pride that automatically assumes that New York City is only better off for so long as it continues to grow bigger? What is the argument, and what are its bases, that holds that New York is better off now than it would be with several hundred thousand fewer people living here, whose absence would relieve the congestion in housing, ease the unemployment figures, diminish the welfare rolls, reduce the general demoralization that is attendant on idleness, trim back the crime rate?

I appear before you as the only candidate for Mayor of New York who has not a word to say in defense of the proposition that New York ought to stay as big as it is, let alone grow bigger. I ask, *Why*? Leave aside all the other arguments, is there an economic argument in defense of this shibboleth? There are 500,000 people on relief in New York today. What do they contribute—I reduce the argument now to purely material terms—what do they contribute materially to New York? It costs a minimum of $700 to furnish public school education for a child in New York. It costs about

$500 per year per person for those on relief; and that much again for public housing. What is the residual benefit to New Yorkers of the sacrifices they endure in order to attract to the city men, women, and children who, in this city—as distinguished from elsewhere—are unemployable, and become structural welfarists? Do we easily justify, in our consciences, luring them into New York by the promise of easy welfare payments? That was the lure of such of our politicians as Vito Marcantonio—and, having got their vote, the politicians let them institutionalize themselves as social derelicts, at liberty to breed children who, suffering from inherited disadvantages, alternatively seek surcease in hyperstimulation—in crime and narcotics—and in indolence—as school dropouts or as poolhall conscientious objectors to work; giving that jaded tone to the city which we recognize as among the most considerable obstacles to its liberation.

I recall a happy event of the campaign, a meeting with Mr. Theodore White, a brilliant man, an irresistible writer, and a super-engaging human being. His standard in approaching people personally— as distinguished from writing about them at second hand—has become whether he has reason "to suppose that they were men of good will,"[3] in which classification (he subsequently wrote to me), he presumed to place me, and hoped that I, having met him, returned the judgment—which I most emphatically do, however puzzled I continue to be by the absence of any sense of shared oppressors. All of which is an aside, the point being that he appeared to be much taken—as by nothing else, I hasten to absolve him—by what I had to say concerning the unnatural size of New York City. He found it an arresting observation, worth serious thought. He did upend me, I remember, by proffering the suggestion that, however radical I thought my observation to be, he had a better one: oughtn't New York City to petition to become an independent and *sovereign* state? I gulped, and quite lost my cool, dismissing his proposal with insufficient reflection, even though I confess to have found the time to smile at the ironic conjunction of proposals made half seriously by Theodore White and altogether in fun by Barry Goldwater. Never mind, he soothed me, he had asked both Lindsay and Beame the same question, and they too had bugged out: which is understandable, considering that Messrs. Lindsay and Beame were running for Mayor of New York, not for President of a new republic. We had other matters to go over (Mr. White was preparing a story for *Life*), and so we agreed to postpone for another occasion a discussion of the difficulties of introducing radical analysis into a general campaign. He did

3. Letter to the author, December 2, 1965.

agree that I had an opportunity the major candidates did not have, but also he agreed that I had certain difficulties in communicating those ideas, in any substantial detail, to the general public. We met before I made the talk which included the remarks above, which were not, so far as I am aware, relayed by any of the communications media (granted, all except for a single daily newspaper were, at that moment, struck down). But I noticed—and I say this fully understanding that Mr. White's professional commitments to the two major candidates necessarily dictated the allocation of space in his article for *Life*—that he ended up in his own piece dealing with the subject as follows: "Knowing himself to be absolved from the dreadful prospect of actually governing the city, Buckley revels in candor: he can muse aloud that New York would be better off if it had less, rather than more, people—if it shrank from eight million to six and a half million." And then his section on my candidacy concludes with a passage which, if I may revel in candor, is a cliché which political typewriters can reel off by depressing a single key: "What, in effect, asks Mr. Buckley, is the purpose of city government? Is it really to care for the worn and the tired, the huddled and hopeless, the refugees who, today, come from the Black South or Spanish Puerto Rico, as 90 years ago they came from Europe to pass through Castle Garden and Ellis Island? Has the city—has, indeed, all American government—promised too much? Should government, therefore, cut and run from its promises?"

Ah, the ideological coda, how it afflicts us all! And how paralyzingly sad that someone who can muse over the desirability of converting New York City into an independent state should, having climbed to such a peak, schuss down the same old slope, when the mountains beckon him on to new, exhilarating runs.

III.

The Political Scene

1. The Republican Party

The tables of organization of New York City politics are far less interesting than the unspoken sociology of New York City politics. The salient features are quickly related, and quickly understood, without the necessity to explore the mazes, or to absorb statistical tables. The most noticeable political fact about New York is that it is a Democratic city and has been one for about as long as can be remembered. It is a Democratic city in part because it is a left-minded city, about which more anon; and in part because the lubricants of a one-party city flow freely, with the result that the Democratic organization is everything that the Republican organization is not. It is merely suggestive to note that there are an estimated twenty thousand Democratic clubhouse workers as contrasted with a pitiable two thousand Republicans, a ratio greatly exceeding the registered Democratic plurality of about three and one-half to one. Democratic judges overwhelmingly outnumber Republicans, and it is generally conceded that such Republicans as there are, are there simply because, at some point, judicial seemliness requires that a second party should be seen, if not heard—if only to provide those comfortable democratic delusions which are formally satisfying. Indeed, of the seven Republican (out of twenty-eight) City Councilmen, five are mandatorily there because the law expressly requires a minority representation by the other party. The most prominent Republican Party leader in the city is Mr. Vincent Albano, the Republican boss of the unbossable county of New York (Manhattan), who was an orthodox Democrat until circumstances impelled him to back Dewey in 1948, from which point he elided gracefully into Republican County leader. Even less noisily he slipped into a position as chairman of the board of a brand-new commercial bank which achieved its charter (the first

40

in Manhattan since 1930) by special action of a Democratic-controlled federal agency. He quickly made a stock killing; the general inference being that a few highly compliant Republicans situated here and there are useful coloration for the Democratic Party, and that those Republicans who cooperate will be remembered, if not hereafter, certainly in this world.

This does not mean that "Republicans" never got elected in New York. Four mayors during this century, the incumbent included, were "Republicans," all of them fusionists and the penultimate, Mr. La Guardia, a gentleman who, like his successor Republican, took considerable pains to endure his congenital deformity with a heroic disregard, leaving him, for all that one would notice, as clean-limbed as a freshly minted Democrat. The upstate Republicans, who have predominated in the governorship since the long reign of Thomas Dewey began in 1942, have acquiesced in the situation—for one thing because the patronage powers of the Governor within New York City are exiguous, for another because Messrs. Dewey and Rockefeller, having measured the odds, appear to have thought it the wiser counsel not to attempt seriously to organize the Republicans in New York City, or even the latent Republicans. So long as New York City behaved sportingly as regards its own elections, the danger was that the Republicans might, by serious attempts to organize New York City Republicanism, so antagonize the very powerful Democrats as to cease to qualify for their discreet cooperation, which has been given to the Republicans from time to time; the most newsworthy recent example was the collusion between Governor Rockefeller and Mayor Wagner in the spring of 1965 on the matter of organizing the Albany legislature.

Besides, assuming it *were* organizationally possible, around what is the Republican Party of New York to organize? The notion that it should organize around certain political ideas different from ideas regnant within the Democratic Party appears to have been discarded as, simply, ridiculous. Would the GOP run on the integrity of its racial stock? It sometimes appeared to be doing so, complained Mr. Leonard Hall, a highly competent political technician, though not competent enough to have secured for himself the Republican nomination for Governor in 1958, at a time when Rockefeller also desired it. Hall added his voice to the chorus of breast-beaters after the ignominious defeat of Senator Goldwater. "We have permitted our party," he said, "to become too exclusive. We have been trying to elect national candidates with the descendants of the people who came over on the Mayflower, and that boat just wasn't big enough. . . . Our party gives the appearance of being an organization of white Anglo-Saxon Protestants." (The WASP vote in New York City is 12 per cent, somewhat less than the Negro vote alone.)

There has been lacking in the Republican Party of New York, everyone appears to agree, a fighting faith through which to distinguish the GOP from the Democratic Party and through which to lure the services of ideological partisans who cannot be commandeered by patronage. Indeed, on those occasions when the Republican Party has won municipal elections it has done so precisely by effacing any distinguishing characteristics of the Republican Party; by tagging along with the idea of Fusion, as was done so successfully by Mr. Fiorello La Guardia, hereinafter not referred to as the Little Flower. The voters of New York, on the other hand, are not immobile. There was, for instance, the insufficiently remembered victory of Mr. Vincent Impellitteri, who, in the special election of 1950, running as an Independent, beat the Democratic-Liberal and (needless to say) the Republican candidate. Mr. Impellitteri ran as himself; as a man who had been denied, brusquely, inhumanly, the Democratic nomination which was popularly supposed to have belonged to him. In any case, he won 1,161,175 votes, as contrasted with 935,000 for Ferdinand Pecora, the Democrat-Liberal, and 382,000 for Edward Corsi, the Republican. It is a matter of minor historical interest that that year, two years after Mr. Dewey practically won the Presidency (and the same year that he outpolled his Democratic opponent in New York City in his successful bid for re-election as Governor), the Republican mayoral candidate in New York City polled 15.4 per cent of the total vote, or less than 2 per cent more than the Conservative Party polled in 1965.

If there was a single conference held by Republican leaders during the winter or spring of 1965 devoted to the subject of whether the Republican Party might amass a series of positions around which to base an opposition to continuing Democratic rule, that session is unrecorded. There were conferences aplenty, most of them in the weeks before the first of March, devoted to the question whether John Lindsay should himself run. As of March 1, Mr. Lindsay, according to the accounts of his biographers,[1] had decided not to, on the grounds that the odds against him were insuperable. Subsequently, after a breakfast meeting with Mr. John Hay Whitney from which he left feeling considerably more resourceful, and after an exhortatory barrage of letters, telegrams, etc., that followed upon a planned leak by his manager, Mr. Robert Price, to the effect that Lindsay was wa-

1. For instance, Messrs. Peter Maas and Nick Thimmesch, writing on January 2, 1966 in *New York*, the magazine of the Sunday *Tribune*, in which they delivered what is commonly accepted as the official Lindsay view of the chronology of the mayoralty campaign.

vering, Lindsay decided that New York did indeed deserve to be saved, and cast his die: but always on the strict understanding that, like his Republican predecessor Mr. La Guardia, he would be running not as a Republican but as himself. His own words, given at a press conference, were that he desired it to be "clear to the whole world" that he was running for Mayor "as Lindsay" rather than as a Republican. The whole world, as we shall see, did not get the message, but the New York swing vote did, and of course, it remains to be decided who was deluded, the Republican Party or the Democratic electorate.

I shall be devoting attention to the dilemma of the Republican Party, in New York City and nationwide, and see no purpose in any anticipation of the argument. What should be stressed at this point is that in the spring of 1965 the high morale of the Republican Party had nothing to do with the prospective exhilaration of a confrontation between two different approaches to municipal government. It was all along assumed that Mr. Robert Wagner would be running for re-election, and the prospect of yet another, redundant term was viewed with despair by many politically and morally energetic men, who, though they found it difficult to criticize the Mayor's general ideas about governing New York, consolidated around the position that a change in personnel was drastically overdue. Later, when Mr. Wagner pulled out, thus guaranteeing that someone other than himself would be the next Mayor—whether Mr. Lindsay or Mr. Abraham Beame, or Mr. Paul Screvane, or Mr. Paul O'Dwyer, or Mr. William Fitts Ryan—the pro-Lindsay coalition I speak of shifted to the derivative position that whereas, to be sure, Mr. Wagner would personally disappear, and presumably with him the awful fatigue of his administration, the point now became to replace Wagner with someone formally unattached to the Democratic Party. Therein—not in a new set of ideas about municipal government but in his person, and in his unalignment—lay the prospects for a refreshed New York, most of Mr. Lindsay's supporters would be saying. It became more difficult to advance that line after Mr. Lindsay sought, and secured, the backing of the Liberal Party, whose iron hold on Mr. Wagner had been manifest, thus renewing formal ties which (the argument had run) Lindsay would be unencumbered by. And then, to add to the difficulties, after one of the most exhaustive searches in political history, Mr. Lindsay designated as his Comptroller—a Democrat, Mr. Milton Mollen, a much-censured associate of Wagner (for whom he had served as Housing Commissioner), whose prestige was at a lower ebb even than Mr. Wagner's. The columnist, Murray Kempton, who had contributed to Lindsay the slogan, "He is fresh, everyone else is tired," although he stopped short of outright disaffection, commented acidly that his jingle had been composed "before Congressman Lindsay decided to begin our municipal rebirth by borrowing his candidate for Comptroller from Mayor Wagner. So it must be amended to say that Congressman Lindsay is not only fresh but, when necessary, he can be downright impudent" (New York *World-Telegram*, August 26, 1965).

But the doctrine held together—even if, intellectually, it was at this point bursting at the seams—that John Lindsay was a free agent. And then, when Mr. Beame was designated at the primary as the Democratic candidate, his placid defense of the status quo and his unbemused affiliations with the Democratic bosses reinvigorated the notion that Mr. Lindsay was uniquely independent.

It is, finally, interesting to recall that the weary Mr. Wagner had only four years before been freshly remandated—as the "reform" Mayor who, by extraordinary moral exertion, had freed *himself* from the bosses, whom indeed he had roundly denounced in 1961, succeeding to re-election as the quintessentially emancipated man. Nobody quite knew what exactly had happened to the reformist momentum that had buried the bosses, and even though Mr. Wagner never did reunite with them, somehow daisies did not spring up on the pavements of New York. It transpired that New York City government without Carmine De Sapio was not noticeably better than it had been with Carmine De Sapio: indeed, to judge from the crystallization of the discontent, New York was a great deal worse after one unboss-ridden term than after the two boss-ridden preceding terms. The reformers' new kick, at least during the period of the Democratic Primary, was the humorless ideologue Mr. William Fitts Ryan; and when he fell, the mantle went to John Lindsay. The Republicans were increasingly maneuvered into the position of believing in John Lindsay qua John Lindsay, as their shriveled justification for their original enthusiasm (he is untied to the people who tied up Wagner) gave way under the weight of one after another entanglement with the same old crowd: the same organization, the same personnel, the same ideology.

2. The Idea of Fusion

When Fiorello La Guardia left City Hall in 1945 he proclaimed, with characteristic self-appreciation, that thanks to himself, "partisan politics, dishonesty, graft, selfishness, favoritism, have been entirely abolished." (By contrast, the Son of God's tenure was a bust.) But allowing for political hyperbole, La Guardia had, it was generally agreed, accomplished the principal mission for which he had been picked by the Fusionists, which was to liberate New York from a city government which had come to view politics as a form of commerce. The good feeling the name of La Guardia popularly evokes is in part owing to his personality—it was La Guardia's color that made his reign so lastingly impressive. But for the serious minded, his name suggests high standards of public service.

He gave Fusion a very good name, in the best tradition of his predecessors Seth Low and John Purroy Mitchel, and it thereafter became a part of a happy legend that those who go beyond their own political parties are the most desirable candidates for municipal office. John Lindsay was to stress repeatedly the nonpartisan nature of his own candidacy, assiduously cultivating the air of transcendence that devolves to a candidate too big for any single party.

In 1933, when New York City government had been so greatly discredited by the Seabury investigations, a Fusion group looked hard for a candidate who would be anti–Tammany Hall, period. Actually, neither La Guardia nor—later—John Lindsay was "above" parties. They disdained only those servile relationships to political parties which, on public analysis, tended to diminish their appeal as idealists. La Guardia, who fought savagely for the Fusionists' endorsement (even as Lindsay maneuvered hard for the Liberal endorsement), had been the reluctant choice of the Fusionists in part because of his unorthodox mien, in part because he was formally a Republican; and it was doubted that a candidate who suffered the liability of that connection could, in a town registered four to one Democratic, beat the Democrats. The Fusionists desired to beat the incumbent with practically anybody at all, and the candidate's own social and political views were held to be utterly immaterial. What mattered were personal integrity and the ability to reform the administration of the city. This was fusion not in behalf of a set of social positions about government but in behalf of elementary reform. For a generation, the political professionals called the civic-minded men who went in for that kind of thing, Goo-goos.[2] The Goo-goos of 1933 were determined to rescue New York, caring not at all about the ideological list of the man they were determined to make the Mayor of New York.

The most prominent members of the Fusion Conference Committee, which was charged with finding a suitable candidate, were, as a matter of fact, political conservatives. Before they formally settled on La Guardia, they had rated as qualified candidates prominent men whose social and political views ranged right across the political

2. Said, by some, to trace back to "Good Government Boys."

spectrum. Judge Seabury, the patrician reformer, was offered the designation, and turned it down on the grounds that to profiteer from the findings of his own committee might have the effect of discrediting his motives. Nathan Strauss, Jr., scion of the famous merchandising family, unidentified with any political ideology, also declined—on the grounds that Herbert Lehman was Governor and to propose another Jew as Mayor might bring on an anti-Semitic backlash. Robert Moses, an independent Republican, was turned down only because Judge Seabury violently opposed him.[3] A ticket including Al Smith and Norman Thomas was seriously considered—Al Smith, who had already begun to question what he deemed the left excesses of Franklin Roosevelt, and had thus emerged as a conservative; and Norman Thomas, the firebrand socialist. Smith said no, as did a half-dozen others. Fusion's very favorite candidate was Joseph McKee, a Democrat of impeccable reputation who had actually served for a couple of months as Acting Mayor after Jimmy Walker quit. But McKee resigned from politics and went into business, whence he was resurrected a few months later by FDR and persuaded to run against La Guardia *and* the Tammany incumbent, Mayor O'Brien, whose daze during the entire period was symbolized by his speech to the Greek-American society in which he confessed his lifelong devotion to "that great Greek poet, Horace."

The Seabury disclosures that brought Fusion to the fore are not to be confused with the routine malversations of public officials. Tammany Hall had been insouciantly bleeding New York, and the place stank. "The gang that had misgoverned the city," Professor Arthur Mann has written,[4] "had made bribery, wirepulling, and influence-peddling into a way of life, from fixing lowly traffic tickets all the way up to buying a judgeship. By 1943, the city's credit was so badly impaired that municipal securities were selling twenty-six points under par."

The job at hand, moreover, was not merely to oust the rascals, but to cause the people to desire that this should be done; to persuade a sufficient number of voters that the whole notion of good government was in jeopardy, that fiduciary standards of public service were actually in danger of deinstitutionalization. Though Seabury was the final hero of the investigations, he had by no means been the crowd-pleaser: the people seemed greatly amused by, and

3. Because Moses was opposed to proportional representation (against which Seabury, in his final years, finally turned); and because Moses was an Al Smith man. Seabury always resented Smith because, he believed, Smith had edged him out of the Presidency. (Seabury was convinced he could have beaten Hoover in 1928.)

4. *La Guardia Comes to Power, 1933* (Philadelphia: J. B. Lippincott, 1965).

certainly were infinitely tolerant of high rascality. The boss of Tammany during another investigation had been Richard Croker, who, when asked what was his opinion of free silver, replied blandly, "I'm in favor of all kinds of money—the more the better."[5] When the dashing Jimmy Walker was asked by Seabury to justify elevating one of his hack predecessors as judge of the Children's Court of Queens, the Mayor said "The appointment of Judge Hylan means the children can now be tried by their peer." But the conscience of the city consolidated, even as the Victorian conscience of London finally reacted against the breezy degeneracy of Oscar Wilde: and the search was on for a truly invincible Goo-goo.

Judge Seabury was primarily responsible for the choice of La Guardia, to whom he had been introduced by Adolf Berle, Jr., who in turn had come to know him through the enthusiastic intercession of the young and influential reformer Newbold Morris. Having got the Fusion nomination, La Guardia was promptly endorsed by the Republican Party. At the outset of his campaign, La Guardia stuck single-mindedly to his mandate. He was running against Tammany Hall, period. He was asked by an association of newspaper editors for his social and economic views and replied that they were immaterial: "The only question is honest and efficient administration of our municipal government." "There is only one issue," La Guardia repeated to his fellow Fusion candidates halfway through the campaign, "and that issue is the Tammany Hall of John F. Curry."

To the Fusionists' astonishment and dismay, Franklin Roosevelt, sensing that Tammany Democracy was at least temporarily out but desiring his very own man in New York, persuaded McKee to run on the "Recovery" ballot, pledging to reform the Democratic Party from within. The popularity of Roosevelt and his New Deal was enormous, with the result that La Guardia faced the awful possibility that he might well lose to McKee, who went busily to work identifying himself with the New Deal. La Guardia feared that McKee would have a special appeal for the city's poor, who were more numerous, even, than the city's Italians, the ethnic base of La Guardia's own strength. As Professor Mann put it, "the task before La Guardia was as clear as it was urgent: to build a bridge between the aspirations of the Goo Goos and the needs of the Disinherited."

Goo-gooism, in other words, would not be enough. So La Guardia went on from his call for administrative purification to welfarist proposals embodied in his famous phrase, "What is needed is government with a heart." He spoke "feelingly" about social justice, said La Guardia, "because I *feel* so strongly about it"—which was cer-

5. *Ibid.*, p. 40.

tainly the very best of reasons for speaking feelingly about it. And indeed, although La Guardia could be accused of any number of hypocrisies and polemical venalities (he prided himself that he could "out-demagogue the demagogues"); and although it is altogether possible that he finally took the election away from McKee only by imputing anti-Semitism to him (which caused FDR, in fright, to withhold the tacit endorsement he had planned), it cannot be contended that La Guardia's unscheduled turn to an emphasis on social welfarism was out of character. He had been known for years as America's most liberal Congressman. He was to go on, his biographer concludes, to "join the liberal political establishment of the 1930's and 1940's." Yet at his inauguration, what he stressed was his original mandate for good government in the technical sense of an honest, just administration. "Our theory of municipal government is an experiment," he said, "to try to show that a nonpartisan, nonpolitical local government is possible." Whereupon he recited the famous Oath of the Young Men of Athens, whose appropriateness is both a tribute to its universality, and confirmation of the essentially non-programmatic character of La Guardia's mandate . . . "We will fight for our ideals and sacred things of the city, both alone and with many. We will revere and obey the city's law and do our best to incite a like respect in those above us who are prone to annul them and set them at nought. We will strike unceasingly to quicken the public sense of civic duty. Thus in all these ways we will transmit this city not only not less, but far greater and more beautiful, than it was transmitted to us . . ."

It is hard to understand the applicability of the Fusion idea to John Lindsay's candidacy. A little oil in the machinery is almost always in order after a long stretch in office by a single administration. But that is Goo-gooism of a completely different order from what was needed in New York after the Seabury investigations. Mayor Wagner's administration was not corrupt, except in the sense that fatigue can be a form of corruption. A close study of the public indictments of Mr. Wagner by Mr. Lindsay confirms that his administrative delinquencies were, by the standards of 1933, utterly trivial. And as if to reinforce the implicit contention that Mr. Lindsay had no deep quarrel with Mr. Wagner, he picked as his running-mates one Liberal—the State Chairman of the Party that had endorsed Wagner's re-election—and one Democrat who was intimately implicated in Wagner's administration. It is as though La Guardia had picked as running-mates two men intimately associated with Jimmy

Walker. If the objective in 1965 wasn't merely the routine objective of bringing in another administration—and we were told the objective was something far more hallowed, calling for the august concept of Fusion—then didn't Lindsay face the difficulties that the reformer McKee faced in 1933? At that time Walter Lippmann, declaring for La Guardia, had written, "Can the machine be sufficiently reformed by men who, until a month ago, were part of it? [La Guardia's Fusion had answered with a resounding "No!" Lindsay's Fusion embraced one of Wagner's highest lieutenants and ran him for Comptroller.] Or is it desirable to overthrow the whole machine of misgovernment and install men who are entirely unentangled with it? [La Guardia's Fusion: "Yes!" Lindsay's Fusion: "No!"] . . . Do the people wish a partial change of control at the top or a radical change of control from top to bottom? [In 1965, the people evidently desired only a change at the top—except for those who were deluded by the Fusion rhetoric into believing that they were voting for radical change of control from top to bottom.] In the McKee [*read:* Lindsay] faction they have men who have been a part of the existing machine, have done business with it, have acquiesced in it, have sustained it, still represent an important part of it, and, barring miracles, must continue to compromise with it. In Fusion [read—see below—the Conservative Party] they have a group of candidates who are the sworn enemies of the machine, owe nothing to it, have every interest in destroying it, and no interest in compromising with it."

Lindsay's Fusion, in a word, was a verbal operation. It was essential in order to hang on to the Republicans while pandering explicitly to the left. If the time for Fusion of the 1933 variety is truly here, one must discard sectarian prejudices. If New York is really going under, Fusion must be called to the rescue: and in behalf of Fusion, Republicans, like the conservative gentlemen on the old Fusion Conference Committee, must put aside their own values as irrelevant until the storm blows itself out. It doesn't make any difference whether the man's social views are those of Al Smith, or those of Norman Thomas; submerge your own ideas, and vote to save New York. Lindsay's Fusion was procedural rather than substantive. Even so, the bugle of Fusion instantly fused together the *Tribune* and the New York *Post*, *Life* and *The Nation*, Richard Nixon and Richard Rovere, Ray Bliss and Ray Walsh, David Lawrence and David Dubinsky, all in the cause of extirpating Wagner from this earth. After the smoke had settled and the Democrats had named their own ticket, Murray Kempton calmly observed that Lindsay's anti-Wagner ticket was one-third composed of anti-Wagner men, while Beame's had evolved as three-thirds anti-Wagner. As for Wagnerism, if it was something other than Wagner, Lindsay was running on it, even while denouncing its eponym.

Wagner's most opportunistic detractors within the liberal community could never quite find a way to state their case against him except in pallid Goo-gooisms. Lindsay's need was to identify the city's dissatisfactions as the direct result of the approach to government of Mr. Wagner. That was never easy to do. Because the trouble in New York was—is—not so much with maladministration as with a frozen ideology. If a public school's standards are lowered because of a precipitate and thoughtless racial integration, what do you call that? Maladministration? If the traffic chokes up not because you *don't* but because you *daren't* control the flow of it into the city, what do you call that? If the middle class begins to flow out of the city because the schools are bad, housing scarce, and taxes high, what is the matter? If the crime rate rises while fresh judicial mores make its detection and conviction harder, what will Goo-gooism contribute to that? If rent control actually causes inequities and depresses the construction of new buildings—what is a Fusion, dedicated to preserving rent control, going to do about that? If labor unions exercise crushing power, what is a cool-cat administrator with vision, imagination, energy, devotion, compassion and genius—who appeared prostrate before a couple of labor union leaders for their support and inveighs against Right-to-Work—going to do about that?

3. The Conservative Party

The Conservative Party of New York was founded in February 1962. The idea had been kicking around for several years. I remember discussing such a party with a few friends in 1955. We were moved to do so by the denial of the New York Democratic senatorial nomination to James Farley—because of pressure from the Liberal Party, which disdained him as too old-fashioned (*read,* too conservative). That was, of course, the Democrats' business, but in American politics the position of the one party tends to influence the position of the other—on the whole a good idea in a political community which tends to discourage political polarization. But the line of the major parties should, of course, reflect substantial bodies of opinion within the consensus of each party. It seemed to me that the neglect of one body of opinion on the political spectrum, even while its counterpart at the other end, because it was effectively organized, was militantly represented, had resulted in distortions in the policies of both major parties. If the Liberal Party, which effectively mobilizes left-opinion in New York, did not exist, neither (I reasoned, and still do) would a Conservative Party need to exist.[6]

The Liberals' influence on the Democratic Party in New York is not anywhere doubted. The influence, in fact, is greater than the vote regularly deployable by the Liberal Party would seem to merit— mostly for psychological reasons. That vote has fluctuated in the twenty years since the Liberal Party peeled off (in 1944) from the American Labor Party in patriotic protest against the ALP's capture by the Communists. Its high point was in 1951, when it won (with the help of a minor party) the City Council Presidency with 659,000 votes. Two years later it got 465,000 votes for its candidate for Mayor, Mr. Rudolph Halley, who had become famous as the principal investigator for the Kefauver Committee (ironically, become famous by the use of tactics roundly condemned by Liberals when they were subsequently used by Senator McCarthy). Its low point was in 1964, when it delivered only 272,106 votes to Mr. Bobby Kennedy, running against Mr. Kenneth Keating. But its power, whatever the fluctuations of its performance, remained high. Its deliberations—which are a colloquy between Mr. David Dubinsky and Mr. Alex Rose— are copiously reported; and Adlai Stevenson, John Kennedy, and Lyndon Johnson, when running for election, or re-election, as President, all appeared in person to accept the Party's endorsement at great big to-dos. The Liberal Party paused to take credit for no less an achievement than the election of John Kennedy as President of the United States, a demonstration which required a certain flair for the use of statistics but which is not uninteresting; any more, for instance, than the Conservative Party's claim—more plausible, as a matter of fact—to having cost the Republican Party the control of the New York State Assembly in 1965 is uninteresting. The Liberals' reasoning was this simple: if the voters who voted for JFK on the Liberal line in 1960 had voted instead for Richard Nixon, Nixon would have carried New York; and if he had carried New York,

---

6. A few conservatives around the country, having become convinced that the Republican Party is for some reason metaphysically useless, have been trying, and will probably continue to do so, to establish Conservative Parties in every state of the Union, looking forward to a national party. They do not recognize that the essential precondition for such state parties is the pre-existence of an equivalent party on the left. It requires the special provocation of a successful left-splinter party to justify direct pressure from a fourth party on the GOP. The Liberals, for the most part, well satisfied with the policies of the Democratic Party, have not felt the necessity to found third parties outside New York, and in all probability will not do so in the foreseeable future. The possibility of a national third party, like Henry Wallace's and backed by roughly the same people for roughly the same reasons, is something else again.

he'd have got a majority of the electoral college. The flaw, of course, is that the voters who voted for Kennedy on the Liberal Party ticket would, most of them, have voted for him anyway; that is to say, irrespective of whether they had been coaxed to do so by the Liberal Party. The Conservatives' claim is, although self-serving, at least one step more plausible. Seven Republicans running for the State Assembly in New York in 1965 were offered Conservative Party support and turned it down. Accordingly, the Conservatives nominated their own people, who amassed, individually, more votes than their Republican opponents lost by. Ergo, if the seven Republicans had accepted Conservative support, they'd have been elected, and the Republicans, with that seven-vote margin, could have organized the Assembly and thus controlled both branches of the State legislature, instead of merely a single branch. Almost-ergo, of course, because there is a weakness in the argument: it is impossible to compute how many votes the seven Republicans might have lost through the alienation of those who are allergic to the Conservative label . . .

But statistical rodomontade cannot detract from the fact of the Liberal Party's enormous influence; or from the Conservative Party's. Indeed, the Conservative Party is already given the (ironic) credit for having elected John Lindsay Mayor of New York by drawing more votes away from Abraham Beame than from Lindsay, as regards which analysis, more anon.

A Conservative Party was finally organized in 1962. Its existence, I think, is a very good example of the fact that however obvious the need, things don't necessarily get done unless someone does them. The Party owes its existence to the energies, physical and moral—I shall maintain—of two young men who set aside their law practices and worked feverishly over a period of months beginning in 1961, ending with the certification of the Conservative Party of New York on Election Day in 1962. J. Daniel Mahoney was then twenty-nine; his brother-in-law Kieran O'Doherty, thirty-four. Mahoney, relaxed, humorous, wise, a peerless conciliator, had been a *magna cum laude* graduate from St. Bonaventure's University and graduated from the Columbia Law School. O'Doherty, intense, fascinated by politics, prodigiously informed, with an infinite capacity for righteous indignation, was a *cum laude* graduate of City College of New York, and received his LL.B from Columbia. They had, as the saying goes, no funds, no machines, no underwriters—and only an inexplicit mandate, but one they never doubted—namely, that a significant number of New York voters felt disfranchised.

"It is by now a mark of advancing years," the young founders of the new party wrote in a memorandum privately distributed on July

4, 1961, "for a conservative to have voted in a Presidential election with enthusiasm. . . .

"Witness the plight of the conservative voter in New York State who approaches the critical 1962 gubernatorial and senatorial elections with the foreknowledge that the Republican Party, the normal vehicle of conservative political policies, will offer him the uncherished opportunity to cast his ballot for Nelson Rockefeller and Jacob Javits. . . ."

The Declaration of Principles of the prospective party emphasized the necessity for realistic anti-Communist policies abroad and, "at home, [opposition to] a crushing burden of taxation for purposes unconnected with defense, [to] never-ceasing inflation, [to] a constantly delaying educational practice [which] combine to transform America gradually but unmistakably into a socialist society, in which the individual person will count for nothing."

The founders put concrete emphasis on ending government support for special privileges to special groups through:

—freeing the workingman, industry, and the community at large from the imperial domination of trade-union bosses, by reducing their monopoly power to a level compatible with the rule of law;[7]

—freeing the farmers from bureaucratic regulation as dependent wards of the government, by eliminating in gradual stages the entire crop control, price control, and subsidy program;

—freeing the energy of American industry, by eliminating specialized subsidies and governmental favors;

—freeing the consumer (who is all of us) from the pressure of constant inflation, which is largely brought about by the curbs of special privilege on American productivity and by the cost of the non-productive bureaucracy which enforces these curbs.

As for the principal political vehicle through which they intended to exert influence, the founders were unequivocal: "We agree that the conservative political movement cannot place its ultimate faith in a third party, but must instead seek its ultimate political realization within the Republican Party."

The New York *Daily News'* James Desmond, who, by avocation, is a biographer of Nelson Rockefeller, got wind of the memorandum and wrote in the *News*, November 16, 1961, that "some far-out conservatives,[8] many aligned with the right wing of the Republican Party,

---

7. I have never seen a better one-sentence statement of the problem.
8. The far-outers, in addition to Messrs. Mahoney and O'Doherty, included Joseph H. Ball, former Senator from Minnesota; Charles Edison, former Democratic Governor of New Jersey and Secretary of the Navy under FDR; Devin Garrity

were surveying the feasibility of entering a candidate against Rockefeller in next year's election. The group, which has been talking informally for several weeks, includes the principal backers of the
National Review, and has been meeting in the magazine's office."
And the conservative columnist and political expert Raymond Moley
remarked that the Conservative Party's sponsors, "no doubt sincere
young people," would in due course recognize how meager was their
experience, and predicted that "their cause will vanish in two or three
months, when the hillsides, along with Christmas jewelry, turn green."

Murray Kempton, getting wind of the organization, predicted
(New York *Post*, November 16, 1961) that "the Conservatives, if they
go through with this, should handsomely reward their enemies. Nothing destroys a dedicated fanatic faster than going into politics, particularly independent politics. . . . It is never wise for any group
which says it speaks for hundreds of thousands to test its statistics
at the ballot." Four years later, the Conservative Party rolled up
340,000 votes in New York City alone.

In 1962, Governor Rockefeller was running for re-election, having
increased the state budget by 44 per cent over the peak reached by a
Democratic predecessor identified in the public mind as a profligate
spender. His methods of financing had been exposed, by diligent
analysis, as relying heavily on sleight-of-hand fiscal manipulation.
(He was given to the device of capitalizing current expenditures so
as to get around the legal obligation that the state's budget balance.)
In 1960, having failed to cop the nomination for himself, he had done
everything he could to torpedo Richard Nixon on the eve of the
Republican Convention in Chicago by springing a series of demands
which rocked the Republican Convention—and Nixon, whom he may
very well have thrown fatally off balance in that close election. (The
Democrats made the most of the schism Rockefeller had publicized.)
For Senator, the Republican Party renominated Jacob Javits, whom
the Americans for Democratic Action had acclaimed with a hundred-
per-cent rating for his dutiful record during the current session of
Congress, and about whom the late columnist George Sokolosky,
while greatly sympathetic to the Kennedy Administration, had thun-
dered that "he has made his own record, and it is not a record for
which a conservative of any hue can vote."

The response of the New York State Republican Party, which belonged, in usufruct, to Governor Rockefeller, was—after courtly pre-
liminaries by the Governor professing his joy at *any* civic-minded

---

and Alex Hillman, New York publishers; Professors Thomas Molnar, Charles
Rice, and Sylvester Petro; journalists Suzanne La Follette, Frank Meyer, William
Rickenbacker, and George Schuyler; and New York attorneys Godfrey Schmidt
and Thomas Bolan.

movements—to do everything possible to abort the establishment of the Conservative Party. Mr. Leo Egan commented (March 12, 1962) in *The New York Times* ("Right Wing Irks GOP") that Governor Rockefeller and his aides were determined not to make the "mistake" the Democrats had made when the Liberal Party was formed. The Democrats had originally viewed the Liberal Party as simply another organizational adjunct, useful for seining extra votes. They did not pause to consider the *quid pro quo,* namely that the Liberals intended to exercise a veto power over Democratic designations, and would proceed to do so.[9] The Republicans, the word went out, must discourage the projected Conservative Party, by pressures rhetorical and legal.

The former were first officially exerted by the Republican State Executive Committee, meeting at the Roosevelt Hotel in June 1962. No Republican," the Committee pronounced, "can be a member of a splinter party and at the same time be a Republican." The leaders of the fledgling party, the Committee threw in, are "political pied pipers who could only betray those whom they lured into their political adventure." At a sticks-and-stones level, Governor Rockefeller ordered his staff to do everything possible to prevent the Conservatives from garnering the fifty signatures per county required to put a party on the ballot. A district attorney from Tompkins County publicly acknowledged, at one point, that he had solicited affidavits of repudiation from voters who had signed the petition; and Rockefeller, asked

9. Leo Egan in *The New York Times,* March 12, 1962:

> The emergence of a militant conservative movement in New York State is raising serious political problems for Governor Rockefeller and other Republican leaders. Depending on how these problems are resolved, they could have a major impact on elections and government in the state for many years to come. In many respects the problems Republicans now face are similar to those that confronted Democrats two and three decades ago when the liberal movement, which gave rise to the American Labor Party and later the Liberal Party, was cresting. The solutions reached then have plagued the Democrats ever since.
>
> Essentially, what the leaders of the new Conservative movement would like (and they have made no secret of it) is a political position in relation to the Republican party comparable to that now held by the Liberal Party in relation to the Democrats.
>
> As things now stand, a Democratic candidate for statewide office in New York has only a remote chance of winning unless he gets a Liberal Party endorsement. [The Republicans] are opposed to letting any minority group get any similar veto power in the choice of Republican state-wide candidates. For this reason their strategy with respect to the conservative movement is likely to be exactly the opposite of that used by the Democrats when they faced the liberal problem. . . . Instead of helping the Republican conservatives attain legal status, the Republican leadership can be expected to use all means at its command to prevent them from achieving this status. . . . Possible stratagems include full use of all the intricacies of the election law; first to prevent the new group from getting the signatures needed to put its candidates on the ballot, and second to prevent it from obtaining the 50,000 votes for Governor needed to achieve legal status.

to investigate, declined comment. Meanwhile, guarding the political store, New York State Republican Chairman L. Judson Morhouse sent out, on August 14, a confidential *aide mémoire* to all county chairmen and vice-chairmen on how to combat the preposterous charges that Governor Rockefeller was not really a conservative. The covering note was more interesting than the attached demonstration, which merely recapitulated in congested statistical form the discredited contention that Rockefeller had proved himself fiscally sound. "It"—warned Morhouse concerning the enclosure—"must be used cautiously and should *not* be published because we do *not* want to emphasize the conservative side so much that we lose some other votes." But along about midsummer, it became apparent that the Party had surprising stamina and a no-nonsense legal adviser—and could not be stopped; whereupon Governor Rockefeller suddenly withdrew his opposition, falling back on the bravely Voltairean stance from which he had originally greeted the Conservative Party's founding, on February 13: "The greater citizen participation we have in public affairs the better."[10] And the big question was now: how well would the brand-new party do at the polls?

The Conservatives named as their candidate for Governor a forty-four-year-old Syracuse businessman, Mr. David Jaquith. Jaquith, a Princeton graduate, president of Vego Industries, a lifelong Republican, president of the Board of Education of Syracuse, had an extensive social and civic background. He campaigned against Rockefeller's domestic policies, stressing that during his free-spending administration as Governor, expenditures had increased by 48.9 per cent and income tax collection by 55 per cent[11] over Averell Harriman's top budget four years earlier. Against Senator Javits, the Conservatives fielded Kieran O'Doherty, the Party's State Chairman, who roasted Senator Javits's record as a fundamental liberal, citing his record in Congress. The Conservative Party climaxed its first campaign at a rally in Madison Square Garden which, although it began a half-hour after President Kennedy's dramatic televised ultimatum to the Soviet Union, nevertheless produced a surprisingly large audience—upward of ten thousand people—and a great deal of enthusiasm.[12]

10. Three years later, State Chairman Daniel Mahoney called on the Governor to declare February 13, 1963, the third anniversary of the founding of the Conservative Party, "Greater Citizen Participation Day," in "lasting commemoration" of the Governor's noble and generous attitudes towards dissenting political opinion." The Governor was not amused.
11. Which figures sounded, two years later in 1964, like the Good Old Days Department. Rockefeller's 1965 budget called for spending 94 per cent more than the Harriman Administration had spent.
12. An interesting essay could be written on Madison Square Garden and politics. It is the symbol of Big Time—and it is greatly feared, because the mere fact of

Javits won in a landslide, well over a million votes. Rockefeller, by contrast, did poorly. The State Chairman Mr. Morhouse had predicted a victory of 800,000 to 1,000,000. Instead, he won by 529,000 votes, 43,000 below his 1958 pluralty. Jaquith polled 141,000 votes which would almost surely have otherwise gone to Rockefeller. The slippage was greatly noticed around the country, and considerably affected Rockefeller's reputation as the undeniable contender for the Republican Presidential nomination in 1964. Homer Bigart summarized the results in *The New York Times*: "In New York the new Conservative Party fell considerably short of the 200,000 votes its leaders had hoped for. David Jaquith . . . candidate for Governor, polled only 118,768[13] votes, and Kieran O'Doherty, Conservative candidate for Senator, only 116,000. The party took comfort in the fact that it drew considerably more than the 50,000 votes it needed to win a permanent place on the ballot." Indeed, Mr. Jaquith, promising that the Party would do better the next time around, observed that "only two or three voters in ten ever heard of the Conservative Party [even] in upstate New York." Regarding this extraordinary success of Senator Javits, Mr. Jaquith remarked, with that political genius for which the Conservative Party is becoming renowned, that Javits's re-election was "just stupidity on the part of the voters."

In 1964, the Conservative Party's principal public contender was Henry Paolucci, a professor of Political Science at Iona College, a diminutive, learned, amiable, talkative, eloquent, versatile nationalist. Senator Keating, following the Rockefeller line, had declared publicly that he would not accept the designation of the Conservative Party if offered to him; and indeed, he and Mr. Robert Kennedy were to spend much of the campaign debating whether Mr. Keating's record in the Senate had been truly truly liberal; so that it is unlikely that Keating, even if Rockefeller had waived his objections, would have wanted the Conservative endorsement. I believe it is accurate to say that the Conservatives would have tendered it to him (a) in recognition of his anti-Communist policy statements during his term of office (par-

---

its use is a taunt to the New York press, which can be counted on to remark the empty spaces, if there are such; and the resulting effect can be greatly demoralizing. The professionals tend to avoid Madison Square Garden as being too risky. New York conservatives have had good luck with it—SRO twice during 1964 for Senator Goldwater, and once in 1962 by the Young Americans for Freedom. But the effort required to fill the Garden is enormous, as also the expense of publicizing the event and trying to lure into it the twenty thousand needed to appease the unoccupied-seat counters. In 1962, the Conservative Party, alone among the political parties, rented the Garden. In 1965, none of the Mayoralty candidates did. The Garden, as a matter of incidental intelligence, rents for ten thousand dollars per night.

13. 118,768 was the original figure reported the day after the election. The final count, however, was 141,000.

ticularly concerning Cuba); and provided (b), he would use his influence with Rockefeller to permit the Conservatives to nominate Goldwater's slate of electors. Rockefeller had meted out an especially spiteful and humiliating blow to the Conservatives by refusing to permit the electors pledged to Goldwater to appear on the Conservative slate, with the ironic consequence that Goldwater, who had been diligently supported by the Conservatives over the preceding years, now that he was officially nominated by the national Republican Party, could only appear on the slate of the New York Republican Party, which was dominated by anti-Goldwaterites; but not on the Conservative Party slate. Meanwhile Goldwater had, of course, to endorse Keating (inferentially rebuking the Conservatives' candidate, Paolucci). Add to all these technical and psychological complications the schismatic determination of many Conservatives to vote for Keating on the grounds that strategic statesmanship required the repression of Robert Kennedy, for anti-dynastic and other reasons.

Of considerable professional political interest were the questions not only of how would Paolucci fare against Keating and Kennedy, but also of how many lesser candidates would win on account of Conservative Party support, or lose on account of Conservative opposition. Although Rockefeller's ban on Republican association with the Conservative Party had effectively bound the major candidates, his hold on lesser candidates was beginning to weaken. No doubt the quite unexpected appearance by Republican State Senate Majority Leader Walter J. Mahoney at the Conservatives' Second Anniversary Dinner in the fall of 1963 had had the desired effect of sending out the word to Republican office-holders that, as a matter of practical politics, the choice would be theirs to make in 1964 whether to accept or decline co-sponsorship by the Conservatives. Senator Mahoney, among the world's most urbane men (and effective public speakers), had said at the dinner, most amiably, in effect, that if you can't lick them (as the Republican Party had tried to do), join them.

In the summer of 1964, at the famous post-nomination Republican unity session in Hershey, Pennsylvania, at which Rockefeller submitted to the discipline of shaking hands with Candidate Goldwater, Rockefeller called a press conference to observe that the Conservative Party "has entered candidates against regular and incumbent Republicans in 58 separate contests for Congress, the State Senate, and the State Assembly," and is therefore "a major obstacle to Republican unity in New York State," incompatible with the spirit of Hershey.

Daniel Mahoney, the Conservative State Chairman, pounced on Rockefeller's statement as a misleading and incomplete summary of the Conservative Party's actual role in Congressional and State legislative contests this year.

More than half of the Conservatives' independent races [he explained] are taking place in safe Democratic districts in New York City. Many of these independent candidacies resulted from a Republican rejection, prompted by the Republican State leadership, of Conservative Party endorsement which [had been] offered to Republican candidates. In several important races, notably the Nassau County race, and the 1st and 5th Congressional Districts, the Conservative Party declined to enter candidates in close races where we would clearly have provided the margin of victory for a liberal Democrat, despite a Republican rejection of our offer of endorsement.

Only in comparatively rare cases is the Conservative Party opposing incumbent Republicans. "For example, the Conservative Party is opposing only two incumbent Republican Congressmen, liberals John Lindsay and Ogden Reid, and five incumbent State Senators. The Liberal Party, whose endorsement President Johnson will accept with the blessing of the Democratic State leadership, is opposing six incumbent Democratic Congressman and eight incumbent State Senators.

Furthermore, the Conservative Party has endorsed 59 Republican candidates for Congress and the State legislature, including 42 incumbents.

Notwithstanding the prevailing confusion, Paolucci polled 203,369 votes, an increase of 75 per cent over the senatorial vote polled by the Conservatives in 1962. (Kennedy beat Keating by 650,307 votes.) Paolucci's vote in New York City was 122,967 votes.

In six Assembly races, the Conservative Party vote either changed the outcome or came within five or ten votes of doing so. Thirty-two members of the New York State legislature were elected with Conservative Party endorsement, as well as Congressman McEwen from the upstate 31st District.

Earl Mazo, replacing Homer Bigart as *The New York Times*' post-election coroner, commented somberly that "an official canvass showed the two-year-old Conservative Party had polled as well in major contests on November 3rd as the Liberal Party, which was founded twenty years ago. . . . Their polling strength is being studied by Democratic and Republican leaders to evaluate the potential impact of the recognized minor parties in future elections." The results of that study have not been made public.

The official Republican opposition to the Conservative Party of New York has centered on the thesis that ideological quarrels should be transacted within the Party, as Governor Rockefeller put it in the midsummer of 1962. The Conservatives have countered that the GOP under Rockefeller has been notoriously insensitive to the existence of reasoned conservatism within the Party[14] and that the probable reason why this is so is the special pressures exerted by the Liberal Party, combined with the collapse of any organized educational effort to lure New York City voters away from dogmatic liberalism—deficiencies which the Conservatives explicitly seek to mend. It is not generally realized that the Republican Party of New York has a highly authoritarian tradition, and that it is very difficult for the dissenter to make his voice heard. Thomas Dewey, for instance, on the eve of the Chicago Convention of 1952, threatened all but public execution for any New York delegate who voted for Taft over Eisenhower. The State GOP is firmly dominated by two or three top Republican office-holders—Rockefeller primarily, and Javits, and now Lindsay—who are impatient of democratic Republicanism.

"At the State level," Daniel Mahoney observed on January 30, 1965, "the Republican Party is simply the Rockefeller Party, as Governor Rockefeller demonstrated when he named his appointments secretary State Chairman of the Party last week. And now John Lindsay has proposed that the Republican Mayoral nominee should control the selection not only of the Republican city-wide ticket, but of every Republican legislative and City Council candidate in New York City. Our election law presumes to entrust these nominations to enrolled Republicans voting in their local primaries, but Mr. Lindsay is prepared to waive this archaic arrangement." It is an interesting conjecture, on which I shall in due course be dwelling, that the effect of the Republicans' closed shop is not only to discountenance a useful bloc of Republican voters but to discourage a potential flow of voters whose background is Democratic, and who might well view the Conservative Party as a way-station to a remodeled Republican Party.

But the final historical responsibility of the Conservative Party of New York will be to answer the question raised in an editorial in *The New York Times* (October 31, 1962). "The Conservatives," it grumbled, "in running a splinter ticket against the Republicans are

14. Which Governor Rockefeller denounced, on July 14, 1963, in the most sundering terms, as "every bit as dangerous to American principles and American institutions as the radical left"—a thunderbolt he did not trouble to direct only at supporters of, let us say, Robert Welch, but at supporters, in general, of Senator Goldwater. The conservatives, Rockefeller went on, "utterly reject the fundamental principles of our heritage," and desire to "subvert the Republican Party itself." Perhaps overcome by the general momentum, he went on to anathematize, while he was at it, the Kennedy Administration as responsible for the "unprincipled opportunism [that] has captured the Democratic Party."

pursuing a willfully destructive course. With their wrongheaded mis-
chief-making the worst thing that could happen to them would be
to succeed." The reasoning is that as the Conservative Party of New
York strengthens, so the Republican Party's strength will diminish,
and thus also will diminish the number of office-holders who do
service to Conservative ideals. That reasoning—it is curious, of
course, that the identical arguments are not raised to urge the liqui-
dation of the Liberal Party—is correct if the big office-holders of the
Republican Party in New York State are indeed furthering such ideals.
If, on the other hand, such calipers as the ADA's are at all useful
for measuring, at least by contemporary political standards, the
differences between conservative and liberal policies (and if not the
ADA's, whose?), then Mr. Javits, Republican, with his hundred-per-
cent ADA record is hardly furthering those ideals; and if fiscal husbandry and a resistance to bloc-pressures are conservative, then Mr.
Rockefeller is hardly satisfying those ideals: and so with Mr. Lindsay.
The Conservative Party becomes a party of nose-spiters only as it
moves, which it has yet to do, against moderate Republicans who in
their public careers have stood up against incontinent liberalism.
There are the sectarians within the Conservative Party, one must
suppose: but they have not made any apparent headway in converting their Party into a utopianist affair, mindless of the here and
now. Meanwhile, in microcosm, the Republican Party's dilemma in
New York is as it is nationwide—only a little more so because New
York, alas, is New York. There are those who wish it were slightly
otherwise, and the year the Voting Rights Bill was passed, and the
re-apportionment decision enforced, was perhaps not quite the year
in which to tell New York conservatives that they alone must not
vote according to their lights.

IV.

Lindsay, Spring 1965

John Lindsay announced that he would run for Mayor on May 13, 1965, after months of brooding about it. His decision was interesting at various levels. Obviously, it was interesting to Lindsay himself. It was interesting, also, to New Yorkers. And interesting, besides, to the Republican community throughout the country.

It is generally agreed that the final impetus to Lindsay's decision was provided by Rockefeller, when he announced, on May 4, 1965, that he would seek re-election as Governor in 1966. Lindsay's extraordinary showing in his 1964 re-election campaign as Congressman for the Seventeenth Assembly District (he got 71.5 per cent of the vote) had given rise to the comment that here was a political comer, and so the question inevitably followed, to what? The Presidency of the United States, of course ("The District's Pride—The Nation's Hope" had been his political slogan during the Congressional campaign); but, presumably, to somewhere in between first. His difficulty lay in a juxtaposition of inconvenient timetables and formidable adversaries. Senator Robert Kennedy would not be up for re-election until 1970; and to wait five long years for the opportunity to run against Robert Kennedy would hardly argue the political sagacity one expects from the nation's hope. He might have waited until 1965 to oppose Jacob Javits in the primary, but such a move, though technically available to him, was out of the question by reason not only of political prudence (Javits had won his own re-election in 1962 by a majority of over one million votes), but of ideological consanguinity. Lindsay's big hope was that Nelson Rockefeller would decide against running to succeed himself as Governor in 1966. When Rockefeller publicly announced that in fact he would run, Lindsay was left without any prospective avenue for advancement until, at the earliest, 1970; and even then, only on the assumption that Rockefeller did not win in 1966 and that, if he won, he would not seek yet another term.

Shortly before Rockefeller's disappointing announcement, Lindsay had proclaimed (on March 1) that "after long and deep thought, I have decided to adhere to my decision not to seek the nomination of my party for the mayor of New York City. Many considerations have led me to this conclusion, including Congressional responsibilities and national legislation of great interest to my district and to me." Rockefeller's subsequent announcement (we have it from Lindsay's biographers), caused Lindsay to decide that, after all, his Congressional responsibilities could wait yet awhile, pending the liberation of New York City.

Lindsay's announcement was interesting to New Yorkers because here was someone who might actually hope to beat Wagner. The early polls showed him running slightly ahead of Wagner in popularity. Lindsay's prowess as a vote-getter had been established, and the general aura that hung over him suggested that, win or lose, here would be a campaign easily distinguishable from the routine Republican attempt to capture City Hall.

I have never seen any evidence that the general excitement caused by Lindsay's announcement issued from any well-wrought expectations by the thinking community of the effect Lindsay's victory might have on the future of New York City, other than the general Googooism of it all—running out the rascals, beating the Democratic machine, that kind of thing. Preliminary editorial comment stressed (a) Lindsay's personal attributes, (b) Wagner's fatigue, (c) the desirability of a change, (d) Lindsay's flamboyant liberalism. But nowhere does one find any public identification of Lindsay with a set of ideas designed to deliver New York from the succubi that had been emaciating the city. The exhilaration centered on Mr. Lindsay as first-rate political horseflesh; nothing more. In the Republican community there was a considerable twitter because, finally, there loomed a prospective Republican victor for the second highest administrative position in the land, and the Republican Party, locally and nationally, ached for any portent of rejuvenation after the great defeat of 1964.

The spoilers, inevitably, asked: What are Mr. Lindsay's credentials as a Republican?

1. Lindsay as Republican

The official position, in American politics, tends to be that a politician is, no questions asked, a legitimate member of whatever party he runs under the banner of, if he wins. As far as the Republican National Committee was concerned, Lindsay was a Republican if only because that is what he had listed himself as being, and had run regularly for re-election as. Very soon after Lindsay announced that he would run, he was publicly adored by Ray Bliss, Chairman of the Republican National Committee, and General Eisenhower and Richard Nixon and other prominent Republicans offered their active support (which Lindsay was, however, careful not to invoke). On purely organizational grounds, it was always that simple—as simple as Governor George Wallace's attempt, in the spring of 1964, to run in the Democratic primaries of Wisconsin, Indiana, and Maryland, against Lyndon Johnson. As a Democrat of record, Governor of the State of Alabama, he had every right to enter the Democratic primaries even in states whose official Democrats were united in passionate opposition to the principles of George Wallace.

Lindsay fared better than Wallace. Wallace was repudiated by important members of his own party—Lindsay was not. It is interesting that even without official Democratic support Wallace succeeded in winning 34 per cent, 30 per cent, and 43 per cent of the Democratic primary vote in Wisconsin, Indiana, and Maryland, respectively. It is inconceivable that he would have succeeded in doing so had he not run as a Democrat; even as Lindsay—to be sure without official Republican opposition—ran, or rather was listed, as a "Republican."

Lindsay is a Republican largely as a matter of baptismal affirmation, even as Wallace is, congenitally, a Democrat. Affirmations are not, of course, enough: it is required that they be ratified by a constituency. The constituency's powers in these matters are, however, largely nominal, of special interest to the locality, but of no necessary interest to the national party. Alabama's overwhelming certification of George Wallace as a Democrat is hardly binding on the Democratic Party of, say, California; indeed, Wallace has been a negative concern of the Democratic National Committee, which runs pell-mell from any implication that Wallace is a representative Democrat. The relationship between the locally certified Democrat and the national Democrat is, in other words, a matter for negotiation. It is a relationship warm or cool depending on whether the local Democrat has plowed fresh political ground, suggesting extralocal means of strengthening the party. Orval Faubus of Arkansas confounded the national contumely of 1957—when he refused to permit the integration of Little Rock schools, yielding only to *force majeure* (ironically, a parachute division led by General Edwin Walker)—by winning re-election after re-election as Governor. But he did not, by his local successes, impress the national Democratic Party, within which he was a continuing, though hardly disabling, embarrassment.

In other words, although a politician is *ex officio* a member of the party whose designation he runs and wins under, he is not, simply in virtue of his local success, a mainstreamer within his party. In Lindsay's case, his public positions have been, roughly speaking, as far removed from the GOP's as Wallace's have been from the Democratic Party's. In addition, it would be impossible to demonstrate that his successive re-elections to Congress were in any way the *result* of his nominal Republicanism. Perhaps the very first time around, when he fought in a Republican primary (in 1958) and, having won it, secured the formal endorsement of the Republican Party, he might be said to have been dependent on his party's endorsement. But having once become a public figure in his own right, he did not need organizational Republican help—any more than he sought it. For one thing, being tapped by the Republican organization in New York City is not to be compared with marrying the boss's daughter. A Republican endorsement in New York will prop you up, but you need to walk alone. What else can be expected in a city over three to one Democratic? Even in Lindsay's own Congressional district, the registration is seven to five Democratic.

Lindsay's home district is probably the most fabled in the United States. It shelters not only just about all the resident financial, social, and artistic elite of New York but also probably the densest national concentration of vegetarians, pacifists, hermaphrodites, junkies, Communists, Randites, clam-juice-and-betel-nut eaters; plus, also, a sprinkling of quite normal people. It is, as I have noted, preponderantly Democratic, although it has a perverse tradition of going "Republican"—indeed has done so uninterruptedly ever since 1937. In that year Bruce Barton (of Batten, Barton, Durstine, and Osborn; author of *The Man Nobody Knows*) was elected Congressman, and although he was a firebrand tory, utterly opposed to the New Deal, he was uproariously popular, even while pledging to devote himself to the repeal of one obsolete law each week, and firmly opposing entry into the Second World War. He was, indeed, *the* Barton of Roosevelt's "Martin, Barton, and Fish," the big political anti-doxology of the late thirties. Barton stepped out of the Seventeenth and ran for the Senate in 1940, lost, and was succeeded by Republican Joseph Clark Baldwin, every bit as liberal as his predecessor had been conservative—so much so that in 1944 Republican Boss Tom Curran flatly refused to endorse him for re-election. Baldwin was enraged. "They said that I did not represent the Republicans in the district. My opinion is to the contrary. They want me on the line on reactionary measures, and I won't do it. You can't be elected by reactionaries in my district. There are only 29,000 Republicans. I was elected [in 1944] with 73,000 votes, which means that some 50,000 independents voted for me." He finished his lament with a wonderful sentence: "For years you had to be a reactionary to get nominated in the Republican Party and a liberal to get elected." Not quite accurate, considering that his predecessor was Barton, and his successor would be Frederic Coudert, who, in the characterization of the historian of the Seventeenth Congressional District, Caspar Citron,[1] "will remain in history as the prototype of the arch-conservative on both the economic and foreign fronts." Baldwin contested Coudert in a primary and was drastically (five to one) beaten.

Coudert lasted six terms, winning his last one by the slimmest of margins. He withdrew partly as a matter of general fatigue, partly because Lindsay had more or less made it plain that he would, if necessary, challenge him in a primary contest; and Coudert, already resentful over the frequency of Congressional elections, did not want yet another political contest on his agenda.

It would certainly appear, from the heavy Democratic registration plurality, that the Seventeenth District is irretrievably liberal, though the fact of Barton's election, and more recently of Coudert's, does not appear to make the district's bias absolutely conclusive, unless it is held that the district forever after consolidated, after Coudert's last term, into liberalism. To be sure, in 1961, as the result of redistricting, the area was enlarged, with the result that a greater number of registered Democrats were drawn into it. At any rate, Coudert's diminishing pluralities and Lindsay's increasing pluralities would appear to suggest that a Barton-Coudert Republican would not have much of a chance in the Silk Stocking District at this point. Lindsay's successor Republican, Theodore Kupferman, ran on a platform which his opponent, the liberal Democrat Orin Lehman, was forced to concede did not differ in any interesting particular from his own.

It is inconceivable to suggest (a) that Mr. Lindsay would have been denied the Democratic designation in the Seventeenth had he at any time, formally renouncing the GOP, desired it; or (b) that his successively increasing pluralities would have been other than still greater, had he been running as a Democrat. What would have been missing is, of course, the piquancy, so stimulating to the jaded taste, that someone of Lindsay's views should call himself a Republican. The squares who pause to wonder why it is generally said with relish

1. Caspar Citron, *John V. Lindsay and the Silk Stocking Story* (New York: Fleet, 1965).

that someone is a "Lindsay Republican" and with disrelish that someone is a "Byrd Democrat" are gloriously unaware of the implications
of the *Zeitgeist*.

Even so, the factual question necessarily arose: What kind of Republican *was* John Lindsay? I say necessarily, because however often
it seemed desirable to parochialize the New York race ("I am not
running as a Republican," Lindsay said over and over again, "I am
running as Lindsay"), he made no discernible efforts—and, to be
fair, could not very easily have done so—to discourage the picture of
himself as the New Image of the national Republican Party. His
friends and admirers simply wouldn't permit it. ". . . One of these
years," a political writer had forecast at the Republican Convention in
1964, "you may see Lindsay at a convention as the candidate." A
gossip columnist had reported that President Johnson and Senator
Kennedy exchanged, in 1965, woeful speculation as to which of the
two was fated to be Lindsay's next adversary. A trustee of Vassar
College presented Lindsay to a Vassar audience as a man "we fer-
vently hope is a President of our country in the making."[2] Miss Inez
Robb has called him "a sure Presidential contender in the seventies—
if the traditional [*sic*] Republican Party is to be saved." Robert Ruark
cabled from Spain [!] that "the Republican Party is starving to death
for men of Lindsay's caliber. . . . He is a statesman, young or not,
and should be around for a lot of years as Congressman, Governor,
who knows? Maybe President." David Dubinsky, chiding Harry
Golden for his refusal to support Lindsay during the campaign, published in full-page advertisements (see Chapter X), his open letter to
Golden: "Suppose we elect Lindsay as Mayor of New York City. What
lesson does this teach to the other Republicans elsewhere who also
would like to be elected? They must conclude that the way for a
Republican to get elected is to act like Lindsay. . . ."

It was a matter, also, of Lindsay's own stated ambitions for the
Republican Party. *"We,"* he had said on November 6, 1964, to the
Wednesday Club of the House of Representatives, which is composed
of liberal Republicans, "are among the Republicans who will have to
rebuild the Republican Party out of the ashes. We hope we can work
with other moderate groups throughout the country to return the
Party to the tradition of Lincoln."

In a word, the appeal to Fusion-for-New York, together with a sort
of intellectual pledge by everyone in the country to disregard the
national repercussions of a Lindsay victory, was always unrealistic.

2. The "political writer," "gossip columnist," and "trustee of Vassar College"
are quoted anonymously in Daniel E. Button, *Lindsay, a Man for Tomorrow*
(New York: Random House, 1965).

If Lindsay won, Republicans in Ohio and California would not be permitted to pass off his victory as meaningless, as merely a triumph of Goo-gooism in a jaded municipal situation. The opinion-making press, which would herald Lindsay's victory as charting the road ahead for a resurgent Republicanism, would not permit it, for one thing. In this sense those Democrats who all along insisted that a victory for Lindsay in New York would work to "Republican" advantage were technically correct; correct in predicting that the Republican Party would inevitably take heed of Lindsay's showing in New York and attempt to profiteer on it. The help-Lindsay-and-you-help-the-Republican-Party objection to Lindsay was superficial only when uttered by highly ideologized liberals—Harry Golden, for instance, and a few members of the Liberal Party—who refused to reflect that, after all, if the Republican Party could be brought to fashion itself after Lindsay, their cherished dogmas would have little to fear from any aggrandizement of the Republican Party.

During his early days in Congress (1958 to 1960, and to some extent even in 1962), John Lindsay did take a few positions, or more precisely did make a few utterances, which had appeal for conservatives—a fact that suggests, as his progressive voting record formally documents, that during his stay in Congress he moved toward, rather than began at, that position of extravagant compliance with the liberal orthodoxy which finally made him a hero, in 1965, to the Liberal Party, to the New York *Post*, and to *The Nation*. For a while, for instance—though his voting record never reflected this concern— he used to talk worriedly about the necessity for fiscal restraint. Which, as is recorded, the editors of *The New York Times* at one point dryly doubted he really, truly, ever really worried about. He once defended Eisenhower on one of those occasions when the President was in one of his frugal moods. "[Eisenhower's] policy is sound," he declared, "even though it is painful and possibly unpopular to insist upon paying for what we get." And again, "The President is correct in insisting upon the Congress's paying for the programs it enacts; spending should be according to priorities of national needs, and pork-barrel approaches to legislation must be avoided."[3]

When John Kennedy became President, John Lindsay was, by contemporary—and certainly by posthumous—standards, positively irreverent. "The President," he said on the eve of the Vienna summit meeting in 1961, "will now meet with Khrushchev *after* disavowing personal diplomacy. He will continue to dole out give-aways after calling for national sacrifice. He will now affirm both a growing economy and a healthy picture in defense after causing gloom and

3. D. E. Button, *op. cit.*

despair with his campaign appraisals. This kind of ambivalence demands our scrutiny." (The demanded scrutiny was not forthcoming.)

On another occasion he actually reminded President Kennedy of the "vigorous support [JFK had promised] of those long-overdue economy reforms [which] would be heartening to every American taxpayer." And, in a general blast which he would not for the world have recalled during the '65 campaign, he charged during the summer of 1962 that "the trouble in Washington today is that the President has never learned how to be President. He thinks he's still running. There is a difference between being a perpetual candidate and being the President of the United States. . . . The fact that he hasn't been able to get his program through his own heavily Democratic Congress [through no fault of Mr. Lindsay's], indicates that the Congress recognizes [sic] more public relations than substance in the President's efforts. If we were treated to less personal image-making, and more concern about basic problems and their sensible solution, we would have better government."[4] That statement was clearly not composed by Lindsay's campaign manager Robert Price, whose efforts during 1965 combined the two imperatives, that Lindsay be identified as a Kennedy Democrat ("For seven years," his principal flyer during the 1965 campaign divulged, "he has represented New York in Congress, where he has supported the programs of Presidents John F. Kennedy and Lyndon B. Johnson"), and that Lindsay's opponents be cast in the role of opponents of better government.

Lindsay had gone on, on that highly forgettable occasion in 1962, to criticize Mr. Kennedy for using tactics which Lindsay was so assiduously to emulate in his own campaign for Mayor: "I blame the Kennedy family for much of it [paralysis in government]. It's gotten so that if you're against the Kennedy family, you're against progress. You can't discuss these things. The party line in the House of Representatives is that if anyone proposes a different or deeper or better approach to, say, the Kennedy civil rights program, then he's against civilization. I don't think the Kennedys realize how much they're shutting off debate." Indeed.[5]

---

4. D. E. Button, op. cit., p. 106.
5. "If I should win the mayoralty of New York it means something important in the country. . . . Mr. Buckley is running against me for precisely [the] reasons [that] his people ran against me last year, in 1964, when I stood for Congress and stood independently and would not support Mr. Buckley—Mr. Goldwater— and Mr. Buckley as a matter of conscience and they tried to destroy me then. They try to destroy us now and the pincer attack, I tell you, is a very dangerous thing because it means that New York City stands the chance of not having a new start simply because a vote for Mr. Buckley is a vote for Mr. Beame . . . most of the advice I received when I decided to run for Mayor was not to run; they said, Mr. Lindsay, if you run you will cut yourself off; New York City can't be governed and worse than that, they will chop you to pieces and if you

For the benefit of the curious, I list in the Appendix B section a brief description of twenty-one bills passed by the Eighty-seventh and Eighty-eighth Congresses, concerning which there are these common denominators: (a) that they were overwhelmingly endorsed by Democrats and overwhelmingly opposed by Republicans; and (b) that John Lindsay was among the tiny minority of Republicans—they ranged from five to thirty-four—who made their passage possible. Lindsay voted with the Democrats, to effect the passage of measures which would not otherwise have passed, a total of thirty-one times. As such, he was runner-up among liberal Republicans in the frequency of his fealty to Democrats-in-a-jam—second only to Congressman Seymour Halpern (New York), who voted thirty-four times with the Democrats. In the Eighty-seventh Congress (1958–1960), he voted with the Democrats, on the critical issues that divided the two parties, 59 per cent of the time. In the Eighty-eighth Congress (1960–1962), he voted with them 78 per cent of the time. During his final session in Congress, he earned a rating of 87 per cent from the Burke's Peerage of United States Liberalism, the Americans for Democratic Action's annual score sheet (which rated him as dependable a liberal as over one-half of House Democrats). On several occasions he voted with a small minority of Democrats for measures uniquely identified as liberal, thus locating himself within the left-most faction of the Democratic Party.

As I say, the attachment to liberal policies was progressive. He voted 31 per cent of the time with the Democrats in 1959, 60 per cent in 1964—during which period the Democrats themselves grew, by commonly accepted standards, more liberal. The (conservative) Americans for Constitutional Action have their own poll—the obverse, pretty much, of the ADA's—which revealed that the median Republican voted with his party 86 per cent of the time on issues of importance to conservatives. On those occasions, Lindsay voted with the party 21 per cent of the time. The range of his votes with the liberal bloc in Congress is merely suggested by: his vote to pack the Rules Committee with liberals designated by President Kennedy, so as to ease the passage of liberal legislation (passed, 217–212); his vote to authorize the President to purchase one hundred million dollars' worth of United Nations bonds, in defiance of the Republican insistence that loans be barred until the United Nations General Assembly adopted the World Court's opinion on financial obligations of members; his insistence that President Kennedy should not resume

---

are elected to Mayor you can't resolve the problems of New York City, and they said it is a dead end. I say New York is the greatest city in the world . . ." (CBS, TV, Sept. 26, 1965)

H-bomb testing until after obtaining the approval of the United Nations; his vote with the majority against the reduction of foreign aid (208–198); his vote with the majority against prohibiting subsidies on agricultural products shipped to Communist nations (187–186); his sponsorship along with a small minority (29) of a bill to abolish, in effect, the House Committee on Un-American Activities; his votes against the reaffirmation of the Monroe Doctrine, against the extension of the provisions of the Sedition Act to Americans abroad, in favor of the abolition of loyalty procedures in defense industries. Lindsay was one of the handful of Congressmen in either party who refused to sign the annual statement by the Committee of One Million opposed to the admission of Red China to the United Nations (for which stand he was explicitly rebuked by his own New York Young Republicans[6]); who expressed public sympathy for the Committee for a Sane Nuclear Policy; who opposed a Constitutional Amendment to permit prayer in the public schools; who voted to increase the minimum wage law, against an alternative suggestion that it be raised, yes, but not to such an unrealistic level; who joined in the liberal attack on the Central Intelligence Agency, in company with those who blamed it for the fiasco in the Bay of Pigs; who favored the so-called Princeton Plan for compulsory integration of the public schools. . . . Apostasy on any one or even more of these issues hardly detaches a man from the Republican Party. But the accumulation is sufficient to justify this generality, that any political technician, presented pseudonymously with John Lindsay's voting record, would, on the basis of existing voting patterns, pronounce that the Congressman in question was, inferentially, a fairly regular Democrat, with a discernible bias to the left.

None of the above is particularly interesting except inasmuch as it plants the categories. It only remains to examine the quality of John Lindsay's thought, to probe his semipermanent digressions from Republican orthodoxy in search of the new role for the Republican Party; to examine the bearing of his thought on the municipal problems of New York City; and, of course, to draw the lessons from it all for the national Republican Party and the two-party system.

As a tactical matter there is no denying that in New York City the suppression of one's Republicanism, let alone one's conservatism, tends to be the smart thing to do. Lindsay's biographer (Button) does not know exactly how to handle the problem. On the one hand Lindsay's transcendence of Republicanism must be presented as a statesmanlike projection of true Republican principle. On the other

6. *The New York Times,* March 10, 1961.

hand a touch of mugwumpery is always charming. He flounders about. "[Lindsay's] campaigns play down 'Republican' identification almost to the point of disappearance,"[7] he notes, "and he follows a highly irregular party line in Washington. Amazement and amusement followed his 1965 declaration [that] he would run 'as Lindsay' for Mayor of New York City." (It is left to the imagination, preferably inflamed, just who was (a) amazed or (b) amused.) After all, the biographer concedes, "For John Lindsay, the device of playing up 'the candidate' rather than 'the party' has been startlingly successful." But as if to guard against the perils of an untoward de-Republicanization, the hagiographer cautiously adds: "Though he established an impressive, ambitious network of district campaign headquarter outposts to be manned by non-Republican volunteers, he identified himself with Senator Javits, former Mayor LaGuardia and others— 'they are Republicans and I am a Republican.'" There were, to be sure, difficulties even then, as for instance when his opponents— Professor Martin B. Dworkis (1962); Mrs. Eleanor Clark French (1964); Abraham Beame (1965)—raised the ugly matter of the eccentric coincidence between Lindsay's votes and those of other Republicans. "The Lindsay record of siding with the Kennedy-Johnson Administration on two-thirds of domestic issues in the two immediately preceding years became his 'failure to support the Administration on one-third of the issues,'" his biographer ruefully observes.[8]

Although, as I have suggested, I do not doubt that Lindsay would have prospered as a Democrat, there is no denying the special quality of the satisfaction that comes from vindicated heterodoxy. Lindsay's opponent in 1962, Mr. Dworkis, wandered forlornly about Manhattan catching people by the collar and proclaiming his comparative purity as a political liberal. He had, remarks Mr. Caspar Citron,[9] grave difficulties.

---

7. Monocle Magazine/The Outsider's Newsletter/80 Fifth Avenue, New York, N.Y.

October 22, 1965

Dear Mr. Buckley:
   Yesterday I received a call from a Lindsay campaign worker who wanted to know:
   ". . . if we can count on your active support during the campaign?"
   "No, I'm afraid not."
   "Are you a Republican?"
   "Yes, I am."
   "Oh, I'm sorry to hear that."
   CLICK
Now just what do you think she meant?

Sincerely,
—Richard M. Beebe

8. D. E. Button, op. cit., p. 221.
9. Op. cit., p. 100.

The odds against Dworkis were not improved by the editorial stands the newspapers took. He feels that they were foreordained for Lindsay, not so much because of the record, but because they felt the need to keep one liberal GOP representative in the House from Manhattan. . . . "We did speak," he recalls, "to the people at the *Post* and the *Times*, and some of the other newspapers like *The Village Voice*—although the editor of the *Voice* was never willing to see us personally."

The New York *Post really* let Dworkis down.

"The editorial endorsing Lindsay said that undoubtedly I was more liberal than Congressman Lindsay, but that it was important to keep a liberal Republican in the House." . . . I asked Dworkis [Citron continued] "what hold he thought Lindsay had on the voters. He said: 'I think Lindsay is regarded as sort of a thorn in the Republicans' side—the promise of a Republican Party that could be put into being—the resurgence of a Republicanism in the image of Abraham Lincoln. A lot of these people think of Lindsay as a sort of Lincolnesque type. Even the *Times*, when he spoke of his own basic, innate fiscal conservatism, really didn't believe him.' "

Indeed, the further his opponents went in suggesting that deep inside him, Lindsay's Republican genes were doing calisthenics against the day of the coup d'état, the tougher the going, up against Lindsay's obdurately liberal record. "From the start, Mrs. French made her mind up to try and pin the GOP badge on Lindsay. She reasoned that as he was, after all, a GOP figure, some Goldwater philosophy would be bound to rub off on him and this would not sit well in the Silk Stocking District."

But the tactic didn't work for Mrs. French any more than, a year later, it worked for Mr. Beame. "The albatross did not stick, and today she feels that she may even have contributed something more to the Lindsay image with this attack. . . ." To be sure, there was the occasional Republican hardnose: "Leaders of several neighborhood Young Republican Clubs . . . [charged] that Lindsay 'has virtually read himself out of the Republican Party' "—this particular denunciation by Republicans was in response to Lindsay's refusal to support Senator Goldwater, the choice of the National Republican Convention—"and attack[ed] his stand as 'a shocking example of political expediency.' "

But no matter. "What a difference election means!" sighs Mr. Citron. "There has been no more talk like that." Indeed, "campaigner Lindsay ended by converting his great liability into a huge and negotiable asset. His independence of the vastly unpopular candidacy of

Barry Goldwater was perhaps the wisest political move he ever made. . . ." And, of course, Citron is correct—nothing, they say, succeeds like success. The Republican Party's admiration for Lindsay as a winner exactly reflects the Republican Party's own ideological promiscuity, betraying its infidelity to what is left of its own philosophy. Indeed, the point might be made that there *is* no extant Republican philosophy, and that Lindsay is its prophet.

2. Lindsay as Moderate

It will remain for a more sure-footed political theorist than John Lindsay to describe what it is exactly that distinguishes, or should distinguish, the Republican Party from the Democratic Party; but pending his appearance, we shall have to do with what we have. I have remarked that Mr. Lindsay, between elections, had talked about the necessity of rebuilding the Republican Party. His most orderly comment to that general effect was published in the *Atlantic Monthly* shortly after Goldwater's defeat in 1964. "To say the party is in 'serious difficulty,' " he wrote, "is to put it mildly. The Republican Party is a pile of rubble at this moment. There will be a hard and long struggle within the party as we try to put ourselves back on the track. But our recovery is indispensable for the two-party system. If there is going to be a decent, constructive opposition, which our government needs in order to function properly, it is going to take a good deal of work on the part of the survivors in the Republican Party. The moderates in particular will have to make a great effort and will have to prevail."[10]

Now in political discourse, rhetoric is ninety-five per cent. So, before we reach the mayoralty campaign, a little infield practice is probably in order. Consider the paragraph above.

1. "But our recovery is indispensable for the two-party system," Mr. Lindsay says. Half true. The recovery of the second party is indispensable provided it offers a significant alternative to the policies, as distinguished from merely the administrative practices, of the party in power. There is never in operation a meaningful two-party system if the two parties are programmatically indistinguishable from one another. Has Mr. Lindsay ever indicated a way by which, simultaneously, the Republican Party might be (a) different from that Republican Party which is a pile of rubble, and (b) different from the regnant Democratic Party?

2. "If there is going to be a decent, constructive opposition, it is

10. Citron, *op. cit.,* p. 123.

going to take a good deal of work on the part of the survivors in
the Republican Party." Now, "decent" is generally accepted as meaning, roughly, the opposite of, well—"indecent." Mr. Lindsay, as we
shall be noting, is not strong on words—more or less anything that
points roughly in the right direction will do. But terminological exactitude is very much in order, if not when one is running for office, at
least when one is running as theoretical reformer in the *Atlantic;*
and the term "decent" must be supposed to have been used by Mr.
Lindsay so loosely as to be meaningless; or in such a way as to distinguish between *his* Republicanism and other people's Democratism,
from which, as we have seen, it is not readily distinguishable; or in
such a way as to suggest that it is *indecent* to oppose, as the traditional Republican Party has done, that tendency of government best
suggested by isolating a few representative points of divergence between Mr. Lindsay and it. Was it *indecent* for Mr. Goldwater to oppose
Title II (the public accommodations section) of the civil rights bill—
notwithstanding his own frequently-stated impulses in support of its
objectives—on Constitutional grounds? Why was *that* indecent,
while Mr. Lindsay's opposition to the proposed anti-pornography bill
—precisely on Constitutional grounds—was, somehow, decent? Why
was Mr. Lindsay's subservience to *his* understanding of law and due
process commendable while Goldwater's was not? Is it manifestly
decent to support, as Lindsay has regularly done, the whole tissue of
federal public welfare bills—in contrast to the traditional Republican
hypothesis that welfare is more efficaciously handled by the local
communities and the individual states? Isn't the quarrel rather over
differing approaches to complicated problems than over relative
ethical stature?

And is it in fact *constructive* to appeal to superimposed political
authority, as opposed to natural economic organization, to dissipate
certain palpable social evils? For instance—to look ahead for a minute—there is the problem of the housing shortage in New York. Is
it "constructive" to pledge, as John Lindsay did during the campaign,
to continue rent controls? Or might it have been more constructive to
pledge their termination? Isn't the problem an empirical one (the
rights of building owners temporarily apart, which rights Mr. Lindsay
has apparently never heard of), namely, *Which* proposal of the two
contending proposals *is* the more *constructive,* in relation to the
objective in mind, namely, the appearance of more housing units?

3. "The moderates in particular will have to make a great effort
and will have to prevail." The rhetorical "moderate." It is apparent
that, in workaday usage, the political categories, as they travel from
right to left, vault over the "extreme" or the "ultra" as applicable

other than to a Communist—or to a conservative. Terminological orderliness would suppose that if one acknowledges the category of an "utraconservative Republican," one must, if only for symmetry's sake, acknowledge the category of an "ultraliberal Republican"—at least in the absence of an altogether arbitrary ordinance prescribing that as one moves left from the ultraconservative position, one traverses moderate territory, then suddenly hits a stone wall—o'erleaping the "extreme liberal" territory which, geographically, one would suppose would necessarily lie between moderate Republicanism and Democratic territory. But the area in question appears to be absolutely unoccupied. I say "absolutely," because for years I have scanned *The New York Times* in search of just *one* "ultraliberal Republican." Not only have I been unrewarded in the *Times*, I have not ever discovered, in all of America, from the mountains to the prairies to the oceans white with foam, a *single* "utraliberal."

Enough. "Ultra" (or "extreme"), although it is an adjective of generic applicability, is exclusively reserved (a) for the unfashionable right (*e.g.*, the Goldwaterites), or (b) as a dainty way of handling the Communist left ("the ultraliberal Paul Robeson . . ."). It is the scarlet letter that identifies and, hopefully, ghettoizes, the politically intolerable; and any definitive study of the rhetorical folkways of our age will quickly note this dead give-away, around whose usage the entire sweep of contemporary political currents can be charted. The Establishment's hard hold over the rhetorical categories is, in political discourse, its most important weapon. How to maneuver, when the odds are thus stacked? "If Mr. Lindsay were any more liberal," I found myself saying exasperatedly at one point in the campaign to a reporter, "he'd be in a zoo." Excessive, yes, yes, I quite understand: but, in a way, a freeish translation of *The New York Times*' solid casting of Mr. Lindsay, in the editorial exhorting the Liberal Party to give him its backing: "[Mr. Lindsay] is in political faith and political position about as close to being a liberal as anybody can get" (*The New York Times,* June 22). As an extreme conservative, I'd have preferred to label him an extreme liberal—except that the species simply doesn't exist. If you don't believe me, ask *The New York Times*.

Loose rhetoric, as I say, makes it difficult to understand just where Lindsay desires to take the Republican Party, always assuming that the concomitant challenge is to take it in a direction other than that in which the Democrats are going. Professional students of Mr. Lindsay's thought are not particularly helpful. "The answer to the question of 'How good a Republican is John Lindsay?'" volunteers Mr. Button, in the spirit of I'm-glad-you-asked-me-that-question, "must be: Intellectually, he is a strong Republican; emotionally, he is fiercely independent; spiritually, he is a progressive and in that sense frequently finds common cause with the Democratic liberal group. But much more importantly [*i.e.*, presumably, *more* important than Lindsay's (a) intellectual, (b) emotional, and (c) spiritual principles, if you can follow this, which I cannot], he is morally and ethically committed to principles he holds to be paramount in value to all other considerations." From here on it is sheerer chaos, but let us move bravely forward: ". . . Thus he is entitled to run, in a campaign of his own making, not merely as a Republican, but 'as Lindsay,' in keeping with his tenet that the office-seeker has a responsibility to survive in the struggle for power—*responsible* power [italics in the original], as delegated by the people."[11]

One senses the difficulties. But let us leave aside emotional, spiritual, *and* paramount problems, and inquire into the nature of the *intellectual* commitment that makes Mr. Lindsay a "strong Republican." The key, one will find, is Abraham Lincoln, toward whom Mr. Lindsay tends to refer all questions having to do with the nature of the Republican Party.

3. Lindsay, Lincoln, and the GOP

"It seemed to me," Linsday advised his biographer, "that it was important that this was the party of the individual—as I saw it, and as I still see it. It's the party of Lincoln, of civil rights, the protection of the person and his liberties against the majority, even against big business or the federal bureaucracy."

Again: "I am a Lincolnian, in that I believe when an individual or a locality can't help itself, it is the function of the federal government to help it . . . to live in dignity and to live decently as human beings. This is the ancient tradition . . . of Republican thought."[12]

"When he talks about his 'Republican heritage,'" Button summarizes, "he means intellectually rather than by family tradition. He says, 'I can't imagine being anything other than a Republican.' Clearly his belief in Lincoln's Republican Party is substantial, not really shaken even by the trauma of 1964, and one of his great tasks as a promising leader and spokesman for that party is to convey the basis of his faith to a growing number of not necessarily convinced voters."

Granted that Lindsay has no greater difficulties in identifying himself with Abraham Lincoln than a modern Democrat has in identify-

11. D. E. Button, *op. cit.*, p. 40.
12. *Ibid.*, p. 17.

ing himself with Thomas Jefferson—historical name-dropping is standard practice among politicians, and one becomes resigned to these arbitrary co-options. But serious students of politics will want, if only for the academic exercise, to go beyond political opportunism to probe the nexus that allegedly binds the old hero and his presumptive heir.

Abraham Lincoln was an infinitely complicated figure, and learned debate still rages about the exact nature of his contributions to the formulation of American political philosophy. It is worth a moment to meditate on the shadow of Lincoln in midcentury politics: but the preliminary point needs to be made that the obligation is heavy on the modern politician who represents himself as the carrier of the Lincoln tradition to explain just what it is that he means by this tradition, especially insofar as it is separable from the Democratic tradition.

It isn't as though Lincoln were a figure, whether profound or simple, whose thought, at whatever moment in history it is consulted, immediately suggests an appropriate approach to a contemporary problem. If a man proclaims himself, to use a simple example, a "Couéist," he is instantly understood to be someone whose optimism is the distinguishing point of his political philosophy, who expects that every day, in every way, things will get better and better. If he calls himself, say, a Comptian positivist, other people know instinctively something about the character and tendency of his thought. If he calls himself a Marxist, once again he communicates something about his thought, and his values.

But if he calls himself a "Lincolnian," he can, by the expert testimony of equally informed scholars, be different and even conflicting things; the question, among scholars, being moot as to which is the authentic Lincoln tradition, at least as regards some very important particulars. At a negative level, the designation is more useful: One thing a self-professed Lincolnian cannot be, is a defender of slavery. But what of the contemporary order of politics? One of the nation's best Lincoln scholars and most ardent admirers of him, Professor Henry Jaffe of Claremont Men's College, was a supporter of Barry Goldwater—who is held, by such as Lindsay, as being the very antithesis of a Lincoln Republican. On what authority? To make matters even more complicated, an able theoretician of modern conservatism, Mr. Frank Meyer, deplores Lincoln as a champion of executive and statist arbitrariness,[13] *i.e.*, an anti-conservative, as the term is currently understood. If the modern politician's invocation of Lincoln is to be taken as other than opportunistic and saprophytic, the invoker

13. *National Review,* August 24, 1965.

must describe what it is about Lincoln that he understands to be the quintessential Lincoln, toward whose ideas he gravitates in the course of waging modern Republicanism, or for that matter, ultra-extreme-right-wing Republicanism.

Lindsay, so far as I am able to discern, has not done this. His references to Lincoln tend to be proprietary, historically snobbish, diffuse, and sentimentalized (*and whashmore, I wanna toast the* gray-test *mother-in-law* who ever lived); not a little evasive; intellectually incoherent. Lincoln's party is *not* the party of civil rights, according to the modern understanding of civil rights—the Democratic Party clearly deserves the title. Lincoln's executive highhandedness during the Civil War is generally frowned upon by those who, for instance, believe that he had no right to suspend, unnecessarily, the citizen's recourse to the writ of *habeas corpus;* or, for that matter, who question the means by which he freed the slaves, without either compensation or due process (Lincoln, himself, a year before he signed the Emancipation Proclamation, expressed doubts that he had the constitutional right to free the slaves; and when, finally, he acted, he readily admitted that he was moved to do so not by doctrinal imperatives but by military expediency). Lincoln was not, in any modern sense, an avid protector of the person and his liberties against the majority (though he was perhaps the most powerful advocate in history of human equality as the necessary basis for self-government). Lincoln simply didn't have the time or the opportunity to concern himself with the existing, or problematical, threat of big business, or, in any systematic way, with the federal bureaucracy, and its bearing on human rights. And certainly Lincoln had no opportunity to weigh, say, the rights of individuals over against those of labor union monopolies—though Lindsay has had such opportunities, and has, almost uniformly, upheld "the majority" over against "the liberties," or "the protection" of the "individual."

The search for points of contact between Lindsay and Lincoln is, to say the least, a romantic pursuit. Lincoln too, in his political lifetime, was asked to run as a "fusion candidate"—with a Southerner as vice-president. And he replied: "As to the matter of fusion, I am for it, if it can be had on Republican grounds: and I am not for it on any other terms. A fusion on any other terms would be as foolish as unprincipled . . . I am against letting down the Republican standard a hair's breadth."[14]

Lindsay complained, after the 1964 campaign, that ". . . [for] the first time in history a major party has failed to find a major ground.

14. Letter to Theodore Canisius published May 18, 1859, in *Illinois Staats-Anzeiger* and the *Illinois State Journal*.

. . . It is essential that the [Republican] party assume proper direction, think of itself as the party of Lincoln."[15] "Let us be diverted," Lindsay's mentor, Abraham Lincoln, said at Cooper Union, "by none of those sophistical contrivances wherewith we are so industriously plied and belabored—contrivances such as groping for some middle ground between the right and the wrong."

Lindsay's consistent support of federal poverty programs, of deficit financing, of redistributionism, of compulsory welfarism, are, one would think, at least in arguable disharmony with Lincoln's famous homiletic, "You cannot bring prosperity by discouraging thrift. You cannot strengthen the weak by weakening the strong. You cannot help the poor by destroying the rich. You cannot establish sound security on borrowed money. You cannot keep out of trouble by spending more than you earn. You cannot build character and courage by taking away man's initiative and independence. You cannot help men permanently by doing for them what they can and should do for themselves."

On the question of civil rights—again, as currently understood—Lincoln must be an embarrassing memory to Lindsay. As a defender of the metaphysical proposition that men are equal, Lincoln was the greatest postbiblical political philosopher. However, concerning the big contemporary issues, Lincoln was not only, according to current terminology, a segregationist but also a racist. "The Republican Party," said Nelson Rockefeller—Lindsay's co-adjutor in New York modern Republicanism—in the summer of 1963, "is the party of Lincoln. It was founded to make men free and equal in opportunity. It is the party of all men, the only national party in America. For that party to turn its back on its heritage and its birthright would be an act of political immorality rarely equaled in human history." "I have no purpose," Lincoln said in the summer of 1858, "to introduce political and social equality between the white and black races. There is a physical difference between the two, which in my judgment, will probably forever forbid their living together upon the footing of perfect equality; and inasmuch as it becomes a necessity that there must be a difference, I am in favor of the race to which I belong having the superior position." The Republican Party which, in the name of Lincoln, Lindsay exhorted at San Francisco in 1964, to emulate the tradition of its founder, did not—most fortunately—ever even consider attempting to harmonize its platform with that of the august Republican Party that nominated Abraham Lincoln for the Presidency in 1860. That platform averred "that the maintenance

15. D. E. Button, op. cit., p. 34.

inviolate of the rights of the states and especially the right of each state, to order and control its own domestic institutions according to its own judgment exclusively, is essential to that balance of power on which the perfection and endurance of our political fabric depends." The Republican candidate so widely deplored by Lindsay as standing *outside* the Lincoln tradition, wrote in 1960:[16] "It so happens that I am in agreement with the objectives of the Supreme Court as stated in the Brown decision. I believe that it is both wise and just for Negro children to attend the same schools as whites, and that to deny them this opportunity carries with it strong implications of inferiority. I am not prepared however, to impose that judgment of mine on the people of Mississippi or South Carolina, or to tell them what methods should be adopted and what pace should be kept in striving towards that goal."[17] Who was in the tradition of Lincoln's Republican Party?

It may be contended that Abraham Lincoln would surely have changed his views between 1860 and 1960. Contended, yes: presumed, no. Neither the Goldwaters nor the Lindsays of 1964 would today accept Lincoln's pessimistic generalities based on presumed differences of a congenital nature between the races, differences of a kind that would bind them together forever—not as slave-masters and slaves, to be sure; but as governors and governed. But if tradition means anything at all, the Lincoln *tradition* on the related question of segregation clearly suggests that the states should retain a measure of authority respecting at least some of the questions nowadays pre-empted in the various civil rights bills by the federal government. So that the credentials of, for instance, the Goldwaters, are historically superior to those of the Lindsays or the Rockefellers on the matter of "Lincoln tradition," in dealing with such matters as race relations. It is, rather, in the Democratic tradition, one would think, than in the Republican tradition, gradually to erode the ancient and, to Lincoln, venerable, allocations of power within the federal community.

At the profoundest level, Lincoln was a moralist; and as such altogether outside the positivist and relativist tradition of contemporary social thought and jurisprudence, the jurisprudence, for instance, of Oliver Wendell Holmes and Earl Warren, heroes of Mr. Lindsay.[18]

16. Barry M. Goldwater, *The Conscience of a Conservative* (Shepherdsville, Ky.: Victor Publishing Co., 1960).
17. *Ibid.*
18. "Historians will deem the Warren Court one of the great courts of our country," Lindsay has frequently said. (D. E. Button, *op. cit.*, p. 57.)

Lincoln's principal metapolitical insight was that for *transcendent reasons* logically explicable, men cannot be considered *other* than equal. From this proposition many others derive having to do with the rule of law and the philosophy of jurisprudence—propositions which are utterly inimical to the most popular philosophical attachments inculcated in the major law schools and departments of philosophy and social science (behaviorism, the movement is, most loosely, called), to which one has yet to hear any objections from people like Lindsay. True, as Professor Jaffe says, "Lincoln was the least doctrinaire man who ever lived." Meaning that Lincoln was not merely a philosopher but a statesman. Accordingly, Lincoln the statesman could write to Horace Greeley, halfway through the Civil War, that he meant, by the war, not to abolish slavery, but to save the Union; still, Lincoln the philosopher meant to save the Union in order to abolish slavery. The unity of statesmanship and philosophy prompted Professor Richard Weaver, surveying Lincoln's career, to conclude that, at the margin, he "reasoned from definition," rather than from "circumstance"; and as such fell in the tradition of the natural law, rather than of the positivism that modern liberalism absolutely depends upon.[19]

Beyond that towering point, Lincoln is up for grabs and has been claimed as a patron by any number of ideological opportunists. The co-option of Lincoln by those who praise the present Supreme Court; who believe that Communists have "rights"; who look to the federal government to prescribe not only the mores but also the folkways of our race relations, to the federal government to formulate our anti-poverty and social-welfare programs; who are forever working to centripetalize our social and political energies—is at best shallow; at worst, nakedly blasphemous; in most cases, merely ignorant. A contemporary liberal Republican of limited imagination would, if wholly honest, more likely find himself saying that he is a Republican *notwithstanding* many of the utterances and attitudes of Abraham Lincoln. A conservative Republican of wider imagination would defend the proposition that Lincoln was a great political philosopher, though inept, at times, in statesmanship and ill-advised in some of his utterances. The safest position would be that of the ideological outsider, the man who, wisely, does not seek wholly to synchronize his own and Lincoln's position; who would agree to go no further than to say that Lincoln was one of the last great teachers of the natural law, but that in matters of practical policy, at a level below that of his major affirmation about human equality, he was sometimes confused and confusing, an eclectic, the most superb rhetorician of his

19. Richard Weaver, *The Ethics of Rhetoric* (Chicago: Henry Regnery, 1953).

century; and that modern exercises in posthumous political reconcili-
ations at the precinct level of political controversy are either playful,
arbitrary, or vulgar.[20]

4. Lindsay and Style

> *". . . Frequently, he writes reviews of new books, for the
> newspapers and magazines; these, like his magazine arti-
> cles and almost all his speeches, have habitually been
> pounded out by Lindsay himself in the recesses of a den
> at home; until the multi-speech demands of the mayoralty
> there was no 'Lindsay-writer.' "*[21]

I feared as much. I remember, in the course of the campaign,
asking a reporter who had been intimate with Lindsay headquarters
why, why with all the money at the disposal of the Lindsay mayoralty
movement, someone could not be found who could suppress the re-
morseless clichés, the ear-clanging phrases, the irretrievable syntax.
. . . The answer was that the money was there all right, and so were
the writers; but that Mr. Lindsay exercised his rights to final-draft
authority, and all by himself inserted those frozen phrases which
caused and cause such great pain to the unwaxed ear.

I would not bring up the matter, except that I have come to believe
that Mr. Lindsay's rhetoric bears on his politics; indeed, that his
rhetoric is an expression of his nature. The news is not by any means
all bad—I mean, the news about his nature. The man with the cliché
for every occasion can be a very good man indeed. Other things, however, Lindsay is not; and those other things some people believe Mr.
Lindsay to be, including, I have the paralyzing suspicion, Mr. Lindsay
himself. And since an understanding of so much of the ensuing
campaign depends, really, on knowing something about the man
Lindsay, a personal exploration is in order. Mr. Lindsay has a real
flair for politics, which I shall in due course record, and bow before;
he has none at all for self-expression: or, perhaps more accurately,
he has absolutely perfect powers of self-expression. A resourceful
verbalist can take a jaded idea and hypo into it one more bloom,
however reluctant; Lindsay can't—because his ideas are tired, per-

20. "A few more like Lindsay," a Republican Congressman is said to have remarked, after one of Lindsay's Congressional re-election victories, "and all we'd
have to do is wave some flags to carry the House and Senate." "This, of course,"
comments Lindsay's biographer—believe it or not—"reflects a projection of the
Lindsay 'image' and the Lindsay 'profile' or the Lindsay 'charm' much more
than it represents an understanding of the Lincolnian Lindsay."
21. D. E. Button, *op. cit.*, p. 23.

haps, but also because his own capacity to formulate is severely lacking in hormones. What is interesting is not the perfectly routine difficulty of devising fresh formulations but Lindsay's apparent tendency to resist them even when they are done in his behalf. I regretfully conclude that this is egomania at work, the conviction that one's own formulations, though manifestly flat, are somehow more desirable than those of others who write, and think, better. Still, this can be set down as a sign of self-confidence, which is not without its political uses. It must have taken extraordinary reserves of self-confidence to reduce to such shambles as Lindsay regularly did the pretty sentences which, there is every reason to suppose, Mr. Lindsay's expensive ghosts delivered to him in the course of duty. I began the campaign by believing that the egotistical passion with which Lindsay stressed the theme that he was born to save New York would probably end up hurting him. For instance—a typical example from the first CBS debate, wherein Mr. Lindsay makes plain the chiliastic nature of his appearance on the municipal scene: "I believe that New York City needs a change so badly that never again in history will we have the opportunity to do it except now. I have been in the forefront of progress. Vote for me on November 2." I was, as usual, wrong; self-appreciation is a cardinal necessity for successful politics. I can be persuaded that a heady self-appreciation will happen to the majority of men when the contest for high office seems to require it. John Kennedy, for instance, was by nature a modest man, but in his campaigning he too came to sound messianic and in no time at all was confiding to his intimates, or so the story goes, that he knew no man better qualified than he to serve as President of the United States; and he so oversold some of his own apostles on the general subject, that some of them went on to commit sins of fulsomeness which, one hopes, deeply embarrassed him.

Consider one of the mannerisms of a generous self-appreciation. Have you noticed how people, as they become important, have difficulty deciding which of the personal pronouns is most appropriate to their own use? You and I, referring to ourselves and our endeavors, say "I": as in "I shall do what I can to help the Red Cross." The minute one goes public, the temptation is to graduate to the royal "We," as it is traditionally called. Now the use of "we" is also common to people in public life who are self-effacing and fear that the failure to go plural will give the impression that they are taking personal credit where credit is in fact due to their entire entourage. Thus a senator who may be the soul of self-deprecation might say, "We are going to do everything we can to help the Red Cross," by which he means he, his administrative assistants, his uncles and aunts, friends and votaries, will jointly do what they all can for the Red Cross. You need to watch out when the politician has got so given to thinking of himself as a collectivity that he is capable of writing in his diary, "At 8 a.m. we got up and took a shower." When that happens, he has elided from modesty to something else.

But there is a point of self-absorption that goes even beyond the "we." It is, of course, the triumphant return to the old-time "I." What matters now is to stress precisely the singularity, in which the collectivity has been subsumed. President Johnson, I remember observing, arrived at that point the night of his first State of the Union message. "Wherever waste is found, *I* will eliminate it," he proclaimed. In fact, of course, he could not have meant that *he* would eliminate it, unless he meant that he would buzz about Washington offices personally retrieving useable paper clips from bureaucratic wastebaskets. He meant: "We"—the members of the Johnson Administration, their subordinates, and their subordinates' subordinates—"will eliminate the waste." The Administration made progress against waste last year, he said—but "*I* intend to do better this year."

Thus it is with Lindsay. His opponent during 1964, Mrs. Eleanor Clark French, complained of it, and recounted to Caspar Citron, "We talked at the Stuyvesant High School one morning, and [Lindsay] said he'd been one of the architects of the [civil rights] act and really implied that he was the one that put it through. One of the students asked him in the question period whether he really meant to imply that he got the act through single-handed. To my amazement, Lindsay said, 'No, I had the help of the Fifth Estate—you people in the audience.' He never mentioned his own party member Dirksen; or McCulloch or Celler—the two who were after all the ones who got it through the House—or Humphrey or President Johnson. I thought it was pretty inexcusable . . . that in public office you have to have humility, and there were times when I felt this humility was lacking."[22]

And then Lindsay would frequently refer to the power and the loneliness and the agonies of the office he sought, even as President Johnson went on to do in his State of the Union message concerning the Presidency. I do believe there is no sentient American who does not *know* how weighty the office is, even those who were born after Harry Truman *really* drove the point home. But there are those who do and those who don't *talk* about things of that kind. There are people who do, and people who don't, talk about how much power they exercise as president of General Motors, how much influence they wield as dean of Harvard University, how much patience they show as husband to Mary Zilch—how great is their integrity, enor-

22. Citron, *op. cit.,* p. 119.

mous their energy, complete their self-reliance. It is a question of taste, but taste is also a sense of proportion, more than knowing whether orange will clash with pink in the drawing room. It has to do with an accommodation to the sensibility of one's fellow men, and an idea of one's own very small part in the order of reality. When that balance becomes disturbed, one fears that the patient's self-involvement obscures reality.

I had already noticed, well before the campaign, that John Lindsay was precociously tasteless on these matters. True, he has had to suffer, from early in his career, from fawners who not only permitted, but celebrated, his earlier pomposities. Consider a selection of phrases from his Congressional career, gathered together, believe it or not, by his biographer as specimens of his fairest blooms.

"I will defend as long as I have a voice in my body" the jurisdiction of the Supreme Court, he said on an occasion when there was never any possibility that the voice in his body might serve as the last line of defense between the Supreme Court and the barbarians. Such a phrase as that one must be reserved for occasions when the melodrama is objectively contributed by great historical circumstances— at which point, but only at which, a banality can have the sound of thunder. It is so with most clichés: "I shall love you till I draw my dying breath" is heartrendingly beautiful—under circumstances which I hesitate even to describe, because to do so under analytic circumstances would be profane. But in routine circumstances—say a letter from Mary Lou to Ringo Starr—it is mere fun, not to be taken seriously. If used by a young Congressman about his defense of the Supreme Court, it is not fun; but it *is* to be taken seriously.

Unfortunately, the I-will-give-all-of-myself bit appears frequently, in one or another variation. Opposing the student loyalty oath provision of the National Defense Act, Congressman Lindsay announced: "I rebel against this kind of requirement. Our history and our constitutional foundations rebel." The order's the thing. Consider it otherwise, i.e.: "Our history and our constitutional foundations rebel against this kind of requirement. So, for that reason, do I." The hierarchy is re-established. Long live the hierarchy.

Or: "I have looked with growing concern" (on the practice of doctoring the *Congressional Record*). "I am old-fashioned enough to believe . . ." (in an accurate record). It comes down to this: you know it's wrong to begin any statement with such self-oriented tusheries, or you don't, and analysis of why you shouldn't is futile. The word is: pomposity.

"I was troubled and angered" (by the Bay of Pigs). Surely, the point with which to begin a discussion of the Bay of Pigs is other than a description of its effect on you?

"I wish to serve notice that I am going to insist as just one member of Congress" (that the President reveal his foreign policy intentions). Now, if you wish to serve notice, say, that as the holder of the mortgage you're going to foreclose, the affected party is going to sit up and take notice. But to "serve notice," that you are going to "insist" on x, y, or z when the world hangeth not on that notice nor do your honorable colleagues is to betray an uncertain sense of your own importance.

"As long as I have a voice in my body, I will speak for what I believe is right"—referring to things in general. Once again, the salvific voice, an appropriate context for the use of which it is difficult to conceive, save possibly as a caption to Michelangelo's drawing of God breathing life into Adam. And isn't it at least the convention that when Congressmen speak, they speak for what they believe is right? Where were the pressures on Lindsay to speak what he believed was wrong?

Then there are the extra-personal clichés, the profligate use of which suggests the failure of the observer himself to recognize the uniqueness he is nevertheless trying to stress.

"I subscribe," said Lindsay as if he were about to add substantially to the sum of human knowledge, "to the theory that the Constitution is a living and growing document." (Incredibly, this sunburst by Lindsay was *not* headlined by the *Tribune*.)

In opposition to the anti-pornography bill, Lindsay volunteered the insight, "Must we burn down the barn in order to catch the rat?" (The answer depends, of course, on one's relative attachment to the survival of the barn, and the death of the rat; as Captain Ahab would have observed.)

When the church in Birmingham was bombed, resulting in the death of four children: "I call"—once again, I; not even "we"; let alone "justice"; or even "vengeance"—"upon Congress to act on legislation and"—one senses its horrible inevitability—"to stop fiddling while the country burns." Re the deficiencies in housing and urban renewal: "It is important," wrote Lindsay in *Harper's*, "to have people who have the brains and courage to point out that the 'king is wearing no clothes.' " Inside quotes in the original. A hungry lawyer would perhaps undertake to contend that "king" in place of "emperor" relieves the phrase of the guilt of banality. More likely, the emperor himself was intended, deposed only by a slip of memory.

Poor Mr. Lindsay. He never had the benefit of a critic's quarter.

"In lighter vein," records his biographer gleefully, "to someone who persisted with questions on the long-range ideas of this new demi-champion, he responded:

" 'Do I want to be Senator?' Sure.

" 'Do I want to be Governor?' Sure.

" 'Do I want to be President?' Let's wait (a Lindsay guffaw interrupted) until I've at least won this election."

Such guffaws, if dutifully echoed by biographers, reporters, television networks, and national news magazines, can make a hit out of any one-nighter.

V.

Buckley, Spring 1965

It was of course expected that the Conservative Party would field a candidate for Mayor of New York; indeed, why not?—John Lindsay's declaration of his own candidacy having established that the Republicans would not be endorsing anyone of conservative inclination. But as of early June the leaders of the Conservative Party had still not finally decided on whom to name. As always there was a general reluctance among qualified candidates, the mission ahead being didactic and disciplinary, the personal inconvenience enormous, and the retaliatory animus high. The Conservative Party had had enormous difficulty in finding suitable candidates during the first year of its operations, in 1962. David Jaquith, a highly qualified candidate, finally consented to run and did extraordinary well. But his personal independence was a fortifying consideration. He was well enough connected socially and institutionally in his own community, his business firm was well enough removed from point-blank pressures, so that he could reasonably expect that even a highly unpopular venture in political point-making would not have the effect of shattering his professional life. The conservative nomination for United States Senator had been offered to a professor greatly disposed to accept it; but on reconsideration he said no, having been advised by a friendly dean that academic reprisals would very likely follow. Kieran O'Doherty, the first State Chairman of the Conservative Party, finally agreed, the deadline looming, to take on the assignment— much against his own will, believing as he did that the Conservative Party's administration should be apart from its ticket, so as not to suggest an impoverishment of candidates, or confuse the separate functions. He ran, did well, and, for his pains, was diplomatically but no less definitively informed by his blue-chip downtown law firm, whose senior partner is a Rockefeller-Lindsay stalwart, that his chances of achieving a partnership in that firm were, so to speak, nonexistent.

Even a minority political party, in order to be effective, has got to have candidates in races where they are conspicuously needed, though the only obligation on a New York State political party that wishes to retain its place on the ballot is to run a candidate for governor every four years who secures at least fifty thousand votes. (It does not matter, incidentally, if the party's designee also happens to be a designee of one of the major parties: just so long as he polls the sacred fifty thousand on the minority party's register.)

Although I had been a friend of the leaders of the Conservative Party and a supporter of their objectives, I had never been an intimate of their counsels and had no day-by-day voice in their deliberations. I knew not much more, in May and early June of 1965, than what *The New York Times* publicly speculated: "The possible conservative mayoral candidates mentioned by [State Chairman] Mr. Mahoney," *The Times* wrote in early June, "are: Dr. Henry Paolucci, who ran against Senator Kennedy last fall; Kieran O'Doherty, who was an unsuccessful candidate against Mr. Lindsay in a Congressional race [in 1964]; George Schuyler, who was the unsuccessful party candidate against Representative Adam Clayton Powell, Jr,; and Suzanne La Follette, who lost in a Congressional race to Leonard Farbstein."

It is a matter of exiguous historical interest what it was that moved me to run, but I suppose it is relevant to this narrative, if to no other.

On June 6, I had decided to run; had decided, to be precise, three days earlier. I thought to begin a diary, which is exactly what I did, the first entry, due to a lack of personal organization, being also the last one. But on that day I did speak into a tape machine for fifteen minutes or so and gave my thoughts on the business of running for mayor.

The opportunity was good (I said more or less) to raise precisely those points which I thought most needed to be raised if New York was to have the opportunity to resolve some of its dilemmas. It had become clear, I reasoned, that the two major candidates would not raise these points. I reasoned further—as if to convince myself— that the "internal cogency of the conservative critique" would be well heard in a city whose major politicians were bound by the prevailing taboos to silence. And I recalled the chronology of my own decision.

Two weeks before, I had written a column for the newspaper syndicate I regularly write for, and also for *National Review*, which I jocularly entitled, "Mayor, Anyone?" "If you live in a large city and desire to run for Mayor [it began], on what platform, pray, will you run? What has John Lindsay of New York decided to run on? One metropolitan newspaper has carefully and enthusiastically recorded his attributes, the most significant of which, some observers have noted, is the brilliance of his teeth.[1] [Yes, that was a qualification solemnly remarked by one major newspaper.] When the press mulcted from Candidate Lindsay the specific ideas he had for New York, he temporarily deserted his Spenglerian observations about the decline and fall of the city[2] and said that (a) he feared the desertion of New York by private industry; (b) he thought something ought to be done about the flourishing narcotic trade here; and (c) he did not believe that sufficient effort had been made to save the Brooklyn Navy Yard.

"Would you like to run for Mayor? [I continued]. Here is a packaged program."

I went on to list ten points "half in fun." I quote them here to my disadvantage—because I fully abandoned some of them, and modified others after myself deciding to make the race. Those I abandoned I abandoned because reflection doomed them as impractical or undesirable for other reasons. I am not a little abashed that I should have thought them sound (even though I did take the precaution of projecting them experimentally), so few weeks and months before deciphering their weaknesses.

1. Crime [I continued in my column]. Teenagers caught and convicted of felonies will be either (a) put in jail, or (b) released in the recognizance of their parents or guardians, who will be legally responsible for recurrent offenses. Said parents would have the right to surrender authority over fractious children by invoking probationary sentences. Communities blockwide or greater which, like the Jewish association that calls itself the Maccabbees and has financed its own watchmen to patrol its own area in a crime-ridden quarter of New York, will be given *pro tanto* relief in their property taxes, sufficient to pay the local police bills. New Yorkers will, in a word, be encouraged to look after their own protection, relieving the municipal police force of an almost impossible job.

The idea of private watchmen as an alternative to rising theft and assault is, I continue to believe, sound. But the business of reimburs-

1. D. E. Button, *op. cit.*, p. 11.
2. Lindsay had delivered his opening statement, intact, in each of the five boroughs of New York, repeating in each instance his determination to arrest the "decline and fall" of New York City, and I remember that the formulation grated terribly. One goes to the rescue of a *declining* city, but surely there is nothing to do about a *fallen* city?

ing communities that hire them out of tax funds is administratively if not impossible, at least awesomely difficult.

2. Narcotics. Anti-narcotic laws for adults should be repealed, and the English system substituted: you can get narcotics for the drug store price of them—provided you come in with a doctor's prescription. Said doctor will renew the addict's prescription or not depending on whether he submits to medical attention. Anyone caught selling drugs to a minor will be subject to fifteen years in prison. Take the profit away from narcotics peddling, and the narcotics peddlers go out of business.

I was not aware of research on the English experiment which was even then being accumulated, and on the basis of which I altogether changed my position (see Chapter VII).

3. Race. Petition the state and federal governments for a suspension of property and income taxes for all Negro or Puerto Rican entrepreneurs who establish businesses, in those areas that have, by federal decree, been denominated as depressed areas. Let Negro entrepreneurs—using white capital and their own—move into such areas with the kind of economic encouragement that has done so much for Puerto Rico in its renowned Operation Bootstrap.

Professor Milton Friedman of the University of Chicago pounced on me, on the grounds that here was the old autarchic heresy. I sought to fight back his theoretical criticisms, but succumbed, finally, to the sheer difficulties of administration: how could you effectively set the boundaries? In Puerto Rico it is easy; hardly in Harlem, or in Bedford-Stuyvesant. Would we be willing to set a racial test in order to establish who was, and who was not, eligible for the tax privileges? And how prevent Negro nominees for white-owned holding companies? Or excursions by the bus-load into Harlem, to buy the week's supply of cigarettes and groceries? Abandoned.

4. Traffic. No commercial vehicle may load or unload cargo between 8:00 A.M. and 6:00 P.M. Double parkers will be fined $10; parkers with diplomatic plates (they are expected to know better), $100. And if Jimmy Hoffa disagrees, why, disagree with *him!*—or get out of the mayoralty race. [Modified—see Chapter VII—in my final position paper on traffic.]

5. Labor unions. Pass legislation imposing criminal penalties on any labor union organization that seeks to prevent any New Yorker from making his own arrangements, on mutually agreeable terms, with any painters, construction workers, plumbers, electricians, or elevator operators. [Sound as a bell.]

6. Gambling. Legalize it. Anybody who wants to bet anything

with anybody may do so, and the prospective mayor wishes every single better the very best of luck. [No regrets.]

7. Taxis. Anybody without a police record may operate a car as a taxi. [Okay, but subject to a gradualized program designed to shield individual taxi owners from the shock-devaluation of their expensive medallions bought during the era of the cartel.]

8. Welfare. Anyone receiving welfare payments who is not a mother looking after children 14 years or younger, or invalided, will report for duty at 8:00 a.m. every morning for street cleaning and general prettification work. No workee, no dolee. [No apologies. The position was to become a point of complicated flurries in the course of the campaign—see Chapter VI].

9. Schools. No one will be required to go to any school outside the plausible geographical limits of his residence. School dropouts under the age of 14 will be sent to special vocational schools, whose administrators will be especially trained. They will be vested with extraordinary disciplinary powers, and charged with (a) teaching literacy, and (b) giving vocational training. Successful graduates of one year's experience will be qualified to re-enter the public schools. [*Res manet.*]

10. The minimum wage law will not apply to children. [Neither should it apply to adults.]

At a staff meeting of *National Review* a few days after this column was written the routine question was raised, as it is every fortnight just before the final deadline for the magazine's cover copy, what to emblazon on the top-left diagonal yellow streamer designed to attract the attention of newsstand buyers. We happened that week to be short of usable titles not already mortgaged on the color-form, which is locked in several days earlier. After a half-hour's paralysis, my sister Priscilla Buckley, who cannot resist a self-deprecatory whirl, suggested "Why not, 'Buckley for Mayor'?" Having, after all, vouchsafed a paradigmatic platform, theoretically useful in any large-size American city, I yielded to the argument that the metaphor "Buckley for Mayor" would be instantly understood; that no reader in his right mind would be likely to infer from the streamer that Buckley was actually announcing that he would run for Mayor and that this was his trial balloon. It was not, as a matter of fact, until a fortnight after the event that I was informed, to my astonishment, that in fact I was legally qualified to run for Mayor of New York, notwithstanding that I was a resident and registered (Republican) voter in Stamford, Connecticut. But my sister, as it happened, had been quite correct. Not a soul mistook the yellow streamer for a Freudian revelation: not even I.

A week or so later, after a long evening's conversation with my colleague William Rusher, publisher of *National Review*, I sat down late in the evening to compose an address to be delivered two nights later at a large public meeting to commemorate an anniversary of Public Action, Inc., and to honor its octogenarian founder, Mrs. Seth Milliken. I had attempted, having informally ascertained that he would be acceptable to the Party's principal officials, to persuade Rusher to run for Mayor of New York on the Conservative ticket. My argument was not only that he was supremely well qualified—he had been an engaged politico ever since undergraduate days at Princeton, was a graduate of the Harvard Law School, had reached a high rank in the New York Young Republicans, was among the small group who founded the Draft Goldwater movement in 1962, is a brilliant contributor on the polemical radio-TV lecture circuit. The answer was "No."

I was enticed, as I began, to pursue my thoughts on the subject of municipal problems and, eschewing national and international issues, resolved to expand on my semijocular column of a fortnight before. I worked on my talk into the late evening. The next morning I called Conservative State Chairman Dan Mahoney, and asked him whether he wanted me as a candidate.

My little one-time tape diary, recorded two days later, shows a number of thoughts, reservations, qualifications, and speculations that were crowding my mind. That tape, as a matter of record, does not once mention the name of John Vliet Lindsay.

I depart from the score at this moment to confront the prevailing assumption that for many years Lindsay had been a special target of mine. Lindsay's biographer, Mr. Daniel E. Button of the Albany *Times Union*, is not alone in suggesting that for years John Lindsay had been an obsession of mine, and of *National Review*. ". . . the bitterest of his political enemies, William Buckley . . . continued his personal vendetta" against Lindsay,[3] Button writes about the year 1964. And again: "The virulence of the Buckley-Conservative drive against Lindsay is, in fact, worth noting. A month before the 1964 campaign came to an end, Buckley's magazine, the *National Review*, published the most detailed of its long series of diatribes against Lindsay, reflecting personal as well as political disdain."[4]

It happens that these charges are incorrect, both technically and substantively. Up until the mayoralty campaign I managed to go whole months at a time without thinking about John Lindsay. As for *National Review*, we have been impartially hostile to liberal Republicans. Why, indeed, should it be expected that we would be otherwise,

3. *Op. cit.*, p. 12.
4. *Ibid.*, p. 222.

inasmuch as ours is a journal of conservative opinion? An examination of the yearly indexes of *National Review* (which list all articles, columns, and book reviews) from the date of Mr. Lindsay's first election to Congress in 1958 until the campaign in 1965, shows only a single entry under "Lindsay, John V."—an article by one Robert Smith (October 6, 1964); not, as Button falsely records, by myself. Hardly suggesting an obsession. The case might better be made that *National Review* was rather behind the general press in monitoring the appearance of a new political comet. I do not deny, and do not regret, that the general tendency of an opinion journal is to be particularly critical of any politician one considers as an interloper in one's own party. I note, for instance, that *National Review*'s criticisms of Wayne Morse tended to move into a different register after he crossed the aisle and became a Democrat, even as many Democrats greeted with relief Senator Strom Thurmond's defection to the Republican Party of South Carolina. Certainly it would be most unusual in an opinion journal to fail to remark the activities of someone considered an anomaly in one's own political party who is suddenly advanced as the beau ideal for the *whole* party. It was difficult enough, during all those years, for many Democrats to swallow Harry Byrd. One can imagine the succeeding issue of the *New Republic* if at some point during his long career it had been proposed by leading spokesmen of his party that Senator Harry Byrd should be nominated as the Democratic candidate for the Presidency.

Beyond that, I had personal ties to John Lindsay, greatly attenuated and largely suppressed during the campaign except on that curious occasion when all the New York press seemed primarily concerned to know whether I had indeed known Lindsay at Yale—about which more anon. There is a tradition in my family—much the same, I expect, as in other people's families—that we are at least presumptively friends of the friends of our own brothers and sisters. John Lindsay and his twin brother David matriculated at Yale with my own brother Jim. David and Jim became fast friends, and of all the personal dislodgments of the campaign I am most grievously concerned over the possibility that it may have sundered that friendship. Jim was an usher at David's wedding and is godfather to one of his children. I knew David (through Jim) well enough at Yale to understand my brother's devotion to him. And when I asked my brother to serve as my campaign manager, he consented to do so, but only after writing to David Lindsay, who was serving his own brother's campaign in Queens. They exchanged amenable letters, agreeing that the forthcoming campaign would simply reflect differing judgments concerning political matters. It doesn't, of course, as a rule, work out quite that neatly; and in due course Lindsay and I would be firing hot lead at each other across our brothers' heads.

I do confess that I developed an idea of John Lindsay which is as unorthodox as his own Republicanism. But apart from my political disagreements with him and my feeling that politically he belongs in the Democratic Party, I had at the moment the campaign began no personal animus, certainly not a shred of that "personal disdain" which his biographer so lasciviously records.[5] And sometimes, I confess, I wondered why my opposition to Lindsay was everywhere characterized as "bitter," whereas Lindsay's opposition to Goldwater never was.

At the Public Action Rally I expanded, in a more serious vein, on the column I had written a fortnight earlier. My eighteen-hour-old decision to run for Mayor was firm in my own mind, subject only to ratification by Conservative Party leaders, to whom I desired to communicate directly the limitations that circumstances and my own judgment would impose on my candidacy, and subject to the extraction of the consent of my wife who, when I telephoned her my inclination (she was in Vancouver with her ailing father), registered an obdurate dismay, by which I was especially moved on account of a disastrous accident that spring, from which she was painfully recuperating. I do not know how, when I had, during the busy afternoon of that day, confided to less than a half-dozen people my tentative decision, *The New York Times* managed to get wind of it. The city editor, Mr. A. M. Rosenthal, of whom I am a secret and penitent admirer, called and asked me point-blank, Was I going to run? I had had little experience in the treatment of the press under such pressures and relapsed defensively into the conventional "No Comment" (which I found as hard to resort to as even now I find it, preferring an utterly frank intercourse).

The Rally itself was a rousing affair, SRO, a band, flags, bunting,

5. To maintain the strictest accuracy, I divulge that my associate William A. Rusher of *National Review* contended with both Lindsay and Robert Price in the New York Young Republican Club during the early fifties, grew to dislike their positions most heartily and to have small personal respect for Price. . . . A confidential memorandum by a Lindsay staffer, Eric Swenson, dated as late as October 3, which fell into my hands, tends to underwrite what I have said. Under the heading, "WFB Attacks JVL," the memo says (italics in the original): "There have been many over the years—*mostly attacks on JVL voting record (HUAC, foreign aid, etc.)*—but these are only of interest in a general way. The point is this: That WFB's chief purpose in running for mayor is not to be elected (see separate listing of his comments on his own race) (?) but to stop the career of JVL. This is not a personal thing (it may be, but I do not think we should use the personal complaint; too easy to sound like a whine), *but rather to eliminate from major elective office a moderate* [sic] *Republican* who would, if elected, become a threat—within the Republican Party—to the Goldwater extremists, of whom WFB is one." Quite correct. Good show, Swenson.

ministers of every faith. Katherine St. George, first cousin of FDR and long-time Congresswoman from the Hudson Valley, gave tribute to the venerable Mrs. Milliken, and the band played on. Senator John Tower from Texas spoke, and decried extremism in conservative ranks. I began my own talk with a reference of purely topical interest, only a few weeks having gone by since the *Tribune* had reported my alleged admiration for the policemen of Selma, Alabama. "I suppose I should point out for the benefit of the *Tribune* reporter, that Mrs. Milliken, whom we are here to honor, is *not* a member of the Selma police force." I went on to suggest a conservative approach to municipal politics.

   . . . As matters now stand, we no longer have the right to decide whether and how to pray in the public schools; whether we desire to join a labor union; how to build our buildings, construct our roads, finance our schools, without crying on the shoulders of Washington and begging it to tax more of our dollars in order to remit us a fraction of them; whether we may send our children to neighborhood schools, or whether we must first consult the Demographic Editor of the New York *Post*. The highest goal of public action is surely to preserve individual liberties. . . .

In the coziness of occasional such gatherings as these, it does not pay to lose sight of the main thing that is going on in the world today—to a lesser extent perhaps in America; but here also. The spirit of the age calls for amalgamating our problems, and delivering them over to a central authority for solving. The spirit of the age contends that extragovernmental solutions to the problems of life are increasingly implausible. And, as a matter of fact, they are. The conservative, as distinguished from the liberal, continues, however, to believe that the presumption remains against state involvement. Obviously the power of government is needed, for instance, to control the traffic problems in New York. Obviously the power of government is needed to decide such questions as what to do when the water reservoirs begin to empty. The question is whether the necessity to increase the powers of government— yesterday there was no traffic problem, no water scarcity—for *specific* purposes, has resulted in unnecessary increases in state power for *general* purposes.

"Consider the situation in microcosm. Granted the municipal government in New York needs to control traffic: is that an excuse for the government of New York to limit the number of cars that can be used as taxis; or, for heaven's sake, to limit the number of people who can ride in a taxi?

Granted the municipal government needs to ration water under certain circumstances; is that an excuse for the government of New York to fix rent controls? Granted the municipal government must decide how to allocate funds for public schooling. Is that a reason for the municipal government to acquire the right to send children to extraterritorial schools?

What is wrong with New York? to get down to brass tacks. Crime, for one thing. But crime seems to have become a social problem, not an individual problem. Just about everything is a social problem—have you noticed? The economist Henry Hazlitt has remarked that it appears to be a part of the spirit of the age that we must worry about everyone else, but never about oneself. But it is no answer to the problem of crime to assume that every criminal merely midwifes a social imperative. That every criminal has been visited by a social incubus that you and I are responsible for, which, having impregnated him, requires, by the laws of nature, the birth of a crime. James Baldwin told me the other day that he does not blame the residents of Harlem for throwing garbage out of their windows, that that is their form of protest. Would we, by the same token, be entitled to throw our garbage out the window when John Lindsay passes by?[6]

It is one thing to be compassionate. And one can be compassionate alike for the president of the New York Stock Exchange who goes to jail for his greed, as one did twenty-five years ago, and for the rapist who is unable to control his lust. But the point is that it is necessary to sequester the transgressors, *whatever* the genealogy of their aberrations. Because individual victims have rights too. But the spirit of the age asks us to diffuse the responsibility for human aberration out among the veins and capillaries of the whole society. Thus James Baldwin—and his followers, and his mentors—are there, always there, to hold society up as the imprisonable entity: and we are asked to punish our institutions, rather than the transgressors against our institutions. Thus it is the policeman in Berkeley, California, representing the law against illegal trespass, who becomes the object of impatience; not the thirty-five hundred students who surrounded and immobilized for thirty-six hours his motor car when he took into it a student who had violated the law: and certainly not the student himself, who is esteemed as an expression of compulsive defiance of unjust laws. . . . Thus the most acute political pressures of the day are leveled against those who seek to maintain the peace, rather than against those who break it. Because it is the social situation that the spirit of the age holds responsible. There is an exact correspondence between the hankering to give over to the state the responsibility for governing our lives and the hankering to hold

6. Reported by the *Tribune* (June 6, 1965), perhaps as condign punishment for my introductory act of *lèse majésté*, as follows: "Mr. Buckley said that James Baldwin, the Negro writer, has told him that Harlem residents threw garbage out their windows as a form of protest. Mr. Buckley suggested that, in the same spirit, other New Yorkers might throw garbage out their windows when Mr. Lindsay passed by. The audience screamed with delight."

blameless individual human beings from responsibility for their own excesses.

We talk about the crisis of the city, and we have one indeed, here in New York. Along comes John Lindsay.

To what effect?

I cannot, hard and diligently though I try, understand the well-springs of enthusiasm for him other than as a personal cult. There is, to be sure, some sort of organizational indebtedness. Mr. Lindsay consents, in his more permissive moments, to use the Republican label. But assuming the label had never been formally affixed to his name, it would certainly not be possible to infer from his voting record that he had ever come near to the Republican Party. The typical liberal Democrat in Congress, on important measures that divide Republicans from Democrats, has not amassed a voting record in any significant way different from John Lindsay's. What does Mr. Lindsay offer to the GOP, other than his glamorous self?

Surely not the recapture of the presumptions of individualism. Mr. Lindsay has not yet said anything at all of any moment, and it is just possible that he will complete his campaign without saying anything at all of any moment, other than that the destiny of New York hangs on its voting for him—which is indeed an awesome pronouncement. What is remarkable about the Lindsay candidacy? That he is a Republican? But that aspect of the matter we are instructed by the candidate himself to ignore, a piece of advice those of us who have studied his voting record can obey without any strain at all. Still, running nominally as a Republican, he gratifies certain organizational instincts, the avarice for vote-getting candidates. But why, if he is a distinctively Republican threat, so much enthusiasm for him from those who normally vote Democratic?

The complex answer is, surely, that there is a sense of psychic composure when a man who is formally aligned on the other side of the political fence endorses all *your* major platforms: it has the effect of relieving you of the disquietude that the existence of alternative approaches to government necessarily pose. When Senator Javits ran for re-election under the Republican ticket, any number of people rejoiced at the fulfillment of their belief that, finally, *everyone* now was acting congruently with the Spirit of the Age.

What might a candidate for the mayoralty ask the people of New York to consider as desirable alternatives to the existing situation?

Half in fun because I am no politician and I respect the difference between my absent skills and their overflowing skills—as, I hope, they respect the nonpolitician's candor, in blissful contrast to their own—I have previously suggested a platform that appeals to me as reformist in nature, yet is rooted in the idea of individuality and order. Consider uniquely municipal needs . . . [A digest of my column followed].

The mechanics of success in democratic elections tend—and this has been widely observed over the years by democratic theorists —to get in the way of the purpose of politics. The purpose of politics is not to re-elect Mr. Wagner, or to launch a national career for John Lindsay; but to do, to the limited extent it is possible to do anything by government action, something for the people of New York, to whom is owed, by good government, the security of their liberties: to work without harassment, to live without a crushing fiscal overhead, to educate their children with minimum interference from extrinsic distractions, to walk confidently in the streets, and sleep quietly at night. Public action is needed to secure these private ends. . . .

It was a politician's speech only in the sense that its author had, subject to a few reservations, decided to run for office. The audience was totally unaware of that decision, and the author was certainly unaware that he would have spoken any differently if he had not anticipated his candidacy. "There was one shout of 'Buckley for Mayor!' from the crowd of about 2800 in the Manhattan Center auditorium," *The New York Times* reported the next morning—under the headline: "BUCKLEY IS EXPECTED TO RUN FOR MAYOR AS CONSERVATIVE."

There never was, that I know of, a less deliberated, less connived at, less complicated entry into any political race. The spontaneity of it all was unbelievable to most of the analysts, who reasoned that here was a hard-planned, nationally subsidized, highly organized campaign to wreak vengeance on John Lindsay, and to hoist anew the flag of Barry Goldwater.

On a half-dozen occasions after the formal announcement of my candidacy (on June 24), newspaper reporters and radio interviewers asked me to confirm or deny the rumor that I had flown to Phoenix, Arizona, a few weeks earlier there to meet with Barry Goldwater and Mrs. Clare Boothe Luce, who urged me to make the race against John Lindsay. It was easy enough to deny the rumor, since it was not true, not even parabolically.[7] I first spoke to Mrs. Luce about my

7. Incidentally, for those of you who have never experienced the sensation, it is an altogether new one to be manifestly—and ostentatiously—doubted, to your face, even when you say something is so because, of your own knowledge, you know it to be so. It is almost impossible to get used to; I say almost, not because I got used to it, but because presumably others have. It is of course true that politicians can look you straight in the face and lie, and there is of course a great and intricate scaffolding marvelously erectible to motivate such lies. Franklin Delano Roosevelt, returned from a meeting with Winston Churchill in 1940,

candidacy (she was later to join a Republicans for Buckley Committee) *after* publicly entering the race. The afternoon before I announced, I called Barry Goldwater, who was in Washington to launch his Free Society Association, and told him that I intended to run, and that my initial declaration would stress that I was a Republican running under the Conservative label because I did not believe that Republican principles, as understood nationally, would otherwise be represented. I did not solicit either Mr. Goldwater's approval or his blessing—although he volunteered the latter, largely I think for personal reasons (we are friends).

During the few weeks between *The New York Times'* announcement that I was expected to run and the announcement itself, I had very few communications, either of encouragement or discouragement. I had none at all from anyone official within the Republican Party, either from its liberal or its conservative camp. I had a telephone call from an old personal friend, advising me that, if I did make the race and was willing to fight hard, he believed that seed money would be forthcoming from conservative Republican circles. And indeed, he came forward with what I considered a breathtaking contribution, rounded up from his closest ideological friends, of nine thousand dollars. I had estimated my budget at an utterly innocent eighteen to twenty thousand dollars simply to guarantee the cost of the internal operation, i.e., a working staff. Professor Paolucci had spent forty thousand dollars in his race against Keating and Kennedy. (I ended up spending over two hundred thousand dollars.) Toward the end of the campaign I received a barrage of letters (organized, I had the impression), mostly from flossy Manhattan addresses, all of them sincere, many of them quite moving, urging me to throw my support at the last minute to John Lindsay. Their strategic thinking (their proposal was utterly impractical under the circumstances) was best embodied in a thoughtful letter from a renowned anti-Communist

---

replied, "No, none at all," when questioned by reporters whether he had made any commitments involving American troops, even as, at his side, a young aide-de-camp, Albert Wedemeyer, carried the President's briefcase, with copies of a commitment to send American troops to occupy Iceland. Richard Nixon looked straight in the face of American televiewers in the fall of 1960 and denied that any plans were being made to liberate Cuba. Arthur Schlesinger, Jr., flatly denied to the press that American armed forces were heavily committed in planning the forthcoming invasion of the Bay of Pigs. Accosted with this years later, Schlesinger dismissed the prevarication as part of the cover story, and confessed that he had not formulated an absolutely satisfactory ethic on the matter of lying to the press. On a later occasion—when much was made, again at the instigation of my friends at the *Tribune*, and thereupon echoed throughout the press—about an alleged appeal I made to the Catholic vote, I was greatly exasperated by the incapacity to defend myself against the charge of having done, or said, or intended to say, something that simply never had crossed my mind.

scholar who wrote me shortly after my announcement, to plant his misgivings squarely.

May I express to you my deep concern at your candidacy for the mayoralty of New York. I have no reason to cavil at your qualifications for this office as compared with the qualifications of other declared candidates. Not being a New Yorker and not having weighed the respective merits of the various candidates, I cannot but abstain from such comparative judgment. Yet, as a Republican, I am concerned with the welfare of our party and its national prospects. It seems to me that we, the members of a minority party, must unite in one purpose, namely, to strengthen the Republican Party and to get Republicans elected. The Democrats have set us an example which we should seek to emulate, though we should not stoop to the unprincipled cynicism which has distinguished some of the compromises of Democratic politics.

I have met John Lindsay. I do not agree with some of his views. I deem him an honorable and intelligent man. I believe that, as soon as the campaign dust settles and he enters upon his mayoral duties, he will turn out to be a good Republican.

You are acquainted with my views on international affairs. I cannot think of anything more important than the making of a strong responsible opposition to this Administration and, *deo volente*, a change of Administration in 1969. In order to achieve this purpose, we must eschew factional disputes and achieve a broader based consensus. I beg of you to keep in mind these long range goals.

With the kindest regards, . . .

I replied:

I have a much higher opinion of John Lindsay than you do. He is not the hypocrite you suppose, who will suddenly discover sound principles on arriving at high office. I beg you to meditate the possibility that it is less easy to deceive *The New York Times* ("John Lindsay is as liberal as a man can be") or the Liberal Party of New York ("John Lindsay is a true and sincere liberal in every respect"), than it is to deceive you who are, as you remind me, not a New Yorker. Your own interest, over the years, and quite enough it is to consume all the energies of any man, is in foreign policy. I give you as an index of the hopelessness of hope that John Lindsay, become eminent, would be a voice for anti-Communist sanity, his denunciation last December of Lyndon Johnson for resorting to "gas warfare" in South Vietnam. You may remember the episode: laughing gas, or some such thing, was used on a single occasion in an effort to disarm a band of VC who had hold of some South Vietnamese prisoners. It is not known what kind of force John Lindsay would approve for use against the Communists there. An editor of *National Review* has conjectured that he would disapprove of anything more irritating than poison ivy.

It is my judgment that John Lindsay will do as much harm to the Republican Party if he is elected and becomes powerful, as anyone who has threatened the Party's role as defender of the tablets in recent history. If the Republican Party is transformed in his image, I shall give you the Republican Party, and go elsewhere. I doubt that you would want it.

It truly pains me to disagree with someone for whom I have such great admiration. I trust that, *Deo* (please note the reactionary capital letter) *volente*, in due course you will reason that I am doing the right thing.

With best regards.[8]

Absolutely no other pressures were exerted on me, positive or negative, other than one which was no pressure at all, but which was my personal initiation into professional political procedures. I was asked by an official of the Conservative Party, between the date of *The New York Times'* announcement that I was considering running and my announcement three weeks later that I would do so, whether I would consent to a public demonstration staged outside my office urging me to run. I was flabbergasted, but sought to act blasé about the whole thing, and finally struck a bargain—that I would consent to the spontaneous demonstration, provided the entrepreneur would consent to my being absent from my office during the hour at which the demonstration was held. We made the deal, and sure enough a spontaneous demonstration in behalf of my candidacy was staged, the TV news people were tipped off, and snitches were carried on evening broadcasts. There is hardly ever any such thing as a spontaneous demonstration, I paused, for the first time, to reflect. Lindsay's advance men—they called themselves Davidoff's Raiders—regularly preceded Lindsay in his peregrinations to organize spontaneous demonstrations in behalf of their hero. Although I was surprised by the technique, I wasn't put off by it. Unless the demonstrators are a paid claque, it would seem fair enough as indications of (a) organizational prowess by the sponsoring organization, and (b) the availability of demonstrators who are willing to give up their lunch hour to join together to make noticeably and noisily a point they would otherwise have to make privately and silently. But I could not bring myself to

8. Several weeks after the election I came upon a copy of a fat book prepared by Lindsay headquarters recording my most heinous doings and sayings over the years—three hundred pages in all. I found there, to my astonishment, a copy of my reply to the professor. I had sent out a half-dozen copies of the correspondence to intimates of the Conservative Party. I wonder whether I am more surprised that Lindsay knew, or that he will be more surprised to know that I know that he knew.

come down from my office and feign surprise, and so gratefully accepted my dispensation from the total discipline.

The first press conference. The birds and beasts were there—reporters, several dozen of them; television cameras from all the networks; newscasters from all the radio stations. The meeting was at the Overseas Press Club. Neal Freeman, a young man (twenty-four) of enormous talent and savvy who had worked at *National Review* during the preceding two years, was in charge of the arrangements. It had been decided that the Conservative Party would not officially participate in the press conference because to do so would be to anticipate the Conservative Party's ratification of my candidacy, which would have been improper. So that it was, formally speaking, just myself and Freeman. A half-hour before the thing began, looking over one of the hundred copies of my prepared announcement, I suddenly noticed that by error the stenographer had reproduced an early rather than my finished draft. Everyone in the office of *National Review* was transformed, during the ensuing minutes, into typists, stencil-cutters, mimeographers, Xeroxers, as we rushed to put together at least a half-dozen copies to give out to those at the press conference with the most pressing deadlines. The few minutes that were to be given over to a hasty conference to attempt to anticipate the most embarrassing questions the press might ask ("What exactly did Senator Goldwater say to you when you spoke to him?" "Why didn't you oppose John Lindsay in the Republican primary?" "Who will compose the balance of your ticket?") were spent typing copy, in some cases hunt-and-peck, stapling, collating.

It was a terribly hot day. The large room was without air-conditioning. Twice I began, twice the television crews stopped me as they made adjustments. Finally, "Okay, go ahead."

I began again:

I propose to run for Mayor of New York.

I am a Republican. And I intend, for so long as I find it possible to do so—which is into the visible future—to remain a Republican. I seek the honorable designation of the Conservative Party, because the Republican designation is not, in New York, available nowadays to anyone in the mainstream of Republican opinion. As witness the behavior of the Republican Party's candidate, Mr. John Lindsay, who, having got hold of the Republican Party, now disdains the association; and spends his days, instead, stressing his acceptability to the leftwardmost party in New York, the Liberal Party. A year ago, Mr. Lindsay declined to support the choice of the national Republican Party—and of twenty-seven million Republican voters

—for President. Mr. Lindsay's Republican Party is a rump affair, captive in his and others' hands, no more representative of the body of Republican thought than the Democratic Party in Mississippi is representative of the Democratic Party nationally.

The two-party system presupposes an adversary relationship between the two parties. That there is no such relationship in New York Mr. Lindsay makes especially clear when he proposes as running mates members of the Liberal and the Democratic Parties. Mr. Lindsay's Republican Party is a sort of personal accessory, unbound to the national party's candidates, unconcerned with the views of the Republican leadership in Congress, indifferent to the historic role of the Republican Party as standing in opposition to those trends of our time that are championed by the collectivist elements of the Democratic Party. Mr. Lindsay, described by *The New York Times* as being "as liberal as a man can be," qualifies for the support of the Liberal Party and of the Republican Party only if one supposes that there are no substantial differences between the Republican Party and the Liberal Party. That there should be is my contention. Yet it is as foolish for a Republican who stands in opposition to those trends of our time to enter a Republican primary in New York City as it would be for Hubert Humphrey to enter a Democratic primary in Mississippi. If Mr. Lindsay is opposed to third parties, perhaps he will take the opportunity to invite the Liberal Party to dissolve.

Accordingly, as I say, I have declared my availability to the Conservative Party, thinking to give the people of New York an opportunity to vote for a candidate who consults without embarrassment, and who is proud to be guided by them, the root premises of the Republican philosophy of government, the conservative philosophy of government.

I shall accept the designation if it is offered to me because I continue to respect the principles of the Republican Party as they are generally understood out over the country. But also because it has struck me as painfully clear, to judge from their public statements, that the major candidates, while agreeing that New York City is in crisis, are resolutely opposed to discussing the reasons why it is in crisis. Their failure to do so—I speak of Mr. Lindsay, and of Mr. Wagner, and of those who compete to succeed Mr. Wagner as the Democratic candidate—is symptomatic of a political disease that rages in New York, and threatens to contaminate democratic government everywhere in the United States. It consists in its most aggravated form, in an almost otherwordly detachment from the real situation in running for political office by concealing any significant mention of any of the significant public issues of the day. To run for office under such circumstances is merely a form of personal vanity. Yet the major candidates are correct in saying that New York is in crisis. New York cries for the kind of attention that is not being given to it by those who coolly contrive their campaigns so as to avoid offending the major voting blocs. But to satisfy major voting blocs in their collective capacities is not necessarily to satisfy the individual members of those voting blocs in their separate capacities.

Mr. Wagner is a humane and honest man. But few will deny that after twelve years of his attention, New York boils with frustration, injustice, and demoralization. The reason being that government designed to placate voting blocs, precisely does so at the expense of individuals. It hardly satisfies the labor union member who is granted special privileges, special immunities, that permit him special advantages, to live in a city where his wife and daughter are not safe because special privileges, special immunities, are granted in turn to another voting bloc. It hardly benefits a man who can earn an average of fifteen dollars an hour wiring a new apartment building, to find that he cannot rent an apartment in that building except by paying a rent that reflects the crushing cost of paying fifteen dollars an hour to electricians.

The passion of the last generation has been to refer our problems to extralocal government agencies, most particularly the federal government. So far has this gone that it has now become impossible to effect true reform in any major city without getting relief from some of the nation's oppressive laws. Two years ago the central nervous system of New York was paralyzed when the newspapers closed down for three months. They closed down as a direct result of the willfullness of a few hundred men using the leverage handed them by a cluster of federal laws. What power did the Mayor of New York, or the beleaguered publishers, have to come to the aid of the public—in the wake of a generation's legislation granting special immunities to the labor unions who are free to conspire together in restraint of trade?

What power does the Mayor of New York have to reverse the crime rate in New York City? More powers, to be sure, than the incumbent has exercised, or than the challenger Mr. Lindsay proposes to exercise. But not enough power, given the series of recent Supreme Court decisions in which the rights of the alleged transgressor are regularly preferred over the rights of the established victim.

What recourse, under the existing prohibitions, has the Mayor or the city's educational agencies to promote a respect for religion in the public schools, the Supreme Court of the United States having ruled against even such prayers as are satisfactory to the spokesmen of the three major faiths practiced in New York City?

The Mayor of New York has, of course, considerable power still left to him, by the courageous exercise of which he could improve conditions in the city. But increasingly the government of New York becomes the vassal of the government at Washington. This trend toward subjugation is not opposed by the major candidates for the Mayor's office. On the contrary, Mr. Lindsay and Mr. Wagner are almost always to be found egging the government at Washington on in its extravagances. And then—necessarily— approaching the government at Washington as supplicants, begging it to return to the city some of the income it has taken from it. Thus Mr. Lindsay, a week ago, actually suggested as a solution to the problem of rising costs in the subway system that it be subsidized from revenues taken from bridges whose construction cost (he pointed out) is furnished ninety per cent by the federal government—with money (he did not point out) taken in the first instance from New York subway riders—whose payments to the federal government, direct and indirect, vastly exceed disbursements by the federal government, in New York City. Against such economic circumlocutions as these, and the attendant mockery of self-government, someone, somewhere, ought to speak out. I propose to do so.

In due course, I shall publicize suggested approaches to some of the major problems that face New York. They will be the result of diligent and, I hope, fruitful study, conducted in consultation with distinguished and experienced scholars and public-minded citizens whose collaboration I shall in due course gratefully acknowledge. The recommendations will be guided by the principles of a free and compassionate society, respectful of the rights of the individual, of the limitations of government and of the needs of community.

At this moment, I am prepared only to suggest the approaches that I will propose to the citizens of New York.

As regards the crime rate, we place no single objective ahead of the necessity to control it. We need, at least until such a moment as the crime rate is reversed, a much larger police force, enjoined to lust after the apprehension of criminals even as politicians lust after the acquisition of votes. Under no circumstances must the police be encumbered by such political irons as civilian review boards—or by any other contraption whose presumptive concern is for advantageous political relationships, rather than for law and order in our streets. The protection of the individual against the criminal is the first and highest function of government. The failure of government to provide protection is nothing less than the failure of government. The City of New York should investigate the feasibility of providing some kind of indemnity for victims of certain kinds of crime.

The ill-feeling that exists between the races in New York is due in part to a legacy of discrimination and injustice committed by the dominant ethnic groups. The white people owe a debt to the Negro people against whom we have discriminated for generations. That debt we rightly struggle to discharge in various ways, some of them wiser than others, and we should continue to seek out ways to advance the Negro, and other victims of oppression explicit and implicit, by sounder means than undifferentiated infusions of politically deployed cash.

To do this is not enough. We cannot help the Negro by adjourning our standards as to what is, and what is not, the proper behavior for human beings. Family irresponsibility; lawlessness; juvenile delinquency—whatever subtle explanations there may be for the pressures that conduce to them—are nonetheless deplorable, and a matter of urgent social concern. In New York, the principal enemies of the Negro people are those demagogues of their own race before whom our politicians grovel. In 1961 a testimonial dinner was held under the auspices of the freshly installed Democratic Administration for Adam Clayton Powell, Jr.; presided over by the chief of protocol of President Kennedy's government, attended by no less than two Cabinet members. Those leaders of the Negro people who cherish resentments, who refuse to deplore misconduct among their own people, who feed on the demoralization of the Negro race, ought to be publicly and explicitly disavowed by the political leaders of the city. It is the ultimate act of condescension to suppose that merely because a man is a Negro, one may not denounce him; that because he is a Negro, it is hardly surprising that he is a poor husband, or an absent father, or a delinquent child. Mr. James Baldwin has said that the Negroes in Harlem who throw garbage out on the streets do so as a form of social protest. It is a much higher form of social protest to denounce such reasoning and the men who make it.

There is turmoil in the city's schools for reasons largely political. The figures, projected forward, suggest a flight from the public schools that may reach the dramatic proportions of the flight in Washington, D.C. The reasons for the flight are not by any means traceable alone to irrational prejudice. Either schools are places where education is the primary consideration, or they are places where the social policies of politicians are the primary consideration. By all means the neighborhood school should be encouraged; the administration of the school decentralized; the uncooperative student sequestered. Special financial inducements should be given to first-rate teachers to persuade them to take on the rigors of teaching undisciplined and uncooperative students. The dilution of education in the interest of a synthetic integration will merely accelerate the flight from the public schools, and leave them without the students who can provide the healthy leadership young people so greatly need from their own companions.

The entrenched labor unions have a hold on the city whose antisocial potential has been demonstrated on such occasions as the newspaper strike, and the more recent paralysis of the Port of New York. Remedial legislation is greatly needed. Meanwhile, the police must be instructed to guarantee the safe passage of anyone who crosses a picket line in order to earn money to feed his family and to satisfy a social need. The minimum wage laws should be abolished, most urgently in their coverage of minors who, denied the work, denied the training, denied the apprenticeships they might enjoy, swell the ranks of the unemployed, and the registers of the police stations. It is inhuman and irrational to endorse an increase in the minimum wage, as the other candidates have done, at a moment when there is unemployment and boredom and waste.

Five hundred thousand New Yorkers receive welfare payments. Those of them who do and are able-bodied, and who are not needed at home to care for their children, should report for duty, in our parks, in our streets, in our development projects, pending their absorption in the labor market. A year's residence requirement should be instituted to discourage the thoughtless flow of men and women into New York, whose incapacity to absorb them heightens their own frustrations, adds to the general demoralization, and continues to add to the high overhead of life for which New York is becoming increasingly infamous.

The beauty and vigor of New York are its principal assets, and are a public trust. The vigor drains away, economically, as the tax rate soars; spiritually, as we live cheek by jowl with problems which we are precluded from solving because of a failure of political nerve. The beauty of New York is threatened by the schematic designs upon it of the social abstractionists who do not look up from their drawing boards for long enough to recognize what it is that makes for human attachments—to little buildings and shops, to areas of repose and excitement: to all those abstractions that so greatly inconvenience the big-think social planners. The obsession with urban renewal must, in due course, be tranquillized, before the city loses its hold on human sentiment.

I intend to do what I can, consistent with minimal resources, to bring these matters up. Hopefully, I will succeed in introducing the other candidates to the New York that seethes with frustration while the politicians conduct their quadrennial charade.

I shall, as I say, in due course elaborate on these observations, and make others relevant to the needs at hand.

I assume that there are many New Yorkers who take seriously the cliché that New York is in crisis, and who are serious enough to recognize that not a blessed reform of any consequence has been proposed by the major candidates. I appeal to them to help themselves and their fellow New Yorkers by voting the Conservative ticket in November.

Excerpts from the press conference

MR. FREEMAN: We are going to have questions now. Please identify yourselves and your paper when you have a question to ask.

FRANK LYNN (New York *World-Telegram*): Have you discussed your candidacy with Senator Goldwater, or do you intend to ask him to campaign for you?

WFB: I do not. I called up Senator Goldwater as a matter of courtesy since we are friends of long standing, not to consult him about running but to inform him that I intended to do so.

MR. LYNN: But you do not intend to ask him to campaign for you?

WFB: No, I don't. I would be delighted if he would, but I don't intend to ask him. If he wants to do it, it will suggest itself to him.

JUDY MICHAELSON (New York *Post*): I couldn't help but noticing in "Who's Who" and "The Register" that you listed your address as Wallachs Point, Stamford, Connecticut. How long have you lived in New York?

WFB: I have lived in New York longer than Bobby Kennedy did when he decided to run.

MISS MICHAELSON: What is your address in New York?

WFB: I don't give it out.

DON SHERIDAN (unidentified): When is the Conservative Party going to meet to make a designation on a candidate?

WFB: Within a week.

PAUL PARKER (WINS): Bill, are you in this campaign to win it or are you in the campaign to, judging from your statement here, perhaps pick away at what you regard as Lindsay's fraud on the party and—

WFB: No. I am in the campaign to get as many votes as I can get, consistent with maintaining the excellence of my position, so the decision, of course, is up to the people, not me. I will not adapt my views in order to increase my vote by ten people, as you have just seen.

ANOTHER SPEAKER: Do you want to be Mayor, sir?

WFB: I have never considered it.

QUESTION FROM THE FLOOR: Do you think that is something that at present should be considered?

WFB: Not necessarily. What is important is that certain points of view should prevail. Whether you or I administer those points of view is immaterial to me, assuming you are a good administrator.

BARRY FARBER (WOR): But you are asking people to vote for you. If you win, will you serve?

WFB: If elected, I will serve.

BOB POTTS (WNDT-TV): Did you say something about what kind of campaign you will run? You are not going to go out and campaign in the streets?

WFB: No, I will not, primarily because I don't have time. I will spend what time I do have on trying to develop as carefully and responsibly as I can those positions that I want to project and will project them wherever the opportunity lies.

RICHARD MADDEN (*The New York Times*): Do you have any preference who your candidates should be on this Conservative line for Comptroller or City Council President?

WFB: Yes, there are prominent candidates being discussed, including Mr. [Lawrence] Gerosa and—but the decisions haven't been finally made.

MR. SHERIDAN: What position would he take on your ticket?

WFB: Comptroller.

MR. FREEMAN [visibly panicked]: Why don't we make that off the record, that last statement?

MR. SHERIDAN [great clamor]: Why? It is on the record.

MR. FREEMAN: Why don't we let Mr. Gerosa answer that statement?[9]

HARRY HENNESSY (WOR): Do you have any specific recommendations for putting New York City on a balanced budget? Do we pay for it by a sales tax, a payroll tax?

WFB: The details of the fiscal reforms will be forthcoming in a paper that is being worked on at this point, so I would just as soon not be more specific than I was [in my opening statement].

MR. FREEMAN: Anything else? Yes?

JUDY MICHAELSON: Do you think you have any chance of winning?

WFB: No.

MISS MICHAELSON: Why are you running?

WFB: I thought I made that clear. I will read you my speech again if you like. It gives you about sixteen reasons why.

MR. LEE (New York *Daily News*): Is this a press conference?

WFB: Whatever you make out of it.

MR. FREEMAN: Any other questions? Yes, sir?

REPORTER FROM *Time:* How many votes would you consider a satisfactory showing?

WFB: When the Conservative Party was founded, the first time around, they got 50,000 votes. Against Mr. Kennedy two years later, one year ago, they got 122,000 votes—for Mr. Paolucci. That is a suggestive range.

MR. SHERIDAN: That is state-wide?

WFB: No, that was city-wide.

MR. SHERIDAN: How many votes do you expect to get, conservatively speaking?

WFB: Conservatively speaking, one.

MR. FREEMAN: Are there any other questions?

---

9. " 'He's crazy,' Mr. Gerosa said when told of Mr. Buckley's suggestion. 'I don't even know the gentleman,' he added. 'Absolutely not—100 per cent not.' " (*The New York Times*, the next morning.) In fact: Mr. Gerosa had been offered the nomination, and was considering it.

End of press conference. The television and radio newscasters thereupon began their own interviews.

Two widely read columnists who covered the press conference confined their reports to personal and picturesque aspects of the candidacy as (see below) the press in general also did. In the *Tribune,* Dick Schaap wrote on June 25:

BUCKLEY FOR MAYOR

William F. Buckley, Jr., is a brilliant man who never lets his intelligence get in the way of his reasoning. He held a press conference yesterday to announce that he is available to run for Mayor of New York City, and he was, as always, magnificent. He talked with his eyebrows. They leaped up first, chased by his bright blue eyes, then his nose, then his mouth. His tongue flicked out of the right corner of his mouth every fifth word, and the taste of the words was delicious. When he said "Adam Clayton Powell June-ee-yore," he made "junior" the harshest word in the language.

Buckley never allowed himself to stumble into simplicity. "We need," he said, "a much larger police force, enjoined to lust after the apprehension of criminals even as politicians lust after the acquisition of votes. Under no circumstances must the police be encumbered by any such political irons as civilian review boards—or by any other contraption whose presumptive concern is for advantageous political relationships."

The words spilled out steadily in Buckley's Connecticut British accent, and they almost ruined Tom Foley, the court stenographer Buckley had hired to make certain that the press did not distort his remarks. "My fingers are killing me," Foley said afterward. "The syllabic content was terrific."

Buckley took no chances. Just in case Foley slipped Buckley had a tape recorder running through the entire conference. The tape recorder was a Uher. It said, "Made in W. Germany." You can carry America First only so far.

In his 15-minute prepared statement, Buckley sliced up John Lindsay and all Democrats, taxes and all labor unions. He is, possibly, the finest debater in the country, and his arguments were devastating. There was only one thing wrong with them. The reasoning behind his arguments makes sense only to people who cannot understand a word he says.

Buckley does not seem to care. He seems to want people to believe him whether they understand his words or not. This is only fair, because he gives the impression that he understands his own words whether he believes them or not. And no one as smart as Bill Buckley could believe everything Bill Buckley says.

The audience was split rather obviously into believers, mostly

Young Americans for Freedom, and non-believers, mostly reporters. Manny Ress, the professional button maker, was giving "Back Bill Buckley for Mayor" buttons to both sides.

"Did Buckley order them," Ress was asked, "or did you just make them up?"

"A couple of them Conservatives came in the place the other day," Ress said.

"How could you tell they were Conservatives?"

"It was easy," said Ress. "They wanted buttons saying 'Cuba Libre' and 'Bomb Hanoi.'"

Everyone was trying for laughs at the conference. When someone wondered where Buckley bought his obviously expensive wool suit, a television technician suggested "Klein's." When a reporter asked Buckley about how many votes he expected to get, the reporter added, "Conservatively speaking . . ." But Buckley had all the best lines.

Only one question really threw him: "Do you want to be Mayor?"

Buckley paused. He pressed his thumbs into the top of his trousers and pushed the trousers down so far the laundry mark on his button-down shirt was showing. "I've never considered it," he said.

"If you win, would you serve?"

He thought it over. "I would serve," he said.

"Do you have any chance of winning?" "No," said Buckley.

Buckley is right, which is too bad. I'd like to see him win. It would serve him right.

And Murray Kempton in the *World-Telegram* on the same day:

We already have had candidates for Mayor various enough to satisfy every taste except the most refined, and the apparition of William F. Buckley may complete the scale.

The truly refined taste, after all, progresses from discontent with each way the thing is being done to the final decision that the thing ought not to be done at all. And Buckley made it plain yesterday that he does not merely disdain the opposition but rather disdains the office itself.

"Do you want to be Mayor?" someone asked him toward the end of the charming languors of his press conference.

"I haven't considered it," the candidate answered.

But anyone who enters a field this crowded has made himself part of the vulgar throng; and when a man answers his city's call to the general mobilization of candidates for Mayor, he is not so much presented to the voters as processed by a permanent induction cadre of television engineers and journalists.

Buckley carried through these indignities as handsomely and containedly as any gentlemen ranker offered his first introduction to the enlisted men's latrine. He also had the kidney to decline the customary humiliation of soliciting the love of the voters, and read his statement of principles in a tone for all the world that of an Edwardian resident commissioner reading aloud the 39 articles of the Anglican establishment to a conscript assemblage of Zulus.

I am sure that there are legions of the poor wandering the streets of this city today with no firm impression except the unwarranted one that the summer after Bill Buckley is sworn in, all able-bodied welfare clients will be summoned to Sharon, Conn., to beat the frogs in the family lily pond so that the Mayor can sleep at night.

Buckley said that he expected—his tone does not justify the verb "hoped"—to campaign whenever he could find the time. His first duty is, he indicated, to the *National Review*, the only magazine which, in Otto Von Hapsburg's opinion, talks sense to the American people. Any candidate deserves to be appreciated who feels a duty not to gallop in pursuit of a job on the time during which he is being paid to perform another. It is a melancholy reflection of our prevailing values, rather than on William F. Buckley, that he feels more responsibility for the *National Review* than John Lindsay feels for Congress, Paul Screvane for the City Council and Franklin Roosevelt, Jr., for anything.

So then, if nominated, Buckley will not serve, but, if elected, he will not run. "I do not propose," he said from the depths of aesthetic principle, "to walk the streets." A visitor suggested that he ought at least to submit himself to the Liberal party selection panel, since he is the first candidate to proclaim that he shares David Dubinsky's distaste for the increased minimum wage. "But that would be just a stunt," Bill Buckley answered. "Do you think I should go to Harlem?"

At last we have a candidate who refused to let the voters intrude upon him. And there is no other way for the voters to enjoy the blessing of a candidate who refuses to intrude upon them.

In general, the rest of the press also personalized the event. The papers (1) touched on the probable effect (nugatory) of my candidacy on the election itself; (2) did a little berating—here-(sigh)-is-another-nuisance- (or, depending on which paper you read, threat-) from-the-extreme-right; and (3) gave generally atmospheric accounts of the occasion.

Thus it would be throughout most of the campaign. These were the three principal preoccupations of the press—I speak mostly of course, though not exclusively, of the *Tribune* and the *Times*, which were the two newspapers in New York "of record." Toward the very end, for reasons that will become apparent, the papers, particularly the *Times*, began to pay more attention to the issues I raised. But at the outset, their treatment was mostly of random phrases or sentences which seemed to have the effect of heightening the scandal-value of the whole enterprise—my interference with what had been programmed as an orderly and ecumenical elevation of John V. Lindsay to City Hall.

The *Tribune* began its story (June 25) by identifying the candidate as a "Right-wing and ultra-conservative debater." The announcement had been made at "an odd press conference." The candidate "admitted . . . amid guffaws that he did not expect to win the office and ventured that he may get 'conservatively' only 'one vote.' . . . He was running, Mr. Buckley said, his brow damp with sweat, his right hand upturned and fingers spread apart, because Mr. Lindsay, 'having got hold of the Republican Party, now disdains the association, and spends his days, instead, stressing his acceptability to the leftwardmost party in New York, the Liberal Party.'" To emphasize the context of that statement, the article went on: "One reaction to Mr. Buckley's breed of Republican came swiftly last night. Not mentioning him by name, Senator Jacob Javits, a campaign chairman for Mr. Lindsay, said to the Rockland County Republican Committee: 'We must show our ability as Republicans to turn back the infiltration of our Party by extremists of the Radical Right (the Senator's capitals) [noted the *Tribune*]—one of the classic challenges of our age.'" And, on the ninth paragraph of an eighteen-paragraph story (paragraph ten resumed discussion of the ideological static of the affair), the following condensation of my opening statement: "In his long announcement, Mr. Buckley talked about the ills of the city, crime in the streets, the poor leadership provided for the Negro in his quest for equal rights, defective schooling, the iron-clad control of labor unions, and the 500,000 relief recipients, some of whom, he said, should work on city projects." The same issue of the *Tribune* carried an editorial.

ENTER MR. BUCKLEY

William F. Buckley, Jr., at least has a sense of political realism. He acknowledges that he's not likely to be elected Mayor; rather, he justifies his candidacy by charging that John Lindsay has all but abandoned Republicanism and the Republican party, and by insisting that his own "conservative" solutions to the city's problems need a public airing. The argument is reminiscent of Mrs. Luce's as she toyed publicly last year with the notion of running against then Senator Keating—a scheme fortunately abandoned, which wasn't very constructive either.

Mr. Buckley has every right to run, just as the Conservative party has every right further to fragment the city's political structure (it begins to resemble France's under the Fourth Republic) by entering a candidate. But the principal political business before the city of New York this year is electing a Mayor; not staging esoteric debates. And the Mayor who governs for the next four years is, as a practical matter, going to be either Mr. Lindsay or whoever the Democratic nominee turns out to be; Lindsay is the one challenger with a chance. Thus, every vote that Buckley succeeds in diverting from Lindsay (whom Buckley seems to have made his principal target) will, in effect, be a vote to continue the Tammany rule.

He may well, of course, have decided that John Lindsay, as a potential national Republican leader, poses so serious a threat to Buckley-style "conservatism" that Lindsay's ambitions have to be checked, and that reconsigning New York to the Tammany maw is simply the price that has to be paid. If so, it's not an approach likely to appeal to the average New Yorker, who, we imagine, would like to consider the mayoralty an office not thus to be trifled with.

The *Times* quoted two sentences from the statement in its opening two paragraphs, and devoted the next eighteen to literate patter about this and that ("Mr. Buckley announced his candidacy in front of a large modernistic painting entitled 'The Merry Company' at the Overseas Press Club, 54 West 40th Street"), and in the same issue fired off the first of a series of Big Berthas that were to pound down on poor old New York, and poor old me, right through to the eve of the campaign.

WHAT MAKES BUCKLEY RUN?

William F. Buckley, Jr., leading apostle of Goldwaterism on the Eastern Seaboard, has offered himself as the Conservative party candidate for Mayor. He regards New York as a city to be saved from crisis and, with his usual diffidence, himself as the man to do it. Whether New York is also ready for Mr. Buckley is another matter. Popular demand that he become a candidate has been thunderously absent.

What makes Mr. Buckley undertake this noble exercise in futility? It can't be "merely a form of personal vanity," because he deplores other candidacies so based. So the only plausible explanation left is that he, and the Conservatives, wish once again to do as much damage as they can to the liberals in the Republican Party. Since one of that party's leading liberals, Representative John V. Lindsay, is a candidate for Mayor now, the opportunity to do a spoiling job on him was irresistible.

Mr. Lindsay, having handsomely survived a previous abortive crusade from the same quarter, when he was running for re-election to the House, is unperturbed; he had expected it. If anything was needed to confirm the soundness of his credentials as a liberal, this opposing candidacy by the editor of the *National Review*, bible of the conservative movement, is gilt-edged proof. Those who may be concerned that this competition will drain off votes from Mr.

Lindsay should now consider what a calamity it would have been if Mr. Buckley, or the Conservatives, had instead endorsed Mr. Lindsay. That would have been a real kiss of death.

Mr. Buckley is glib, assertive and usually impossible. His kind of Republicanism suffered devastating repudiation at the polls here and throughout the nation last November. We are sure the voters will show the same excellent judgment again this year.

To this editorial I replied a couple of days later:

The Editor
New York Times
New York, N.Y.

Dear Sir:

Every man has the right to ask rhetorical questions, but so, one supposes, does every man at whose expense they are asked have the right to make the effort to undeceive those who are led astray by them. To judge from your editorial column, "What Makes Buckley Run?" (June 25), you would have your readers believe that I am running for Mayor primarily in order to displease the New York *Times*. I could be coaxed into defending the proposition that such a career is among life's nobler callings, but I am in fact running not in order to annoy you but to propose certain reforms for the City of New York which are not being proposed by any of the other candidates. If you are curious as to what these reforms are, you need go no further than the city room of your newspaper to consult the nine-page statement that I made on announcing my availability, and disclosing the program I will run on: not a single plank of which was reproduced in your news story. I am running on a program that will (1) seek to restore law and order by increasing the police force, encouraging it to do its duty and the city judges to do theirs; (2) lower taxes by effecting efficiencies and introducing a residency requirement in order to qualify for welfare benefits; (3) require work from able-bodied beneficiaries on relief who are not directly concerned with looking after their children; (4) disavow and discourage those of their leaders who encourage racism, lawlessness and despair among the Negro people; (5) petition Congress for legislation that would permit New York to free itself of the binding hold on some of its vital functions, e.g., the newspapers and the waterfronts, now exercised by the monopoly labor unions; (6) decentralize the city schools and substitute education for racial integration as their principal function; and (7) tranquillize the mania for urban renewal and city planning of the kind that is dehumanizing the city.

You say that my kind of Republicanism "suffered devastating repudiation at the polls . . . last November." That is true—only

800,000 New Yorkers voted for the Republican candidate. But it is also true that New York continues to be misgoverned. There may be a cause-and-effect relationship here. Meanwhile, permit me to call to your attention that as far as I know from reading the New York *Times*, I am the only candidate who proposes those major reforms. Which is why Buckley is running.

Very faithfully,
[WFB]

Only the New York *Daily News* (on June 26) editorially welcomed my candidacy:

> The half-dozen or more Democratic aspirants for the mayoralty are in a war of words which boil down to: "I'm more liberal than you are, you such-and-such."
>
> John V. Lindsay, Republican candidate for Mayor, is wooing the Liberal Party and snooting his own party so effectively that the Liberals are reported making ready to endorse him next Tuesday.
>
> Into this fracas has now barged William F. Buckley, Jr., an unashamedly conservative Republican and editor of the unashamedly conservative magazine *National Review,* which (free ad) in our opinion consistently prints some of the finest writing being done in English today.
>
> Mr. Buckley says he will run for Mayor on the Conservative Party's ticket, though he doesn't much expect to be elected. His chief aim is to inform the voters as to what true Republicanism is, and how phony is the Lindsay brand of Republicanism, in the Buckley view.
>
> This editorial commits *The News* to no candidate or party in the upcoming mayoral election.
>
> But we are delighted to see Bill Buckley jump into the fight, and thereby stir the local "liberals" of all categories to slavering, slobbering rage. They've been asking for this sort of challenge from a fearless conservative for a long time, and we're overjoyed to see them get it at last.

At the outset, several observers reasoned, as we have seen, that the Conservative candidacy might in fact help John Lindsay. Whether they did this, as in the case of the *Times*, merely by way of trying to find a silver lining, I cannot say. However, none of the analysts at this time played around with the point they posthumously jubilated over, *viz.* that the Conservative candidacy ended up drawing as many votes away from the Democrats as away from John Lindsay—perhaps more. Rather, at the outset, the point several-times made was that the Conservatives' entry into the race would precisely illuminate Lindsay's liberalism. "While Mr. Buckley seemed to be campaigning against Mr. Lindsay, some Lindsay strategists contended that the Buckley candidacy might help the Republican nominee. Mr. Lindsay has pitched his campaign to independent Democratic and Liberal voters, instead of relying on traditional Republican voting strength." (*Times*, June 25.) The *Times* editorial quoted above made the point backward, by suggesting how much more it would have hurt Lindsay if he had been backed, rather than opposed by, the Conservative Party. The New York *Post* made the same point. And the same day, a story in the *Times* even suggested that "the reported Liberal swing towards Mr. Lindsay was said to have been given added momentum by the entry of William F. Buckley in the race." It is odd, in the light of the subsequent acrimony, that this piece of analysis was totally forgotten during the panic of late September and October when it was generally assumed that the Conservatives would cost Lindsay the election.

The question was also raised, and quite naturally, How many votes was I likely to get? I walked into the press conference determined not to exhibit the usual neurotic confidence of all political candidates, strong and weak, popular and despised. I had reasons personal and philosophical for declining to perform the usual ritual of self-confidence. The first of these was that I felt no self-confidence, other than in the cogency of my views, and would have found it personally and professionally embarrassing to go about town speaking nonsense about my own expectations. Besides, I didn't at any point want to suggest that the vote I would get would reflect the potential conservative vote in New York City. I knew I could only hope to mobilize a small fraction of the voters who, for instance, had gone for Goldwater a year before, lacking as I did the support of a major party, the lavish publicity given to a Presidential candidate of a major party, and the enormous personal popularity of Goldwater.

Even so, I quite clearly overdid it—by answering, jocularly to be sure, in reply to a provocative question, that "conservatively," I could only be sure of "one vote." Even though I did go on to say to the radio and television interviewers that I would attempt to get as many votes as I could consistent with my position and my resources, the crack about getting only one vote rattled around New York and the messages began to pour in during the next few days that that statement had made me an "unserious" candidate, had greatly hurt the Party. I argued that I *was* an "unserious" candidate in the formal sense of the word, *i.e.,* I had no chance to win and would not, therefore, by definition pass as a "serious candidate," that I was "serious" only in the sense that the undertaking was very serious indeed. But the pressures mounted and I promised to attempt a clarification at the next scheduled press conference, a week later, called to introduce my running-mates, Mrs. Rosemary Gunning (for President of the City Council), and Mr. Hugh Markey (for Comptroller).

I only succeeded in making matters worse. I said then that although I did not expect to win, I would work as though that were the objective. "What would you do if you *were* elected?" a reporter asked. "Demand a recount," I said: and in turn *that* phrase rattled around, making my cohorts gloomier than ever.

I must have been asked fifteen hundred times in the course of the ensuing four months how many votes did I think I would get, and did I believe I had any chance to win the election. I stuck obdurately to my original formulation—that Dr. Paolucci, an excellent candidate, had secured 120,000 votes in New York City only a year before: that he had waged a fine campaign; that in fact I had difficulties he did not have inasmuch as I was running on municipal issues rather than national or international issues (it is easier for a New York conservative to vote against Red China than for the end of rent control in his apartment building). I even permitted myself to say, under the acutest pressure, that it would be a miracle if I won, but then I did believe in miracles. . . . I did not, however, succeed in controlling the temperature of my associates, most notably that of Kieran O'Doherty, who was to serve as the Party's press aide and whom I would constantly come across, the stars dancing in his Irish eyes, confidentially predicting to a cluster of newspaper reporters that I would win the election. For old times' sake he would add, on spotting me—"by a narrow margin."

And, finally, at the very first press conference, a question arose, the ramifications of which were to touch almost every point of the campaign. At that point in June, John Lindsay had been campaigning ardently for over a month, and not a day went by in which he failed to make a personal appeal to a racial, religious, or nationality group, usually by the indicated equivalent of plopping an Indian warchief's headdress on his head, puffing on a peace-pipe, and saying something on the order of, Me-um like-um Navajo people. Asked whether I would campaign on the sidewalks of New York, I said no, that time forbade it, adding, "I will not go to Irish centers and go dancing. I will not go to Jewish centers and eat blintzes, nor will I go to Italian centers and pretend to speak Italian."[10]

10. Ha ha!—a reporter who remembered this statement accosted me halfway through a press conference I was conducting in Spanish—wasn't I violating my pledge? No, I answered: I am not *pretending* to be able to speak Spanish: I *do* speak Spanish. And in any case, how do you communicate with Spanish-speaking voters who do not speak English? —in French? And *anyway*, what I was busily engaged in telling the Puerto Rican community, in that press conference, was that other than in the field of education, the fact of their being Puerto Rican was immaterial; that they should neither ask for, nor receive, any special favors.

I do not know of anything harder in politics than to escape the coils of racial and religious opportunism. At one point in the campaign I paused long enough to observe that it had then been implied by roughly the same set of people that I was anti-Catholic, anti-Protestant, anti-Jewish, and a religious fanatic.

VI.

Race, Religion, and Politics

(A) A PASTICHE

> *"No subject is more intensely discussed in the privacy of any campaign headquarters, either state or national, than the ethnic origins of the American people and their bloc-voting habits."*
>
> —THEODORE H. WHITE,
> *The Making of the President, 1960*

> *". . . the Conservative candidate came right out in the open on crime in the streets, drug addiction, protest demonstrations and all the other code words for race prejudice."*
>
> —JOSEPH KRAFT, New York *Post*, October 29, 1965

1. The Practicing Politician

(*The New York Times*, September 25, 1965)

LINDSAY AIDE IS LINKED TO "PLOT"
TO SWING DEMOCRATS TO BUCKLEY

A former campaign worker for John V. Lindsay said yesterday that he had been asked by a district coordinator for the Republican-Liberal Mayoral candidate [Lindsay] to solicit votes for William F. Buckley, Jr., the Conservative nominee.

Walter A. Swift said he had been told this strategy would enable Mr. Lindsay to reduce the votes that Abraham D. Beame, the Democratic candidate, might get from normally Democratic but conservative Irish Catholics. . . .

In a section of the tape purporting to be a discussion with Mr. [Wyn] Kramarsky . . . manager of Milton Mollen's campaign for Controller on the Lindsay ticket . . . [Kramarsky] was quoted as saying that he had been unaware of what Mr. [Elliot] Saron wanted

Mr. Swift to do and that he did not consider it "smart politics." . . .

(Excerpts from transcript of tape recording distributed
to the press)

(Telephone rings)

SECRETARY: Mr. Mollen's office. [Milton ("Pat") Mollen, candidate
for Comptroller on John Lindsay's ticket.]

SWIFT [Walter Swift, Bronx Coordinator of "Democrats for Lindsay"]: Is this Pat?

SECRETARY: Yeah.

SWIFT: Is Wyn there? [Wyn Kramarsky, Campaign Manager for
Mollen]

SECRETARY: He was due in an hour ago and just phoned and said
he'd be another half-hour. May I take a message?

SWIFT: Yeah. I'd like to talk to him about that Inwood situation.

SECRETARY: Uh-huh. Shall I have him call you? Where?

SWIFT: I'll be at the club—733-4545. I'll be here until nine-thirty.

SECRETARY: Okay. I'll tell him.

(Telephone rings)

SARON [Elliot Saron, Manager, Lindsay HQ at Dyckman Street.]:
Hello.

SWIFT: This is Walter.

SARON: Walter, how are you?

SWIFT: Fine. How's everything?

SARON: Fine. Walter, what are you doing tonight? Are you working,
or do you want to come down—have a couple of drinks?

SWIFT: Nah, I'm not . . . I got to get hold of Wyn. There are about
three questions I want to ask you before I say anything one
way or the other—on that thing. Is this basically your own idea
or is this an idea that is okayed and approved and everything
else from down there?

SARON: No, [Wyn] Kramarsky thinks it's a good idea. He also spoke
highly of you.

SWIFT: And the other—that answers two questions. I was also
going to ask you how much Wyn knew.

SARON: Wyn knew it; Wyn knows it. And I spoke to Wyn twice. I
called him up yesterday to wish him a happy New Year [the
Jewish New Year, September 27, 1965].

SWIFT: Look, I'm going to be talking to Wyn later on before I give
you an answer on it.

SARON: Third question?

SWIFT: Give me a brief breakdown again on just exactly what you
expect of me and what you expect I am going to be able to
accomplish.

SARON: All right. This is a traditional Irish Catholic Democratic area [a section of extreme northern Manhattan in the Fifteenth Assembly District], with the exception of some of the more, shall I say, well-policed E.D.'s [Election Districts] which have Jewish voting populations. The Conservative vote may run ten votes a district, twenty votes a district. But they are nothing spectacular. These districts, such as the one in Park Terrace area, are districts [in] which Keating would come up a hundred votes, a hundred-fifty votes over Goldwater. The Marble Hill district, there is a Conservative vote in the stretch roughly starting between Nagle Avenue and Broadway—Broadway, Nagle—do you know the area?

SWIFT: Nah, I don't know that area.

SARON: Well, Nagle Avenue—Broadway there runs in a circular direction, sort of like an arc, and Nagle Avenue runs—they both run north-south, but they go up in a wide shape, sort of like a triangle. After you get to that triangle, from there all the way up to the East End of Manhattan, with the exception of a couple of districts along Inwood Hill Park, which is predominantly Jewish, and housing project, you get an Irish Catholic stretch—but Irish—from the shanties. There's a lot of E.D.s up there that are predominantly Jewish. There's not much of a Conservative vote among the Jews. They'll get maybe five votes a district, but what the hell! Anybody would get four votes a district. I'm not concerned with the Jewish vote in the southern half. That's another problem which will be met by sending Jews around insisting Lindsay is better for the Jews than Beame is. At least for those who would be affected by such an appeal. The rest of them you simply have to be rational with. But in that stretch in Inwood and in the stretch of Manhattan called Marble Hill—you've heard of it, I presume?

SWIFT: Yeah.

SARON: There's a strong Conservative grain. You have Election District after Election District, and in about twenty-five instances, Goldwater running well ahead of Keating. Hard to fathom, isn't it?

SWIFT: [Unclear]

SARON: You understand it?

SWIFT: Yeah.

SARON: Now there's reason to believe that a lot of these Irish could be swung off the Democratic line to the Conservative line. We had—Lindsay had the same experience in '64 and didn't know it—until I told him before the election where the Conservative strength was. In Yorkville in the Tenth, [conservative candidate] Kieran O'Doherty ran, got a greater portion of the total vote than he did in the Ninth—all the Irish Democrats; because they're interested in such things as censorship, banning *Fanny Hill,* and that sort of crap. And I can't go out and make a presentation and be hypocritical about it. The only thing we could possibly do is plant this Buckley literature under Democratic doors. Buckley is out to ruin Lindsay. I mean that's the open purpose. A lot of his supporters think that is what they're going to do. So with a little bit of guidance in the right direction, they could help Lindsay and not know it. Because they're sufficiently unsophisticated—because, you know, they've got such blinded mentality— you know, you could pull this off. What I would say—you know, get in there and act like an idiot for approximately three weeks. It would be a condescension on your part. But, hell, it's a condescension to go fight for your country, when you get down to it—you know, carry a rifle in a foxhole. But on the other hand, let's face it, it's work that has to be done. Any of my local personnel would be recognized immediately. If I sent any Jews in there they'd get murdered. Any of my Jewish personnel from other parts of the city. I would have to send in somebody else. I've never met you, but from the description, physically, and your background in the Army, you might be able to fit in very well with them. You know, without anyone knowing you're going against your thinking; and put that Buckley literature under Democratic doors.

SWIFT: In other words, you want me to actually become a member of the local club?

SARON: Yes, join them; work with them. Click heels with them.

SWIFT: And draw what votes I can away from Beame to . . .

SARON: Buckley. Lindsay's not going to get them. But if Buckley gets them, fine. That's one less vote for Beame. So it's one less vote I have to worry about. It will be a tremendous contribution for the cause, frankly. The Democratic Club there, which is mostly Irish and Conservative Irish, is not going to be out for Lindsay. . . . These are the most vicious sons-of-bitches God ever put on this earth. I mean don't let anyone ever tell you you are different. It's something—they should get all those Irish names over to Buckley. I don't care; Buckley, Schmuckley—as long as they're not voting for Beame. If we campaign for Buckley—it's strictly among the Irish—see they're going to try to shoot the Republicans. In other words, you accidentally make sure the literature goes under Democrats—I mean, listen, true, Beame's got O'Connor [running-mate, on Beame's ticket, for President of the City Council]. Let them switch from Buckley to O'Connor because the only thing that I can see—any other sort of rationale —well, I mean Buckley-O'Connor; that's fine. I don't give a damn about Frank O'Connor. I mean Costello [running-mate, on Lindsay's ticket, for President of the City Council] is a fine fellow and all that sort of thing, but the point is *Lindsay*. That's the big one. And the second thing is, you say, "Look, Buckley is the only Irishman running," and that sort of thing. That's the

only solid Irish slate. There are some—you see, they'll come
down, and they might as well vote Buckley and then they will
vote Markey [running-mate, on Buckley's ticket, for Comptroller];
then they'll go over to O'Connor. You know why?

SWIFT: Why?

SARON: Well, they're normally Democrats.

SWIFT: Where does that leave both Mollen and Costello? It leaves
them out in the cold.

SARON: It hurts Costello. They'll probably swing back to the Democratic line on O'Connor. They won't swing back *before* O'Connor.

SWIFT: Yeah.

SARON: You know why?

SWIFT: Why?

SARON: Did you ever hear of the Irish voting for an Italian? Procaccino [running-mate, on Beame's ticket, for Comptroller]? The
only place that Procaccino could conceivably run ahead of the
ticket is in an Italian neighborhood. I mean, really.

SWIFT: Yeah, but what is Mollen?

SARON: Mollen's Jewish.

SWIFT: They're liable to go Italian before they'll go Jewish,
though.

SARON: No, no, no. The name Mollen—they see a name like Procaccino—it's something which they think you put spaghetti on.
They won't go for Mollen. I'm saying they'll go for—they'll stick
with *Markey*, this bunch, and then go over to *O'Connor*. They
won't go over to *Mollen*. You see, Costello is Irish, but an Irish
liberal in that neighborhood usually gets creamed. I'll tell you
what happened in two instances: 1948, Javits won the Irish
vote against Paul O'Dwyer. But Javits won it because O'Dwyer
was nominated by Democrat and American Labor. And Javits
gets up and speaks at the Church of the Good Shepherd. They
got 2000 Irishmen sitting there, and he says, "Where do you
stand on foreign policy? With Henry Wallace or Harry Truman? I
happened to support Governor Dewey and he's anti-Communist."
You know? That's all the Irish had to hear. That was '48. 'Fifty-
four they voted for Javits again, but that was against Franklin
Delano Roosevelt, Jr., and Eleanor was having a little row with
Cardinal Spellman that year. 1962: the only area where Fitts
Ryan [left-Democratic candidate for his party's nomination] got
badly beaten in the primary was up in Inwood by Herbert Zelenko. Zelenko came out in favor of aid to parochial schools,
fighting Communism, and Fitts Ryan comes out as a big liberal.
Even though he was Irish they figure he's a traitor. In 1963
Blaikie beat O'Dwyer up there because they figured O'Dwyer was
still a left-winger. This year O'Dwyer convinced them he wasn't
a left-winger. He won one election district with the Irish. But
O'Dwyer was beaten by Blaikie in that area up around the

Fifteenth. In Inwood, the primary. So you got an idea of how it votes?

SWIFT: Yes, but you're running into stiff trouble because Beame hasn't come out as a liberal in any sense.

SARON: That's irrelevant. Buckley is coming out as a real Irishman.

SWIFT: Yeah.

SARON: And there's a clear-cut choice for these idiots.

SWIFT: What's that click on the phone?

SARON: I don't know. It's not at this end. You want me to call Kramarsky on this?

SWIFT: Uh—

SARON: Why don't you wait and call Wyn on it? I think it's very important, and the point is, it's the craziest goddamn district in the city. I was the only—me and one other Assembly District leader had requested the piece of literature which is known as *The Maltese Falcon*. You know what that is?

SWIFT: No.

SARON: The Grand Cross of the Order—it's a big Catholic fraternal order. That was the only thing he could do with it. And I was the only leader to request it. The Republican Club in my district, for Christ's sake, is so f—ing right-wing it isn't even funny. That's the one district, the Fifteenth Assembly District, at least, particularly certain portions of it, the only Assembly District where Barry Goldwater was running substantially ahead of normal Republican vote. The normal Republican vote up there runs maybe a hundred votes in an Election District. Goldwater was getting twice that, for Christ's sake. My, that's why I asked— [*laughing*] that's what my problem was. . . . Where you'll be smack in the heart of that belt. . . . Every other store's an Irish store, Irish religious goods, Irish groceries; there are sixteen hundred gin mills to one grocery store in the neighborhood.

SWIFT: Yeah.

SARON: They still have wakes there, you know.

SWIFT: Yeah.

SARON: They don't exactly have wakes in the old style, but what happens, next to every funeral parlor there are two gin mills.

SWIFT: Yeah.

SARON: And they go into the tavern. They bring their children to the tavern at one o'clock in the afternoon.

SWIFT: Yeah.

SARON: The mothers beat the s—t out of their youngsters. You know—

SWIFT: Yeah, but what's this got to do with the election?

SARON: No, but this is the tone of the area, which you are going to be in.

SWIFT: . . . Well, there's two things. In the first place, I'm not Catholic; I'm Protestant.

SARON: That doesn't mean a goddamned thing. As long as you look
—you see, what they are—they're interested not too much in
Catholicism; they're interested in the crazy ideas which they
espouse. . . . Do you have a car?

SWIFT: No. Well, we'll see whether Kramarsky is going to pick up
the expenses on it . . . on whatever I have to spend over there.
I'm not going to spend it out of my pocket.

SARON: I think Kramarsky will. . . . Don't worry about the money
part of it. Either Kramarsky—if Kramarsky doesn't swing it,
we will swing it out of our petty cash.

SWIFT: Yeah.

SARON: It's worth our while to do it.

SWIFT: Yeah.

SARON: Any other questions, Walter? . . . If they ask you your
religious affiliation, "Well, I'm Protestant." And if they ask you,
you're from upstate New York.

SWIFT: I was in the army.

SARON: Tell them you were in the army. Tell them you made
Sergeant; they'll eat that up.

SWIFT: Okay.

SARON: Were you in any combat actions?

SWIFT: Yes; I was in Korea.

SARON: Oh, yes, you fought Communism in Korea. Good man! I
didn't even know that. Oooh! Good man! Excellent! You're perfect for this thing. And you're blondish, I understand?

SWIFT: Yes.

SARON: You look relatively rugged?

SWIFT: Yes.

SARON: Good; good man.

SWIFT: How does it affect me if the news gets out in my own area?

SARON: That I don't know. Wyn never said anything about that.
But frankly, I'll tell you something we—if you weren't a Con-
servative-for-Buckley in there—first of all, your name won't go
on any literature.

SWIFT: Yes, I know.

SARON: Don't worry about that. You just join it and start working
along with them, you know. That's it.

SWIFT: All right, I'll call Wyn back, and then I'll see what—then
I'll give you a call, either if I get through with him early enough
I'll give you a call later; if not, I'll give you a call tomorrow.

SARON: Okay, fine. I appreciate that, Walter.

SWIFT: Okay.

SARON: Bon seer! 'By now.

SWIFT: Good-by.

(Telephone rings)

KRAMARSKY: Walter? Wyn.

SWIFT: Yes.

KRAMARSKY: Shoot.

SWIFT: On this thing regarding the Inwood thing—

KRAMARSKY: How does it strike you?

SWIFT: I don't like the idea of going into somebody else's camp and spy for somebody else. It's one thing to go in and spy for your own people, but it's another thing altogether to go in and spy— pull in votes for Buckley. In fact, I have no use for this whole operation as a result of this conversation. . . . [Swift took the story, and the tapes of his telephone conversations, to Beame headquarters.]

2. Balancing the Ticket

"For the first time [1933], an Italian, an Irishman, a Jew, and a white Anglo-Saxon Protestant ran on the same ticket for the four top positions."
—ARTHUR MANN, La Guardia Comes to Power, 1933

(New York *Herald Tribune*, July 1, 1965)

BUCKLEY HAS A "BALANCED TICKET": MARKEY, MRS. GUNNING—ALL IRISH

The ticket that the conservatives fielded yesterday was all Irish, but Mr. Mahoney, an Irishman himself, saw nothing invidious in that. As he introduced the candidates, he noted that his party does not seek to balance tickets for any particular electorate.

Mr. Mahoney, a conservative-type Conservative, said of the all-Irish happenstance: "We didn't give it any thought," and observed that all three of the Buckley-Gunning-Markey slate "are from different backgrounds." . . .

(Excerpt, address by WFB at Third Anniversary Dinner, Conservative Party of New York, October 7, 1965)

Back a few weeks ago, when Mr. John Lindsay was looking for a Democrat to fill out his ticket, there was considerable speculation as to who he would be, there being agreement only on the single proposition that he would most certainly be Jewish. Why? Because Mr. Lindsay is Protestant, Mr. Costello is Irish: therefore, the Third Man had to be either Italian or Jewish. However—I give you the analysis, even as published, by the professionals—since Mr. Lindsay is depending very heavily on enticing a great number of Jewish voters, and since the Italians are mostly Catholic, and are therefore represented religiously through the medium, however imperfect, of Mr. Costello:—then, it followed, that the Third Man would be Jewish. And thus, of course, it went in constructing Mr. Beame's ticket. Mr. Beame risked only the absence of a Protestant. But if you have to slight someone, the professionals say, slight a member of the majority: they don't care that much.

Our own ticket, I am informed, is composed of three Catholics. I know you will find it unbelievable, but let me tell you the truth: namely that I was not aware that Mrs. Gunning was a Catholic until I read that indeed that is what she is, in the blaring headline of the *Tribune's* heavy reference to the Conservative Party's "unbalanced ticket."

3. The Sting of the WASP

(New York *Herald Tribune,* October 15, 1965; from account of appearance by candidates before PAT, Queens)

[Mr. Buckley] underscored the fact that Mr. Lindsay is a "white Protestant." Mr. Buckley, and the rest of his ticket, are Roman Catholics.

(New York *Herald Tribune,* October 16, 1965)

. . . Thursday night at a Parent's and Taxpayer's meeting, Mr. Buckley underscored the fact that his own all-Catholic ticket was opposing Mr. Lindsay, a white Protestant. Yesterday, the Flatbush Minister's Council denounced Mr. Buckley's remarks. A statement issued on behalf of 15 Brooklyn ministers by Rev. Joseph C. Holbrook of Grace Reform District Church said:

"I would like to not simply deplore the injection of this religious name-calling into the race for Mayor, I would like to denounce it as cheap and underhanded. Appeals for votes on the basis of religious affiliation have no place in American public life today."

Commenting on a statement reportedly make by Mr. Buckley that he "hopes to exercise a position of cultural leadership" . . . Mr. Holbrook said: "We would suggest to the candidate that his unethical attack on Mr. Lindsay's religious affiliation makes him a poor choice for such leadership."

(Letter to the New York press by James L. Buckley, campaign manager for WFB, October 23, 1965)

Dear Sir:

. . . your editorial writer seemed to accept as a fact the erroneous charge of Mr. Costello that Mr. William Buckley "introduced religion into the campaign" at a speech he delivered in Queens on October 14th.

For the benefit of the voters and the archivists, permit me to record that the myth Mr. Costello has been reporting had its origin in reports first carried in the *Tribune*, and later elaborated upon in the *World-Telegram*, to the effect that on the evening of October 14th, while addressing "a predominantly Catholic audience" Mr. William F. Buckley, Jr., "underscored the fact that his own all-Catholic ticket was opposing Mr. Lindsay, a white Protestant."

The facts are: (1) The particular audience in question, composed of members of the Parents and Taxpayers Association in Queens, was predominantly Protestant.

(2) Mr. Buckley made not a single mention, direct or indirect, of the religious affiliation of himself or of any member of his ticket.

(3) His only reference to Mr. Lindsay's religion, after devoting preliminary remarks to the unfortunate tendency of Mr. Lindsay and Mr. Beame to think in terms of bloc-voters, was as follows: "Mr. Lindsay, it is not too late to make yourself plain. I beg you to say, I, John Lindsay, forty-three, white, Protestant, of sound mind and body, do believe in the principle of the neighborhood school."

Dr. Costello has yet to call the Conservative Party for a transcript of Mr. Buckley's remarks at Queens. Perhaps he will do so when the burden of his work lightens, some time after Election Day?

Yours faithfully . . .

(PAT Candidates' Night, Richmond Hill High School,
Queens, October 14, 1965. Excerpts from extemporaneous
remarks by WFB)

Mr. Chairman, etc.:

. . . I think it is true that people have become accustomed to thinking that New York voters are merely blocs to be moved around according to sophisticated polls which are supposed accurately to measure the extent to which all of us are affiliated with some bloc or other. We are supposed to be Catholics or Jews or Protestants or bricklayers or non-bricklayers or typists or whatever. . . . A social theorist [Wyndham Lewis] about ten or fifteen years ago said "You know, if you classify people enough different ways, you deprive them completely of their individuality." If somebody is exclusively moved in virtue of his participation in this bloc or in that bloc, creating enough blocs in which each one of us belongs, in the end we are all treated as categories. . . . Increasingly we *are* treated as categories. . . . There is supposed to be catnip for each one of us— each one of us is supposed to respond rabidly to a particular stimulus. And under the circumstances you have in New York politics . . . a situation in which . . . every[body] is a pin on the wall . . .

and you get these master strategists and they figure how they can deliver your vote by giving *you* this much catnip and *you* this much catnip and the other person that much catnip.

. . . the traditional practices of politics [ask] . . . how many Jewish people are there? how many Italian people? how many Protestants?—not Protestants, come to think of it; they don't count —how many people are moved by Harry Van Arsdale, how often is it necessary in the course of a working day to genuflect to David Dubinsky, how often is it necessary, in order to prove that you don't have any racist prejudices, *not* to criticize Adam Clayton Powell, Jr.? . . .

I can look Abraham Beame in the face and John Lindsay in the face, two or three feet from them, and I can say to them, "Mr. Beame, Mr. Lindsay, if we believe in a moral reform for New York City, can't we at least begin with the proposition that Adam Clayton Powell, Jr., is a scoundrel and a rogue?"

Whereupon, they will immediately and briskly engage in a debate over who first proposed a review of the sales tax. You can say to Mr. Lindsay, "Mr. Lindsay, it is not too late to make yourself plain. . . . I beg you to say I, John Lindsay, forty-three, white, Protestant, of sound mind and body, do believe in the principles of the neighborhood school and am opposed to school busing." And he will launch into a rhetorical peroration on the beauty of school parks. Or you can say to Mr. Beame, "Mr. Beame . . ."

4. Will the Real Catholic Stand Up?

> " 'I think it ought to be very clear,' [Costello said], 'that my statements were in response to what Buckley said. When he got up on a public platform and boasted that all the top members of his ticket were Catholics—and also pointed out that John Lindsay was a white Protestant—I was disturbed and angry.' "
>
> —Interview with Dr. Costello, by James Wechsler, New York *Post*, October 21, 1965

(*The New York Times*, page 1, October 16, 1965)

COSTELLO ASSERTS VOTE FOR BUCKLEY IS ANTI-CATHOLIC

Says Conservative Opposes Church Stand
on the Poor,
Minorities and UN

REPLY IS UNDER STUDY

Dr. Timothy W. Costello who is running with Representative John V. Lindsay for City Council President, charged yesterday that a vote for William F. Buckley, Jr., the Conservative party candidate for Mayor, would be an anti-Catholic vote.

Mr. Costello, who like Mr. Buckley is a Roman Catholic, said that the Conservative's views on the poor, on minority groups and on the United Nations were in conflict with those of the Catholic Church.

He also charged that Mr. Buckley had ridiculed encyclicals issued by Pope John XXIII and that this showed he had "delusions of grandeur." . . .

At Fordham, Dr. Costello, who received three degrees there, said he refused to accept the possibility the Catholic community would "fall prey to doctrine of ignorance, fear, hatred and intolerance."

"It is time we ripped the sneering clown's mask from William Buckley and revealed his negative, divisive preachings as the threat they really are to peace on earth, to the progress of the nation, the uplifting of our City, and the propagation of the social doctrine of the Catholic Church itself," he said. . . .

(*National Review*, July 29, 1961, an editorial, unabridged)

The large sprawling document released by the Vatican last week on the 70th anniversary of Leo XIII's famous encyclical *Rerum Novarum* will be studied and argued over for years to come. It may, in the years to come, be considered central to the social teachings of the Catholic Church; or, like Pius XI's *Syllabus of Errors*, it may become the source of embarrassed explanations. Whatever its final effect, it must strike many as a venture in triviality coming at this particular time in history. The most obtrusive social phenomena of the moment are surely the continuing and demonic successes of the Communists, of which there is scant mention; the extraordinary material well-being that such free economic systems as Japan's, West Germany's, and our own are generating, of which, it would seem, insufficient notice is taken; and the dehumanization, under technology-cum-statism, of the individual's role in life, to which there are allusions, but without the rhetorical emphasis given to other matters. There are, of course, eloquent passages stressing the spiritual side of man, as one would expect there should be. But it is not unlikely that, in the years ahead, *Mater et Magistra* will suffer from comparison with the American Catholic Bishops' hierarchy of emphases, in their notable annual message of November 1960.

(*La Tribune de Genève*, Geneva, July 23, 1965; excerpts from an article on the New York election)

. . . The indignant Goldwater Republicans immediately rendered John Lindsay the inestimable service of opposing him with

a list of ultras under the direction of that same William Buckley
who a short time ago called good Pope John XXIII, "that fellow-
traveling foreigner."[1]

(Reply, by WFB, to Timothy Costello,
October 17, 1965, unabridged)

I find it hard to believe that Mr. Lindsay's representative should
have attacked my religion. Perhaps the Liberal Party has become so
used to taking over New York political movements that now it
proposes to take over entire religions. To imply that I am anti-
Catholic is as convincing as to imply that Mr. Beame is anti-
Semitic—which at this rate Mr. Lindsay will be doing next week.
One of the meanings of the Vatican Council is to stress the freedom
within the Church, which encompasses men of many political
faiths, now as before. If I am a bad Catholic, I shall be punished
by Someone I fear far more than the New York Catholic voter. To
whom I say this: I don't want you to vote for me because I am a
Catholic. I want you to vote for me because of the positions I
take. And I pledge you, my fellow Catholic, this: that *I* will never
disgrace the Catholic Church by introducing the religions of the
other candidates as issues of the campaign.[2]

(Editorial, New York *Daily News*, October 19, 1965)

LOW BLOW COSTELLO

Timothy W. Costello, Liberal Party candidate for City Council
President on allegedly Republican John V. Lindsay's mayoralty
ticket, saw fit last week to toss a charge of anti-Catholicism at
William F. Buckley Jr., Conservative nominee for Mayor. Both Doc
Costello and Mr. Buckley are Roman Catholics.

Buckley proceeded to answer the idiotic charge with surgical
skill, leaving Costello only a shred of his political scalp.

Costello's accusation was tops in bad taste, if nothing worse, and
it is to be hoped that religion will not again be dragged into this
mayoralty campaign by anybody. There are plenty of real issues to
discuss, and time is running out, what with the election coming
just two weeks from today.

---

1. *"Ce communisant étranger."*
2. Excerpt, column by James A. Wechsler, New York *Post*, October 21, 1965
after interview with Timothy Costello: ". . . [Dr. Costello has] provoked William
Buckley into a frenzy of grotesque indignation unrivaled since the late Sen.
McCarthy solemnly accused his critics of resorting to the un-American practice
of unjust accusation."

RELIGIOUS ISSUE (Editorial, *The New York Times*, October 19, 1965)

We confess to surprise at finding ourselves in agreement with William F. Buckley Jr. on anything: but we share the conviction of the Conservative party mayoral candidate that it was wrong for one of his political opponents to introduce any aspect of religion or religious views into the campaign.

When Dr. Timothy W. Costello, Republican-Liberal nominee for Council President, asserted that a vote for Buckley would be an anti-Catholic vote, he was injecting into the debate a consideration that ought not be there. We hope all the candidates will spend the two weeks left discussing the real issues, not artificial ones.

5. Is Moynihan a Racist?

(From: *Beyond the Melting Pot*, by Nathan Glazer
and Daniel Patrick Moynihan, M.I.T. Press, 1963)

. . . The rate of illegitimacy among Negroes is about fourteen or fifteen times that among whites. When we find such an impossible situation as that discussed in the New York press in 1960, in which babies are abandoned in hospitals by their mothers, and live there for months on end, for there is no room for them anywhere else, most of them are Negro children. . . .

More Negro children live apart from parents and relatives; more live in institutions; more live in crowded homes; more have lodgers and other related and unrelated persons living with them.

Broken homes and illegitimacy do not necessarily mean poor upbringing and emotional problems. But they mean it more often when the mother is forced to work (as the Negro mother so often is), when the father is incapable of contributing to support (as the Negro father so often is), when fathers and mothers refuse to accept responsibility for and resent their children, as Negro parents, overwhelmed by difficulties, so often do, and when the family situation, instead of being clear-cut and with defined roles and responsibilities, is left vague and ambiguous (as it so often is in Negro families).

We focus of course on one side of the problem—there are more unbroken than broken homes among Negroes, more responsible than irresponsible parents, more nonworking than working mothers, more good homes for children than poor ones. There is a whole world in which these problems do not exist. But the incidence of these problems among Negroes is enormous, and even those who escape them feel them as a close threat. They escape, but family, relatives, friends, do not. . . .

We do not propose a single explanation of the problems that

afflict so many Negroes; obviously, if the schools were better, the students' performances would also be better. If housing and job conditions were better, there would be less illegitimacy. If the police were fairer, there would be less arrests of Negroes. If Negroes had better jobs and higher incomes, fewer of them would be sentenced, fewer criminals would be made in prisons and reformatories. All these things are true. And since it is easier to do something about education, housing, jobs, and police administration than many other things, there is where we should put our emphasis, and there is where we begin. But I think it is pointless to ignore the fact that the concentration of problems in the Negro community *is* exceptional, and that prejudice, low income, poor education explain only so much. . . .

. . . The image of the Negro is still predominantly that created by the problem element. But it is also true that the Negro middle class contributes very little, in money, organization, or involvement, to the solution of Negro social problems. Conceivably, institutions organized, supported, and staffed by Negroes might be much more effective than the government and private agencies that now deal with these problems.

. . . But the worst of it is that important tasks, necessary ones on the agenda of American Negroes, are shirked and ignored. These are tasks that conceivably no one but Negroes can do. It is probable that no investment of public and private agencies on delinquency and crime-prevention programs will equal the return from an investment by Negro-led and Negro-financed agencies. It is probable that no offensive on the public school system to improve the educational results among Negroes will equal what may be gained from an equivalent investment by Negro-led and Negro-financed groups, and an increase in the numbers of Negro teachers and principals. It is possible that no effort to change the patterns of the Negro lower-class family will be effective at a time when the white family is in disorder, when strong families of whatever kind. native and ethnic, show signs of disintegration; but if anything can be done, it is likely that Negro agencies will be far more effective than public agencies and those of white Protestants.

Succeeding the period of accommodation, then, and the period of protest, one can detect the need for a period of self-examination and self-help, in which the increasing income and resources of leadership of the group are turned inwards. And already a few voices are raised to make just this point. . . .

MEMORANDUM

TO: WFB
FROM: Gertrude Vogt [Secretary to WFB]
DATE: April 30, 1965
An aide to Mr. Patrick Moynihan of the Department of Labor

called and asked for a copy of the column in which you "called Mr. Moynihan a racist." Shall I send him the column?
[Yes—WFB]

Dear Mr. Moynihan:
Here is a copy of the column your office has requested.

Sincerely yours,
Gertrude E. Vogt, Secretary to
William F. Buckley, Jr.

ON THE RIGHT—Wm. F. Buckley, Jr.
Distributed by George Matthew Adams Syndicate

For Release Thursday, April 15, 1965 or thereafter.

ARE YOU A RACIST?

I recently heard a man denounced as a racist for having observed that the rate of illegitimacy in New York is fourteen times as high among the Negro population as among the white. I was not, of course, surprised, having become accustomed to hearing the epithet loosely used: but I did remark the irony that it should now be used against a prominent liberal Jewish sociologist, Mr. Nathan Glazer, who recorded that datum in a book, *Beyond the Melting Pot*, which he wrote in collaboration with an Irish Catholic, and which copped an award from one of the learned societies—which would not be caught dead trafficking in racist literature.

One of the troubles with keeping epithets fresh is that it is very tempting to exploit the opprobrium that attaches to them: for political purposes, or for generally malign purposes—to do the other fellow in, for whatever reason. The word "racist" has been rendered especially horrible because it evokes the ghastly shadow of Adolf Hitler, whose entire ideology was racist, which is bad enough: but who, unsatisfied merely to acclaim the superiority of his own race, set out to exterminate an entire other race. If Hitler hadn't scourged the world by his presence and his ideas, it is unlikely that the word racist would be around as an everyday word; certainly it would not carry the weight of disapproval it now does.

And even in spite of Hitler, the meaning of the word is changing. It changes in part because of its licentious use. Any word can be deprived of its sting if used commonly enough, indiscriminately enough. "Why you old bastard, where have you been?" is said every day by people in greeting to their very best friends. If everybody who believes in social security legislation is called a Communist by enough people, the word, deprived of all exactitude, will lose its meaning, and its sting.

If everyone who says the Negroes in New York breed more

illegitimate children is a racist; if everyone who says the Irish have a better sense of humor than the Swedes is a racist; if everyone who says the IQ of the average Jew in New York is higher than that of the average Anglo-Saxon is a racist—then it will turn out that most people are "racist." And in a democratic society, where most people, by the divine dispensation of Jean-Jacques Rousseau, John Stuart Mill, and Oliver Wendell Holmes, are good, then by definition to be a racist, according to that sense of the word, is all right, Jack.

The meaning of the word is indeed diluting. In 1933, the definitive Oxford English Dictionary, for instance, did not even list it. The Seventh Webster Collegiate Dictionary says that a racist believes that race is *"the* primary *determinant of human traits and capacities and that racial differences produce an inherent superiority of a particular race."* That is a tough definition, and anyone who is a racist in that sense cannot, for instance, be a Christian; inasmuch as a Christian may not believe in the "inherent superiority" of any one of God's creatures over another: on the contrary, he is committed to believe in the inherent equality of all men.

But the Third Webster's Dictionary, the more modern of the two, defines the word differently. Racism here is *"the assumption that psycho-cultural traits and capacities are determined by biological race,"* which is *"usually coupled with a belief in the inherent superiority of a particular race."* Note the important evolution. "Determined" is, rhetorically, a demotion from the word "primary." No longer does the word require belief in the inherent superiority of one race over another; it is merely observed that "racism" "usually" is coupled with such a belief.

What will the dictionaries of tomorrow say? It depends a great deal on how the word is used in the hectic days ahead. If every sociologist who puts down figures about illegitimacy rates or crime rates is marked down as a racist, then the entire data-collecting profession will inherit the word. If everyone who believes in states' rights is automatically set down as a racist, then the word will further dilute in meaning. And if the word finally becomes meaningless, what word shall we come up with to distinguish, say, between Harry Byrd and Adolf Hitler? Those who throw the word around for tactical advantage should ponder that one.

6. Negroes, Crime, and Police

(Excerpts from Theodore H. White,
The Making of the President, 1964)

With this, one arrives at the terrifying figures of family decomposition. In general, across the country, Negroes bear ten times as many babies out of wedlock as do white families. Nationally, one fifth of all Negro children are illegitimate. But in the big city this figure soars—so that in central Harlem, according to the last available figures, more than two fifths, or 43.7 percent, of all children were born out of wedlock in 1964. The pace of decomposition in that community can be indicated by noting that as recently as 1956 illegitimacy was already a frightening phenomenon at a rate of 33.2 percent. *More than half of all Negro children* in central Harlem today come from homes where one of the two parents is permanently absent.

. . . Out of these broken homes and loveless breeding warrens come, first, the delinquents—and then the criminals. Thus as they mature, like the postwar *besprizorni* of Russia, they make a larger and larger social problem. Their terrorizing of the New York subways is a condition generally referred to statistically—as, for example, in the report of the New York Transit Authority that in the year 1964 alone major crime on its underground system had jumped 52 percent from the previous year. No figures on adult crime are broken down in New York by race; but unofficially the mayor's office makes available the estimate that 80 percent of all crime in New York is committed by what are called "non-whites" —Negroes and Puerto Ricans, generally of the late teens and early twenties.

These teen-agers are an element that no one knows how to handle. In New York City, 5,481 illegitimate Negro children were born out of wedlock in the year 1954. By the year 1963 this number had jumped to 11,809. There are, thus, today in New York well over 100,000 Negro youngsters, ranging in age from infants to the late teens and early twenties, denied love or dignity or patrimony or tradition or any culture but television—and they rock around on the deck of an unstable society, their bread given to them by underpaid welfare workers, their hopes zero, their mothers despised, their hearth the gutter, a subculture in a general American urban culture which itself does not know where it is going.

Few Negro leaders care to discuss the situation publicly, but among the most courageous of them is Roy Wilkins, executive secretary of the NAACP. In an eloquent outburst of dismay, he wrote, "The teen-age Negro hoodlums in New York City are undercutting and wrecking the gains made by the hundreds of Negroes and white youngsters who went to jail for human rights. These punks . . . these hot-shots, tearing up subway cars and attacking innocent people, are selling the Freedom Riders down the river. They are helping Mississippi. These foul-mouthed smart alecks are really beating up the six-year-old Negro girls who dared to go to school in New Orleans through a screaming crowd of white mothers. The Harlem and Brooklyn morons . . . are cutting and slashing at the race's self-respect, something they can never rebuild with their knives, their baseball bats, their brass knuckles and their filthy language."

(Testimony by William F. Buckley, Jr., to City Council of New York concerning proposed Civilian Review Board for Police Department)

July 13, 1965

[Excerpts]

What are the givens of the situation? They are: (1) There *is* more and more crime. (2) There is *not* any documented rise in instances of police brutality. (3) A larger percentage of the crimes being committed are being committed by members of a minority group, namely New York's Negro population, a cause of considerable concern to the Negroes themselves.[3] And (4) The pressure to encumber the police comes primarily from members of that minority group affecting to speak for the whole of it, who for political reasons have gotten endorsements from men whose private judgment probably opposes the suggested civilian review board.

. . . Surely it is relevant to remind ourselves that the principal victims of lawlessness are the Negroes themselves. The dilemma lies in the fact that unthinking Negro leaders are flogging the Negro population in an attempt to make them believe that they are, as a race, the specially selected victims of a concerted police brutality. Yet to the extent they succeed in doing so, they harness the Negroes' political strength towards arrangements—a less effective police force—which militate against peace and justice for the law-abiding Negroes, an overwhelming majority, who live in the city. If the police find that yet another encumbrance is put in the way of duty, *all* of us will suffer who live within the reach of the criminal—and his reach nowadays is into every cellar in every tenement house, and into every penthouse in every skyscraper—but they will suffer most who live in areas where lawlessness is most active: specifically, in those areas in which there is the heaviest concentration of Negroes.

It is one thing to observe that it is no wonder that so many

3. Theodore H. White, *The Making of the President, 1964*, page 230: "No figures on adult crime are broken down in New York by race; but unofficially the mayor's office makes available the estimate that 80% of all crime in New York is committed by what are called 'non-whites'—Negroes and Puerto Ricans, generally of the late teens and early twenties. . . . Let there be no mistake about it: these junior savages are a menace most of all to decent Negro families, penned by white prejudice into the same ghettos with the savages; it is the good Negro child who is first beaten up by the savage, the decent black family which suffers from the depredations of the wild ones."

Negroes commit crime. "What we do not tend to realize," said the Sheriff of Chicago recently, commenting on the crime rate among Negroes in his city, "is that most of the Negro delinquent children have never in their entire lives met a single decent human being." It is one thing to say that the white people of this city, as of Chicago, should accept—as I believe we should do—a moral responsibility for contributing to the helplessness and despair that breed ignorance and lawlessness [among so many Negroes]. But it is something altogether different—it is a total distortion of civilized thought—to deduce from whatever is the extent of our corporate responsibility for the high rate of Negro crime, that Negro crime is other than criminal. That broken homes, because they are Negro broken homes, are any the less broken. That illegitimacy, because it is Negro illegitimacy, is any the less illegitimate. However understandable it may be that it is as a result of *my* delinquency as a parent that my son has become a thief, thievery is wrong; and the supreme duty of civil society is to prevent that thief from marauding against innocent citizens.

That is the function of policemen. That and only that. It is the function of *others* to devise the means by which to discharge the debt we have to the Negro people. That debt is not discharged by succumbing to pressures, generated by the frequent exaggerations of a few misled leaders, to render more difficult the job of the policeman. Let those leaders use their leadership to urge on their people a racial pride of the best kind, of the kind that encourages hope, the hunger for knowledge, the appetite for industry, and excited concern for the rights of others. Let those leaders, instead of berating the police, encourage the police to apprehend, and isolate, the criminals in their midst, and, simultaneously, let them urge those who will listen to them, that the surest way to avoid embarrassing confrontations with the policeman, is to obey zealously the laws that are written to protect everyone in New York, black or white, rich or poor, young or old.

If you gentlemen submit to synthetic pressures to cure an imaginary evil, at the risk of undermining the pursuit of a demonstrated evil—which is that this is an unsafe city to live in—you will doubly damage the prospects for New York. First, by reducing the effectiveness of the police at precisely the moment when all our ingenuity should be devoted to devising means of increasing their effectiveness. And second, by exacerbating the relations between the races. If crime continues to rise, and if the Negro crime rate continues to rise relatively, latent racial animosities will smolder. If yielding to pressure that is generally understood to be primarily Negro pressure, you take steps whose consequence is that crime shall increase, then so will resentments and ill-will increase.

RIGHTS AND WRONGS

(Excerpts from a syndicated column by Roy Wilkins,
Executive Director,
National Association for the Advancement of Colored People,
November 14, 1965)

. . . much of [Buckley's] support was among the people hostile
to the Negro civil rights movement. Most of these happened to be
traditionally Democratic. Buckley opposed any changes in school
administration to correct racial imbalance. Buckley deified the police, pooh-poohed brutality charges, inveighed, in his super-clever
way, against crime and identified the latter, without saying so,
with the Negro surge.

Many of the slick Buckley nuances were not clear to all Negroes
(as they were unclear to many whites), but Negroes understood,
first, that Buckley supported the police completely: whatever the
circumstances, the police were right and the Negroes wrong. . . .

7. Negroes, Demagogy, and the "Backlash"

(From Theodore H. White, *The Making of the President, 1964*)

. . . In New York, Adam Clayton Powell, Harlem's leading black
racist, began to invite riots. It was as if Southern white crime required Northern Negroes to take vengeance on Northern whites.
And as outrageous statement succeeded outrageous statement,
television and press began to require even more dramatic and
violent statements in a competition of threat and violence by which
Negro leaders sought the attention of the nation. "Miscalculation
of the moment of truth which is upon us," threatened the Reverend
Gardener Taylor, leader of a Negro church in Brooklyn, "could
plunge New York, Brooklyn, Philadelphia, Chicago, Detroit and
Los Angeles into a crimson carnage and a blood bath unparalleled
in the history of the nation."

. . . by and large, Negroes elected by the civil vote of the Negro
communities are among the finest men elected by free politics
anywhere in the country. Headlines are claimed by such egregious
and frightening elected exceptions to this rule as Adam Clayton
Powell of New York. Yet for every Powell there are five others in
every city as well educated and responsible as the finest white
legislators of the country. . . .

(New York *Post,* July 28, 1965)

WILLIAM BUCKLEY'S ATTACK ON POWELL STIRS NEGROES

An attack on Rep. Adam Clayton Powell as a "scoundrel and an
opportunist" was made last night by Conservative William F.

Buckley at a meeting of prominent Negroes gathered to hear him and four other candidates for Mayor. . . .

Turning to the subject of Powell, Buckley contended that the Harlem Congressman was harming the Negro cause and asked why his constituents continued to re-elect him.

One of the 150 men in the audience jumped up and said Powell had worked to end segregation in the armed forces during World War II and also cited his record as chairman of the House Education and Labor Committee. Buckley retorted:

"Yes, but he wrote a column for the *Daily Worker* 20 years ago and called many of his colleagues in Congress Fascists."[4]

When the man continued to object, Buckley said:

"I'm not here to engage in a spitting contest with you, but if any statement in the world is safe to make, it is this:

"Adam Clayton Powell is a scoundrel and an opportunist."

. . . After the speeches, Brooklyn attorney George Fleary declared that "Buckley has insulted every man in this room" and the repudiation vote followed.

4.   July 29, 1965

Dear Mr. Buckley:

Congressman Adam Clayton Powell, Jr., has requested me to advise you that unless you make immediate public retraction or apology for the false, defamatory, and widely published statement that, "he wrote a column for the *Daily Worker* 20 years ago," you will be sued for damages.

As you are no doubt aware, the statement appeared in the public press on July 28, 1965, and you were quoted as having made the remark on July 27, 1965, when you appeared before The 100 Men, Inc.

It is Mr. Powell's opinion that you have effectively conveyed to the public and to his constituents, a charge that he is a Communist.

Very truly yours,
Henry R. Williams /s

August 10, 1965

Dear Mr. Williams:

In reply to yours of July 29, I confess to having made a technical error, though apparently one that is of greater consequence to you than to Congressman Powell. While I said during the question period at the meeting of One Hundred Men, Inc. that Mr. Powell had written a column for the pro-Communist *Daily Worker* twenty years ago, I should have said instead that he wrote a column for the pro-Communist *People's Voice* twenty years ago. If you believe there was a substantial difference between those two publications, I suggest that your quarrel is not with me but with your client. At Madison Square Garden on January 10, 1944, the *Daily Worker* held its twentieth anniversary celebration at which Congressman Powell was one of the featured speakers. He is reported to have evoked much applause when he referred to his own paper, the *People's Voice*, in which he wrote a regular column, as "the Lenox Avenue edition of the *Daily Worker*." In reply to your specific question, do I charge Mr. Powell with being a Communist, my answer is No, I do not believe Mr. Powell is a Communist—he is too opportunistic to be anything so unpopular at this moment.

May I take the opportunity to advise you to spend your efforts in behalf of Mr. Powell in attempting to intimidate people less familiar than I with Mr. Powell's public record? And am I to infer that for the purpose of bringing libel suits, Mr. Powell is prepared temporarily to suspend his routine contempt for the courts and the processes of justice?

Yours faithfully,
[WFB]

(New York *Amsterdam News,* October 23, 1965)

NAACP ASKS VOTERS REJECT BUCKLEY BID

New York City voters were called upon this week to reject the appeals to "racist emotionalism" being waged in the mayoralty campaign of Conservative William F. Buckley, in a resolution unanimously adopted last weekend by delegates to the NAACP State Conference of Branches in Schenectady, N.Y. . . .

The NAACP resolution on Buckley called his campaign "cynical," and said it was based "upon a demagogic appeal to man's baser prejudice while in his cavalier disregard of the facts he continuously makes subtle and overt appeals to racist emotionalism."

(Excerpt, column by Jimmy Breslin,
New York *Herald Tribune,* October 22, 1965)

. . . all along, his statements and inferences, in New York cuteness, have asked for a little white backlash at the polls. . . .

(New York *Herald Tribune,* October 21, 1965)

BUCKLEY'S STAND ON A "WHITE BACKLASH"

William Buckley Jr. said yesterday that he welcomed a "white backlash" aimed at resisting the special pleading of certain leaders in the Negro community. Mr. Buckley, the Conservative Party candidate for mayor, specifically cited Rep. Adam Clayton Powell Jr. and Bayard Rustin, director of the A. Philip Randolph Foundation and a leader of the March on Washington.

He said that Mr. Powell "constantly played on the entrenched hostility in the Negro community to all white people" and that Mr. Rustin had proposed upsetting the entire American economic structure to advance the cause of the Negro.

Mr. Buckley, who addressed a packed luncheon audience at the Overseas Press Club, said there was also another kind of backlash that he deplored: the backlash against Negroes in general "for making justifiable progress."

(*The New York Times,* October 21, 1965)

. . . Mr. Buckley said at an Overseas Press Club luncheon yesterday that he would welcome any white backlash that represented a repudiation of Negro leaders like Representative Adam Clayton Powell.

When he was asked if he would welcome a white backlash because of a belief that Negroes were getting too much, he replied emphatically, "Most certainly not."

He said that Negroes should be given opportunities to advance to justice and to "the kind of special treatment that might make up for centuries of oppression."

He accused Mr. Powell of constantly making "importunate demands" and of fostering hostility between Negroes and whites.

8. "What Exactly Did You Say?"

(Excerpt, New York *Post* account, "William Buckley's Attack on Powell Stirs Negroes," July 18, 1965)

"It is incorrect (Mr. Buckley said to the 100 Men Inc.) that the American conservative is animated by hostility to the legitimate aspirations of the Negro race. The Jew with his crooked nose, the Italian with his accent, these were nothing like the disadvantages you suffered. But socializing the country is not the answer."

Anti-Defamation League of B'nai B'rith

315 Lexington Avenue, New York, N.Y. 10016

July 30, 1965

Dear Mr. Buckley:

We have seen no comment by you published about the July 28th New York *Post* report of your statement at a meeting of "The 100 Men Inc." May we, therefore, inquire of you directly whether the following, attributed to you, is accurate, inaccurate, or perhaps out of context:

"It is incorrect that the American conservative is animated by hostility to the legitimate aspiration of the Negro race. The Jew with his crooked nose, the Italian with his accent, these were nothing like the disadvantages you suffered. But socializing the country is not the answer."

Sincerely,
Arnold Forster

Washington Star Syndicate

July 29, 1965

Dear Bill:

What's this crap in the *Post* about the "Jew and his crooked nose," etc., etc. What's going on? It sure surprises me.

Yours,
Harry Elmlark

August 2, 1965

Dear Harry:

I don't blame you for being surprised. I was too, though the

surprise is lessened by the fact of the story's having appeared in
the New York *Post* . . .

What I was asked, and what I said, was this. Halfway through
the question period, a gentleman got up and asked whether I could
compare the difficulties of other minority groups in rising up out
of poverty, with the difficulties faced by the Negroes. I replied that
No, the difficulties could not be compared, that the plight of the
Negro was far worse. I then enumerated the other principal minority groups, giving an invidious characteristic in each case: the
Jew with his crooked nose, the Italian with his bumbling accent,
the Irishman with his tendency to drink. I described, in other words,
three dominant prejudices against three major ethnic groups: the
Jews as pictured in the literature of Shylock—the money-lender,
the usurer; the Italian as the incorrigible alien, who never adapts
to his new country; the Irishman as the shiftless drunkard. Notwithstanding these prejudices, they rose swiftly in America. The
prejudice against Negroes is far more obstinate, far more comprehensive: and their challenge far more difficult. . . . Fortunately,
I have a tape of the damn thing. If it hadn't been for the inexplicable omission of the Irishman (which tends to make the account
racially self-serving), I'd have thought the reporter merely incompetent, rather than malicious.

Best (hastily),
Bill

C: Mr. Arnold Forster
Anti-Defamation League
315 Lexington Ave., N.Y. 16

(Paul O'Dwyer, Democratic candidate for mayoralty
nomination, on Barry Gray Show, WMCA,
August 23, 1965)

. . . Mr. Buckley, I heard you say one time, very recently, that
the Negroes in Harlem throw the garbage out the window *so they
can wallow in it*. That is exactly what you said. I don't know about
the others—about how they reported it. But I know what I heard.
WFB: Don't tell *me* what I said. Do you want to hear what I said?
O'DWYER: I was there, sir, and listened to you. I heard you. I was
at the Committee of 100 downtown, and you used that exact
expression—that they threw the garbage out the window so they
could wallow in it. I remember very distinctly . . .

(Excerpts from tape of meeting before The One
Hundred Men, Inc., July 27, 1965)

WFB: . . . You suffer disadvantages that the white man did not suffer. The Jew with his crooked nose, the Italian with his accent, the Irishman with his drunkenness or whatever—they had a difficult time. But it was nothing like the great disadvantage you have suffered and which we white people need to face as a charge upon our conscience that we need to expiate . . .

QUESTION: Mr. Buckley, having in mind your reference to the hardships that other minorities had to face in New York City— the Jew with his crooked nose, the Italian with his accent, the Irishman with his drunkenness—can you equate the hardships that these other minorities suffered to the hardships than confront the black American today in the light of his history? . . . And if you cannot equate these hardships, what would you as Mayor propose to do to create the kind of climate in the State of New York that would evidence the discontinuance of calculated obstacles and oppositions and selective discrimination against the black minority?

WFB: Yes sir. As I told you I cannot equate the disadvantages of those two groups, and indeed I said that, in the course of my preliminary remarks. I mentioned that there had been disabilities and disadvantages on the part of Irishmen, Jews and Italians, but that, quotes [*quoting myself*] "they could *not* compare"— and therefore by definition I did not equate them. That is why I really feel that there is a special burden, a *special* burden, that the white man must discharge as he seeks some kind of a law of expiation. But here is where I would disappoint you. I would disappoint you because I take a different view of the function of government from the view you do. I happen to believe that the truly important things in this world are not accomplished by government. It would be inconceivable for me as a conservative, who believes in the integrity and inviolability of the individual, to take any contrary position. John Kennedy was not supposed to be a conservative—he was a liberal—and he said "Ask not what the government can do for you; ask what you can do for the government." I maintain that if you put every politician in New York who appears before you groveling and unctuous and prepared to turn the entire apparatus of New York and put it at your disposal on a silver tray—you will not substantially augment the happiness, the security, the sense of accomplishment of your own people. The job of the Mayor of New York is a limited job, and I beg you to disregard as either a hypocrite or as a romantic, any man who appears before you and says "Elect me as Mayor of New York and four years from now you will have arrived at Utopia." The *principal* problems that are faced by Negroes today, and that were faced to a lesser extent by other groups, are *not* solved by government. They are solved by the leadership of their own people. Will *you* kindly tell *me* what the government has proposed to do, for instance, about the problem of illegitimacy? Is the government supposed to go out and administer some sort of a birth-control program, or insist that people, after the first illegitimate child, subject themselves to certain kinds of operations to make a recurrence impossible? What is it a government is supposed to do, for instance—*you* tell *me*—to keep people from throwing garbage out of their windows in Harlem? I asked James Baldwin why some people do that, and he said "Why that's a form of social protest." This is an answer that is inexplicable to me. Why should people throw garbage out their windows?—in order themselves to wallow in it? You don't wallow in it. I don't wallow in it. But why excuse the fact [that some people do]? The Mayor of New York has got to be modest in his pretensions. He must not approach the Negro people and say "I will transform your life." He must say, "I will give you justice and opportunity, and then it is up to the moral leaders of the community—the teachers, the newspaper men, the ministers, what they used to call the Lords Spiritual—to crack down on discrimination everywhere it shows its hideous head, to argue *against* discrimination, to give the people compassionate opportunities; above all to preserve a system of freedom and mobility which will permit a recurrence, vis à vis your own people, of the phenomenon that emancipated other minority groups."

9. On Stirring Race against Race—Part I

(Martha Dean Show, WOR, October 7, 1965)

JOHN LINDSAY: . . . in the last analysis, the Buckley candidacy, translated in the streets, is promoting tension; it's promoting tension between the people, group dislikes, group hatred, person against person, people against people, race against race—the worst kind of antagonism. And if the Buckley point of view, which is negative and backward, were ever to achieve ascendancy, it would literally mean that the streets would be totally unsafe instead of fifty per cent unsafe, the way they are now. It would mean bloodshed in the end because that's what it would come down to. And the sad part about it, the tragedy of it, is that whereas in 1964, Mr. Goldwater attracted, whether he knew it or not, some of these extremist elements, I am not sure he knew the full consequences of it or that he knew they were being attracted. Mr. Buckley of Connecticut, on the other hand, sniped from the sidelines, as he *does* know the consequences of his acts . . .

("The Race for Mayor," a Debate, WNEW,
October 10, 1965)

JOHN LINDSAY: . . . Mr. Buckley, stripped again in his candidacy,
it comes down in the streets to group against group, person
against person, neighbor against neighbor, and race against
race. . . .

(New York *World-Telegram*, October 15, 1965)

LINDSAY LABELS BUCKLEY ADVOCATE OF HATE, VIOLENCE

Rep. John V. Lindsay today accused William F. Buckley, the
Conservative Party candidate for Mayor, of advocating "a radical
philosophy full of hatred and division and violence."

(*Meet the Press*, NBC-TV, October 17, 1965)

JOHN LINDSAY: . . . And stripped of all its sarcasm and its comedy,
the Buckley candidacy represents group against group, neighbor
against neighbor, and race against race.[5]

(WINS, Radio News Conference, October 31, 1965)

Q.: As an observer here, do you believe, with many others, that
Mr. Buckley represents a balance of power between those two
men [Beame and Lindsay]? If there is going to be a substantial
Negro vote, is there a possibility that perhaps the Buckley vote
could defeat that?

JACKIE ROBINSON: Well, I am very much concerned about this particular aspect, Jim, because, number one, this is New York City.
If they get a substantial number of the votes here in this city, it
could only mean that we have a lot more bigots than we figured
that we had here in New York City, and we have already decided,
with the talk of the Klan coming into New York, that we've got
to get ready and prepare ourselves for the ultimate. Everything
is so subtle that Buckley talks about, when he talks about busing,
when he talks about welfare, when he talks about everything
that pertains to the Negro. It's subtle, but you know exactly

5. "I do believe that the people of New York are entitled to resent the imputa-
tions of Mr. John Lindsay that anyone who, like myself, favors a vote for Mr.
William F. Buckley, is bigoted, or racist, or is engaged in an attempt to destroy
the Republican Party. I am a New York voter, a Republican, a former keynoter
at the Republican National Convention and a former Republican Congresswoman, and I care deeply for the future of my Party. I also care for the future
of the democratic process and believe that Al Smith and Fiorello LaGuardia
would be appalled as much by the debased tactics of Mr. Lindsay as they would
be at the failure of decent New Yorkers to rise up in protest against them. Mr.
Lindsay's categorical refusal to grant the good faith of those who oppose him
is destructive of the mutual decencies that candidates owe to one another, and
is rather in the tradition of a Huey Long or a Senator Bilbo, than of a man who
seeks election in a city that prides itself on its liberalism."—CLARE BOOTHE LUCE,
October 29, 1965.

what he's talking about, you know who he's aiming to, and he is no more looking to win this election than the man in the moon, but what in my view he's after is to cut down the Republican Party so that Conservatives can come here and take over, and Buckley can be their spokesman. So I say very frankly to you that if Buckley and the other people who are supporting him garner a substantial number of votes here, you can look for problems in this city. And we're going to organize because you can't afford in New York City to have this kind of a man and the people that are supporting getting more and more people over to their side without taking some action yourself. When, in this country, in 1965, we are allowed to have people go out and murder with impunity, it could happen right here in New York, and we're not going to sit back and take it. . . . I think Negroes have to protect themselves and I am calling upon the Negroes, just after this election, let's get together and let's get prepared. I'm sure that civil rights organizations can't get involved in it, but there are a number of people who are ready to get prepared and we're going to do so.

Q.: What type of action would you take, Mr. Robinson?

JACKIE ROBINSON: I don't know. I just talked this over with about four people, and they all agreed, and one fellow who owns a ballroom, he says, "We will get our ballroom, and we will take it over, and we'll make our decisions so as to what we are going to do, but we're not going to stand for people"—I love Dr. Martin Luther King: I work for him; I go wherever he asks me to go, but I'm not one that's going to turn the other cheek. I've lived too long now. I've suffered too much, and I tell you very frankly, I can see this thing happening, and if the people of New York will support Buckley, and give him a substantial vote, I think you can look for serious problems in this city.

(*Searchlight*, NBC-TV, October 17, 1965)

MR. PRESSMAN: Mr. Lindsay has just said that you are running a racist campaign. Your reaction?

WFB: Well, he went out of his way to say that *I* am not a racist. What he said is that certain people of racist persuasion are agitating for me. Now, Mr. Pressman, I honestly don't know what to make of the situation. I saw for instance in the newspaper yesterday a reference to somebody claiming to be a supporter of mine who made some reference to "not wanting niggers in Prospect Park." Now I know enough about newspaper reporters to know (a) that that episode might not have existed at all, or (b) that he might have said something very different. But in case such a person does exist, I want to say something to him: "Buster, I don't want your vote. You go off to the fever

TOP: A communion breakfast, followed by a furor. *Left to right:* Mayor Robert F. Wagner, Police Commissioner Michael J. Murphy, Patrolman Peter J. Conlon, WFB.

BOTTOM: Candidates Rosemary Gunning, WFB, Hugh Markey.

TOP: In airplane, with Neal Freeman, en route to National Press Club.
BOTTOM LEFT: With James Buckley at recording session.
BOTTOM RIGHT: At home, between speeches.

Throughout my public career I have worked for unity within the Republican Party, regardless of shades of opinion within the broad principles which ~~constitute the~~ characterize our Party. Today, in New York, there is only one candidate for mayor who is running on Republican principles, and who is ~~proud~~ proud to identify himself with ~~those principles~~. In my opinion, Bill Buckley is the only true Republican running for mayor of New York, and I urge all good Republicans to support him this November.

Oct. 9, 1965

The unused endorsement, signed B(arry) M(orris) G(oldwater).

BOTTOM LEFT: New York *Herald Tribune*, October 30, 1965.
BOTTOM RIGHT: Minneapolis *Tribune*, October 29, 1965.

New York Herald Tribune

Long, Minneapolis Tribune

Will the real liberal please stand up?

Why are the reactionary forces of Conservatism determined to destroy John Lindsay's candidacy for Mayor of New York?

Beame lays claim to the proud banner of liberalism. Why doesn't Wm. Buckley concentrate his fire on Comptroller Beame?

The answer is simple. Beame is <u>not</u> carrying the liberal banner in this campaign. John Lindsay is.

Says who?

The Citizens Union says so.
Americans for Democratic Action says so.
The New York Post says so.
The Liberal Party says so.
The N.Y. Times and the Herald Tribune say so.

Flyer, distributed by "Democrats for Lindsay · Mollen · Costello."

The debates. TOP: Lindsay, Beame, WFB, U.S. flag. MIDDLE: Abraham Beame and friend. BOTTOM: Beame makes a point.

Cornell Capa, Magnum

Press Conferences. TOP: Kieran O'Doherty (center, sitting). James Buckley (standing, between posters). BOTTOM: NBC's Gabe Pressman at mike.

DAILY NEWS

NEW YORK'S PICTURE NEWSPAPER ®

7¢

10¢ OUTSIDE L. I. AND SUBURBS

Vol. 47. No. 91   Copr. 1965 News Syndicate Co. Inc.   New York, N.Y. 10017, Tuesday, November 2, 1965★   WEATHER: Sunny and cool.

AT THE GATE

LBJ, Humphrey Push Beame; Dem Chief Koch for Lindsay

(NEWS foto by John Tresilian)

A Kiss for the Dark Horse. Arlene Luterman plants a kiss on Conservative Party mayoral candidate William F. Buckley at his headquarters, 25 W. 45th St. Buckley, Democrat Abraham Beame and Republican-Liberal John Lindsay, wound up their campaigns yesterday. *—Story on page 3; other pictures in centerfold*

Election Day.

"SOMETIMES I JUST FEEL LIKE HANGING UP MY SNEAKERS"

New York Herald Tribune

Mauldin, Chicago Sun-Times

Werner, Indianapolis Star

swamps and get yourself your own candidate, because I'm not your man." The Negroes in the city—the city belongs as much to them as it belongs to any white man. There is no place for racism in New York City and there is nothing that I have ever said or ever will say that will give any kind of help or encouragement to racism.

MR. PRESSMAN: Do you feel that there are any people supporting you who have racist ideas?

WFB: I don't doubt it for a moment. I don't doubt that there are Communists supporting Mr. Lindsay. We know there are racists in New York, don't we? We know there are Communists in New York. There are presumably Nazis in New York. There are vegetarians—there are kooks of every kind in New York. And each one of them is going to find his own candidate. The point is—is it correct to infer from the existence let us say of a Communist voting for Mr. Lindsay, that Mr. Lindsay is a Communist? Obviously not. There were people in that Vietnam parade yesterday calling for surrender in South Vietnam wearing Lindsay buttons. Am I therefore justified in saying that Lindsay represents the forces of surrender in South Vietnam? Obviously not. That is the way of the demagogue, and I am trying to resist demagoguery, and I wish that Mr. Lindsay would succeed half so well.

MR. PRESSMAN: And you repudiate any racist backing? You don't want it. . . .

WFB: I don't even need to repudiate it, Mr. Pressman. To repudiate it is to acknowledge that there is some burden on me even to go into the subject. And there *is* no such burden.

10. Only Brutes Have Brutish Instincts

(*The New York Times*, August 10, 1965)

MOYNIHAN SCORED ON ETHNIC VIEWS

Aide in Beame Race Assails Screvane Running Mate

The president of an Italian-American organization denounced yesterday a book written in part by Daniel Patrick Moynihan, a Democratic candidate for City Council President.

Paul R. Rao, Jr., who heads the United Italian-American League, described the book as a "mass of twisted facts, contorted conclusions, and hearsay statements." He said he questioned Mr. Moynihan's fitness for "responsible public office."

The book, written two years ago by Mr. Moynihan and Nathan Glazer, a sociologist, is called "Beyond the Melting Pot." It is a long analysis of five ethnic groups in New York City—the Negroes, Italians, Puerto Ricans, Jews and Irish.

. . . Mr. Moynihan said that his study was now in use as a text-book at 143 colleges and universities, including both Harvard and Columbia. He quoted the following assessment by the Rev. Joseph Fitzpatrick of Fordham University in *America* Magazine:

"The authors are not 'anti-anybody.' Their devotion to the people they discuss is obvious, and they write in order to help them seize the great opportunities of the future."

"If there is any one thing that sins against the spirit of the people of the City of New York [Mr. Moynihan continued], it is the effort to exploit and worsen the relations between ethnic and religious groups for gritty political purposes."

(Editorial, *The New York Times*, August 11, 1965)

POLITICAL LOW NOTE

When sociologist Nathan Glazer and political scientist Daniel P. Moynihan completed two years ago their study of the major ethnic patterns in New York City they admitted at the outset that some of its readers might be offended. In the preface to "Beyond the Melting Pot" they wrote that the book "cannot but on occasion give offense to those very persons for whom we have the strongest feeling of fellowship and common purpose." To be of scientific value the study nevertheless had to describe the facts not as some would have them, but as they really are.

Now Mr. Moynihan is seeking the Democratic nomination for President of the City Council on the ticket headed by Paul R. Screvane. Paul F. Rao Jr., campaign chairman for the opposing slate headed by Abraham D. Beame, has seized the occasion to use the book as a basis for questioning Mr. Moynihan's fitness for office.

Mr. Beame and his personal campaign manager, Edward N. Costikyan, have disavowed Mr. Rao's charges, but the damage is done precisely as Mr. Rao intended it. Mr. Moynihan's commendable striving for straightforward authenticity in his book—which is used, incidentally, as a text in 143 colleges and universities—has become a basis for slurring him at precisely the time when it was hoped it would do him the most harm. Mr. Rao has further strengthened the blow by saying he is speaking for the Italian-American League, of which he is president.

This is a clear case of trying to divide the voters along purely racial lines. Mr. Rao is guilty of precisely the offense he so gratuitously charges to Mr. Moynihan.

(October 21, 1965, letter addressed to WFB)

Dear Mr. Buckley:
Last night, on Barry Gray's show, Mr. Daniel Moynihan was

being interviewed, and he said that "everything Mr. Buckley has said on the Negro question is a plagiarism taken straight out of my book, *Beyond the Melting Pot.*" . . .

(s) Terry Schmidt[6]

(Excerpt, editorial, *The New York Times,*
October 23, 1965)

SUPER-PATRIOTISM A LA BUCKLEY

For weeks William F. Buckley Jr. has been pandering to some of the more brutish instincts in the community, though his appeals to racism and bigotry have been artfully masked. . . .

(Letter to *The New York Times,* by WFB,
October 29, 1965)

To the Editor:
. . . On the more general point you raise, that I have been "pandering to some of the more brutish instincts in the community" through my "appeals to racism and bigotry," which, however, have been "artfully masked": pray, why not unmask them? I have not, as it happens, said a single thing about the Negro problem in Harlem that hasn't been said by others whom you have not, so far as I am aware, done one of your hippopotamus-walks over.

Daniel Moynihan, for instance, whose credentials are by your standard in very good order, accused me the other night of lifting all my observations about the Negro problem from the book he wrote with Prof. Nathan Glazer, "Beyond the Melting Pot." He is quite correct; except that I didn't "lift" them in the bad sense of the word: I have eternally quoted him as an authority. . . .

What brutish instincts am I appealing to? Come, now, my fair-minded friends, tell me. Are these appeals so artfully disguised that they are only penetrable by your editorial writers? If you will be good enough to advise me what are the brutish instincts to which I appeal, I promise to be so compliant as to attempt to persuade you that they are not brutish at all, that rather they are good, decent instincts, good for you, good for New York City; or else, failing that, I shall publicly repent.

(Excerpts, editorial, *The New York Times,* replying to
letter from WFB, October 29, 1965)

. . . He is no racist himself; yet, he delights the prejudices of certain listeners by slurs on Negroes; "I would go to Harlem to a

6. The tape of this interview no longer exists, but Mr. Barry Gray has confirmed, from memory, the accuracy of the quotation in this letter.

place where garbage is regularly thrown out the window and call a rally and ask the people to stop." He urges a "white backlash" against Negro leaders ranging from the demagogic Adam Clayton Powell to the vastly more thoughtful Bayard Rustin. He calls upon John V. Lindsay to identify himself as "white, Protestant." In a letter published on this page today Buckley appeals for a definition of the "brutish" instincts to which he is appealing. Those instincts are fear, ignorance, racial superiority, religious antagonism, contempt for the weak and afflicted and hatred for those different from oneself.

11. On Stirring Race against Race—Part II

(Excerpts, Address by WFB at Third Anniversary Dinner, Conservative Party of New York, October 7, 1965)

. . . I have been very much interested in some of the paradoxes and ironies that have emerged in the course of the campaign; interested philosophically, and also interested politically. One of these relates to the whole business of what goes under the name of "racism." New York is said to be racially the most sensitive city in the world: and yet I do not at this point know whether to believe this, or whether not to believe it; or, in any case, just how to understand what is meant by "racism."

The other candidates, sensitive as they are to ethnic sensibilities, do not dare to acknowledge that there is in fact a problem in New York of a kind which cannot be effectively diagnosed, except insofar as a racial vocabulary needs to be used. There is for instance a special problem of illegitimacy and broken homes among Negroes in certain areas of New York. But to mention this would appear, to judge from the prevailing silence on the subject, to say things which are racially invidious. The paradox is intellectually striking. On the one hand, the Liberals are committed to the proposition that protracted unemployment, discrimination, and the historical emasculation of the Negro male by the white community, have caused the phenomenon of the broken home (an historical analysis with which, by the way, I happen substantially to agree); yet on the other hand, they seem to be saying that to mention the fact of Negro illegitimacy is to insinuate that Negroes are racially disposed to that special weakness. What they say, then, is: White people are responsible for producing situation X. However, situation X does not exist.

Why are they afraid, having firmly advanced the first position, to acknowledge the data which in fact substantiate their own findings? namely, that there are tragic results from generations of discrimination?

But mention the fact that Negro illegitimacy is a grave social problem, mention such a thing in front of, say, Mr. Beame, and Mr. Lindsay, and they will either simply vanish from the room in a cloud of integrated dust; or else they will turn and call *you* a racist! The very same gentlemen who believe that you can't *hope* to appeal to a Catholic voter unless you present yourself alongside a Catholic running-mate; who believe that no Jew in New York will vote for you unless you prop up a Jewish running-mate and show him off, and chew away on a blintz, morning, noon, and night; these same gentlemen are pleased to condemn as racist those who could not care less what is the race, or the religion, of those who appear on the ticket; or who do not for a moment suppose that merely because a family is Negro, there is a congenital disposition to promiscuity.

Consider, for instance, the situation in Harlem. How are we supposed to describe that problem? If we are, having consulted our atlases, entitled to generalize that Harlem is an area in which, predominantly, Negroes live, mustn't we then be prepared to say that Harlem's problems are, to that extent, problems which Negroes particularly face? What is the conservative position as regards such problems? It is, so far as I can see, a problem which is to a relevant extent, a "Negro problem." It is a problem that cannot be intelligibly specified unless we are willing to use words which the politicians, because they fancy themselves as anti-racist, are unwilling to use.

You have here the dilemma. It consists in declining to face certain problems of racial significance on the grounds that to face them in their capacity as problems of racial significance, for some reason makes you a racist. What needs to be said, for instance as regards Harlem, cannot be said unless one is prepared to defy the taboos, and speak about the Negroes as a group of people who do have special problems which are not exhaustively enumerated merely by cataloguing the long record of white inhumanity to the Negro race.

What needs to be said is something of the following order. (1) The Negroes in the United States, and in Harlem, suffer from accumulated indignities and privations which we as white people are to a considerable extent responsible for. We need to go on to say, (2) We are required to believe, as conservatives who accept the fact of the brotherhood of man because we are creatures of God, that the Negro is in the most important respects the equal of every one of us. We must say, (3) that inasmuch as it is the case that the Negro is especially disadvantaged in our society as a result of his oppressive legacy, then it is our duty to do what we can to liquidate those artificial disadvantages. But if we are prepared to admit that we are responsible for producing an undesirable situation, then are we not committed to acknowledging that an undesirable situation exists? To acknowledge, for instance, that the crime rate, and the illegitimacy rate, among Negroes is higher than among non-Negroes. An example. Mr. Patrick Moynihan, a Catholic Liberal Democrat (I give his religious and ideological pedigree only because there are those who would find it relevant, even though I do not), and Mr. Nathan Glazer, a Jewish Liberal, wrote in their remarkable book, *Beyond the Melting Pot*, that the situation in Harlem was dire and dreadful, and that the moment has come when, the government's competence in these matters having been largely exhausted, leaders of the Negro people must take on the responsibility of helping their own people and dispelling the illusion that what is left to do is primarily up to the white man to do. To effect that transfer of power requires that our politicians cease to be contemptuous of the Negro race. This is the subtle face of racism in New York politics, reflected in the notion that a political ticket must be racially balanced. We must transcend the subtle racism imbedded in the rituals of New York politics. Recently Mr. Sargent Shriver said at a public Congressional hearing, "I am delighted to be in any cathedral where the distinguished minister from Harlem, Mr. Adam Clayton Powell Jr., is in the pulpit." Here is an involuted form of racism. It is the short form for: "Even though I, Sargent Shriver, know, and everybody else knows, that Adam Clayton Powell Jr. is a demagogue, whose power and reputation have been built on a cultivation of hatred between the races, nevertheless I recognize that he is a Negro leader, and therefore I must treat him as though he were a qualified object of universal admiration."

I say the moment has come to treat the problem maturely, to say that the racists are those who treat people primarily as members of a race. One of the principal burdens visited upon the Negroes in Harlem, the fact of Adam Clayton Powell Jr., is of the making of white people only insofar as it can be maintained that we continue to be responsible for him because such persons as Sargent Shriver hypocritically sing his praises; and such persons as John Lindsay, who accost us dripping with moral credentials, decline to utter a word of him. I say: let us not only do what we can, individually and corporately, to help the Negro people by acts of individual generosity. Let us also help those many Negroes who deeply desire a helping hand in the establishment of standards of decency and hope hardly furnished by our treatment of Adam Clayton Powell as though he were a cherished part of the New York skyline.

We Conservatives say, in short, that the Negroes have especially aggravated problems. Those problems are in part of our making. But those problems are in part of the making of Negro demagogues, and the Negroes who tolerate them. We need not only a reformation of the attitude of whites towards Negroes, we need a reformation in the attitude of some Negroes towards Negroes. Let us move towards a chivalrous candor, based on a respect for the essential equality of human beings, which recognizes reality, and speaks to reality; and disdains those synthetic and reactionary attitudes toward races and religions the symbol of which is the balanced ticket, and the great silence about conditions in Harlem.

(B) MANIPULATING THE JEWISH VOTE

It was a tiny studio, thirty feet by thirty, totally inadequate for the legion of photographers, reporters, staff. The broadcast was to be live, and the candidates posed for the cameras for several minutes, the rules of the debate were respecified (a theme, to be dropped by the moderator, two minutes each for the candidates to comment on it, working clockwise from Beame, to myself, to Lindsay, according to the draw); the producer ejected as many bodies as he could pry out of the room, leaving it packed, so much so that other than the principals and the moderator, most were forced to stand: and off we went.

Was this a city of fear? asked the moderator intending a discussion of the police problem. Beame rattled on about what had been done to increase the size of the police force, etc., etc., and it was my turn. I had decided to touch on the most untouchable subject in New York.

"I agree that this is a city of fear, and I believe that John Lindsay is doing everything in the world that he can do to cultivate that fear. Every newspaper in New York is talking about his neat operation of the past five or six days. And that operation is explicitly leveled at the Jewish voters of New York City. Mr. Lindsay has been trying to say to them, in his special kind of shorthand, 'Do you realize that Buckley is really in favor of concentration camps?' This single maneuver is intended to take votes away from Mr. Beame on over to himself. . . . [Thus] Mr. Lindsay . . . [characterizes] all my attempts to solve some of the pressing problems of New York as [calling for] one or another form of concentration camps, summoning up all kinds of Nazi versions of horror, aimed especially at members of the Jewish race."

Lindsay was visibly stunned. His turn came next, and after a considerable pause, he reverted to the subject of the police, ignoring the challenge. On it went around again, dealing with diverse subjects, Beame, Buckley, Lindsay, Beame, Buckley, Lindsay, Beame, Buckley, Lindsay—whereupon as if finally reached by a delayed fuse, he exploded: . . . "First of all, Mr. [Moderator], I'd like to say this to

Mr. Buckley, that Mr. Buckley's statement that I in defending myself against his ultra attacks and those of his people and his supporters in this campaign, that I am appealing to Jewish voters, is an offensive and irresponsible comment and I'll ask him not to make it again." *Ce n'est que la vérité qui blesse.* It came back to me; Mr. Beame, during his two minutes, stayed very well out of the way, and I remember an instant's temptation to reveal the names of the three prominent reporters—whom Lindsay could have reached over and touched without getting out of his chair—who had clinically discussed Lindsay's operation with me just a few minutes before. I resisted the temptation because I didn't want to embarrass them. My timing, I later thought, was off. I could have said, without any fear at all that Lindsay would have called me on it: "Mr. Lindsay, do you want me to give you right here and now the names of three prominent reporters from *The New York Times*, the *Tribune*, and the Washington *Post*, who were discussing your appeal to Jewish fears with me as recently as fifteen minutes ago? Perhaps you will want to forbid *them* to publish their analysis?" Lloyds of London would have given a million to one that old JVL would have changed the subject. I said, instead, angrily I fear:

> Somewhere along the line, Mr. Lindsay, in the course of his self-infatuation, decided that he could give me instructions about what I might say and what I might not say. You *did* hear him [I was addressing the moderator], a moment ago, *instructing* me not to repeat a certain charge? Well, I'm *going* to repeat it. . . . I can find Mr. Lindsay five hundred references published in the press during the past two weeks to the effect that he is trying to appeal to the Jewish voters.[7] And he is trying to appeal to the Jewish voters by *scaring* them. He is trying to do to the Jewish voters what the Ku Klux Klan has been trying to do to the white people in the South, keep them scared. . . . Mr. Lindsay is saying in effect to the Jewish voters, "Vote for me—because this is, over here, an ultra-rightist, who is trying to bring bloodshed to the city, whose statements are reminiscent of, quotes, 'some of the worst moments in history.' " What do *you* think he's talking about? Everybody else knows [what he is talking about] and Mr. Lindsay can't have it both ways. . . . Now let Mr. Lindsay, having finished giving me instruction, per-

7. Well, a dozen. Sample: "To win in November, Lindsay must strengthen his appeal with these wavering Jewish voters . . ." (Samuel Lubell, October 11, 1965). "In trumpeting the charge that 'A vote for Buckley is a vote for Goldwater,' the Lindsay camp seems to be appealing to . . . Jewish Democrats who are likely to be alarmed by nothing so much as a threat from the right wing" (Richard Witkin, *The New York Times*, October 26, 1965). See also: New York *Post,* October 21, 1965; *National Observer*, October 25, 1965; Samuel Lubell, New York *World-Telegram*, October 13, 1965 and October 26, 1965; *The New York Times,* October 28, 1965; etc., etc.

haps receive one from me: Cut it out, Mr. Lindsay, and I'll cut it out. Stop this . . . business about the ultra-right and concentration camps. . . .

"BUCKLEY CHARGES LINDSAY APPEALS TO JEWISH FEARS," the *Times* headlined the next day, recounting the exchange. Followed by a background paragraph:

> From the beginning of the mayoral campaign, political leaders in both parties have concluded that Mr. Lindsay would have to attract the votes of large numbers of Jews, otherwise Democratic or independents, if he was to stand any chance of defeating Mr. Beame, himself a Jew.

The Washington *Post* ran a more detailed story October 29. Again the writer, Mr. Julius Duscha, recounted the exchange; and continued:

> Dressed in their basic campaign blue, the three candidates shook hands and came out fighting for 55 minutes as a moderator asked them questions while reporters, jammed into the small room, took notes.
>
> The discussion revolved around the key Jewish vote in Tuesday's election, which, if Lindsay wins, will turn him overnight into a national Republican figure.
>
> Jews cast a third of the vote in New York, and the most political observers here believe that the Jewish vote will spell the difference between victory and defeat for Mr. Lindsay.
>
> When Mr. Lindsay entered the race for Mayor last spring, he counted heavily on the Jewish vote. He is popular among Jews because he reminds them of John F. Kennedy, whom they supported, and speaks of issues in the intellectual terms New York's Jewish voters like to hear.
>
> But when Beame won the Democratic primary last September, he presented Jewish voters with a painful dilemma. New York has never had a Jewish mayor, and Jewish voters now had to choose between Lindsay and Beame, a lackluster bookkeeper from Brooklyn who is nevertheless one of their own.
>
> Polls and other political soundings have indicated that Beame is running extremely well in Jewish areas and is cutting deeply into the margins Lindsay had expected in those areas.
>
> To counteract this trend, Lindsay has shifted his campaign strategy to an all-out attack on Buckley as a right-winger who calls up memories of "some of the worst moments in history."
>
> The Lindsay strategy is aimed at convincing Jews that his defeat by Beame—Buckley has no chance of winning—would be interpreted as an encouragement to right-wing groups throughout the country, many of which are anti-Semitic.

. . . It is believed that the race for Mayor is extremely close with the election only a few days away, and the charges and counter-charges hurled during the debate seem to bear out the nervousness in both the Lindsay and Beame camps.[8]

The maneuver by Lindsay (and later by Beame) was a conjunction of design and opportunity. I provided the opportunity; but the plan was originally that of Dubinsky and Rose, leaders of the Liberal Party, who hotly urged on Robert Price, Lindsay's manager, and on Lindsay, from the very outset, that he conduct a campaign "against the radical right," that being a tested hobgoblin in New York, as witness the Goldwater debacle of a year earlier. Price resisted, his contention being, at that point, that Lindsay's candidacy was best served by flatly ignoring his Conservative opponent, which Lindsay proceeded assiduously to do. Price's strategem was manifestly inconsistent with his subsequent decision that Lindsay should agree to appear with both Beame and myself in a series of scheduled debates. Lindsay, in the first debate, was badly hemmed in by the dilemma. He tried bravely to ignore my presence, by referring only to Beame during the first three-quarters of the program, and answering only Beame's genteel taunts; but, finally, he gave up—had to, the situation having become theatrically intolerable—and started to denounce the there-tofore invisible candidate seated across the table. But even after that debate, and the succeeding one, I was an "unperson" in his press conferences and other than at face-to-face meetings, and it was not until the first newspaper poll was published, which gave the Conservatives an astonishing ten per cent of the vote, and until after Lindsay had faced at public meetings noisy anti-Lindsay demonstrations, that the decision was made to alter the strategy. The *Times* front-paged the decision:

LINDSAY AND BUCKLEY DUEL—ATTACK SHIFTS TO BUCKLEY

John Lindsay, the Republican-Liberal candidate for Mayor, dropped his seeming unconcern about William F. Buckley Jr. yesterday by delivering a stinging denunciation of the Conservative candidate.

8. The article finished: "Only Buckley seemed to be enjoying himself in the radio studio." (I wasn't enjoying myself; I sensed that, in fact, Lindsay had got the better of the situation, that though he had forced me to say what was in fact true, I had nevertheless hurt myself rather than Lindsay. By merely affirming that some Jewish votes were deployable, I wounded more feelings than the candidate who had tried to deploy them.) ". . . after Beame, who holds a degree in accountancy, accused Buckley of initiating 'a vicious conspiracy,' Buckley airily said; 'it seems I'm involved in so many conspiracies that it takes an accountant to keep track of them.' "

Mr. Buckley answered in kind.

. . . Until now, Mr. Lindsay had concentrated almost all his political fire on the Democratic candidate, Controller Abraham D. Beame, and had tried to ignore Mr. Buckley, treating him somewhat as a noisy but essentially harmless mosquito.

But recent newspaper polls have shown Mr. Lindsay trailing Mr. Beame, with Mr. Buckley showing unexpected strength and possibly holding the balance of power.

One poll taken by the *Tribune* and still in progress, showed today that Mr. Beame was leading with 44.3 per cent of the vote, followed by Mr. Lindsay with 36.9 per cent and Mr. Buckley with 11.2. Another survey, done for the *World-Telegram* by the political analyst Samuel Lubell, indicated that Mr. Lindsay's chances were being jeopardized "by a major split in the Republican vote."

Conversations in the Lindsay camp yesterday tended to confirm the impression of many political observers that the attack on Mr. Buckley was an acknowledgment that he was a serious threat and could draw off enough votes to cost Mr. Lindsay the election.

The question inevitably arose at Lindsay headquarters: What, precisely, to do? The Dubinsky-Rose Smite-the-Right strategy was obvious, but what specifically to pin it on? Hardly my proposals on how to meet the transit crisis. And there had been no endorsement from Senator Goldwater to chew on. . . .

Lindsay seized on two openings. In my position paper on welfare, I had recommended a "pilot program to explore the feasibility of relocating chronic welfare cases outside the city limits."

Consider, [the paper said, in what were to become the most controversial paragraphs I wrote in the course of the entire campaign] for instance, the mother with three illegitimate children. She costs the city in direct welfare payments about $2700 per year. If her children are of school age, their schooling costs the city a minimum of $2100 per year. If she and her children live in subsidized housing, she may receive a subsidy that may cost the city as much as $1000 per year. The cost to the city of that family's share of the police, hospital, welfare overhead, etc., is incalculable; but it is considerable.

It is indisputable that such a family needs special services, special opportunities, special protections, a special environment, special teaching. To provide it within New York is especially difficult. Housing in New York is scarce. Temptations are abundant. Demoralization is a special problem. Disadvantaged children, and incontinent mothers, might be better off—and certainly New York would be better off—in the country, with special schools, and special supervision, aimed at true rehabilitation. New York City has nothing to gain from keeping such persons within its metropolitan limits.

Let New York continue to accept the burden of their education, and board, and housing—but in another area. It is conceivable that it would greatly ease any number of New York's problems: the housing problem, the school problem, the crime problem, the narcotics problem: if welfare payments to such chronic cases were made available elsewhere, in areas established by New York City as great and humane rehabilitation centers. . . .

The free translation of this suggestion by John Lindsay and Senator Javits:

"Senator Javits . . . accused Mr. Buckley of advocating 'sending people on welfare to concentration camps.' " (*Times*, Oct. 19)

"Mr. Lindsay said his Conservative opponent . . . had advocated 'deportation camps' for welfare recipients. . . . 'The vile implications of what Buckley advocates, and Beame sees fit not to condemn,' he said, 'would destroy the last fiber of decency for every minority-group member and all citizens of New York.' " (*Tribune*, October 26)

"Senator Jacob Javits [charged that Buckley] wants to send welfare people to 'concentration camps.' " (*Times*, Oct. 29)

"John Lindsay angrily labeled this a proposal for 'concentration camps.' " (N. Y. *Post*, Oct. 31)

I managed to add fuel to the situation by the advocating, in a position paper on the narcotics problem (see below) the forcible detention of narcotics addicts, it having become finally clear to me that narcotics addiction is a contagious disease: and this, of course, renewed the fever. But by this time, Abraham Beame's participation was clearly overdue. He tried to make up for the lost time by summoning the press on Friday afternoon, October 29, and reading his statement. The *Times* headlined:

BUCKLEY A CLOWN / BEAME DECLARES

Democrat Assails "Sinister"
Views of Conservatism

And reported:

Abraham D. Beame, [the article began], the Democratic candidate for Mayor, called William F. Buckley, Jr., yesterday a sinister "clown" whose campaign exploited fear, prejudice and hatred.

Mr. Beame insisted that the Buckley role as "spoiler" dedicated to the defeat of John V. Lindsay was "a sham and a fraud." Actually, Mr. Beame declared, Mr. Buckley's major effort has been directed at luring voters from the Democratic candidate.

"A vote for Buckley is not just a wasted vote—for he obviously cannot win—but it is a vote for Lindsay and national Republican philosophy, a vote to encourage the wild-eyed radicals of right extremism," Mr. Beame asserted.

"Perhaps the most dangerous facts in the New York campaign this year have gone unexposed because of the mask of humor. Comparatively few New Yorkers have taken William Buckley seriously because of an attitude of 'it can't happen here.'

"Nevertheless, behind his warped humor and twisted wit are sinister and evil philosophies. Mr. Buckley has not hesitated to conjure up repulsive images in the Machiavellian hope that a snicker would cover the deadly serious intent of his proposals.

"This Clown Prince of Politics has appealed to the base instincts of mankind. He has campaigned on a program of fear and prejudice, of hatred of neighbor for neighbor—concepts which have always been repugnant to New Yorkers. I believe his philosophy and program go beyond Goldwaterism.

"For example, Mr. Buckley's suggestion of concentration camps for drug addicts is frightening. Drug addicts today; which group would he quarantine tomorrow?" . . .

Back of the Beame broadside apparently was the realization in his camp that Representative Lindsay, the Republican-Liberal candidate, had a good thing in the theme that Mr. Buckley was a "spoiler" seeking the defeat of Mr. Lindsay and the eventual takeover of the Republican party by the radical right.

Just before Mr. Beame gave his views at a news conference at the Summit Hotel, his campaign manager, Edward N. Costikyan, conceded that in recent days many voters, frightened by warnings of an upsurge of the radical right, had swung to Mr. Lindsay. However, he contended, the trend was being reversed as voters realized that the rightist extremists had no chance of getting control of New York.

Mr. Lindsay commented last night that Mr. Beame had "belatedly discovered the ultra-reaction and the snarl of bigotry that lies behind the quip façade of William Buckley." . . .

The evening of the following day, I addressed the Conservatives' final rally of the campaign at Queens and acknowledged Beame's broadside, relating it to what had become the central theme of the campaign:

. . . Poor Mr. Beame. I am told I have neglected him. Perhaps I have. So, perhaps, will the voters of New York. Mr. Beame thought himself up a frenzy yesterday. In doing so, he appeared to be secretly jealous of Mr. Lindsay, because it was Mr. Lindsay who first discovered that anyone who is in favor of neighborhood schools; who opposes the politicalization of justice through a civilian review board; who scoffs in disbelief at the suggestion that the federal government is going to finance New York City's mania for spending tax dollars; who favors taking positive action to relieve New York City of the curse of drug addiction—it was Mr. Lindsay who first discovered that these ideas are best summed up in the haunting evocation of "concentration camps." So Mr. Beame lathers himself up and informs the city that "Mr. Buckley's suggestion of concentration camps for drug addicts is frightening. Drug addicts today; which group would he quarantine tomorrow?" (My answer is: lepers.)

Mr. Beame, you will have noticed, spent the first four weeks of the campaign resenting Mr. Lindsay's unfairness. Didn't Mr. Lindsay say that Mr. Beame was responsible for making New York City the heroin capital of the world? Mr. Beame's voice quivers with rage and resentment, a rage and resentment which I took to be a true reflection of his feelings. Mr. Beame was defended by gentlemen of the left and of the right, against so unfair an insinuation.

He even imported Franklin Roosevelt, Jr., to defend him against Mr. Lindsay's subsequent charge that Mr. Beame had prayed for an early death for Mrs. Roosevelt and Mr. Lehman, which indeed if it was the case, surely suggests that Mr. Beame's prayers are hardly efficacious, since Mrs. Roosevelt and Mr. Lehman took their own time in passing on to a better world. So Mr. Roosevelt, Jr., came to New York to denounce Mr. Lindsay—quite rightly, I believe, since Mr. Beame over the years clearly and consistently identified himself with the policies of Mrs. Roosevelt and Mr. Lehman—and to shrive Mr. Beame of any perfidious activities.

So we all felt sorry for Mr. Beame. That, it seems to me, is a little harder to do at this point. It has become a little bit like feeling sorry, as a result of all the insults hurled at him, for Drew Pearson. Now I repeat, Mr. Beame is, I feel quite sure, a very nice man, but I am no longer very sure that he is an honorable man, at least if one supposes that honor has any role to play in politics. If he does not know the difference between a quarantined hospital for sick people, and a concentration camp, I suggest that he ask someone who has been in a concentration camp what that difference is. If he feels that anyone who wants to quarantine drug addicts, because modern research clearly establishes that it is addicts themselves who spread the poison, is the kind of person who would want to quarantine other people just for the sake of it, then he must harbor deep suspicions of all doctors, and health inspectors, and statesmen who through the ages have believed that it is indeed the responsibility of society to protect itself from infectious diseases. By Mr. Beame's standard, Florence Nightingale was at heart a fascist. (As a matter of fact, Lytton Strachey was the first to make that discovery; but Mr. Strachey never asked the people of London to make him their Lord Mayor.)

The answer, of course, is that Mr. Beame believes no such thing, but that someone around him persuaded him yesterday or the day before yesterday, that he was losing the contest to hobgoblinize the conservative population of New York City. I can see it now. "Abe," someone says, "Lindsay is getting a lot of publicity on the concentration camp bit. Why don't you upstage him, and suggest that the Conservative Party plans concentration camps for *every-one* in New York City?" Come on, Abe, show the voters that *you too* can be a demagogue. Mr. Beame replies, "I owe a great debt to New York City. I grew up in New York City. New York City sent me to college. I have worked for the city for thirty-five years. . . . I am the experienced candidate. . . ."[9] Yes, yes, Abe, just here. . . .

I expect that is how it went. And thus Mr. Beame showed himself fully qualified to earn the trust and respect of the voters *The New York Times* approves of. . . .

The next morning, at noon, the candidates assembled together with the two Marxist candidates for an hour's television show sponsored by the League of Women Voters—a wild show, it turned out to be, in part because literally all the mayoralty candidates were fore-gathered, for the first and only time, including the Socialist Worker and the Socialist Labor. I took my place between Mr. Lindsay—and Mr. Beame. He turned to me and whispered: "Bill, I was really sorry about that business Friday. I mean, about that *word*. When I read the statement to the press, I actually left it out." (Shades of Mr. Truman!) "Goddamnit, Mr. Beame," I whispered back, "What kind of good could that do—the press release went out with 'the word' in it—all the papers and radio and TV ran it—'concentration camps'— and I gave you hell for it last night at Queens." "I know," he said sadly, and went back to his notes.

I never before, or since, felt more keenly the benumbing cynicism of politics, and its devastating effect on people. My rage wasn't at Abe Beame, who so clearly had yielded to a committee document, which he dumbly endorsed; but at what it had done to him to sign it, since he now felt constrained, because of an irrepressible decency, to whisper his apologies to his antagonist. I was wild with impotent indignation and only remember pledging that some day I would record, for those who care, that the transparent cynicism of all that concentration-camp talk was not called by a single one of the egregious metropolitan moralizers who were busy identifying the advent

9. These were the lines with which Mr. Beame usually opened, and closed, his public appearances, *i.e.*, his public signature.

of John Lindsay with a better day, a cleaner day, for New York politics, stressing his moral and spiritual superiority over the little bookkeeper whose conscience was the only one that stirred during those final bitter days.

There was a final surprise, two months after the election. It was at a large party, and the birds and beasts were there. The city editor of a major metropolitan newspaper, whom I have known slightly and pleasurably over the years, approached me amiably.

I thought, he said (in declining to quote him directly, in the absence of a transcript, I observe his own newspaper's high ethics)—I thought, he said, that you were a bright guy, but you sure fooled me. That last speech—that one phrase—cost you a hundred thousand votes.

I literally had no idea what he was talking about.

You know—the business of the "vision of a new order." It lost you one hundred thousand votes.

I professed an astonished ignorance, and I do believe that he thought I was being coy. I wrenched it out of him. A "vision of a new order" is associated in the mind of every Jewish voter over thirty-five years old (he maintained) with Anne Morrow Lindbergh's book *The Wave of the Future, A Confession of Faith* (1940) hailing (his word) the forthcoming fascist order; and it was the opinion of this sophisticate that the use of those five words had sharply estranged, on Election Eve, 100,000 Jewish votes that would otherwise have come to me. He would not believe me when I told him that in the sixty days since the election I had not heard another soul mention the apparent indiscretion. (My exact words had been, in the wind-up talk televised on Election Eve: ". . . if the Conservatives roll up a substantial vote, it is the beginning of a new dawn for New York. I am not asking you to vote for me, but for a vision of a new order.") Now it was actually being suggested, by one of the most urbane and influential journalists in New York, that this had been a red flag flourished (however inadvertently—therein, he said, I had been merely "stupid") in the face of the Jewish community.

I disbelieve his analysis, let me note.[10] But I remain in awe that

____

10. Shortly before this manuscript was finished, I received a letter, the only letter on the subject I ever received, from a gentleman who used the stationery of the 92nd Street Young Men's and Young Women's Hebrew Association: "Bill baby," it began; ". . . It is common knowledge that the Nazis used the term 'New Order' to describe the Third Reich. I cannot accept as pure coincidence your utterance . . . to the effect that: 'a vision of a new order' was in sight. Just what were you trying to say Bill, baby? No one chooses those terms without a knowledge of their former meaning and significance. Not even you. Especially not you."

he should have thought as he did, which must mean that there are others who thought the same thoughts. CBS reported—I have no way of knowing whether it is so, but no reason to believe CBS would report other than the truth as its own researchers saw it—that I got only 3 per cent of New York's Jewish vote.

The afterthoughts. Let us not moralize, merely inquire. The usefulness for political purposes of the other fellow's racial or religious slurs, real or alleged, is tediously well known. The best known example in American political history is, of course, the Catholics' resentment of the "Rum, Romanism, and Rebellion" crack, the failure to disavow which is said to have cost James Blaine the Presidency. In contemporary history, La Guardia accused his opponent of anti-Semitism in 1933. Herbert Lehman accused John Foster Dulles of anti-Semitism in 1949. Samuel Stratton, seeking the Democratic gubernatorial nomination in 1962, was accused. Roughly everybody accused Barry Goldwater of (objective) anti-Negroism in 1964. Paul Rao of the Beame Team accused Moynihan of the Screvane Train of anti-Italianism. "The students at Benton," Randall Jarrell wrote in his novel,[11] "yearned for the discovery of life on the moon, so that they could prove that *they* weren't prejudiced against moon-men." It is probable that for so long as groups of voters exist who are religiously or ethnically identifiable, political technicians will seek means by which to move them *qua* members of their creed, or race, and that the day after the day after tomorrow, a Saron will be calling a Swift, whether with or without the permission of his Kramarsky, to suggest means by which ethnic or religious or nationality group A can be brought to transfer its allegiance to B. And, that being the way with human beings, it is likelier that such movements can be stimulated by causing the group to be angered by A, than to be attracted by B: because—it is reluctantly conceded by most democratic theorists— voters tend to register their protests, rather than their affirmations: which, one pauses to observe, is not a bad convention.

The dilemma is part of the long shadow of the politics of the universal franchise. Once committed to the notion that anyone with (say) a sixth-grade education can vote—more, that anyone who can vote, should vote—it becomes necessary to accommodate to the fact that prejudice and passion and narrow self-interest are the proximate movers on Election Day for a heavy percentage of the voters. John Stuart Mill, so often thought of as the theoretical patron of the idea of the universal franchise, is not widely recognized as the author of the startling reservation, that of course he assumed that everyone who *did* vote, would vote with reference to the best interests of the

11. Randall Jarrell, *Pictures from an Institution* (New York: Knopf, 1955).

community as he saw it, rather than merely his own. Mill, as Professor Harry Jaffa has so dramatically demonstrated ("On the Nature of Civil and Religious Liberty," *The Conservative Papers* [New York: Doubleday, 1963]), would have been disappointed in the workings of his axiomatic democracy at various times and places in the twentieth century. He would have been shocked at the extent to which the accommodation to the narrowest and most irrational concerns of the voters had gone—not by those modern politicians who are commonly accepted as demagogues but by those who are commonly accepted as not being such. *"Drug addicts today; which group would he quarantine tomorrow?"* The question is whether an attempt should be made to jam the dialogue between the demagogue and the masses: by the society's *ex officio* censors, the columnists, the editorial writers, the ministers, the preachers, the professors—again, the lords spiritual. "I once thought it would be amusing," Albert Jay Nock wrote, "to attempt an essay on how to go about discovering that one is living in a dark age." Surely one might begin by opening the newspapers and observing whether anybody is there, active and impartial, interfering with the flow of demagogy. I do indeed dream, wistfully, of a vision of a new order. But I also recognize that this may be a form of rationalist utopianism, and that rationalists have as much business in politics as—to use the most absurd example that comes to mind— I do.

VII.

The Position Papers

The prediction (mine) that the two major candidates would differ from one another only in the appoggiaturas was, it turned out, correct. *The New York Times* made the point apodictically. On the Sunday before Election Day, the *Times* ran a long compression of the candidates' positions under the headline: "CANDIDATES FLOOD THE VOTERS WITH POSITION PAPERS BUT REVEAL FEW DIFFERENCES." Subhead: "Liberal Mantle Hotly Contested. Buckley Has Become Issue as Well as Candidate in Lindsay-Beame Debates." And the lead:

> With only three days to go, the mayoral candidates have given the voters an unparalleled number of position papers, issued with State Department solemnity but revealing few basic differences.
>
> Both [Mr. Beame and Mr. Lindsay] have claimed the liberal mantle. Moreover, each has challenged the other's liberal credentials and has accused the other of collusion with William F. Buckley Jr., the Conservative party candidate.

And a quick précis of some of those differences:

> Both [Lindsay and Beame] have proposed wholesale expansion of city services, especially to the poor, and both have relied heavily upon federal and state funds for financing. . . . Mr. Buckley also proposes change, but in the opposite direction. He seeks to reduce government services, contends that many problems cannot be solved by government, and urges that New Yorkers be encouraged to help themselves rather than rely on government. . . . He dissents from the nearly identical positions the major candidates have taken on a series of issues. He urges [for instance] gradual elimination of rent control—opposed by the two other candidates—and an increase in the 15-cent subway fare, which is also opposed by both Mr. Beame and Mr. Lindsay. He proposes a one-year residency for welfare recipients, also opposed by both major candidates.

169

Mr. John Kenneth Galbraith remarked to me while I was engaged in writing this book that surely I agreed with him that it made no difference, except in terms of national political repercussions, what were the formal political attachments of a mayor of New York. His point was that New York needed fresh leadership and imaginative ideas, and that "ideological"[1] approaches are irrelevant. As is not un-common, Mr. Galbraith is half correct. It is difficult to deduce from the reticulations of ideology just exactly how to cope with the transit problem of New York. But "ideology" does contribute relevant *assumptions*, in this case that the municipality has a right so to order its internal arrangements as to produce a harmonious traffic situation; and that that right is not to remain unexercised merely on the grounds that to do so would inconvenience highly organized and politically expressive aggregations, *e.g.*, merchants and labor unions.

In the course of the campaign the Conservative Party issued ten position papers, intending to issue twelve.[2] They treated: water, wel-fare, education, fiscal affairs, crime, taxation, housing, pollution, narcotics, and transit. They were, in the posthumous description of *Newsweek,* "needle-pointed." The sociologist Paul Goodman called them "occasionally . . . inventive."[3] The *Wall Street Journal* (Novem-ber 4, 1965) called them "concrete remedies" to the city's problems. And yet they were, though "needle-pointed," creative, and "concrete," nevertheless "ideological" in the sense in which Mr. Galbraith uses the word. They were—or at least sought to be—realistic: in that they sought to restore movement, to break up the log jam that had been caused by the conflicting interests of (a) politico-sociological ab-stractions, (b) organized political power, and (c) reality.

1. I put the word in quotations not only because Mr. Gailbraith used it, but be-cause I feel toward the word the abhorrence systematically encouraged by Pro-fessor Eric Voegelin (*The New Science of Politics,* University of Chicago Press, 1952), who persuasively insists that "ideology" is the antithesis of "philos-ophy," and that etymologically and historically the ideologist (more usually, the "ideologue"), is the man who clings to *a priori* abstractions irrespective of their relations either to right reason or to empirical evidence. The language has not yet provided a word which is safely removed from the doctrinaire fall-out of "ideological," Webster to the contrary notwithstanding. He permits "ideology," in one of its meanings, to convey simply, "a systematic scheme or coordinated body of ideas or concepts especially about human life or culture . . . the in-tegrated assertions, theories, and aims that constitute a sociopolitical pro-gram. . . ." Webster never read Voegelin, would not have been the same if he had.
2. The missing two (1) labor relations (it was to have been subtitled, "Let's Run Harry Van Arsdale Out of Town"; Van Arsdale is President of the Central Labor Council, and the ganglion of repressive, oligopolistic, and even, at times, terroristic, labor union power); and (2) "A Plan for Community and Conserva-tion Nature Centers." A shortage of time prevented their final drafting—and spared us, at least, the charge that we proposed concentration camps for nature-lovers.
3. *New York Review of Books,* December 23, 1965.

A vital assumption of conservative thought is that a certain tidiness in economic arrangements is desirable, from several points of view. That tidiness contributes a knowledge of what it is that a community is up to, which knowledge is indispensable to realistic appraisals, in turn essential to informed judgments, in turn a prerequisite to enlightened democracy. The maxim used to be: "There is no such thing as a free lunch." Professor Milton Friedman, a top libertarian theorist, has revised that maxim in deference to the sophisticated objection that any voluntary exchange (I give you my butter, you give me your shoes), presupposes an incremental mutual benefit which, in rigid philosophical terms, must be thought of as "free." He reached back to a far older maxim: "Always look a gift horse in the mouth." The meaning of which is that the "free" lunch one's children receive at school may be "free" in the highfalutin sense we have identified, but is not "free" in the sense most people believe it to be. Someone paid the dairy for the milk; and if the tax base is broad, as it most clearly is in the United States, that person is more likely than not, the economic razzle-dazzle having been unscrambled, you-know-who.

It is, then, a matter of importance to know the net economic meaning of what we do because a knowledge of the truth is important. Secondly, it is important to know what is the economic truth in order to observe the canons of *equity*. The presumption, in conservative thought, is that that which is yours, is yours. There are myriad reasons why, and myriad circumstances when, a part of that which is yours should be taken from you—whether to go to the government because the government performs certain indisputably essential services in your behalf (for instance paying the police and the army) or to other people—because said other people are otherwise forlorn. The circumstantial arguments quite expectedly rage as to whether this or that is a necessary function of the government under these criteria; whether this or that person is indeed helpless; whether the kind of help this person demonstrably needs might not be made available by voluntary, rather than by coerced, contributions to his welfare. It is the *presumption* which is important to bear in mind, the presumption that what is the individual's is his, unless the evidence clearly supports that it needs to be taken from him—in which case it should be taken from him by impartially designed laws unanimated by class prejudice. Here the presumption touches the metaphysical, *i.e.*, in its insistence that the individual's property is to begin with a part of himself; that property is, as Aristotle put it, one of the "predicables," *i.e.*, attributes, of the human being.

And—third—a conservative assumption is that the *private* arrangement tends to be superior to the public arrangement because (a) it is more flexible, permitting an infinity of adjustments based on an infinity of preferences; because (b) it is less categorical, and therefore less arbitrary; because (c) it is less wasteful, in that it is disciplined by the competing pressures of alternative modes of activity; because (d) it is more ingenious, in that it encourages a continuing competition for a variety of approaches; and because (e) it resists the natural tendency toward the centripetalization of power in government, which is the prime historical oppressor, and needs therefore constant domestication.

And, finally, the presumption is in favor of *the individual* measured as such; *i.e.,* irrespective of his political leverage. Political leverage tends to gravitate to the wealthy, to the influential, to the organized, to the (upper case) Minority. The presumption, under the rule of law, favors the individual irrespective of his political power, whether exercised through the manipulation of his money, of his labor union, of his race, of his religion, of his ideology. And an individual's right is no less so because individuals, coming together, might form a majority. We are increasingly trained to grieve only over the rights of (certain) minorities.

Those presumptions, in favor of realism (economic truth), private property (equity), the private sector (as opposed to the public), the individual (as opposed to the bloc), greatly illuminate the problems that have plagued New York. For instance, it is simply unrealistic to suppose that New York can hope to take from the federal government more than it gives to the federal government. It will not manage to do this until it succeeds in building up a preferential relationship to Washington which is antisocial in nature, *i.e.,* effected at the expense of other cities and other areas whose representatives in Washington are less influential than New York's—a development which the Constitution explicitly sought to prevent by establishing the Senate of the United States.

Inexplicit redistributionism runs counter to one of the conservative presumptions. To give to the poor because the poor cannot otherwise make do is one thing. To give to the poor merely because they are poorer than you is, by conservative standards, something you should do on your own behalf, not on your own and also your neighbor's.

To ask the government to do something which might very well be otherwise effectively accomplished by nongovernmental action argues against one of the presumptions. It is especially contrary to conservative presumptions to propose that a higher echelon of government should undertake a job which could perfectly well be done by a lower echelon of government (in violation of the principle of "subsidiarity").[4] (Is it really necessary to secure federal money for a study of juvenile delinquency in New York City)?

There are of course other features of the conservative syndrome, perhaps not exactly in the rank of presumptions. Call them attitudes —which bear on municipal problems. Conservatism is, for instance, notoriously anti-milleniarist; with the result that, to use James Burnham's example, conservatives know that you *can't* do away with Skid Row. They know, also, that some human beings, as Albert Jay Nock stressed in his heuristic lectures at the University of Virginia, are educable, others only trainable.[5] Conservatives believe that there are rational limits to politics, that politics should not, in the lofty phrase of Voegelin, attempt to "immanentize the eschaton." And conservatives believe, along with Dr. Johnson, that the "end of political liberty is personal liberty."

The following are digests of the position papers issued to the press. They sought to reflect the assumptions listed above. Inevitably, they are to some extent arbitrary; and, indeed, some of them were opposed, in some particulars, by members of the Conservative Party's high command. They are not therefore to be understood as final distillations of conservative thought: but they are, so far as I know, indisputably conservative-minded. At the third anniversary dinner of the Conservative Party in October, I took the precaution of making the point that "the position papers as issued necessarily reflect, finally, my own recommendations, from which, I hardly need remind them, Mrs. Gunning, and Mr. Markey, Mr. Mahoney, and Mr. O'Doherty, the county chairmen, and the Conservative Party, are wholly free to deviate, in any particular, now or later. No one, I am sure, believes that any of these proposals substantially defies conservative axioms. But here and there, there surely are alternative ways of doing things, all within the spirit of conservatism."

1. Why the Drought?

Water

September 30, 1965

The existing reservoirs of the City of New York are adequate for the present population of the city.

4. A part of Catholic social doctrine, enunciated by Leo XIII and endorsed by every one of his successors. The principle holds that public agencies ought not to undertake a job that can be done by a private agency, and that no higher (*i.e.*, more centralized) public agency should undertake to do something a lower public agency can handle.
5. Albert Jay Nock, *The Theory of Education in the United States* (New York: Harcourt Brace and Co., 1932).

—The rated capacity of the existing water supply is 1.8 billion gallons per day.

—Normal consumption is 1.3 billion gallons per day.

—Estimated avoidable waste is .4 billion gallons per day.

—Conclusions: the reserves of water are sufficient for New York City's needs even in such drought situations as that of 1965—provided the wastage is eliminated, or drastically reduced.

The existing water crisis must be dealt with as a separate matter. The measures appropriate for coping with the current emergency are irrelevant to the strategic problem. The temporary measures recommended by Water Commissioner D'Angelo in conjunction with those proposed by federal agencies, will probably eliminate the need for rationing water in November.

However, the current emergency is less of nature's making than of New York City's. Nature's fluctuations have not been so severe as to account, by themselves alone, for a water shortage. If the use of water had been reduced by the same proportion (20 per cent) as Philadelphia reduced its use by universal metering, New York's existing water supply would be easily adequate, notwithstanding the drought; and the annoying restrictions now being put on the public consumption of water would be unnecessary.

The strategic problem is to relate the use of water to the supply of water. New York City has the largest water-supply system in the world. We have enough water, in normal years, to permit even a lavish waste of it. But we do not have enough water to permit waste in drought years.

In drought years, New Yorkers must minimize not their consumption of water—there is no drought on record so severe as to require a reduction of the approximately 50 gallons per day that the average individual uses—but their waste of water.

Proposal: The only sensible way to regulate the waste of water is to charge for the excess use of water. That requires metering. (At the present time, only 24 per cent of New York water—principally the water available to industrial users—is metered.)

New York should instantly embark upon a program of universal metering, as most of the major cities of the United States have done.

The Building Code should be revised in such a way as to require meters to check the flow of water into all new dwelling units.

Meters should be installed in all family-owned buildings.

Meters should be installed in all apartment buildings, at the source.

The cost of the meters and their installation should be borne by the city; and, as is the case with other public utilities, should be passed on to the consumer over a period of years in the form of depreciation charges reflected in the basic rate structure.

The special problems of metering individual dwelling units within an apartment building are considerable. A formula should evolve whereby the landlord apportions the cost of water equally among all tenants. However, the individual tenant would reserve the right to meter the outlets leading into his own apartment, and pay the cost of the water he uses, rather than his percentage of the whole. The extra cost of such special installations would be shared with the individual tenant in accordance with a reasonable formula to be established by the city.

The present charge for metered water is approximately one cent for 50 gallons (the average daily use per person). The cost for water should fluctuate according to the supply. When the supply is abundant (which is most of the time), the price of water should be no more than the nominal cost to the city of providing it. As the reservoirs diminish, the price should rise—so as to put a premium on water conservation and encourage the location and repair of leaks.

The following is a hypothetical case:

If the reservoirs are at the level of 80 per cent or higher on June 1, water should continue to be made available at one cent per 50 gallons. If the level should fall under 80 per cent, the price of water should rise to three cents per 50 gallons.

If the level should fall under 60 per cent all water after the first fifty gallons, which should continue at the three-cent rate, should be priced at ten cents per 50 gallons.

Under the worst conceivable circumstances, then, an individual could continue to have his daily fifty gallons at nominal cost.

Water metering would encourage consumers to locate and repair leaks, and to turn off their faucets when water is not needed. A single leaky faucet can waste 100,000 gallons of water per year. A leaky toilet will waste 13,000 gallons per year. Such wastage would prove costly under the proposed arrangements.

It has been estimated that the initial cost of universal metering would be $85 million. The alternative solution—the building of an additional reservoir—would cost a minimum of $200 million, resulting in a higher per capita cost to the average New York taxpayer, and in the construction of a reservoir which under normal circumstances would be totally redundant.

Neither Lindsay nor Beame would come out for water metering. Their positions and my own, which I will not repeat, were, as digested by the *Times* on October 31: "Beame—Wants to augment city's leakage detection force, to study reduction of loss by evaporation,[6] and to develop new supply sources; to tap underground water in Long Island; to sink wells along water mains coming from upstate reservoirs, to add water to present supply."

"Lindsay—Proposes intensive campaign to eliminate underground leakage[7]; requiring all newly constructed industrial recirculating systems; consolidating functions of Board of Water Supply, with Department of Water Supply, Gas and Electricity[8]; tapping Hudson River above Hyde Park; reinstating Chelsea pumping station for emergency use."

2. A Vicious Cycle

Welfare

October 1, 1965

Government welfare programs are justified only as a means of providing emergency relief for the needy that cannot be, or is not being, provided by nongovernmental sources. As a general rule, the more affluent the society, where the surpluses of private agencies and individuals grow, the less the theoretical need to depend on government welfare. Meanwhile a welfare program ceases to operate in the community interest when it:

encourages participation in it by persons who have no plausible claim to that community's care;

encourages participation as a permanent condition, rather than as an expedient to be terminated as quickly as possible through gainful employment or other form of private support;

encourages degenerate and socially disintegrating attitudes and practices;

neglects to provide jobs for participants who are able to do work, thus denying them the opportunity, and the discipline, for self-help;

is administered so as to create unnecessary bureaucratization and waste of public resources.

The Indictment: By all these standards, New York City's welfare program is moving in the wrong direction. As regards the size of the commitment, the city continues to authorize staggering increases in

6. Indeed, why not?
7. *Idem.*
8. *Idem.*

public welfare outlays despite a general rise in prosperity and living standards. During 1965, the city's welfare programs will cost $629,969,572. (Although the city, state, and federal governments each pay approximately one-third of the total sum, economic archaeologists can easily trace the entire sum to taxes paid by New York City taxpayers.) This figure represents an increase in the cost of New York City welfare during the past five years—notwithstanding a stable population, in contrast to an inflation of 11 per cent and a real-wage increase of 18 per cent—of 97.5 per cent.

Moreover, the existing programs countenance specific abuses:

Unlike most cities, New York imposes no residency requirement on welfare recipients. The result is that thousands of persons who either do not desire to work, or who cannot work, come to New York, often with large families, leaving areas where unemployment is less severe than here; where housing is less scarce; where their families are in a position to provide help; and stream into this festering city.

The Department of Welfare requires a recipient's outside earnings to be deducted from his monthly allowance. This commendable impulse towards frugality has manifestly undesirable results. Consider the family of five (man and wife, unemployed, with three children), for instance. It is entitled, under the welfare laws, to a monthly payment of $250; yet if the father should earn $200 in outside work, in any given month, the family's allowance is reduced by that amount, and its welfare payment becomes $50. What is more, outside earnings—unlike welfare payments—are subject to income tax. The result is a clear economic inducement to idleness.

A substantial number of welfare recipients (the minimum figure is estimated at 3 per cent, and even that makes fifteen thousand people) are able-bodied, are not involved with child care, and yet are permitted to share in the public largess without being asked to perform work on public projects, or even to enlist in vocational training programs. The city thus positively contributes to their demoralization.

Aid to Dependent Children accounts for approximately one-third of the Department of Welfare's budget, and nearly two-thirds of all persons receiving public aid in the city under the welfare program. Moreover, in the year 1965, two-thirds of the children receiving ADC are illegitimate.

The welfare program can act in such a way as to promote broken homes, because if a family is reunited, or if the mother marries the father, and a breadwinner comes to the household, welfare payments are liable to stop. Illegitimacy, and promiscuity, are therefore subtly promoted by the existing arrangements.

Proposals:

1. A one-year residency requirement should be instituted immediately, and notice of its institution should be widely publicized.

2. Welfare recipients should be allowed to retain a sufficient proportion of outside earnings so as to provide them with the incentive to seek gainful employment.

3. All qualified welfare recipients, as a condition for welfare payments, should be assigned to work on public projects, neighborhood rehabilitation projects, etc., for which they should receive a few extra dollars per week, to take care of the cost of transportation, lunch away from home, and some pocket money for miscellaneous expenses. Alternatively, recipients should be required to participate in vocational training programs.

4. The Aid to Dependent Children program should immediately institute vigorous investigating procedures designed to cull from the relief rolls persons who are procuring payments by fraud, or who are otherwise ineligible. (In the District of Columbia, such a clean-up effort reduced the ADC caseload by 1778, or nearly one-third.)

5. A pilot program should be instituted to explore the feasibility of relocating chronic welfare cases outside the city limits . . . [proposing the rehabilitation centers for certain chronic welfare cases, as described in chapter VI].[9]

The *Tribune* published a lengthy criticism of my position paper by Lindsay lieutenant Charles Moerdler, then President of the New York Young Republican Club, now Buildings Commissioner in the Lindsay Administration. I reproduce excerpts from it, and my reply, together with the polemical bumps and grinds which are, at this distance, merely distracting, but suggest some of the heat of the campaign.

October 13, 1965

To The Herald Tribune:

The welfare program proposed by Conservative party mayoral candidate William F. Buckley Jr. demonstrates that his candidacy is based upon a demagogic appeal to man's most base prejudices.

Mr. Buckley proposes the establishment of "rehabilitation" camps outside New York City to which certain welfare recipients and their children would be "relocated." The suggestion is reminiscent of the "labor camps" which mark man's darkest hours.

Mr. Buckley's oversimplified, yet extreme, solutions also demonstrate ignorance of the facts.

Thus, it now occurs to Mr. Buckley to suggest "a working in-

9. See also Appendix C.

centive system that would permit recipients [of welfare] to keep a portion of outside earnings" with only partial diminution of their welfare payments. His "discovery" became law on July 20, 1965.

Mr. Buckley's next panacea is the familiar cry for a one-year residency law. Following a comprehensive study, the Moreland Commission found last year that at least 80 per cent of all recipients have lived in New York for more than five years and of the not more than 7 per cent who have lived in New York for less than one year only a minuscule portion could fairly be even suspected of having come to New York with a view toward collecting welfare payments. The cost of administering the Buckley policing program far exceeds the savings he could hope to effect.

Mr. Buckley next suggests that "able-bodied welfare recipients be required to work on city projects because they owe the city something." Sections 164 and 349-b of the Social Welfare Law already stipulate that failure to perform a work relief assignment disqualifies an employable person from the right to relief.

Mr. Buckley's last proposal is a supposed solution to the problem of Aid to Dependent Children, which in 1964 accounted for some 58 per cent of all welfare recipients, and the percentage goes up annually. Many of the dependent children are unwanted illegitimates. Yet, Mr. Buckley's only solution to this problem is the assertion that some "frauds" might be unearthed which could cut down the problem posed. We recognize the reason for Mr. Buckley's unwillingness to come squarely to grips with the problem, for the only conceivable solution lies in family planning and for purely political reasons Mr. Buckley lacks the courage to speak out on that subject. Nor does he speak out on the extreme proposal of some of his far Right supporters that the answer lies in the forceful taking of illegitimate children from their unwed mothers.

Mr. Buckley's cavalier disregard of the facts and his penchant for "easy answers" demonstrate that he is not a serious candidate for office; rather, his single purpose is to wreak vengeance upon those in the Republican Party who welcome the 20th century.

Charles G. Moerdler

October 15, 1965

New York Herald Tribune:

Mr. Charles Moerdler, President of the New York Young Republican Club . . . has accused me of a lack of political courage ("*O Geordie, jingling Geordie, it was grand to hear the Baby Charles laying down the guilt of dissimulation, and Steenie lecturing on the turpitude of incontinence!*").

1. Specifically, he criticizes my welfare proposals. He chooses to designate the rehabilitation center I suggested as a pilot program for certain kinds of welfare cases, "rehabilitation camps." "Reminis-

cent," he continues darkly, of "the 'labor camps' which mark man's darkest hours." I don't know why the prospect of rehabilitation for drug addicts, chronic breeders of illegitimate children, wretched young punks without mothers and fathers who desperately need the kind of personal care they cannot get in New York City, all of whom suffer for lack of decent living conditions which are hard to get in New York and costly: why an attempt at rehabilitation should remind Mr. Moerdler of labor camps.

2. Mr. Moerdler cites the Moreland Commission as saying that not more than 7 per cent of those who receive welfare payments came to New York during the preceding 12-month period. Well? Seven per cent is 35,000 people, consuming 42 million dollars in direct welfare payments, and twice that in city services. Mr. Moerdler scoffs at the very notion of a one-year residency requirement. Very interesting. But less so, I should think, than that a special committee appointed by Governor Rockefeller (the State Citizens' Committee on Welfare Costs) which extensively inquired into the subject, reported back to Governor Rockefeller on April 29, 1965, and recommended: a one-year residency requirement.

3. Mr. Moerdler seems to believe he is informing me of something when he tells me that Sections 164 and 349-b (he means 350-b) of the Social Welfare Law "already stipulate that failure to perform a work relief assignment disqualifies an employable person from the right to relief." The Conservative Party's position paper asks for an *enforcement* of the law, asks that able-bodied workers be "required" to work. The law in question has been on the books for six years. Mr. Moerdler fails to note that it has not been acted upon; that the discretionary power to act on it or not was given to the Welfare Department.

4. "We recognize the reason for Mr. Buckley's unwillingness to come squarely to grips with the problem" of illegitimacy, says Mr. Moerdler; for "the only conceivable solution lies in family planning and for purely political reasons Mr. Buckley lacks the courage to speak out on that subject." I am not quite sure what Mr. Moerdler is trying to say, but let me try to find out. Is he saying that as a Catholic, I would decline myself to do something which is forbidden to me to do by the Catholic Church? If so, the answer is he is quite correct. It does not take political courage to contravene one's own religion, it takes moral infidelity, of which I do not propose to be guilty inasmuch as I put the moral order above the political order. If Mr. Moerdler is trying to suggest that I would interfere with the dissemination of birth control information to persons whose religion does not forbid the use of it, he is quite incorrect (and lest he should at this moment be cackling with glee for having ambushed me into making this statement, allow me to inform him that I made it to Mr. Theodore White a month ago,

with permission to publish it, which he intends to do, in a pre-election issue of *Life* magazine).

[WFB]

And then Mr. Beame.

Mr. Beame made a technical criticism concerning my position on residency requirements in a letter addressed to me and released to the press:

October 1, 1965

Dear Mr. Buckley:

I do not agree with your solutions to the problems facing our city. I believe that 20th Century New Yorkers are anxious for 20th Century solutions to our problems.

For example, your insistence that the absence of a residency requirement for public welfare has created major problems simply does not accord with the facts. The facts are that less than 2% of the welfare budget goes to recipients who have lived in the city less than a year and that every cent of the amounts paid to support these unfortunates is reimbursed by the State.[10] Moreover, I do not believe that any Mayor is going to allow people to starve to death on the streets of New York whether they have been here one month or one year. If by any chance you were elected Mayor I am sure you would not allow them to starve to death either. . . .

I replied:

Dear Mr. Beame:

. . . You say that only two per cent of last year's welfare budget went to persons who had been residents of New York City less than one year. Question. (1) Why, then, did the cost of welfare rise by 12%, even though unemployment decreased? Question. (2) Why did the cost of welfare rise by almost one hundred per cent during the past five years? Question. (3) Of the other 98% of welfare disbursements, how much went to persons who came to New York only because there was no residency requirement here? Considering the high relative costs of welfare in New York, and the high incidence of it, why are you so sure that we have nothing to learn from the 46 states of the Union that *do* maintain residency requirements of one sort or another? It is obvious to me as it is to you that no American should be permitted to starve to death. But I do not believe that people should be encouraged to schedule their own starvation to begin immediately upon arriving in New York City.

10. The State receives *its* money in considerable part (about one-half) from taxes levied on those who live and work in New York City, a fact which every accountant is aware of, and many non-accountants.

The positions of the other candidates, again as digested in full by the *Times*:

> Beame—Opposed residency requirement; stresses more personal work with clients, with emphasis on rehabilitation; urges reduction of paper-work. Would seek federal funds to raise welfare allowances.
> Lindsay—Opposes residency requirement; stresses rehabilitation of clients; urges better salaries for welfare investigators, [reduced] paper-work. Goal: "Break the chain of despondency that carries over from generation to generation."

3.   Whatever Became of Education?

The Schools

October 5, 1965

New York's public schools are not providing the education they should. That is the judgment of the market place, as witness the increasing number of parents who are making extraordinary sacrifices in order to remove their children from the public schools and send them to private or parochial schools.

In Manhattan alone, the percentage of white children who attend the public schools decreased, between 1946 and 1964, from 62 per cent to 34 per cent.

There is a continuing flight of middle-class families from the city, largely because of general dissatisfaction with the schools. Conversely, the inferior quality of the schools militates against an influx of middle-class families to the city.

Although only one out of seven children aged four to fourteen in New York City is Negro or Puerto Rican (the two most disadvantaged groups educationally), two out of seven attending the public schools in this age group are Negro or Puerto Rican. And if the trend continues at its present rate, Negro and Puerto Rican children will constitute a majority of those attending the city's schools within ten years.

The drop-out rate in city schools is high (as high as 50 per cent among Negro children), suggesting a lack of motivation which is undoubtedly owing in part to unsuccessful teaching, inadequate discipline, and low morale.

Notwithstanding the brilliant achievements by graduates of some of New York City's schools, the average performance is shockingly bad. Some 23 per cent of youths educated in the public schools fail to pass the Selective Service test, which requires thirteen-year-old proficiency in reading and writing.

Even the highest salary scale in the country for teachers ($5300 minimum to $11,000 maximum), and the highest per capita expenditure per child ($700 per elementary school student, $1200 per vocational school student) have not created a high morale among teachers and students, let alone satisfaction among parents.

Proposals:

1. The purpose of education is to educate, not to promote a synthetic integration by numerically balancing ethnic groups in the classroom. In today's all-white neighborhoods, it is reasonable that the schools should be overwhelmingly white. In today's Negro neighborhoods, it is reasonable that they should be overwhelmingly black. Mature, self-confident, and mutually respectful relations between the races are more a by-product of sound moral education than the automatic result of integrated schools; and the integration of neighborhoods—and of their schools—will inevitably follow upon the establishment of that mutual respect.

If the public schools become little more than social laboratories for the promotion of integration, the parents most ambitious for the educational advantages of their children will, if they can afford to do so, send their children to private schools; those who cannot afford to do so will continue to send their children to the public schools but will become bitter, and even hostile, toward the minority groups whose pressures they hold accountable for unnatural arrangements.

In either event, the cause of integration will suffer: in the first case because the most highly motivated students will be lost to the public schools, and will not, therefore, contribute their energies and leadership to the setting of high academic standards; and, in the second case, because integration effected by compelling children to attend schools in neighborhoods other than their own (usually termed "busing") will cultivate hostility rather than diminish it.

2. The importance of maintaining the neighborhood school can not be overemphasized. The neighborhood school is essential to maximizing the potential of public education for several reasons. The neighborhood school promotes parent-teacher contact, which fosters parental responsibility; it enables the older children to escort and look after their younger brothers and sisters; it develops community interest in the community school. The neighborhood school is inherently sound, regardless of whether the neighborhood is integrated. Accordingly, there are weaknesses in the so-called "school park" idea, which tends to ignore the neighborhood principle.

3. The Board of Education should address itself courageously to the special needs of students of differing race, background, and train-

ing. As an obvious example, Puerto Rican children should be taught English before being plopped in classes conducted in English. If tests reveal that Negro children freshly arrived from the South need special training in special disciplines (*e.g.*, mathematics), they should not be deprived of that training merely to pay obeisance to abstract ideas concerning equality. The Board of Education, in other words, should free itself of ideological prejudices, and give children the education they most need, and can best profit from.

4. The rigid centralization of the administration of the schools is a grave mistake, making for unnecessary bureaucratic rigidities, top-heavy administrative costs (for every nine teachers, there are five nonteachers on the educational payroll), a lack of spontaneity in individual schools, and an undesirable routinization of the curriculum. The administration should be broken down, giving more authority to the boroughs, to the school districts, to the individual schools, and to the individual teachers.

5. The maintenance of classroom discipline is a major problem. Many classrooms are chaotic because teachers do not have the authority to maintain order. Special disciplinary authority should be granted to a board within each school, at which the administration, the teachers, and the parents are represented.

6. Intellectual progress must be stressed even at the expense of pseudo-democratic equality. Mass promotions, notwithstanding the failure of individual members to qualify, damage not only those who earn their graduation into the next class, but those who do not. A synthetic age-grade correlation, on the basis of which children are placed in a class according to their age, irrespective of whether they are prepared to enter that class, is obviously harmful.

7. It may be that the time has come to change the means of selecting the nine members of the Board of Education. They are now selected by the Mayor, from a list proposed by various organizations. Perhaps they should be elected, two from each Borough, in the same manner as councilmen-at-large, in order to permit substantial debate on issues of educational policy. That is the way the members of the Boards of Education are selected in all other major cities, permitting public debate, and a mature relationship between the parent, and the school. However, the Board of Education should not be given independent taxing authority.

Both Beame and Lindsay opposed the State legislature's recent measure calling for nominal ($400) contributions by students at the city colleges toward their own education, a practice in effect in the public colleges outside New York City. Lindsay's stand in favor of "mandated free tuition" was prominently displayed in much of his literature.

Here, I thought, was clearly a collision point between sound and unsound social practice. The argument can be made—indeed I would support it and did so during the campaign—that there are the few for whom two hundred dollars per academic year is marginal, *i.e.*, that the necessity to raise those two hundred dollars would make the difference between their being able to go to college or not. I pointed out to Messrs. Lindsay and Beame at our first debate that several New York City banks had broadly advertised their willingness to lend the money at nugatory interest to students in good standing at the city colleges, to be repaid over a considerable period in the future. It might make sense, I pleaded, to establish the mechanism which would identify those cases of special hardship that needed the full tuition payments. But that it hardly made sense to institutionalize mandated free tuition for everyone. Most college students, as a result of the value of their college education, will predictably be earning income, a few years hence, in excess of that of many who are currently taxed in order to furnish the subsidies. How to justify such regressive redistributions?

But neither Beame nor Lindsay would touch it—it was mandated free tuition or bust.

At a large rally at Queens College, at which a surprising number of the students had shown themselves extremely friendly, a question came up from the floor: "Do you favor mandated free tuition?" I answered: "Most positively not." The crowd unanimously and lustily booed me. "Do you realize," I persisted, "that you are asking men and women who are, many of them poorer than you, and poorer than your parents; many of whom earn less money than you yourselves will be earning in the course of a few years, to make sacrifices in your behalf?" Boo! "If you don't believe me," I said, "go to your economics teachers and ask *them*." Boo! "All right," I said, "*don't* go to your economics teachers, and *don't* discover the economic realities— you'll find it much easier on the conscience *not* to know who is sustaining the hardship for your free education." Applause!—as a matter of fact. On one occasion, lunching with a board of egregious editors, I said that I could not think of a single word or deed of political courage shown by Lindsay during the spring, in the course of publicizing the general positions on which he would wage his campaign, and that that absence of leadership had contributed to my decision to enter the campaign. I named three symbols of a lack of that courage: his endorsement of a continuation of the fifteen-cent subway fare; his endorsement of a continuation of rent control; and his call for mandated free tuition (in direct opposition to the views of the liberal Republican Governor, Nelson Rockefeller). One wonders: if Americans under twenty-one are under no circumstances to pay for anything at all; nor, increasingly, Americans over sixty-five—just how heavy a burden can be carried by Americans between the ages of twenty-one and sixty-five who are a minority (34.9 per cent) of the total population?

On the sensitive matter of "busing": the recent political history of the issue had been turbulent. Busing was first advanced in 1963 by the civil rights groups as a means by which students in New York public schools could be relocated, with the view to accelerating racial integration. The proposal was resisted by a group called the Parents and Taxpayers Association (headed by Mrs. Rosemary Gunning). After a series of unsuccessful attempts to arrange a hearing before Superintendent of Schools Dr. Calvin E. Gross, the parents organized a boycott at the beginning of the school year (1964), at which time over 300,000 students stayed away from school.

The lines hardened; but some unexpected voices were being heard in opposition to busing as a means of effecting integration.[11] In the heated election of 1964, during which opposition to busing was at its height, everyone waited to see how Robert Kennedy, running for the Senate, would square off on the subject. He defused the subject with magnificent skill, by coming out against "unreasonable busing"— leaving it for the multitudes to argue, and to agree to disagree, on what is, and what isn't "unreasonable."

Lindsay was as afraid of the subject as Kennedy, and he too hedged. I induced him, after saturation bombing, to say, at the end of one television debate: "I don't think that busing is the answer to the question of integrating the schools." But a year earlier (March 19, 1964), speaking before a Civil Rights Rally sponsored by the United Civil Rights Organizing Committee, Lindsay had said: "It seems to me clear that the Princeton Plan, for example, is a sound approach in contiguous areas. This is combined with careful 'busing out' in order to relieve the pressure in the badly overcrowded schools." Moreover, the so-called Allen Plan adopted by New York City's Board of Education in June 1965, called for what amounts to the trans-shipment of students at certain age levels, largely with the view to spurring racial integration. And Lindsay had supported the Allen Plan. And, besides, Lindsay was enthusiastic about the idea of educational parks. "How does he propose to transport school children to those

11. For instance, Mrs. Agnes Meyer, widow of the former owner of the Washington *Post* and a prominent liberal, who wrote to *The New York Times* (July 2, 1963) to opppose busing as a goal of the integrationists, among whom she had for years been in the front rank.

great 'education parks' which he promised to build last Sunday?" I asked. "By helicopters?" Lindsay would not budge from his ambivalent position any more than Kennedy did; and, presumably, for the same reasons. The issue is dormant, but explosive.

The positions of the other candidates:

Lindsay—Wants to build educational parks; to modernize school construction; to free teachers from non-teaching chores; to increase prekindergarten program from 7,000 to 40,000; to increase to 100 the number of all-day neighborhood schools; to provide massive reading programs for 300,000 children who are two years or more below grade level; to organize vocational and academic high schools into comprehensive high schools; to improve teacher training. . . .

Beame—Proposes building coordinated system of comprehensive high schools; speedier acquisition of school construction sites; improving physical facilities; building educational parks, on an experimental basis.

4. The High Price of Mismanagement

Money

October 7, 1965

The figures are widely known. New York City is in dire financial condition, as a result of mismanagement, extravagance, and political cowardice.

The budget for fiscal 1966 is $3.9 billion. The increase over the previous year's budget is $521 million. This increase is 75 per cent greater than any previous increase, and is equal to the total increase over the first five years' budgets of the Wagner Administration. It projects a deficit of $312 million, over three times as great as the deficit ($92 million) during the preceding years.

The Wagner Administration justifies the anticipated deficit by expressing confidence that a constitutional amendment will be passed in November, 1966, permitting a rise in the tax rate on real estate from $4.41 per $100 assessed to $5.66 per $100 assessed. The projected increase in tax revenues would, it is supposed, be sufficient to cover the deficit. Even Comptroller Abraham Beame opposed the "borrow now, pay later" proposal; and, indeed, the city's official credit standing, as measured by the interest rate it is required to pay on its bonds, fell in the summer of 1965, when it was adjudged, by professional assessors, something less than the highest-rate credit risk. Debt service accounts for $550.9 million (nearly 15 per cent) of the total budget. Mayor Wagner is apparently willing to live with this crushing burden on the taxpayer. "I do not," he says, "propose to permit our fiscal problems to set the limits of our commitments to meet the essential needs of the people of the city."

During the period in which the costs of government rose so dramatically, how did the average New Yorker fare? Between 1954 and 1963, local taxes increased by 84 per cent. During the same period, average income rose only 53 per cent. Since World War Two, local taxes have increased twice as fast as local income. In 1955, the city budget was $200 per person. Today, it is $500 per person.

The sales tax, raised a year ago from 3 per cent to 4 per cent, proved a disaster. Instead of bringing in an anticipated extra revenue of $92 million, it brought in only $57 million. It is estimated that, as a direct result of the one-per-cent increase, $1 billion worth of business that would otherwise have been done in New York was done outside New York. Notwithstanding, the tax was raised yet another percentage point this year.

The commercial occupancy tax of 5 per cent is, in effect, simply another tax on business, and another deterrent to business. The gross receipts tax levied on the gross business done, irrespective of expenses, is both a bureaucratic nightmare and a deterrent to marginal businesses.

The result of high and inequitable taxation has been a migration away from the city of those who are both hardest hit by taxes and most mobile—the small businessman and the manufacturer. During the last five years, the city has lost approximately 75,000 industry jobs by reason of manufacturing firms' leaving the city.

Under existing arrangements, neither the public nor the public's expert representatives have sufficient time to review the Mayor's budget. It need not be submitted until April 15, and the City Council and the Board of Estimate must hold public hearings on it by May 10. There is insufficient time to generate public interest in the budget, and insufficient time to focus on its inadequacies. A two-thirds vote in both the Council and the Board is required to veto any item in it. All of which, taken together with Mayor Wagner's extraordinary parliamentary powers, has made it extremely difficult to force him into a rudimentary regard for fiscal responsibility.

Proposals:

1. New York City must discontinue its present borrowing policies, and learn to live within its income, before it goes bankrupt. There is,

Mayor Wagner to the contrary notwithstanding, no "essential service" that cannot be provided by reasonable taxation in the wealthiest city in the world.

2. It is a general rule of sound government that the actual cost of services should not be disguised. The present tendency to throw all New York City's services into the hopper, fostering the illusion that the services are free, is inimical to a mature understanding of the processes of government and of the economy. Where feasible, city services should have a price tag. The exceptional hardship case should be handled by outright subsidy.

3. The commercial occupancy tax, the gross receipts tax, and the multifarious nuisance taxes and license fees that plague manufacturers and small businessmen should be eliminated and replaced by a single nonprogressive tax on business enterprises, the details of which will be fully described in a future paper.[12] The five-per-cent sales tax should be reduced, the point of diminishing returns having been approximated. The reduction, accompanied by a restoration of confidence in New York City, could stimulate business sufficiently to generate tax revenues equivalent to the original expectations of the five-per-cent tax, and more.

4. A one-year residency requirement for eligibility for welfare benefits should be instituted. (See position paper on Welfare.) Forty-six states currently have residency requirements of one sort or another, and, with 500,000 people on relief, the city can ill afford not to follow their lead. While no one in the city should be permitted to go hungry, neither should people be encouraged, as they are under present arrangements, to come here to be poor.

5. The Citizens Budget Commission has outlined several detailed economies which should be effected. . . .[13]

6. While the Citizens Budget Commission proposals would reduce expenditures by over a quarter of a billion dollars, it is clear that no comprehensive solution to the city's fiscal problems is conceivable in the absence of a readjustment in the flow of revenue from the states to the federal government. The so-called Heller Plan, which calls on the federal government to return to the states part of the money they contribute to it, implicitly acknowledges that if the states, let alone the cities, are to govern themselves adequately, they must be left with the financial resources to do so. New York City could well afford its extravagances if the flow of money to Washington, D.C., for nondefense spending were reduced.

Accordingly, New York City should establish a permanent lobby

12. See below.
13. For a total saving of over $250,000,000.

in Washington to press for relief from oppressive taxation. The lobby would be entrusted to pressure the city's representatives in Congress to vote No on legislation which would have the effect of further draining the resources of New York City's citizens; and to remove the strings on existing programs which tell New York how to spend the money which the federal government deigns to return to the city.

John Lindsay, in August, issued a "10-Point Program" for the "economic rejuvenation of New York" which, to quote Randall Jarrell, had to be seen, not to be believed. Sample (Point 10): "Emphasize fair-priced housing, including middle income housing, physical safety on the streets, better schools, parks, recreational facilities, air and water purity, cultural endowments, efficient traffic and anti-discrimination measures to encourage persons who work in the city to live, shop and pay their taxes here."

I analyzed, or rather reacted to, the Lindsay program:

. . . Clifton Fadiman once remarked of one of Gertrude Stein's novels, that anyone searching for orderly sequence in her thought would have to settle for her consecutive pagination. Mr. Lindsay has tried to construct 10 points for the economic rejuvenation of New York by the simple expedient of numbering ten paragraphs of emptiness (1) through (10) consecutively.

The technique is to say nothing that anyone could conceivably disagree with. Don't raise taxes. Do encourage businessmen. Don't spread unemployment. Do encourage employment. By all means, appoint committees. Encourage technology. Bring business and labor together. Love education. Bring in federal money, encourage low rent housing, clean the streets, reduce crime, . . . revere life; and, especially, revere John Lindsay. . . . He cannot bring himself to describe a single program that would be unpopular with a single person. But progress cannot be made in New York unless someone is willing, even at the risk of annoying Camels, to say a word for Lucky Strikes. The fact that not a single human being this side of Bellevue or of the offices of the *Daily Worker* can find a syllable in Mr. Lindsay's "program" to disagree with finally confirms its irrelevance.

For once, I was not alone. On August 25 the *World-Telegram* published an editorial, "Plenty of Nothing."

John Lindsay ticked off a 10-point program for the economic rejuvenation of the City. William F. Buckley Jr., the Conservative party candidate for Mayor, called it "10 paragraphs of emptiness."

But why pick on Lindsay? Except for Buckley, who doesn't care what rash proposals he makes since he's not really trying to win, the entire field of mayoral candidates has been serenading the public with sweet, vague nothings.[14]

In the weeks that followed Lindsay's economic manifesto, the city waited for suggestions by Messrs. Beame and Lindsay on how they would pay for the grandiose things they had in mind for New York. Toward the end of the campaign Mr. Beame, who after all is a professional accountant, expressed incredulity at the long list of projected benefactions by Mr. Lindsay, and at the last public debate challenged Lindsay to describe just how he could effect them, inviting him, as others had done, to specify what new taxes he contemplated. Lindsay declined to come out in favor of a New York City income tax. Earlier, he had rebuked his running-mate, Timothy Costello, for his superior candor in publicly suggesting that just such a thing, a city income tax, might prove necessary to finance the Lindsay program. "John Lindsay" (*Tribune*, August 23) "put himself at odds yesterday with Timothy Costello, the number-two man on his ticket, by condemning the concept of a city income tax as an 'absolute last resort.' The Republican-Liberal candidate for Mayor said a city income tax 'would terrify middle-income groups. New York City would then be a city of the very rich and the very poor.'" Exactly six weeks after his inauguration (the last resort?), Lindsay officially proposed a city income tax.

I proposed a new business tax, the so-called value-added tax.

5. The New Business Tax

October 14, 1965

The life-blood of any community is its payroll. The size of that payroll, however, is to a significant degree affected by whether local taxes on business enterprises within a community are equitable in their application, and simple in their computation and administration. It is not so much the total of the taxes collected from and through business that has driven paymasters out of New York City. Rather, it is the way these taxes have been distributed and collected.

In New York, the business community (using the word in its

14. I wrote the *Telegram*: "Now, it happens that I *am* trying to win, however unlikely it is that I shall succeed in doing so. It also happens that, having committed almost my entire adult life to the search for political wisdom, I am especially appalled at the prospect of political rashness. Indeed, I would sooner risk the displeasure of a voter than I would that of my muse, who is more demanding. So: if you will be good enough to point out to me which are my rash proposals, I agree instantly to abandon them. Fair enough?" The *Telegram* did not accept the invitation.

broadest sense to include all enterprises undertaken for profit, whether involving the sale of services or the manufacturing and sale of goods) is burdened by a bewildering patchwork of special taxes and fees which must assume a substantial part of the blame for the exodus of business from the city.

The multiplicity of existing taxes (gross receipts taxes, sales and use taxes, utility and conduit taxes, occupancy, cigarette, amusement and hotel room taxes, and a host of others) all carry with them a burden of paper work which few individual proprietors can cope with, without costly outside assistance, and which create an overhead burden which is a serious deterrent to the attraction of new business to the city.

During the period from 1948 to 1962, over 15,000 businesses left New York. Between 1950 and 1964, manufacturing employment dropped 16.4 per cent, from 1,038,000 to 868,000. Yet these were years of unprecedented business growth in the country at large.

Most of these taxes place a flat burden on the mere fact of doing business in New York, irrespective of a particular business's economic productivity. The gross receipts tax, for example, imposes the same tax burden on a food wholesaler working on a one-per-cent gross margin as it does on a manufacturer working on a ten-per-cent margin.

What is required, then, is the adoption of a new concept of taxation which will permit New York to collect from the business community its just contribution to the cost of running the city; a concept which will be equitable in application and simple in administration.

Proposal:

It is therefore proposed that, as a substitute for all existing taxes presently levied on or through business enterprises, including the three-per-cent city sales tax, New York City adopt what is known as a "value-added tax." This is a concept which in recent years has been gaining increasing favor, especially in Western Europe, as a substitute for all other forms of business taxation; in fact, in varying forms, this tax has been adopted by France and West Germany, as well as by the European Coal and Steel Community.

This approach to taxation is based on the concept of a business unit as one in which an individual or group of individuals are engaged in the production of goods or services for sale, and as a result of whose work economic value has been created. The nature of this tax has been described as follows: "The value-added tax is conceptually the height of simplicity . . . it utilizes as its base the economist's concept of value added by manufacturing or commercial activity.

Value added, in simplest terms, is the gross business receipts of the firm minus the cost of previously taxed goods and services purchased from other businesses. The tax can be applied to business and professional services as well as tangible goods."[15]

The very simplicity of the tax makes it possible for the smallest shopkeeper or the largest manufacturer to compute his own value-added tax liability without a battery of lawyers or accountants or special systems of bookkeeping, as the tax is based on the fundamental business realities of cash receipts and cash payments. To illustrate this simplicity, a form of tax return which could be used in the computing of a value-added tax for New York City is attached to this paper.[16]

The principal advantages for New York City and its business enterprises of the proposed form of taxation may be summarized as follows:

(a) It would maintain a broad tax base (which recognizes the obligation of any business enterprise to contribute to the cost of the city services it enjoys), and yet apply only to the actual added increment in economic value created by any individual business.

(b) It would eliminate a thicket of taxes, often arbitrary, which has created a significant administrative burden both on the city's enterprises and on the city government.

(c) It would reduce the problem of policing business taxes to that of merely verifying cash receipts and cash expenditures.

The *Times'* final digest of the major candidates' fiscal papers:

Lindsay: "Although I pledge a return to fair tax standards, I cannot, as a responsible candidate, promise a broad reduction of taxes." Wants to repeal or equalize the sales tax and to repeal the gross receipts tax and replace it with a more equitable business tax. Favors offtrack betting and state lottery. Also against "borrow now, pay later."

Beame: "No responsible person could tell you what kind of taxes we'd need" because of the uncertainty of the extent of federal and state aid. Wants to repeal or equalize sales tax and to repeal or equalize the gross receipts tax 4 per cent, to repeal gross receipts tax and substitute tax based on profits; to tax federal and state-owned property; to review tax exemption of Triborough Bridge and Tunnel Authority; to tax 11,500 real estate properties confiscated

15. Richard E. Slitor, Federal Executive Fellow, The Brookings Institution, in a paper delivered at a symposium on value-added taxation conducted by the Tax Institute of America in 1963.
16. The sample form is in Appendix D.

by city for nonpayment of taxes. He is against the "borrow now, pay later" theory. Favors offtrack betting and state lottery.

6. In New York It Pays

Crime

October 13, 1965

The first mark of the civilized community is the ability to control its criminal element. By this standard New York City has lapsed into barbarism. Last year, 1761 major crimes were committed for every 100,000 of the city's population. During the first three months of this year the rate of crime increased 6.6 per cent over the same period of 1964. Such conditions, to be sure, constitute a "scandal"; but simply to repeat that cliché is scandalously to understate and to depersonalize a very real outrage daily perpetrated on the peace of mind and body of every law-abiding New Yorker.

The basic cause of increased crime is, of course, the increasing moral and social disorder that mark contemporary society, and is thus less a problem for civil magistrates than for our churchmen and educators. (It is ironic, under the circumstances, that it has been judged by our highest civil magistrates a crime against the Court of the United States to mention the name of God in the public classrooms.) But the problem has been greatly aggravated by factors over which the city government does have control, or influence:

The city's law-enforcement facilities are inadequate. The police force is too small to cope with burgeoning crime. Current proposals (Lindsay's) to abolish two-man patrol cars, moreover, would make matters worse by diluting the effectiveness of the present force, and by jeopardizing police security. More policemen are needed.

The present Administration is doing nothing to resist the derogation of the law enforcement agencies. The disparagements of the police have created a crisis in morale and a swaggering disrespect for the policeman as the symbol of the public order. Yet far from resisting such assaults, the Wagner Administration has taken the course of appeasement: the proposed Civilian Review Board is nothing less than an agreement to elevate the campaign to discredit the police to official city policy.

Current welfare and housing policies have resulted in an undue concentration in New York City of idle and demoralized persons in an environment which breeds crime and criminals. No program to restore law and order to the city can be effective without coming to grips with New York's grave social problems (see Position Paper on Welfare).

Above all, crime has been encouraged in the city, as elsewhere, by the policies and practices of the courts. Too many judges appear to have forgotten that the primary purpose of courts of justice is to assert the demands of the public order—by meting out convincing punishment to those who transgress against it. This purpose is consistently frustrated in New York by fastidious procedural requirements that impede convictions of the guilty, and by lax sentencing policies that fail to provide an effective deterrent to crime.

To be sure, much of the trouble in bringing criminals to justice can be traced to decisions of the United States Supreme Court—for instance, the *Mallory, Mapp,* and *Escobedo* cases—which, if they indeed extend the implicit rights of the accused as guaranteed by the Constitution, raise the question, to which our judges have not addressed themselves, whether the Bill of Rights, as presently interpreted, sufficiently provides for the effective maintenance of law and order. Former Police Commissioner Michael J. Murphy has put it this way: "*We* are forced to fight by Marquess of Queensberry rules, while the *criminals* are permitted to gouge and bite."

But some of the courts of New York City have gone far beyond the specifications of the Supreme Court. They have institutionalized what commentators have taken to designating as "turnstile justice." They have applied the rules of search and seizure, and other evidentiary and procedural requirements, with an extravagant, often ludicrous technicality. As one newspaper has observed, "the law itself has created so many escape hatches for criminals that nine postponements and a half-dozen separate hearings to suppress evidence or controvert a search warrant are not unusual before a case is ready for trial." The result is that our judicial system blinds its eyes on countless occasions to demonstrable guilt, and turns loose upon our streets the drug pusher, the sex offender, the mugger, the thief. The fact is that crime in New York City, both juvenile and adult, does pay. It pays, in large part, because the city's judicial system has defaulted on its primary duty to protect the public, in favor of an obsessive solicitude for those individuals who are responsible for breaking the peace of the city.

Proposals:

1. Additional policemen should be hired. Many of them could be hired from among retired policemen, to relieve younger men currently deskbound. To assure the police force a maximum efficiency, it should be provided with the most advanced technological tools now

available, so that its equipment is at least as sophisticated as that now routinely employed by the criminal.

2. The new Administration should oppose the establishment of a Civilian Review Board, and should encourage the police to do their duty, and back them up when they do it.

3. The new Mayor and other city officials should bring vigorous pressure to bear on local judges to abandon criminal-coddling policies, and resume the administration of justice. The Bar Associations and other civic groups should be urged, with the support of the communications media, to mobilize an irresistible public demand that the courts of law join New York City's fight against crime.

4. Parole and probation procedures should be tightened to assure the confinement or surveillance of convicted criminals for long enough periods to guard the public safety. Studies should be conducted to determine whether enough parole officers are employed by the city to do an effective job and whether civil service regulations should be revised so as to ensure that officers not qualified or not disposed to administer the law strictly can be replaced.

5. The special treatment now accorded to juvenile criminals should be re-examined in all its ramifications. Specifically, existing legislation should be revised to permit severer punishment of juveniles who commit serious crimes. Youth must cease to be an excuse for vicious attacks on fellow citizens.

6. As a further deterrent to juvenile delinquency, legislation should be enacted requiring the publication of the names and addresses of juvenile offenders guilty of serious offences, and of their parents. This practice was recently adopted by Judge Lester H. Lobel in Helena, Montana. Subsequently, juvenile crime decreased by fifty per cent. While a community like New York can hardly expect such startling results, improvement would almost surely result. "The parents," Judge Lobel observed, "can't stand the heat. I have today about a thousand parents who are about the best probation officers any court can have."

7. As the protection of the individual from acts of lawlessness is a first responsibility of government, to the extent that the law-abiding citizen is victimized by the criminal, the government has failed in its duty to him. Legislation should, therefore, be enacted providing for the indemnification of victims of personal assaults and other crimes of violence.

8. Legislation should be enacted to provide (a) enticing bounties for informers who furnish information leading to criminal convictions, and (b) financial compensation for witnesses in criminal trials.

These measures are necessary inducements for wider citizen participation in the defense of the city.

Of all of the crises now gripping New York, the emergence of Crime Triumphant is the gravest. The challenge to a new Administration could not be plainer: it is to make New York habitable.

There were a few scattered comments to the effect that I desired to modify the Bill of Rights—which, as a matter of fact, are half correct—and I herewith decline to terminate this sentence where logically it should be terminated, in order to make it just a little harder for the above few words to be excerpted out of context—the current movement to fanaticize certain provisions of the Bill of Rights has of course the effect of diminishing certain other provisions of the Bill of Rights. This law of the projection of rights to the point of irreconciliability, an ancient intuition, has been brilliantly demonstrated by Professor Sidney Hook in his little book on *The Paradoxes of Freedom*. You cannot, Professor Hook maintains, extend any two freedoms indefinitely because there is a point at which they are likely to collide with each other. He gives many examples, among them: (a) the freedom of the press on one hand, and on the other, (b) the right to a fair trial; the conflict of interest between the two, at a certain point, being manifest. Another obvious example is the right to practice religion and the right to protection from religious indoctrination.

The position paper on crime sought to identify a crystallizing dilemma. The series of recent decisions by the Supreme Court reifying derivative rights of defendants that trace to the Bill of Rights are highly defensible extrapolations. For instance, if one has the "right" to counsel as of the moment one becomes *de facto* the accused, then it would appear that that right exists irrespective of whether the suspect knows of its existence; hence the Supreme Court—in its *Escobedo* decision, for example—and the Third Circuit Court in its *Russo* decision correctly develop the Sixth Amendment. The question, however, should collaterally arise: what corresponding right exists for the public prosecutor whose duty it is to affirm the rights of the aggrieved? The rights of the party of the first part are increasingly developed, while those of the party of the second part are relatively neglected. In England, Sir Hartley Shawcross has been waging a passionate campaign attempting to rectify the imbalance, his startling contention being that the day is past when the court is most usefully engaged as mere umpire between defendant and prosecutor, that radical revisions of the old rules are in order, revisions that aim at conscripting all parties concerned to the ascertainment of the truth. The truth is, after all, what is desired—*did* John in fact kill Jane?—and he boldly asks whether the adversary system is the most productive form of jurisprudential epistemology. For the hell of it, I spun out these considerations to a fidgety deputation from the Citizens Union of New York, a nonpartisan gathering of right-, or better, good-minded persons whose function was to ascertain, and then to report to the people, whom, in the higher interests of New York, they should vote for.[17] The four lawyer-interrogators who—frankness requires me to confess—were clearly there to interview me only so that they could report that they had been there to interview me, and thus document their formal open-mindedness, nodded in more or less excited confusion—agreed, yes, that radical analysis was probably in order, yes—but quickly and with evident relief guided the discussion back to the fashionable sociological platitudes of the day and never again lost their hold of the conversational leash. So that the discussion, which had begun on the theme of law enforcement, turned to crime and the bearing on it of (a) unemployment, (b) insufficient housing, (c) race relations, etc.—all of which have much to do with the causes of criminals and nothing whatever to do with their apprehension or conviction.

It is conceivable that dilemmas of the kind I felt like talking about tend to occur last to lawyers, whose training commits them to the old precepts; and that may be a reason why the legal profession, of which John Lindsay is a member, has done so little reformist thinking on the subject. It is rather the philosopher Sidney Hook who comes through with the definitive destruction of the same Hugo Black whom Lindsay venerates. On the other hand, Shawcross (who was Attorney General of England in the postwar Labor government) and Mr. C. Dickerman Williams, who almost singlehandedly stopped[18] the establishment of the emerging doctrine that no adverse inferences of any sort are to be drawn from the use of the Fifth Amendment, are lawyers; but an organization like the Citizens Union depends, for its prestige, on its respectability; and respectability in New York, as in most other parts of the country, tends to be confined within the limits of tolerability set by, *e.g., The New York Times.*

In the days ahead the dilemma is bound to harden. Either the Supreme Court will, as unfortunately has been its recent wont, more or less laze up to different specific cases in different ways, leaving the question of what are and what aren't the rights of parties in dispute, in boundless incertitude; or else basic laws will have to be rewritten,

17. Answer: Lindsay
18. "Problems of the Fifth Amendment" *Fordham Law Review,* Vol. 24, 1955.

perhaps even a Constitutional Amendment or two, aimed at clarifying the rights of the public against those of the defendant. A lot can be done about law enforcement in New York City—as I indicated in the Position Paper—under existing arrangements; but, I fear, there is a lot that can't be done.

The most original reaction to the paper was—as usual—Murray Kempton's; he blazed away (October 14) at the specific proposal that "enticing bounties" should be proffered to informants against crime. He tooled off, in his engaging, otherworldly overdrive:

> Buckley has a richly defined sense of irony, and there is always the chance that he advances these ideas in the hope of destroying every liberal illusion by parodying it. But it is more likely that his real charm is not his wit but his innocence. Poor Bill Buckley has never been a liberal. Being a liberal is a dreary experience but it can be a splendid education. This century has been a continual trial and failure of liberal notions. The prime article of its faith has been that, if you pay a man well enough, he will do things that pride or sense of public obligation should have made him do in the first place. There is every excuse for Bill Buckley to believe in this century; he hasn't been there. . . .
>
> Every evidence of our senses should have taught us by now that pride in one's work has nothing to do with wages and conditions of labor. A man must do his job because he believes that he will go when he dies to one or another form of hell if he doesn't, or he will never do his job at all. A teacher who has to be bribed to go to Harlem was no teacher when she held out for the money and will be no teacher after she takes it.
>
> Money is a necessity but it is never an inducement. It is what people take after they have exhausted every means of grace or hope of glory. When a man can talk only about money, he is either desperate or dead. . . . So until now, you and I were presumably the sort of persons who would watch an old lady get mugged in the street and do nothing about it because there was nothing in it for us. But now Bill Buckley will put something in it for us. He would redeem the bad citizen by making him a good bounty hunter.

It is a profanation, in which I have had on several occasions to indulge, to advance on Kempton's thought with compass, scissors, and tape measure, and it is the sign of his special genius that he inevitably leaves his critics feeling like Philistines. But—but.

(1) The point in offering monetary inducements to those who have information of use to the prosecutor is not to confirm that we live in

a virtuous society, but precisely to confirm that we do not. (2) So, then, our society is, by the highest standards, admittedly unvirtuous. And therefore (3) the question is whether to confine oneself to the writing of elegies on the unvirtuousness of that society, or to accept the fact of our disgrace and—to use the ugliest available word—bribe those who know, to tell us what they know which we need to hear if we are going to prevent Mr. Jones from mugging a second old lady. The assumption (4) that bounties have no effect on human behavior is neither liberal nor antiliberal, it is antihistorical (was Judas Iscariot a liberal or a conservative?).

Kempton's reference to the teachers was a continuation of his grand theme—he had previously jumped me for the suggestion that teachers should be paid extra money to persuade them to go to Harlem to take on the education of the most intractable students. His objection was consistent—namely that no teacher has 'the right to consider himself a public servant unless he is willing to do the public's saying.

> The root of the trouble [he began with his inimitable swoop] is that our civil servants are union men first and public employees second at a very far remove. To take a case, a year or so ago, the Board of Education announced that it proposed to assign its best qualified teachers to the Harlem schools. The persons so described went at once to their union, which at once protested, and the plan was abandoned. . . .
>
> One great trouble with our educational system is that teachers can demand and be given the comfort of teaching only those children who are easiest to teach, which is an aspiration so low that no professional who gives way to it should be appeased if only for his own sake. . . .
>
> Ordinarily Buckley would, I should think, be ashamed to appeal to desires this unworthy. But now he is a candidate. One supposes that he ought not to have taken that first step. He offered us hope because he alone has the posture from which to talk a certain kind of sense about our situation. But that is a posture for critics and not for candidates. Its survival was too large a hope even from Buckley.[19]

I wrote him at the time (rather sloppily), on this matter of major importance to New York—the improvement in the education of the least educated:

19. By the time the campaign had drawn to a close, I had, apparently, finally re-convinced Kempton that, after all, I was otherworldly enough to suit him. "The process which coarsens every other man," he wrote on October 28, "has only re-fined Mr. Buckley . . . [as] another friend said last night, fond as he has always been of Bill Buckley, he's even fonder after finding out that he's *not* really a politician."

. . . the subject isn't quite as easy as you suggest, for the reason that [many] teachers are willing to teach only the brighter students, and in genteel surroundings. I, for instance, would fail your moral-qualification test, because I would decline to teach the less bright. I would evangelize among the less bright; but I wouldn't [*myself* undertake to*]* teach them how to read. What I would do is what an awful lot of New York teachers do every year (Lindsay will give you the figures): I'd quit, and go teach somewhere else. The solution [should have written: "an approach"] is to pay special salaries . . . to tempt the very good teachers to do what they aren't disposed to do.

It is easy, of course [I wrote, elsewhere, under Kempton's spur], to rail against the teachers in question for refusing to accept an assignment that would not only have taxed their ingenuity as teachers, but would have had the effect of recalling however faintly something of the idealistic genealogy of their profession (the word "rabbi" means "teacher"). But teaching is not, for most of those who go into it, a priestly calling, a pledge made before God and Man to go out and extirpate ignorance from the globe. Most teachers teach because that is a way, not totally disagreeable, to make a living, and to lead a busy life.

For many teachers—like the New Yorkers in question—the prospect of commuting to disagreeable sections of the city, to grapple with inertia, indiscipline, and hostility (see, for instance, the recent book, *White Teacher in a Black School*[20]), is not what they had in mind at all when deciding to teach. It is all very well to say that the teachers should be told to do as they are told, like good civil servants. But you cannot treat a teacher—or a civil servant—as you can a nun or priest, who has taken a vow of obedience. The teacher, even assuming his union had let him down and told him to obey the Board of Education, would probably have done what so many other teachers in New York do every year. Quit.

There is a lot of money bustling about New York in pursuit of a better city. I cling to the belief that more of it should go to induce a better education for those who need it, and to elicit more information for those who need such information in order to prevent physical harm from coming to persons so innocent, or so perverse, as to live in the city.

The *Times*' digest of the other candidates' positions:

Lindsay—Calls for twice the present number of patrol cars, now 1,600, and three times the number of motorcycles, now 165. Would increase police force by 2,500 to authorized strength. Would put one man in patrol cars in most areas. Wants to emulate Chicago

20. Robert Kendall (New York: Devin-Adair, 1964).

communications system; to use two-way walkie-talkie radios for all foot patrolmen; to create a single emergency telephone system, with one digit dialing, to reduce paperwork, to improve police morale by offering pay incentives, overhauling promotion policies and reforming Criminal Court calendar procedures; to modernize police stations; to add four civilians to three police officers now on police review board.

Beame—Wants to put the policeman back on the beat. Proposes increasing the number of patrol cars, using one patrolman in cars in some areas; shifting policemen from clerical jobs; utilizing modern equipment; initiating a program of prevention and rehabilitation; emulating Chicago's communication system; increasing lighting of streets and parks; initiating single digit dialing for the police. Proposes citizen participation in police review board, but offers no plan.

7. Opportunity for Liberation

Housing

October 19, 1965

The first thing to recognize is that the nature of the problem is typically misrepresented, or misunderstood, with the result that the city is typically asked to make an irrelevant response.

There is no housing shortage, as such, in New York City.[21]

There is an overabundance of "luxury" and moderately priced dwellings.

There is a critical shortage of decent, low-priced housing facilities, which can be overcome at a relatively small public expense once the nature and basic causes of the deficiency have been brought into focus.

The second thing to recognize is that the problem will never be dealt with successfully until those responsible for city planning have been emancipated from some demonstrable superstitions:

The vaunted federal Urban Renewal Program has *not* resulted in an increase of decent, low-priced housing. Indeed, the overwhelming evidence suggests that Urban Renewal has actually reduced the number of units available to lower-income dwellers, to say nothing of the program's disintegrating impact on the social and economic life of the city. By addressing the complexity and diversity of modern cities with a sophistication pitched to the blade of a bulldozer, Urban Renewal has managed to destroy thousands of low-rent housing units, while removing many of the former occupants to even less desirable

21. For supporting statistics see Appendix E.

neighborhoods where rents are frequently higher. But not only does the program, at best, merely transplant slums, with a net loss of low-priced units: its principal victims are Negroes, Puerto Ricans, members of minority groups who are least able to assimilate the strains of forcible relocation.

Housing:

Rent controls, over the long run, are *not* responsive to the needs of those who depend on low-priced housing. The greatest potential source of relief for current inadequacies are those older properties that are now rent-controlled at rates from $50 to $100 a month. Yet many of these properties have been withdrawn from the market by landlords who cannot afford to rent them at the controlled rates, and therefore sell them to luxury developers. Still other housing of this kind needs renovation and modernization. Yet thanks to rent controls, and to the red tape and other obstructive practices of the Rent and Rehabilitation Administration, landlords cannot properly maintain and improve their properties. It is little wonder that responsible private investors have been driven from such properties, only to be succeeded by speculators and slumlords who exploit them to the fullest and thus annex them to the city jungle.

Rent controls, moreover, foster a number of specific inequities.

They favor large landlords over small landlords. The complex administrative processes of rent control are beyond the resources of the individual proprietor; large real estate operators, by contrast, maintain staffs equipped to discover and exploit every loophole in the regulations, and possess the requisite funds for fighting unfavorable rulings through the courts.

Controls discriminate against the young, mobile families that are likely to require new leases on premises that have qualified in the past for rent increases. By comparison, some tenants who have remained at the same dwelling for many years pay rents unjustifiably low. (In some cases the rent disparity runs as high as 150 per cent for identical facilities.) Others, who have become well-to-do and live outside the city, maintain their rent-controlled New York apartments for their occasional convenience in town.

Controls immobilize elderly persons whose families have grown up and who would therefore prefer to occupy less spacious premises were it not for the higher rents that might be charged for new premises. This immobility contributes, in turn, to the shortage of medium-to-large dwelling units, and forces the families that would normally rent them to remain in uncomfortable small quarters.

The federal government is *not* an "additional" source of funds for satisfying New York's housing requirements. On the contrary, under the current arrangements with Washington, New Yorkers must pay over to the federal government three dollars (toward the welfare pool) for every dollar the city receives for federal "assistance." Moreover, that dollar is normally returned only on the condition that New York conform its policies and practices to a tangle of bureaucratic regulations that typically have little relevance to the real needs of the city. It follows that to the extent that the city must depend on public funds for housing, or for any other purpose, a prerequisite of sanity is to disabuse New Yorkers of the illusion that they are on the "receiving" end of federal aid.

Proposals:

1. New York City should immediately opt out of the federal Urban Renewal Program. In place of the block-buster approach to deteriorating neighborhoods, the city government should energetically foster a city-wide program for the rehabilitation of existing structures and their surroundings. In place of artificial, paternalistic schemes spun out of the ideological prepossessions of social engineers, future city planning should give the widest possible berth to organic community development, spurred by the private initiative of those who inhabit the neighborhoods in question. New Yorkers should aim for a rich diversity in the various communities that make up our city—as the only possible avenue of civilized progress.

2. A program to renovate and modernize older dwellings should be made the keystone of the city's efforts to overcome the shortage of decent, low-priced housing. If this program is pursued with sufficient energy, the city may be able to satisfy current housing requirements without further recourse to public funds.

3. To this end the Mayor should set in motion a thoroughgoing investigation of the practices of the Rent and Rehabilitation Administration, designed to expedite private initiative, and to liberate private investors from bureaucratic harassment.

4. To the extent additional public housing is needed to meet the immediate needs of lower income groups, the city should weigh the economies of buying out marginal "luxury" housing already in existence, as an alternative to building new units. Many of these existing units are an economic drain on their present owners, thanks to a large number of vacancies. And since they were built at costs lower than obtain for current housing, their acquisition would represent a sound public investment. Some of these units, indeed, may be available at foreclosure sales.

5. As an indispensable means of integrating community life and

of providing congenial residential atmosphere, the city should mobilize a convincing live-and-play-at-home campaign, which would encourage the evolution of hundreds of self-contained working and recreational communities.

6. Rent controls, a twenty-year-old relic of the war emergency, should gradually be eliminated. Precipitate abandonment of controls would, of course, entail disastrous consequences for many tenants.

7. The logical first step in the elimination of controls is to decontrol units as they become vacant; such a policy would not inconvenience current tenants. It would, however, permit gradual improvement and modernization, encouraging landlords to renovate entrances, common halls, and so forth.

8. The Rent and Rehabilitation Administration should be required to present to the City Council next April (1966)—when current rent controls are due for renewal—a staged program looking forward to the total elimination of controls over a five-year period. The plan should include recommendations for protecting the interests of tenants living in housing to be decontrolled, as well as detailed justifications for retaining such controls as are temporarily to remain in force. The adoption of such a plan would be solid inducement to landlords now fleeing the regimentation of public programs to renew their involvements in the housing business.

9. To assure the satisfaction of future housing needs, the city should encourage the investment of private funds in low-priced housing developments. But to lure the maximum venture capital for low-priced housing back to New York it will be necessary (a) to reduce the cost of construction by denying the monopoly labor unions the right to exact inordinate fees (see forthcoming Labor Paper),[22] (b) to reduce the heavy tax overhead on New Yorkers (see Fiscal Paper), and (c) to take elementary steps to discourage the thoughtless flow of immigrants into the city (see Welfare Paper). Future reliance by New York City on private capital for this purpose will not only assure more humane and dignified living conditions for New Yorkers who will occupy new housing; it could also generate a historic breakthrough in what hopefully will become a national campaign to emancipate housing from the status of a government business.

No particular flurry in the press. The occasion is, I think, apt to record how some positions get formulated; or, at least, how they did in this particular campaign. The role of the inter-office memo: Mrs. Rosemary Gunning is widely identified, by those who oppose her, as a sort of *tricoteuse* who hates Negroes; she rose to prominence as a

22. As noted, it did not materialize.

result of her successful organization of Queens housewives against compulsory busing. She is middle-aged, buxom, amiable; in her public statements tending a little to the banal because, I came to discover, that is the medium in which she believes, no doubt correctly, that public politics is spoken. I later discerned that although her political judgments were often faulty (she tended to overoptimism), her intellectual rigor is remarkable; and on every issue, she would leave a compassionate overlay. We used to meet, every week or two, together with Hugh Markey, forty-two, the candidate for Comptroller, a Staten Island businessman with a fine sense of humor and proportion, incorrigibly modest; with my affable brother Jim, forty-two, the campaign manager, the superconciliator with the deadest eye in the conference business for keeping the point of the discussion just high enough to be always visible in the hurly-burly; with Kieran O'Doherty, thirty-eight, obsessed with the political implications of it all, the self-denying evangelist, tactically the pessimist, strategically the optimist; Dan Mahoney, thirty-three, serious, amusing, galvanizing, poised; Neal Freeman, twenty-four, omnicompetent administrator, profoundly committed to the campaign, personally and professionally; and Mrs. Gunning, methodical, humane, immensely knowledgeable, always advancing the concern of the people among whom she lived, whom she knew so well.

And she knew housing well. She has sent around, in dirty-mimeograph, a series of observations on a number of subjects. Her knowledge of rent control is better than that of anyone else I know or know of; and the burden of her analysis struck me as devastatingly informative, tending to show how, as always, the big boys always, always, manage to get theirs; tending to show, by empirical demonstration, how true is Milton Friedman's observation that the workings of most big-think welfare measures, the obvious exceptions being obvious, tend to accrue to the benefit of the middle-rich, or the big-rich. Her analysis of rent control—boisterously supported by Lindsay and Beame as designed-to-protect-the-poor—was the kind of political sociology that truly informs, for which reason, with admiration, I publish herewith extensive excerpts:

> Rent Control: Vito Battista [perennial United Taxpayers' Party candidate] has bled publicly for years on the lack of principle, justice and constitutionality in current rent control and its burdens on landlords, especially small owners. He has left most of the city unmoved. Most controlled tenants, having had substantial rent increases because they have "big" landlords, do not believe him. This is also true of non-income homeowners, many of whom bought because of rent problems and who have relatives concerned with

them. In fact it was the rent control issue which helped substantially to defeat Lefkowitz when it was artfully introduced by Wagner at the end of the campaign [1961]. (He and Rockefeller panicked at Wagner's charges instead of fighting back, because neither of them really knew the subject.)

We must realize the terror the possibility of an unlimited increase in rent presents to most controlled renters. . . .

We must therefore present our rent control position primarily on the basis that it is the greatest delusion being offered the tenants; that present rent control administration does the tenant incalculable harm because under it the large landlords—covering most apartment and tenement house tenancies—never had it so good and the tenants never had it so bad. This is truly the fact because the law favors speculators and hamstrings investors. . . .

We cannot escape the rent control question in this campaign because it has been raised and it is a legitimate city issue. If we appear to be doing well, it will be sprung on us at the last minute, as they did to Lefkowitz. We must therefore educate the great bulk of New Yorkers—the tenants—on how adverse rent control and public housing is for them. Don't worry about the [little] landlords; they know how bad it is. And people who struggle each month to pay their present rent will not be interested in the principles and philosophies involved. People tell me they will vote for us but they wouldn't if they thought we could win because of our position on rent control. . . .

I replied in an inter-office memo:

. . . I must confess I do not comprehend parts of the last paragraph of page 5 in Rosemary's memorandum. I do not see how one reasons that rent control *helps* the landlord.

Mrs. Gunning replied:

Rent control has been extremely helpful to the large real estate operators (which is why it has remained).

Many tenants felt a blissful security in their low rents only to be dismayed by a notice to move because their building was to be demolished or renovated into twice as many apartments. This resulted from the fact that owners could not operate at even 1950 costs on 1943 rents. . . . [The new owners] assembled plots on which to build large apartment buildings or renovated buildings into twice as many apartments by dividing the large apartments into two—all decontrolled. Yorkville and Chelsea were especially victimized. Many low rent properties in good condition met the bulldozer for uncontrolled luxury apartments which took their place—and have many vacancies, but the rents are high enough to pay off for most. These tenants all had to pay higher rents in, sometimes, distant neighborhoods. They would have preferred, if they had realized what was going to happen, to pay a moderate increase which would have retained their former owners as investors.

The present relocation provisions of the Rent and Rehabilitation law grew out of these hardships. (Demolishing and renovating owners must relocate the tenants.) You will note that the broadest reason for federal subsidies for rent is for relocatees. It looks like Uncle Sam is going to the aid of "private enterprise" which must relocate tenants in the coming rush of new buildings under the Housing Bill. . . .

Since it was obvious owners could not operate with the rising costs and in order to meet the legal dangers this presented, the state, which then administered rent control, permitted landlords to apply for rent increases for their buildings provided they did not produce a 6 per cent return on their investment plus 2 per cent for depreciation. Recent owners were permitted to use as their investment base their purchase price, but long-time investors had to use an obsolete rate based on assessed valuation. (It was a change-over to the current equalization and a fairer equalization rate, which caused the controversy in the last mayoralty campaign. Wagner pretended that large-scale increases were being allowed; the fact was—for reasons hereafter set forth—it affected very few long-held properties and very few applications had been submitted under it. Since neither Rockefeller nor Lefkowitz understood the problem, they panicked and a moratorium was established and rent control was turned over to the city.)

Only an accountant, whose books are set up to accumulate the information required (detailed schedules, receipts, etc.) could prepare these applications. The small owners could not afford the fees. Up to 15 per cent a year increases were allowed each year. While the small owners found the fees and the returns impossible [to pay, and to fill out], the large operators, with appropriate staffs, were able to avail themselves of this and the tenants received a yearly "hardship" increase. When the building was on a top return, they simply sold the building and the next year's "hardship increase" application was based on the new higher purchase price. In some buildings, this became a yearly occurrence, until the city took over. Now applications can be made only after a building is owned two years and only every two years, but it still favors the speculator because the purchase price may be used only if the building was purchased after 1958. Long-time owners—investors—are treated strictly on the assessed valuation. Assessed valuation in Queens— 50 per cent of value, in two-family houses—only a third of value. The assessed valuation rate is a little higher in other boroughs but only in Manhattan do they approach real value.

Consequently, simply by buying and selling periodically—no

problem to large corporate owners—bi-annual increases are assured to these owners. Since they have "captive" tenants, who are denied the benefit of free competition in rentals, they provide a minimum of services and buildings which used to be "nice" in the moderate rental field, now just escape being slums. Modernization and rehabilitation by private owners require so much red tape, uncertainty and injustice in rent increases for them, as well as long delays, they have practically stopped—so slums have grown faster in New York City in the past thirty years (depression and rent control) than ever in the history of the city.

Speculators have bought up low-income property because investors had to unload and no investors except large operators buy in New York City, so we now have more slumlords than landlords. They simply mulct the low-income properties, letting them deteriorate, knowing the city will eventually take them over for slum clearance, etc. By doing no maintenance work, giving a minimum of services, they soon get back their small investments, reap a good profit and even pay the fines, etc., which is why the city cannot possibly maintain a sufficient inspection force.

In addition new tenants bring a 15 per cent increase. (A 15 per cent "voluntary" increase is allowed for a two-year lease. No one rents except with such a "voluntary" increase, so there is every inducement in having tenants move.) Minimum service can therefore safely be furnished. Rents have gone so high in the most undesirable apartments, from which tenants move as soon as they find something better, as well as even some good ones, they are renting at below the maximum rent fixed by the Rent and Rehabilitation Administration. Because there are now vacancies, there is competition.

While the foregoing is an over-simplification of the problem— not every, and perhaps even only few, owners actually increased each year or each two years, and many owners, resenting the red tape and harsh controls, want an end to rent control—the fact is that most large operators will admit, off the record, they have done all right under rent control. Remember they now operate with practically no vacancies whereas 10 per cent vacancies are normal in ordinary times. The real hardships to owners under rent control are to the small owners, especially those who are unwilling to sell because it is their home too and who must tolerate impossible tenants they cannot remove.

However, the bulk of rent-controlled tenants in this city have received increases and all believe the only reason the owner does not increase is because he has no grounds—he must [the tenants assume], be making at least 5 per cent plus 2 per cent. Did you read [William] Fitts Ryan's blast on rent control? One point he made was right—they should stop breaking up the larger apartments into small units. The families need them. I objected to this at one of the hearings and, quoting my language, without giving credit, the Administrator ruled that in future renovations, there must be a certain percentage of four-room apartments for families. This was not my suggestion—I wanted the seven-room apartments left with a suitable increase for larger families.

Because the politicians are mostly afraid of the Tenant Organizations, who control votes, we have tried to get set up special rules and units for buildings under sixteen, even ten and eight, units, where the landlords have some votes—the deciding votes in some areas. Attached is a résumé I prepared with my civic organization for use by Affiliated Property Owners of Brooklyn and Queens to present to their Councilmen. We presented it to ours but nothing much happened with the other groups. My experience has been that most small-property-owner groups talk, but take little practical action. This was prepared in 1962. You will note even then new units exceeded the increase in population.

I am awaiting the latest figures, which will be for 1964, but you can see how little we need more public housing or government-assisted private projects. You can also see that the 5-per-cent vacancy rate must [already have been] exceeded which the law provides for the end of rent control. But the juggled figures Mrs. Gabel procured have been accepted by the Courts and the City Council. There was—so we were told—a return from the suburbs by a flight of families because of the school situation. I am trying to track down some authority for the figure being circulated that 30,000 white middle-income families moved from the Bronx during the past year. We know from PAT the large exodus of families in our affected areas. Unfortunately too many would rather move than fight. They tell us, with some justification—who can fight when their children are being beaten, molested and receiving inadequate education?

That is my idea of an inside picture, utterly free of ideology; a case history of how lacking in harmony with reality, and how contrary to the intended social objective, a welfarist measure—rent control—can turn out to be. Yet for all her realism, Mrs. Gunning betrayed herself as a Platonist: "We must therefore educate the great bulk of New Yorkers—the tenants—on how adverse rent control and public housing is for them." Indeed. Analysis as intricate as the foregoing simply isn't the stuff of thirty-second blurts on radio and television. Even condensed in full-page newspaper ads, such analysis tends to repel the casual newspaper reader, who instantly assumes that here is merely the real-estate lobby, arguing its special interests. Here is the kind of analysis the responsibility for whose comprehension devolves uniquely upon the opinion-makers, who then, on their own time, and invoking their own prestige, must attempt to make others

understand. The same opinion-makers, by and large, who were praising John Lindsay as the man of freshness and penetration and courage did not themselves exhibit the qualities they heralded in their
candidate. The record shows that *The New York Times*, for instance,
has opposed the continuation of rent controls. But the difference between formal and active advocacy is the difference between doing
something about rent control and not doing something about rent
control. So that, without any observable reproach by New York's
major opinion-makers, sure enough, both Beame and Lindsay endorsed the indefensible continuation of rent control in New York
City.

The *Times'* digest (for reasons unknown there was no mention
in the summary of Lindsay's and Beame's call for a continuation of
rent controls—or of my own recommendation for their abolition):

> Lindsay—Proposes four year program to build at least 160,000
> low- and middle-income apartments, with the aid of more than $2
> billion from Federal and state governments. Would direct Housing
> Authority to submit step-by-step program to construct or renovate
> 50,000 low-rent apartments during the next four years, with private
> companies building 50,000 low-rent apartments. Would boost mid-
> dle-income apartment construction to 60,000 units over next four
> years. Wants strict enforcement of housing codes by a Department
> of Housing Maintenance.
>
> Beame—Calls for immediate construction of 115,000 low- and
> middle-income apartments. Would eliminate income limit in low-
> rent housing, which forces those who earn more to move elsewhere,
> and raise the rent. Would use city's pension funds to finance mort-
> gages for privately constructed housing, and build more vest-
> pocket housing. Urges updating building code.

8. Where Is the Government Hiding?

Pollution

October 21, 1965

Here is a legitimate concern of government—a classic example of
the kind of thing that government should do, according to Lincoln's
test, because the people cannot do it as well or better themselves.

The pollution problem, however, is one that eminently qualifies
for local solutions, devised and implemented by the communities
directly affected. The federal government has no legitimate concern
with the purification of New York City's air and water. The challenge
is clearly addressed to the city itself, and to those geographically con-

tiguous communities and states that share in both the creation of the problem and its consequences. Yet for years the government of New York City has been little more than a bemused observer of the accumulating filth in the waters that wash the city's shores and of the soot and noxious fumes that saturate the air.

The city's most conspicuous dereliction in the matter of water pollution has been its failure to prevent the dumping of sewage into the open water during rainy periods. The cause of the problem is clear: both rain water and sewage are presently carried off by the same drainage system, and the existing sewage treatment plants are inadequate for handling the combination of rain and sewage during heavy rains. As a result a large amount of raw sewage flows into the open water—notably in the Jamaica Bay area of Brooklyn and Queens, and in the upper East River and Eastchester Bay area of the Bronx. In 1959 the Commissioner of Health, the Commissioner of Parks, and the Commissioner of Public Works proposed a realistic plan to deal with the problem at an estimated cost, over a ten-year period, of $150,000,000. Six years later, the project is still at the talking stage: the only significant change in the situation is a revision of the cost estimate, which—thanks to an inflation of construction costs—has risen to $158,130,000, and is sure to go higher. While enabling legislation has been enacted to defray a portion of this figure, the city government has not mustered sufficient political courage to impose the direct levy on sewer-users that is essential for adequate financing.

Cesspool conditions in the Hudson River are equally notorious. To be sure, the city's responsibility for devising a solution is more remote since most of the pollution occurs upriver. Still, the maximum impact of the pollution is felt in New York City. Even so, the city government has so far reacted with little more than whining complaints against Washington's failure to promise more funds for vague control-projects over which the state governments of New York and New Jersey have been wrangling for years.

The city's response to air pollution—a menace that is familiar to every New Yorker—has been even more ineffective. We all know that air pollution is a contributing cause of respiratory disease—of chronic bronchitis, of pulmonary emphysema, of lung cancer. We have learned that it may also become a cause of fatal lead poisoning. We know it damages many kinds of plant life and trees. We know that even art treasures have felt its ravages. And we are aware that the problem is particularly acute in this city. New Yorkers unavoidably inhale an amount of the cancer-inducing hydrocarbon benzopyrene equivalent to that inhaled by a two-pack-a-day smoker. New York

City's air contains more sulphur dioxide than that of any city of the United States—twice as much, for instance, as Philadelphia's. In money terms, the annual damage from air pollution in New York City is estimated at $520,000,000. Yet despite this mounting evidence of the destructive effects of air pollution, the government of New York City has been content with empty gestures—the ritualistic appointment of committees, study groups, and the like.

While air pollution is traceable to many causes, private as well as public, a major factor is the transportation and refuse facilities owned and operated by the city itself. The city government is to be censured for failing to encourage control-initiatives by industrial polluters, and for failing to enact legislation dealing with such private pollution sources as automobile exhaust. But above all the city must be indicted for failing to reduce its own contribution to the contamination of the air.

Proposals—Water Pollution:

1. The answer to the overflow of sewage and storm water during rainy periods is twofold—to build new sanitary sewers in some areas, while using existing sewers exclusively for storm water; and in other areas to build overflow basins for the deposit of storm-caused sewage excesses, which could then be chemically treated before being dumped into the open water.

2. This modernization of New York's sewage system should be financed primarily by a moderate increase in sewer rents. In 1959, it was estimated that the necessary funds could be made available by increasing the current rate of 5 cents per 100 cubic feet to 15 cents, resulting in a cost of seven or eight dollars per year per householder, thus equalizing the charges for sewage disposal and for the use of water. A somewhat larger rate increase may now be required to meet higher construction costs—a consideration that bids the city to begin construction of the new system at the earliest possible moment to avoid still higher levies. As the proposed system would be self-amortizing, the initial capital cost could be financed through the sale of bonds without impairing further the city's credit.

3. The elimination of water pollution by private industrial sources cannot be accomplished by legal fiat without running into problems. The major one is the large economic commitments of industrial polluters in existing waste-disposal practices. Drastic penalties might halt production; but they might also drive the offenders from New York, thus removing vital bases of the city's economy. A prudent approach therefore requires a judicious combination of inducement and sanctions designed to strike a balance between the ideal of total

depollution on the one hand, and the economies of the imperfect purification techniques now available on the other.

4. As a negative sanction, the flow of pollutants from industrial sources should be monitored, and the offenders assessed at a set rate based on the amount of pollutants that enter the water flow. The rates should be high enough to encourage purification measures, yet not so high as to drive the polluter from the city.

5. In addition, the city should furnish positive inducements to industrial pollution control by offering real estate tax concessions— as a supplement to those offered by state law—to polluters who agree to install purification devices. The city should also offer its services in helping to obtain financing for private pollution control measures.

Proposals—Air Pollution:

The city should immediately institute a systematic program for the reduction of air pollution originating in city-owned property.

1. The most conspicuous offenders are city-owned buses. As an interim requirement, exhaust should be more adequately filtered and engines modified to reduce offensive emissions. However, the long-term solution—summoned successfully by other American cities— is to substitute liquefied petroleum gas for the fuel presently used. Burned properly, LPG does not emit noxious fumes. Since conversion of existing equipment to LPG would be expensive, the city should adopt a policy of exhaust control and engine adjustment for existing equipment, and undertake to replace retired buses with vehicles equipped to burn LPG.

2. Control devices should also be applied to other city vehicles— sanitary department trucks, fire engines, police cars, street sweepers. It would be unrealistic for the city to insist upon pollution-reduction in privately-owned vehicles (see below) unless the city takes comparable steps with respect to its own vehicles.

3. Municipal incinerators account for close to 20 per cent of the soot in the city's air. Incongruously, not one of the city's eleven incinerators meets the legal requirements for pollution control that govern Consolidated Edison plants. Obviously, the city should modernize its incinerator equipment, and thus observe the same standards that are imposed on private industrial operations.

4. The city should institute a staged program for eliminating the private burning of garbage. Eventually all garbage should be removed by truck and burned in the modernized municipal incinerators.

5. The city should prohibit the burning of bituminous coal—a fuel that dirties the air with tons of soot daily.

The principal offender among private polluters is, of course, Consolidated Edison. In the summer months, for instance, Con Ed is responsible for nearly all of the sulphur dioxide in the air, and in the winter months for nearly one-third—not surprising statistics given the fact that Con Ed burns approximately one-half of all the fuel in New York City. Con Ed, however, has taken admirable initiatives to minimize air pollution, having spent over $100,000,000 for this purpose—more than any other company in the world. Further conversion of existing facilities to natural gas is a partial answer in the short run. But significant progress toward reducing the company's contribution to air pollution will not be achieved until public attitudes have become acclimated to the use of nuclear energy as the primary power source for Con Ed operations. The city government should therefore take the lead in disabusing the public of the imagined perils of nuclear facilities, and encourage the company to supplant existing power facilities at the earliest possible moment with atomic energy plants.

6. Other industrial air polluters should be dealt with in the same fashion as water polluters. A realistic program of assessments against pollution, and tax relief for pollution control, would go a long way toward eliminating contamination of the air from private sources.

7. The city should require that all new cars sold in New York be equipped with a pollution-reducer device similar to those now prescribed by law in California. The requirement would add approximately $50 to the price of a car, but would eliminate nearly 80 per cent of the hydrocarbons and about 60 per cent of the carbon monoxide that is now exhaled by private vehicles.

8. In addition, the city should weigh the feasibility of requiring that all private supply and commuter vehicles not bought in New York be equipped with pollution-reducer devices, as a condition for entering the city. Constitutional objections might be raised, but in all likelihood the requirement could be successfully defended as a reasonable exercise of the city's police power to protect the public health.

It hardly needs to be added that these proposals cannot achieve truly effective pollution control in most areas unless they are accompanied by similar measures in neighboring communities, particularly in the industrial complex of nearby New Jersey. The city government should therefore take vigorous and widely publicized initiatives in urging other communities to follow suit, and where direct coordination and cooperation is indicated, to join in establishing the relevant inter-government machinery. The difficulties of securing effective intercommunity cooperation should not be tolerated as an excuse for taking no action at all, in the light of such effective examples of inter-state cooperation as the New York Port Authority.

One suspects that the foot-draggers are deliberately inviting intervention by Washington, as the most convenient political course. A conservative Administration would firmly exclude such attitudes as incompatible with the dignity, independence, and resources of New York City.

The pollution- and air-control paper did not cause any particular stir, nor did those of Lindsay and Beame which, always excepting the usual dependence on the federal government, were sound. Indeed, here was probably the single area of social concern respecting which a tri-partisan program emerged.

The digest:

[Water Pollution]
    Lindsay—Says "In a single sentence, the repellent, disgraceful condition of New York City's waters is caused almost entirely by the city's failure to provide adequate sewage treatment plants to cope with all its vast and mounting production wastes." Proposes all new sewerage systems be double systems, and urges baffle systems at beaches. Supports bond issue.
    Beame—Proposes that all new sewage systems be double systems, to handle sewage and rainwater separately. Urges conversion of existing single-sewer systems into double systems, and baffle systems at beaches wherever possible. Supports bond issue.
[Air Pollution]
    Lindsay—Proposes annual outlay from $5 to $5.5 million for air pollution control; increasing number of inspectors by 50 per cent to 66; conducting block-by-block survey of all air pollution sources in the city; systematically improving city's 2,000 incinerators. Proposes that by 1969 all industrial stacks be equipped with control devices, and urges tax rebates as incentive.
    Beame—Proposes equipping buses and other city vehicles with after-burner devices; initiating regional and interstate control; enlarging Department of Air Pollution Control; having strict enforcement and stiffer penalties; upgrading substandard incinerators, and starting public education campaign.

9. Narcotics Is a Plague

Narcotics

October 25, 1965
    It is not widely enough recognized that the problem of narcotics addiction is both individual and social. It is still less well understood that in narcotics, the individual and the social problems fuse.

It is obvious what are the devastating effects of addiction on the individual addict's life.

It is less certain exactly what is the extent of the social damage done by addicts. Mayor Wagner, reporting at the White House Conference on Addiction in 1963, puts the cost to the community in crime, treatment, and added police protection, at an incredible one billion dollars, an amount equal to almost one-third the present city budget.

Narcotics peddlers, reaping profits of 600 per cent on the sale of drugs, are said to route these huge profits into other underworld operations, helping to finance the structural underworld.

It is practically impossible to "cure" a narcotics addict who does not desire to be cured. Former addicts return again and again to the habit even after being coaxed back into health at great pain and expense.

It is not feasible to dispose of the social problem by making drugs generally available under doctors' prescription. A typical addict always desires more of the drug than a responsible doctor, concerned with the addict's physical health, is willing to give him; and therefore the black market continues.

The key insight into the narcotics problem evolves from meditating this datum: that it is the addicts themselves who spread the addiction, more so even than the professional pushers. They do so by enticing others who are psychologically weak, or misinformed as to the gravity of what they are being invited to taste; and the hook having been taken, more often than not a life is ruined. But the ruined life seeks in turn to multiply the ruination of life. And so the disease spreads in geometric proportion, and permits us to generalize that: *narcotics is a contagious disease.*

Proposals:

1. It being the case that narcotics is a contagious disease, which has already victimized in New York City between 40,000 and 80,000 persons, it becomes necessary to treat it as a plague.

2. New York should undertake to quarantine all addicts, even as smallpox carriers would be quarantined during a plague.

3. The narcotics problem is properly a federal problem because the contagion is country-wide. It is true that New York City, which houses an estimated fifty per cent of the nation's addicts, is the highest point of narcotic concentration. But an addict in New York City can, and frequently does, contaminate an individual who lives elsewhere. There are, of course, federal antinarcotics laws. But they are purely punitive in nature. They are immature, in that they are not designed

to cope with the whole problem. The federal government, then, should, having collected the money from the several states, administer the massive quarantine centers, with the view to extirpating the disease.

4. The federal government should pass laws based on the emergency powers taken by the state in plague situations, which would among other things invoke the authority to administer tests to suspected addicts, so as to determine whether an individual is addicted.

5. Addicts should then be separated into two general groups: those who desire to be cured, and those who do not. The Synanon and the Daytop treatments, already extensively tested, should be emulated for those in the latter category. The former should also be sequestered.

6. The drug methadone should be widely experimented with as a palliative. Preliminary results have been highly successful. The methadone alternative is not properly speaking a cure, in that addicts continue to need a daily dose of a drug, however beneficent, in order to eliminate narcotic-hunger. However, the methadone drug does not appear to have significant harmful side-effects, and therefore should be indulged, even as caffein is indulged as a substitute for alcohol.

7. It is undesirable to specify, in anticipation of hard studies conducted by experts who can bring together knowledge of available facilities, physical, medical, psychiatric, and other, exactly, and in detail, how to proceed. It need merely be repeated and repeated again that (1) addiction is a contagious disease; (2) that it has reached plague proportions; and (3) that it has graduated into a social, indeed a federal responsibility; so that we correctly look to the central government to use its unique authority to protect us, even as it would in case of plague.

I have mentioned the uses to which my suggestion for quarantining addicts were quickly put by Mr. Lindsay, and then Mr. Beame. In February 4, 1966, Governor Rockefeller went to the state legislature and asked for the power to quarantine drug addicts for a period of three years.[23]

The other candidates:

Lindsay—says: "The solution to drug addiction will not be found in the prisons; it will be found in the hospitals." Urges crackdown on pushers; the construction of a comprehensive New York City hospital for drug addiction and more rehabilitation centers. Op-

23. Although his reasoning did not rest on the insight that narcotics addiction is contagious.

poses administering drugs to addicts. Proposes extension of methadone experiment.

Beame—says: "Take the profit motive out of the narcotics system" by setting up Department of Narcotics Treatment Centers in
each borough. Proposes empowering selected city hospitals to administer drugs to addicts, with psychiatrists and social workers
engaged in rehabilitation; establishing a Narcotics Advisory Board,
a federal narcotics hospital in the city, and setting strict sentences
for pushers.

10. The Key Is Experimentation

Transit and Traffic

October 27, 1965

There are any number of proposals kicking around to increase the
facilities for automobiles entering New York City. These are of two
kinds: (a) parking areas within the heart of Manhattan, and (b)
parking areas along the city's borders, especially where the tunnels
empty and the bridges touch ground. We oppose the first, for the
reason that experience shows that the demand always exceeds the
facilities; that to construct X facilities for more cars to come into the
heart of Manhattan, will result in X plus Y cars coming into Manhattan. Facilities of the second kind are less objectionable provided they
are not so abundant as to result in clogging up the entrances into
the city.

The only way to move large numbers of people into Manhattan is
by the use of rapid transit facilities. An example of the physical problem: five square feet are needed in a subway car in order to accommodate someone coming into New York. Six hundred square feet
are needed to accommodate someone coming into New York by automobile (if he drives at moderate speeds); 1200 square feet if he is
to be permitted to drive 60 mph on the public throughways. However,
existing rapid transit facilities are overcrowded during the rush hours,
particularly between Queens and Manhattan.

The traffic problem within Manhattan is a major menace to commerce, to convenience, and to morale. Experience suggests that the
elimination of as few as 10,000 to 20,000 private automobiles from
Manhattan, a mere 2 to 3 per cent, would materially alleviate the
traffic problem, as witness the decongestion during the several days
this spring when 10,000 taxis disappeared during the strike.

Experience suggests that for every private vehicle entering New
York, one potential tourist or shopper is deterred from entering New

York. There ought, then, to be a net advantage to New York's commerce in discouraging the kind of congestion that keeps people away from the city.

New York City ought to be convenient primarily to New Yorkers—who work here, live here, and pay the costs of the roads and the costs of the public facilities.

The regulation of traffic coming into New York City poses legal problems which are not, however, insuperable.

To discourage out-of-city traffic from coming in over the toll bridges and tunnels would appear to violate the indentures on the basis of which bond-holders were lured into making investments in these facilities. However, it does not follow that even to raise the rates substantially would result in decreasing the total revenues. More likely, it would cause doubling up in automobiles entering the city. The average passenger-occupancy per car entering New York is 1.7. It is easy to see that if twice as many people could be persuaded to use the same car, and each car were required to pay more than twice the existing rate, revenues would increase, not decrease.

There remain the Constitutional and the New York legislative problems. Article 1, Section 8 of the Constitution grants exclusive powers to the Congress of the United States to regulate interstate commerce. New York City, in order to restrain out-of-state cars, would need to petition Congress for such authority as is needed to cope with the existing problem. It being manifest that New York City's purpose in doing so is not to impede commerce but to promote it; not to penalize visitors from out of state, but to facilitate their passage through the city, it is unlikely that Congress would balk at granting New York powers so elementary to its self-protection. As regards traffic flowing into the city limits from New York State, it would be necessary, under New York State laws, to demonstrate that the proposed toll is reasonably related to the cost of providing the facilities being charged to extra-territorial motorists. That demonstration should not be hard to make, considering the heavy financial costs to New York City of providing streets, road maintenance, road clearance, lights, police, transit expediters, etc. Alternatively, state legislation would be needed to confirm, or grant, New York City's authority.

Proposals:

1. *The key is experimentation.* Private automobiles registered outside the city limits of New York should be discouraged from entering Manhattan during the business hours. All channels leading into Manhattan should charge tolls to all cars whose license plates are from outside the city limits. A preliminary charge of $1 should be

levied, and should be raised, if necessary, sufficient to diminish the flow of cars by ten thousand units, or more if necessary. These tolls should be suspended after 7:00 in the evening, until 8:00 in the morning, and altogether during Saturdays and Sundays.

2. One lane on each bridge and one lane in the Holland or the Lincoln Tunnel should be reserved for express buses coming into the city. Passengers should be given free tokens good on any bus or subway to take them from the point of disembarkation in Manhattan to their destination. The express buses might, or might not, take care of the overflow from Queens. If not, an additional tunnel would have to be built.

3. Between 30th Street and 60th Street, an experiment should be launched permitting truck deliveries of nonperishable goods on staggered days: *e.g.,* on odd-numbered streets, Monday and Wednesday; on even-numbered streets on Tuesday and Friday. Thursday might, for the time being, be open to deliveries on all streets, because (a) Thursday is the heaviest shopping day; and because (b) the success of the alternate-day rule could be gauged by comparing the flow of traffic on other weekdays with the flow on Thursdays.

4. The Transit Authority should be required to charge transportation fees sufficient to pay the cost of operating the city's subways and buses. New York City politicians have deluded the public into believing that in fact it pays only 15 cents per ride. In fact the people pay, in their capacity as taxpayers, the full cost of the rides they take on buses and subways. Proposals to subsidize the subways from excess funds accumulated by the toll bridges are irresponsible because (a) the transfer of such excess revenues is illegal; and (b) even if it were not illegal, the subsidy from accumulated surpluses would be exhausted in a year. It does no service to the taxpayer to give him a ride on the subway for 15 cents and then to add taxes to his milk, bread, and cigarettes. Subway fares and bus fares in Cleveland, Washington, St. Louis, Milwaukee, Los Angeles, Philadelphia, Detroit, Baltimore, Houston, and Chicago are at twenty-five cents per ride. The New Yorker must be informed of the hallucination of the cheaper fare. The price of public transportation should rise sufficiently to meet the cost of providing it. However, this cost could and should be considerably less than the raw figures suggest: if (a) the overhead of operating the buses and subways were reduced by effecting efficiencies in management, and reducing the political overhead; and (b) a single labor union (the TWU) were deprived of the monopoly stranglehold by which it exacts wages in excess of the going market wage for workers of equivalent skills; and deprived of its powers to prevent progress through automation. There is no reason

why the white collar worker, the janitor, the elevator operator should pay the cost of subway fares that reflect subsidies for transit operators, merely because Mr. Quill has the power to strike the transit facilities of New York. The increase in the use of the public facilities, resulting from a heavier toll of out-of-town facilities, should increase revenues, resulting in a lower transit fare than would otherwise be necessary.

5. The impoverished members of the community should be given free bus and subway tokens. It is preferable to subsidize them directly in the use of rapid transit facilities than to conceal the true cost of the use of those facilities from the average New Yorker, who is indirectly paying the cost of the subsidy.

6. A few minor annoyances: Automobiles with diplomatic license plates should not be immunized from traffic and parking regulations. The federal government has recently served notice on the various embassies that their diplomatic immunities do not extend to protection from municipal traffic regulation. The law should be vigorously enforced to prevent such demoralizing blatancies as double-parking in narrow streets by cars attached to foreign embassies and legations.

7. There are not enough taxis in New York, considering the present congestion. It is conceivable that if the traffic cleared, the existing taxi supply would be sufficient to cope with the demand. If not, several steps should be taken: (a) taxis should be permitted, as in Washington, D.C., to take multiple passengers; (b) more taxi medallions should be issued; and, in any case, (c) arrangements should be made to make it possible to reserve a taxi by telephone, in order to cope with the problem of the crippled, and of those who need to arrange for a taxi at a designated time and place.

8. I also recommend the construction in Manhattan of a "Bikeway," to run, to begin with, down the length of Second Avenue, from 125th Street to 1st Street. The Bikeway, twenty feet wide, would run twenty feet above ground, on both sides of the street. Crosstown spurs would feed into it from 125th Street, 91st Street, 56th Street, 35th Street, 12th Street, and 6th Street. If the Bikeway proves popular and economical, an additional north-south bikeway should be constructed down the length of Seventh Avenue. Ramps would permit bicyclists to mount the Bikeway at every block. At every block, parking areas would swell out from the Bikeway to permit bicyclists to park their bicycles and chain them to posts. Crossways would be built to correspond with every IRT subway stop, permitting bicyclists to make U-turns.

The purposes of the Bikeway are (a) to ease the traffic problem; (b) to provide New Yorkers with an opportunity to exercise and so to stimulate their health; and (c) to provide pleasure for those who take pleasure from the sport and desire to turn it to functional use in going to and from work, to shop, to go to movies and theaters, etc.

The estimated cost of the initial Bikeway down Second Avenue and the six crosstown spurs, is $14 million. Users should be charged fifteen cents for access to the Bikeway. Bike parking should be free. At the average rate of bicycle travel (15 mph), a bicyclist could travel one hundred city blocks in 20 minutes. If 50,000 persons used the Bikeway 250 times per year, amortization should be possible in ten years.

I had the devil's own time with this paper, objections to this-or-that recommendation from all sides. There was: the Constitutional problem (Article I gives Congress exclusive power to regulate inter-state traffic), and how we would walk around that; the problem of the merchants who want their deliveries every day and who are frightened at the prospect of discouraging transient shoppers; the unions, who want round-the-clock access to every point in the city for their truck drivers and delivery men; the bondholders, who frown at the suggestion of any diminution in the tolls collected by the bridges; the working population, which frowns at the prospect of raising the subway fare. The paper was an effort, successful I (naturally) like to think, to conciliate those differences while still insisting that something *can* be done about the traffic, *i.e.*, that it is not in the category of unattainable objectives (like, *e.g.*, ideal race relations). But *ex hypothesi*, nothing can be done about the traffic problem except by interfering with existing habits—which have resulted in the existing chaos; which generality, I suppose, reduces to something like the rule that in order to do something about anything, it is necessary to do something. I found that such an approach to a city problem, intellectually axiomatic, had become almost revolutionary in its implications: to be sure among political liberals, who tended to weigh, always, the bloc-factor; but to a startling extent also among conservatives. I sat fascinated among my brethren as a few of them advanced reasons for finding *some* excuse for pledging, *e.g.*, that the subway fare would not be raised. Fascinated that the reasons should be advanced, but fascinated also that I was tempted by them. Fascinated that I found myself voluptuously fingering highfalutin justifications for overriding the venerable presumptions—when there was, really, no finally plausible reason for doing so.

For instance: why not argue that the rapid transit facilities of a city are merely an extension of the non-rapid transit facilities, *e.g.*, the sidewalks; and who is about (other than, say, Ayn Rand) to suggest that tolls be set up to collect a copper every time you walk out on the street and use the sidewalk? The argument—and here is the fiercest aspect of the problem—is *not* altogether implausible.

Or again: if a city reasons that its prosperity increases in ratio to the number of persons it induces into its stalls—isn't there an argument here for absorbing the transportation cost of those who are disposed to come into the city—always, of course, within reason?

Or again: If the principal obstruction to free-flowing commerce within New York is the traffic congestion within its streets, isn't it sensible to induce people to come into New York other than in automobiles and—*pace* Murray Kempton—isn't the profit consideration the foremost people-mover we know of; *i.e.*, if subways and buses were absolutely free, wouldn't that discourage people from the relatively expensive alternative of arriving in their own automobiles?

I did conclude that, philosophically, the case is stronger for abolishing rapid transit fares altogether than for pegging them at a price that shields their actual cost. But other considerations stand in the way of the free-fare solution, considerations that are biologically related to the presumptions I listed at the beginning of the chapter. The fact of the matter is that the subways and the buses need to be paid for, and questions both of equity and of clarity arise: Who? Who should pay for them? The obvious answer is, by experience, also the most reliable; in this instance, that the public-subsidy principle needs to be opposed as close as possible to its roots, or else the justification becomes harder and harder to formulate for opposing it anywhere this side of the totally socialized economy built around Marxian postulates, which have proved economically inefficient and socially totalitarian. The argument can be made for charging the identical fare for a ten-block ride on the subway as for a ten-mile ride, on the grounds that the cost of administering differential fares probably would exceed the additional revenue (although in London they apparently calculate otherwise). But to charge *nothing* for the fare is of course tantamount to charging everyone for the fare; and to charge everyone for the subways, in a broad-based tax situation such as exists in New York and in almost all other major cities (the era is long gone when the maharajahs or the bankers pay the principal cost of public welfare), is to raise the general overhead of life even as a mobile is raised, all its parts maintaining their relative distance from one another, but all of them nevertheless ending up higher than they began. And the result is to disguise the true cost of things, on the basis of which intelligent, purposeful, and individuated economic decisions can be made. To distribute, for instance, the entire annual cost ($333 million) of the operation of the transit system on the shoulders of all New Yorkers would mean a fresh tax, or a higher rate of tax; whether on property, on sales, on income, on whatever. What would be the consequences of such an added tax on the general economic behavior (and derivatively, the noneconomic behavior) of the residents of the city? No one of course can tell; which is itself a towering consideration. It must however be acknowledged that there would indeed be *some* effects, inasmuch as economic factors do affect human behavior. When the New York City sales tax was raised by one per cent the confidently anticipated extra tax revenue of about $100 million clocked in at just better than one-half—because economic man went out and maneuvered in his own self-defense, in this case by routing an estimated one billion dollars' worth of his spending outside New York City, with grievous consequences for New York City merchants and, derivatively, for the city tax-collectors. How do the planners assimilate such a datum, and move forward on the basis of it? At what point will they concede that the people have got away from them? At the point at which they begin to yap about the decline and fall of their city?

And if free subways, why not free electricity?—people have to see, don't they, in order to do business? Free water?—hygiene is socially important, isn't it? Free telephones?—indispensable to commerce. And of course one runs up against Mr. Friedman's axiom about the free lunch: everybody is busy paying everybody else for their free perquisites. The resulting insulation from economic truth not only tends to disorder harmonious economic adaptations to spontaneously arising needs; but tends, also, to induce that semi-ignorance which, increasingly, gives rise to the politics of unreason, which indeed is the politics within which most modern politicians prosper. The federal government can, of course, more easily than a municipality, get away with economic mystifications—thanks to its enormous resources, its authority to run endless deficits, and the impenetrability of its budget (an item as large as two billion dollars for the Central Intelligence Agency remains to this day invisible in the interstices of the hundred billion dollar whole). In a mere city it is different. John Lindsay pledged and pledged and repledged that he would not raise the subway fare. Within three months of taking office, *The New York Times* was reporting (March 7), "The Mayor also hinted that the city's 15-cent transit fare might have to be raised." (It was—on July 5.)

The transit crisis in New York struck me, and still does, as the crowning symbol of democratic impotence. More brilliantly so than any other problem. The most thoughtful men do not yet know for sure what it is that drives men to crime, or to narcotics, or what it is that keeps children from desiring to learn to read. But everyone knows why one cannot move around in New York City during certain hours;

and it is unrealistic to hope that those other, profounder problems can be advanced upon, if such others as traffic—concrete, fathomable —cannot be. And yet—as the saying goes—it gets worse and worse. For the lack of will. And that lack of will derives from the fear of the consequences of alienating any large, or powerful, voting bloc. It was hard enough for me, with nothing to lose, and convinced from the outset of the general reliability of a set of coordinated assumptions, to argue down an occasional criticism from within my own group: how very much more difficult for a Beame, or a Lindsay, to blurt out the truth, which is that people have got to pay the cost of what they demand to have from the government.

A footnote about my Bikeway. It happened that it was the last of my series of proposals, and my timing was obviously defective. I have been told that its release, at the eleventh hour, finally convinced a great many voters—I have heard the figure put as high as the legendary 100,000—that my campaign was, finally evaluated, frivolous. The implicit criticism being that with so many grave things to talk about, one should not talk about bicycles, bicycles being built for two, and that sort of thing. One member of the high command of the Conservative Party all but got on his knees begging me to leave the bicycles for another year. I obstinately made the point that (a) the idea was itself first-rate (it is, I think); (b) that it does no harm for a candidate—particularly a Conservative—to have an off-beat idea or two, and that so far as one could tell, it didn't necessarily mean the end of the world—hadn't John Lindsay come out for floating swimming pools back in August? And (c) what-the-hell, I was going to say what I thought ought to be said. I gather that I showed, when I released the proposal at a press conference, a sense of knowing that some would think I had taken up the fiddle while the city burned. "One of its [the transit paper's] elements," wrote Murray Kempton, "is an overhead bikeway down Second Avenue. 'You could get from 125th St. to First St., [the candidate said], if anyone should want to get there, in 20 minutes.' 'Shall we,' a visitor asked, 'call this the Buckley Bikeway?' 'Yes,' Buckley answered. 'My finest hour.' The smile was wild shared delight. 'I did have trouble getting it through the Conservative Party bureaucracy.' "

The Conservative Party bureaucracy, I hasten to correct myself, was not by any means unanimous in its opposition, although as I have noted, a prominent member of the Party was heavy-laden with grief and premonitions and, I now agree, its release was miserably ill-timed. One should not end a campaign with grace notes. I remember the evening of that press conference, which I spent at the home of an old Negro election-district boss in Bedford-Stuyvesant, former Pullman porter of indefatigable political energy and utterly total recall, who had promised to deliver me the entire Bronx, or whatever, and had got together his family and a few lieutenants. We sat about the living room while his warm and hospitable wife in the kitchen below sent up a torrent of sandwiches, cakes, drinks, cigars, as the old gentleman rambled around in his copious memory telling us of this and that. His daughter-in-law, a sophisticated, slightly cynical, more than slightly bemused nurse's aid from a local hospital, told me at one point: "You know, I was for John Lindsay until today." "What," I asked, delighted, "did John Lindsay do today?" "It was that ridiculous bicycle scheme," she said. I paused. But only for a moment, let the devil record. "That *was* ridiculous, wasn't it," I exclaimed— changing the subject, and concluding that as of that moment, I had really and truly become a politician, and how would I formulate *that* sin at my next session with my confessor?

Lindsay—Proposes building new East Side subway line, extending subway lines in Brooklyn and Queens, and building new rapid transit system in Staten Island; consolidating many transportation agencies; air-conditioning new lines; retaining 15-cent fare; computerizing traffic control; added cross-town express streets; overhauling subway stations to increase cleanliness, comfort and conveniences; expanding Meter Maid force.

Beame—Wants to channel Triborough Bridge and Tunnel Authority surpluses into Transit Authority to save 15-cent fare; to seek state subsidies, similar to those received by commuter railroads; to install electronically controlled systems; to expand network of peripheral parking facilities near bridges and tunnels; to build additional garage space; strict enforcement of double parking rules.

VIII.

The Candidate and "His Supporters"

It was over and over again alleged during the campaign that "Buckley supporters" were rowdies, hoodlums, vandals, etc. The charge was first elaborated on September 9, in a front-page story in the *World-Telegram* with headline stretching across the entire width of the front page—"RIGHTISTS HARASS LINDSAY." And the story:

> Rep. John Lindsay and his campaign workers through the city are being victimized by "vicious right-wing hate tactics," a source close to the Republican-Liberal candidate disclosed today. Windows in volunteer storefronts have been smashed, telephone lines have been slashed, mail has been opened and destroyed, and several aides have received threatening letters, the source said. In addition, volunteers distributing pamphlets on the street have been "roughed up," telephone lines have been "jammed" with thousands of calls, and "impostors" are infiltrating the Lindsay ranks. . . . The harassment campaign actually began in June when Lindsay himself received threatening telephone calls. The source said one caller warned: "John Lindsay must be killed. We have to kill him." . . .

Etc., etc.

I confess I did not take the story seriously, reminding myself that it was probably as accurate as the report of what I had said to the police at the Communion breakfast a few months earlier.[1] But I was told the newspapers would expect a comment and so sped off to headquarters and issued a brief reply:

> Mr. John Lindsay, through his agents, has in effect accused the Conservative Party of superintending a program of malicious har-

---

1. The author of the *World-Telegram* story resigned from his newspaper after the election to become press chief for Mayor John Lindsay, who had not, after all, been killed by right-extremists.

228

assment of him and his campaigners. He alleges that windows in his volunteer storefronts have been smashed, . . . that his mail has been opened and destroyed, that impostors (by which I assume he means Republicans) are infiltrating the Lindsay ranks, that large quantities of mail have been misdirected by espionage, that planted typists have made intentional mistakes which have fouled up distribution lists, and that anonymous gentry have telephoned threats on his life.

I decline to go through the motions of disavowing these activities, because to do so under the circumstances would be to suggest that they are in some way mine to avow or disavow. Mr. Lindsay, according to his complaint, was accosted by one placard that accused him of being a Communist. It is no more necessary for the Conservative Party to repudiate vandalism, blackmail, and intimidation, than it is for Mr. Lindsay to disavow the charge that he is a Communist. The Conservative Party of New York would never impute pro-Communism to Mr. Lindsay, and only regrets that he has permitted his agents to impute vandalism to us.

There are crackpots in New York, as there are crackpots everywhere. They do not pick exclusively on Mr. Lindsay. As regards threats against Mr. Lindsay's life, I will match him threat for threat.[2] . . . As regards eavesdropping, I register herewith my compliments to the doll who listened from the adjacent table to everything I said to and heard from my staff at dinner the other night at a restaurant, and then, as we rose to go, sweetly announced herself as John Lindsay's personal aide.

John Lindsay has nothing at all to fear from crackpots. He has a great deal to fear from rational and intelligent men. Mr. Lindsay complains that Conservative Party workers have been assigned to "follow Lindsay volunteers" and "destroy pamphlets Lindsay workers have distributed." I herewith call on all Conservative Party workers to distribute Lindsay literature alongside my own, confident that anyone who contrasts the two will vote the Conservative Party ticket in November.

That tended to quiet things down for a little while, but in due course the charges were raised again, and again and again; and there was the celebrated incident at Queens College. The three candidates were scheduled to speak at intervals of one hour. I spoke first, and left. Lindsay appeared. He was, apparently, treated roughly—it was on that occasion, waiting for the hall to quiet, that he announced, "I remember waiting for an hour for politeness to set in at the Cow

2. I had about four; and, at the suggestion of the police, agreed, during October, to be accompanied on my public rounds by a plainclothesman. I had agreed to the same thing during a fortnight in April, after the Communion breakfast, an anonymous caller having announced his intention of blowing up *National Review's* offices "within 48 hours." But there were no physical assaults on me during the campaign.

Palace last year" (he was referring to the bad-mannered reception given to Governor Nelson Rockefeller by the galleries at the Republican Convention in 1964). "Lindsay made several attempts to be heard, finally seized a rare moment of silence to say, 'I had planned to allow this meeting one hour. So I will stand here for at least that hour if you do not permit me to speak without interruption before then.'" (The report is by John Dreiske of the Chicago *Sun Times*.) "He did stand there for 40 minutes before the hecklers finally, grudgingly permitted him to make a short address. Then he left the hall with the Buckleyites' taunts ringing in his ears."

Now this was the identical meeting—Queens College, October 8—which the New York *Post* had also covered (the other New York papers were on strike); and its headline and lead were, "STUDENTS JEER CANDIDATES AT QUEENS RALLY. . . . Mayoral candidates John Lindsay and William F. Buckley Jr. Friday night faced a jeering, unruly Queens College audience at a meeting which appeared almost evenly split between supporters of the two men." There was no further mention, anywhere that I noticed, of the fact of my having been heckled. On the other hand, it became a part of the stigmata of John Lindsay, beginning on that occasion, that, for daring to fight for the future of New York, he was regularly and noisily abhorred by right-wingers, at all public occasions.

Now Lindsay did speak a great deal more often than I did. Moreover, my public appearances were mostly at Conservative Party rallies, so that Lindsay probably did, in the course of the campaign, hear more cat-calls than I did, though I heard a number. Even so, the inferences he and so many others drew, to the effect that Conservatives were uniquely bad-mannered, are logically unwarranted.

On another occasion Lindsay and I appeared, *seriatim*, before representatives of the Parents and Taxpayers Association, which was as clearly predisposed in favor of me as, say, the Liberal Party Convention was predisposed in favor of Lindsay. The *Tribune* reported on October 15:

> John Lindsay faced the most hostile audience of his mayoral campaign last night. For 15 minutes, 800 people sat silent at the PAT meeting he addressed in the conservative heart of Queens. Then they erupted with boos, hisses, and shouted heckling when he mentioned his proposal for a police civilian review board. "Down with Lindsay—Shoot him in the back!" screamed a heckler as the Republican-Liberal candidate left the auditorium. Orange Buckley buttons were flaunted [an odd choice of words: how does one flaunt a button? By wearing it on one's nose?] by two-thirds of the audience. . . . Before the meeting, held in the auditorium of Richmond

Hill High School, 16 policemen with two motorcycles and eight bullhorns had been assigned. Outside the hall Shelly Byalick, of 1156 W. 10th St., Brooklyn, a William Buckley Jr. supporter said: "Here's the gang that's for John Judas Lindsay."

And the headline:

"LINDSAY BEFORE PAT—A 'JUDAS' "

Connoisseurs will recognize the technique—a single man, outside the hall, name and address thoughtfully provided, used the word "Judas": and, hesto presto, the entire organization is given the responsibility for that evaluation: ("LINDSAY BEFORE PAT: A 'JUDAS' ").

A skillful reporter will note, for atmosphere's sake, the activities of the crackpot, the eccentric, the emotionally possessed; but a conscientious reporter will carefully integrate these data so as not to convey, if such was not the case, that the crackpot's was the voice of the audience. Booing and hissing is pretty conventional behavior in America, particularly at political meetings: it is the means, the only one democratically available to everyone regardless of race, color, or creed, of expressing disapproval of a particular point—though the tradition is that having booed, one quiets down and listens, at least until the candidate provokes a fresh boo. Individualized and highly anomalous protests are more often recorded by newspaper reporters if they are amusing ("Lindsay is an oxymoron!") than if they are merely sick ("Down with Lindsay—Shoot him in the back!"). And the reason is obvious. There is a large public appetite for, and tolerance of, political high jinks, but very little for public meanness. A single individual acting perversely can, if the spotlight is focused on him, contaminate an entire meeting. Such an individual, moreover, may be acting on his own perverse impulses: or—the idea of the *agent provocateur* is clearly not beyond the scope of the imagination, for instance, of the inventive Mr. Saron (see chapter VI)—in the political interests of the individual he is ostensibly berating. "All right," Senator Kennedy is reputed to have said in the closing days of the campaign to a few friends, "suppose I am a Republican candidate for Mayor. Just how much would I pay to get myself booed in Wall Street in the last week of the campaign? And those Buckley people do it for Lindsay for nothing!"[3]

---

3. Quoted by Murray Kempton, October 29, 1965. As a sophomore at Yale University (1947), together with a small band of the faithful (not including John Lindsay), I attended a Wallace for President rally at the New Haven Arena bearing placards rendering variations on the theme: "We're For Peace: Give Russia the Atom Bomb." My conscience is in repose about this episode because it was clear to me and my companions that the Communists were (as, for instance, *The New York Times* subsequently admitted), running the Wallace campaign, and that the

In England, eccentrics are universally recognized as such. Transcending faction, they are expected to home in on all public political meetings. They are largely ignored, except as instruments on which the speakers can hone their wit. A recent and typical account in the London *Times*, for instance, suggests the superior perspective of the British press in their treatment of such eccentrics, however malevolent their doctrines. Colin Jordan is England's George Lincoln Rockwell. Yet Jordan's activities are generally treated with that benign toleration that expresses the society's self-assurance. The *Times*, whose reputation is that of the stuffiest newspaper in the world (page one was until recently devoted exclusively to classified advertisements), remarks in its coverage of a speech before a predominantly Conservative audience by the Labour Foreign Secretary Gordon Walker, running for election in his constituency, that Jordan stood up and performed a Hitler salute, that thereupon. someone threw a lighted firecracker onstage, and a general scrap ensued. "Mr. Jordan and his acolytes were [eventually] . . . pulled out, still struggling, like stubborn teeth being extracted. One man took off from six feet away and dived head first into the melee as enthusiastically as a spring-bok loosed forward, going into a maul. The leader of the Nazis, bleeding profusely from mouth and nose, disappeared from the hall, feet not touching the ground, trying to shout 'Heil Hitler.' The platform party reassembled apprehensively. Mr. George Brown [the Minister of Economic Development], with wagging finger and obvious enjoyment, dealt massively with the interrupters, isolating them, getting them to make their points singly, and then shooting them down in flames. . . . The police made no arrests." Neither the *Times* nor any other English newspaper, headlined, "Gordon Walker Denounced by Hitlerites at Conservative Gathering."

Although in its editorial pages *The New York Times* made frequent references to the base nature of Conservative voters, its own news stories greeted with refreshing perspective and skepticism the routine business of heckling, the charges of vandalism, etc. A story early in September (September 4, 1965) by Mr. Eric Pace actually used the word "enliven" in its headline: "Cookies and Song Enliven City Race. Slogans Also Are a Fringe Benefit of the Campaign." "Supporters of William F. Buckley Jr.," the story went on, after discussing the eating habits of the principal candidates for the Democratic nomination, "plump the slogan 'Buckley for Mayor; Lindsay for Blintzes,' charging that John V. Lindsay's eating habits are meant for political consump-

---

placards in question were candid expressions of the implicit objectives of the Wallace movement. But I could see the mischievous leverage a crypto-adversary can apply at a public meeting by being much, much more royal than the king.

tion"—a pleasant pun, and—note—no labored attempt to insinuate anti-Semitism, or any other grand malevolence into the slogans. Pace went on:

> Mr. Buckley, in challenging Mr. Lindsay to a public debate, [has] said "I would even undertake, so as not to distract him from his principal occupation as a campaigner, to provide Mr. Lindsay, during the commercial breaks of any program on which we appeared together, with a photographer and a blintz."
>
> Food presents candidates with more than digestive perils; a faux pas while eating can cost votes. Campaign staff members are haunted by the legend (denied by those concerned) that Robert F. Kennedy, on being given a pizza during his senatorial campaign, publicly asked for a fork. . . .
>
> More exotic than the cookies, however, are some recent campaign slogans. Overlooking Bryant Park, a 30-yard Lindsay billboard echoes the film "Mary Poppins" with "John Lindsay is Supercalifragilistic Expialidocious." Listeners to Greek radio programs will soon be urged: "Psifisate ton (vote for) Abe Beame."
>
> The legend on Lindsay subway posters ("He is fresh and everyone else is tired") has spawned irreverent versions. At least one poster has been altered to read—in apparent reference to Mr. Lindsay's prosperous parentage—"He is rich and everyone else is poor."
>
> It has been proposed that Mr. Beame, who is 5 feet 2 inches tall, adopt the slogan: "He is short and everyone else is tall." One pro-Buckley placard read "John Lindsay is an Oxymoron."[4] Webster defines "oxymoron" as "a combination for epigrammatic effect of contradictory or incongruous words."

But this was a light interlude in a campaign which sought, in its description of eccentric behavior, always to be conscripting the eccentrics, or the crackpots, in order to make points in behalf of, or against, someone or other. The *Times*, after Mr. Pace's amiable report, ran a feature story on the headquarters of the three candidates. The picture of Lindsay headquarters showed, on the wall, a Buckley poster, inked in with a Hitler moustache and hair-do, wearing a swastika armband. No comment, no fuss. One can imagine the furor if the Buckley headquarters had shown a Lindsay poster with a hammer and sickle draped about his neck.

It was essential to the effect desired by Lindsay's supporters to stress and restress that the Conservatives were hoodlums, haters. A Chicago columnist carried the word abroad:

> As I approached a gray station wagon allocated to the press for

4. I had at some previous point referred to the "oxymoronic backing of Lindsay by the Liberal and the Republican Parties."

the Lindsay campaign in New York last week, I asked a campaign aide:

"What's that smear on the door and window?"

"Eggs," was the reply. "Those Buckley kids are always throwing eggs at any car carrying Lindsay signs."

I asked if he was quite sure the egg-throwers were supporters of William F. Buckley Jr., John V. Lindsay's ultraconservative opponent.

Oh, yes, the aide replied, the Buckleyites had identifying literature with them.

There was much evidence that the Buckleyites were really a far-out group, behaviorwise. By and large they were, like their leader, young, highly educated, extremely literate and non-beatnik but very smarty-pants. And, to put it mildly, ill-mannered and rude.

They even went beyond rudeness on several occasions and inflicted physical injury on Lindsay. Several Buckleyites made it a point to maneuver directly up to Lindsay and then stab at him with the pins of Buckley campaign buttons.

Lindsay aides told me that this stabbing business penetrated Lindsay's clothing several times and resulted in minor bleeding with the possibility of infection ever-present.

Another technique by the Buckley partisans caused distress at Lindsay meetings. Soon a pattern developed which showed clearly there was a prearranged schedule of heckling extending right up to election day.

The Buckley people marked a single Lindsay meeting each day and made detailed plans for attendance in considerable numbers. The forays were organized with detailed instructions for the type of heckling, duration, language to be used, and methods of distributing literature. . . .[5]

The congestion of utter nonsense in this column and in other reports prompts me to refocus on the running charges of Conservative misbehavior which I had so airily dismissed during the campaign.

1. How can one tell if such charges are true? A deeply serious question. After the original *World-Telegram* story charging vandalism, rape, and regicide, the Conservative Party took the precaution of instructing its captains around the city to telephone to police headquarters to inquire whether any complaints had actually been lodged —it being, after all, against the law to smash windows and cut telephone lines and threaten mayhem and murder. There was not a single complaint on record. The allegation that the heckling of Lindsay was a concerted affair done under Conservative supervision was palpably ridiculous. Nothing could hurt us more than such heckling (as Bobby

5. Chicago *Sun Times*, November 5, 1965, columnist John Dreiske.

Kennedy would note—see p. 231); and it was therefore obviously not in the interest of the Conservative Party, ethics aside, to stimulate such politically disadvantageous publicity.

What then do you do when a reporter asks you to comment on this or that act of verbal or physical hoodlumism attributed to your supporters which, if in fact it happened, is manifestly inimical to your own interests? As I said earlier, to disavow can have the psychological effect of suggesting that you are disavowing your own—so that a disavowal is itself incriminating. John Lindsay had a fleeting encounter with the problem when the *Times* reported (October 22), that "The police are investigating reports that a car or cars are touring predominantly Jewish areas, with a loudspeaker blaring: 'Don't vote for Beame; vote for Lindsay. To hell with the Jews.' . . . A Lindsay aide," the story reported, "was 'furious' about the new incidents and [said] that they 'fit a pattern of harassment that has been going on for several months. . . . The aide [get this] declined to blame the reported incidents on any specific group. [And this:] In recent weeks, however, Mr. Lindsay and his aides have complained specifically about some of the tactics employed by the followers of Mr. Buckley, whose politics are right-wing." Anyone who has eyes to see, or half a brain to reason with, is herewith cordially invited to make the elision: that Buckley supporters were manning the (alleged) soundtrucks. I say alleged, because none was ever chased down, notwithstanding "police investigation" sought by Lindsay's infuriated aide.

The more subtle point is, of course, that misbehavior from which you yourself may concededly shrink might nonetheless be the logical consequence of positions you take. As, for instance, it was here and there maintained that the Freedom for Dirty Speech movement at Berkeley was a natural offspring of the anarchic movement sponsored by Mario Savio and his Free Speech Movement. At this point, reason, conscience, and self-restraint are all that we have to rely upon, the burden resting on those who postulate a nexus between a sane position and an insane extension of it to make their demonstration. The liberal fanatic will contend that anyone opposed to compulsory busing is subjectively anti-Negro. A conservative fanatic will contend that anyone who is in favor of abolishing the House Committee on Un-American Activities is subjectively pro-Communist (see below). The burden falls, as most burdens do, on the lords spiritual of the community. They will vocally disavow, if they are doing their duty, or fail to disavow, if they are neglecting their duty, fanatical or opportunistic extrapolations.

2. How, in purely human terms, can one expect a minority to act toward someone who has publicly questioned its motives and derided

its intelligence? John Lindsay appears before the Parents and Tax-payers Association, whose principal official Mrs. Rosemary Gunning is known to them all as a deeply humane and intelligent woman utterly lacking in race prejudice. She is candidate for President of the City Council on the Buckley ticket. Lindsay has several times labeled Buckley supporters as racists, hoodlums, and reactionaries. What kind of treatment can he expect? Mr. Paul O'Dwyer said on the radio (See chapter VI) that he was greatly surprised that at a meeting of Negro community leaders, given my (alleged) lack of sympathy for Negro objectives, I had been treated courteously. Never mind that I had never evidenced that lack of sympathy: O'Dwyer's observation is theoretically interesting. As is the question, What kind of a reception could Nelson Rockefeller, addressing galleries of people against whom he had for months been railing as cretins and worse, reasonably expect from them? It is easy to say that ideally you should stand still and be polite and attentive when addressed and cozzened by the same man who that same morning berated you as a racist and hater. I grant that Rockefeller—and, later, Lindsay—*should* have had respectful attention; but it is unrealistic to expect that a typical audience com-posed of flesh and blood regularly whiplashed by them would behave, on being confronted by them, like Coldstream Guards being reviewed by the Queen.

And, finally (3) I am fascinated by the ease with which a casual remark by a single supporter can be manipulated for image-creating purposes. A short, bright, engaging review of a day-in-the-life of each of the candidates appeared *seriatim* in *The New Yorker* during Oc-tober. It was my turn. I walk (the writer records) to the doors of the Overseas Press Club where I am scheduled to speak. "A woman . . . declares, 'I think he's very courageous.' Another woman adds, 'I like what he stands for.' 'Against welfare,' says a fourth in a tall magenta hat, 'and not making New York a haven for . . . well . . .' She says no more." Now great big grown-up people can effect the enjambement without strain. The lady in the magenta hat was anti-Negro! At a meeting with the distinguished editors of a distinguished newspaper, the dark point was explicitly raised, and I knew there was no easy answer, save the old *tu quoque* argument—which is not necessarily irrelevant. What kind of thing *do* people, taken at random, *say* when suddenly questioned about why they intend to vote for John Lindsay? Or for Abraham Beame?—Or, for that matter, for Abraham Lincoln? There are two levels at which people respond. The first is frivolous— "He's so cute," concerning, say, John Lindsay. Or—"He taught my father accounting," concerning, say, Abe Beame. Or, conceivably—

"He opposes Steve Douglas, and I can't stand Douglas," concerning, say, Abraham Lincoln.

Other replies, more generalized, will suggest extra-personal motives —indeed, will suggest a political position. But these positions, given the vernacular, are more often than not sloganized, and as such subject to the criticisms that most slogans are subject to—which however does not necessarily mean that the voter satellized by the slogan is necessarily superficial, or venal. The lady who said she didn't want New York to be made a haven for ". . ." was not necessarily anti-Negro in any racist sense. Nor was her ejaculation necessarily less thoughtful than, say, the Ph.D.'s who pickets the White House with the placard: "Stop Murdering Innocent North Vietnamese." Both suggest positions which may be infinitely complex, infinitely thoughtful; and no one can simultaneously defend the practices of democracy and maintain that it is any more wrong for the lady in the magenta hat to express herself as she did than, say, for John Lindsay to go to Nathan's publicly to eat a blintz: on the contrary, I would sooner defend the act of the former than of the latter, because the lady is not posing as a leader of men, whereas Lindsay is.

There is very often a substructure of analysis and value judgment sustaining many sloganized political ejaculations; and it is an act of snobbishness, usually tendentious, to ignore the fact. The lady in the magenta hat could very well have been thinking something like this: the Negro population of New York City (never mind for the moment *why*; any more than, for the moment, we were required in the thirties to meditate *why* the Great Depression became, in Democratic terminology, the "Hoover Depression")—is responsible for an inordinate percentage of the crime, of the broken homes, of the poverty, of the rowdyism in the schools: let's not have a municipal government which, because it is politically expedient to do so, adopts a see-no-evil, hear-no-evil attitude towards these existential verities; a government which seeks, because to flatter them as potential voters is the politically profitable thing to do, to make New York a cynosure for them; a government which lures them into coming here by the promise of lavish welfare, permissive treatment in the courts, etc. I sigh fatalistically at the improbability that the point can successfully be made, but attempt nevertheless to say that an analysis of that order is not "anti-Negro" provided the reasoning is *a priori*. If it is *a posteriori*, reasoning from crime and broken homes to Negroism, rather than from Negroism to crime and broken homes, the reasoning is racist; otherwise it is sociological. There is no denying that there are people in New York who are anti-Negro; or that there are people in New York who are anti-Semitic; or that there are people in New York who are anti-Catholic—in the racist and religious senses of the word. I inquire, rather, into the assumptions on the basis of which pejorative generalities about the nature of a candidate's constituency are arrived at. The Inquiring Photographer, a New York City institution which delivers the *vox populi* for the New York *Daily News*, asks questions of the people it interviews, the answers to which are often superficial or wrong-headed. These answers, in twenty-five words or less, are not intended to be taken as conclusive transcriptions of the interviewees' *Weltanschauungen*, but neither are they interesting merely as expressions of personality. The people's slogans, their clichés, often sit, however uneasily, or self-consciously, at the top of a structure of values and discriminations which are not lightly to be dismissed, at least not more lightly to be dismissed than the democratic system. It is easy to laugh at, or to deride, the proximate factor that brings this or that citizen finally to the decision to vote for this or that candidate; and I myself often do it. My own favorite example (reported in *The New York Times*, November 1964) is the lady in New Hampshire who, although a life-long Republican, announced finally that she would cast her vote against Goldwater. Why? she was asked by a neighbor. "Because if elected, Goldwater would take away my TV." "No, no," the neighbor remonstrated, "not *your* TV, *the* TVA." "Well, that's very reassuring," she said, "but I'm not going to take any chances." The Inquiring Photographer does not frequently call at the house of the philosopher. "Why are you a conservative?" someone once asked the late, self-effacing Richard Weaver, professor at the University of Chicago. He declined to answer: but, under relentless pressure, finally obliged: "Because conservatism is the paradigm of essences towards which the phenomenology of the world is in continuing approximation." Professor Weaver would have voted for me in New York, in 1965, along with the lady in the magenta hat: and, in an odd sort of way, very likely for the same reasons, differently grasped.

In summary: it is easy to ridicule the statements of typical voters as, often awkwardly, they stammer out the reasons for their preferences; and even easier to despair at their analyses, when they make their analyses. And it is especially easy to apply a double standard, to disdain the moral and rational powers of the one class of voters— because its choice of candidates is different from your own—and enthuse over the other—because its choice is also your choice. "Admiration," Ambrose Bierce reminds us, "is our polite recognition of another's resemblance to ourselves."

IX.

Notes (after the Fact)
from a Diary (Never Written)

1. Headquarters

August 30. We got around, finally, to opening a formal head-quarters. A cheery affair, marred by a glass partition's crashing under the weight of volunteers standing on tiptoe to listen to the fight-talks, cutting up a couple of bystanders. We were worried about the rent but managed to pay it promptly. Here all the staff meetings were held, and the press conferences, and here the volunteers came to do the mailings and coordinate their activities. Lindsay and Beame had vast spreads at the Roosevelt and Summit Hotels respectively. In mid-campaign, reporters from the *Times* did color-pieces on the three headquarters. The piece on our own, written by McClandish Phillips, was headlined:

BRIGHT, YOUNG AIDES OF BUCKLEY ARE SPIRITED, STYLISH AND WITTY

. . . Buckley-for-Mayor [ran the story] headquarters in midtown is largely populated and run by a mint-new crowd of right-wingers: young men and women who are bright, stylish, spirited, well-schooled, articulate, attractive, and easy to get along with—suggesting a sort of "New Frontier" elite of the political right.

They have wit. There is an old print at the Buckley headquarters showing lower Manhattan and New York harbor more than a century ago, with low village dwellings and great sailing ships at anchor. Beneath is a hand-lettered legend: "Artist's sketch of lower Manhattan as it would appear following implementation of William F. Buckley's plan for urban renewal." . . .

Headquarters for the Buckley campaign is Room 1003 on the tenth floor of 25 West 45th Street. A green door with a brass mail slot and a pane of cloudy glass opens into a large room flooded with fluorescent light. Much of the space is occupied by folding tables and chairs used in mailing operations.

The place is draped with red, white and blue bunting. Sandwich shop phone numbers hang near the wall coil telephone. . . .

Nearly 3 million pieces of literature will be distributed before the election. Night and day the busy hands fly, stuffing envelopes with campaign tracts in the midst of a low murmur of conversation. Hundreds of letters have to be stamped by hand. Workers lick the stamps and pat them into place. "I'll keep going until my tongue sticks to the roof of my mouth," a college-age volunteer vowed.

Jane Metze, who is 24 years old, runs the office. She is a dimpled honey blond with an oozy voice, and laughs easily. Miss Metze, who came out of St. Joseph's College in Manhattan, did volunteer work last year in a small Goldwater campaign office on Main Street in her home town, Harriman, N.Y. After the Goldwater defeat she became secretary of the local Conservative Club.

The top man in the Buckley campaign is James L. Buckley, a 1944 Yale graduate who is three years older than his 39-year-old candidate brother. He works in his office at the Catawba Corporation, the Buckley family enterprise that provides financial and administrative services to companies engaged in oil and gas ex-explorations.

James Buckley is a jaunty man with a crew cut, youthful in looks and manner, with some of his brother's characteristics: much of the same flashing humor: a gift of language and facility of expression; the grand manner engagingly wed to a natural friendliness.

"We had some trouble at the start because so many people thought this campaign was just a lark and they were not going to throw money down a rathole," he remarked. "We began with the smallest possible nucleus—three people—and we've been relying very heavily on spontaneous generation since then.

"The campaign is running itself, it really is."

Neal Freeman, a 25-year-old Yale graduate of 1962, has served for almost two years as aide and confidant to Mr. Buckley, and is known in the campaign as "the keeper of the body." It is he who lines up campaign appointments.

Mr. Freeman is executive director of Republicans for Buckley and a member of the executive committee of the Young Republican National Federation. "We don't have a million things like Dentists for Buckley and Sky Divers for Buckley," he says. "We don't go in for that sort of thing."

In another cubicle sits Donald G. Pemberton, 30, who serves as head of Youth for Buckley. A Brooklyn insurance man who also runs a secretarial service, he is state chairman of the conservative Young Americans for Freedom.

James A. Bentley, a soft-voiced native of Alabama, said he had "never been in a political campaign in my life" but felt he "could not live with myself unless I did something to help restore the

city to a sound basis." He took leave from his management con-
sulting firm.

Jim Buckley put him in charge of door-to-door work. His method
has been to cull out the brightest and most personable of the
volunteers who have walked into headquarters and commission
them as doorbell-ringing captains with authority to choose their
own teams. He said he would have 400 teams out visiting at the
peak. Nearly 1,000 volunteers were said to have "just dropped in"
to offer help.[1]

The original estimate had been that to mount our operation we
would need a staff of five people. It grew to thirteen. Priority was
given (a) to the production of essential literature; (b) to election
posters; (c) to radio spots; and (d) to newspaper advertising. Money
was allocated, as it came in, to these uses, and in that order. If more
money had come in, and in time, we'd have spent it on television
spots, which are universally acclaimed as greatly effective. We tested
"White's Law," as we came to call it, and found it, in our case, accurate. It is described by Theodore White in *The Making of the President, 1964*, and says that money for a campaign tends to come in after
it is needed, and that therefore a successful campaign manager will
make commitments, provided they are reasonable, on the expectation
that as the fever builds, support will come in. We undertook to live
by White's Law, but carefully. And the money did come in to pay
our debts, and even to leave us a surplus of a few hundred dollars.
At the end, it turned out that the cost per voter for John Lindsay was
$2.24, Beame $2.08, Buckley $0.72.

2. Beame Wins the Primary

September 15. Abraham Beame won the Democratic primary, an
upset victory over Paul Screvane, who had been the favorite, and
against whom Lindsay had apparently planned his strategy. A blow to
the Conservative Party. Beame, the incumbent Comptroller, opposed
the deficit-budget of Mayor Wagner, and a lot of Democratic fiscal conservatives (the Lawrence Gerosa-type, who stuck with Gerosa in 1961
when he ran independently for Mayor) will be drawn to Beame,
whereas they probably would have deserted Screvane, who is President of the New York City Council, as merely an extension of Wagner.

The press wanted a comment on Beame's victory. I wrote one out:

The victory of Mr. Beame over the other Democratic gentlemen

1. *The New York Times*, October 16, 1965.

is both encouraging and discouraging. Encouraging because Mr. Beame does have a reputation as a penny-counter, raising the question why he did not become a nervous wreck during his association with the Wagner Administration; instead of that, he flourished during a period when the expenses of city government rose by 14 per cent. Discouraging because Mr. Beame has projected a campaign in which he will attempt something more difficult even than balancing the city budget: namely, to paint John Lindsay as a conservative.

Mr. Beame was probably nominated because a great many New Yorkers feel increasingly insecure as a result of the riotous spending of my predecessor, Mr. Wagner. But whereas Mr. Beame has repeatedly stressed the necessity to balance the budget, he is not well known for specifying the economies necessary in order to make this possible. He sometimes gives one the feeling that he would be perfectly satisfied if New York City spent the entire sum total of its citizens' earnings, provided it first taxed them, so as neatly to balance the budget.

I do profoundly hope, although I must confess to a pessimism on the subject, that Mr. Beame will not afflict New Yorkers with the fiction, cultivated during his campaign and stressed during the height of his ecstasy last night, that John Lindsay is "the candidate of Barry Goldwater and Richard Nixon." That is about as accurate as to charge that Beame is the candidate of Chester Arthur and Grover Cleveland. The differences between Mr. Beame and Mr. Lindsay are biological, not political. They will strive very hard, in the days ahead, to discover points of disagreement: indeed, they may even succeed in genuinely disagreeing over Mr. Lindsay's proposal for floating swimming pools. In our debates together, towards the end of this week, on WMCA and CBS, it will be manifest that the gentlemen actually disagree only on the question of whose ambitions should be furthered in November. I shall be there to maintain that not Mr. Beame's, not Mr. Lindsay's but New York's ambition should be furthered.

Murray Kempton took up a phrase in my release, wrung out of it what (only) he could; and went on to predict a Lindsay victory against Beame for the very best reason advanced during the campaign for voting for Lindsay:

MATTER OF BIOLOGY[2]

"The differences between Mr. Beame and Mr. Lindsay are biological, not political."

—WILLIAM F. BUCKLEY JR., *yesterday*

That is the most sensible thing any surviving candidate for

2. Kempton, September 16, New York *World-Telegram*.

mayor has said so far in this campaign. And to hope for any sensible statement from any candidate henceforth, we seem to be stuck with Buckley. That is not to be construed as an endorsement of William F. Buckley; I should lose all respect for him if he ever endorsed me, and I trust him to hold my dignity as high.

It has been the only consistent dedication of poor stewardship to keep persons like myself and Mr. Buckley out of public office. But we're not going to have a statesman, and we should be grateful that from now to November, we shall at least have the company of a good critic. . . .

The reasons *are* biological. This election makes no political sense. The Democrats have fought through a Darwinian struggle in the jungle and the survivor can claim to be the fittest by right of battle, but he is hardly an example of the logic of nature.

The best argument for a Republican mayor is the dismal performances of the incumbent Democratic Mayor. But, after the primary, the Democrats have presented us with three candidates who are all dedicated enemies of Robert F. Wagner. The Republicans on the other hand have a ticket two-thirds of whose members are still proud to proclaim themselves loyal friends of the Mayor.

The Republicans might seem to have some claim on a chance to try and run the city; they are the only party, after all, which has no complicity with the unfortunate past and the unpleasant present. But Lindsay has done nothing to indicate that he is a Republican so far except to attack Nelson Rockefeller. There is an argument— there is in fact a strong necessity—for a two-party system in this city, but it is hardly satisfied by a campaign between a Republican ticket 66 per cent pro-Wagner and a Democratic ticket 100 per cent anti-Wagner.

Buckley is eminently correct: the difference between Lindsay and Beame is biological. That is why, as a neutral, it is hard for me to believe that Lindsay will not win. Beame is an accountant; my own accountant gives me the best service at the most ridiculously low rate of any businessman I deal with. Without him, I should today be a chattel slave of the federal government. But it remains a melancholy fact that our most intimate moments are in the spring when I call him and say: "Do you mean to say that there is no way I can keep these bandits from making me pay them $700 I haven't got?" There is no way; my accountant is right; he is good for everything else, but he is, by profession, no man to build a dream on. . . .

As for Lindsay, it is my duty not to lie, at least when I think I'm lying. He has pressed no claim on reason so far in this campaign which suggests that he would be a good mayor. But what a splendid fellow he otherwise is. Just as a man he is magnificent and that is enough in a candidate to convey illusions. Illusions are biological and not political in origin.

3. Soft on Communism

September 28. I doubted we could get through the campaign with-out the subject's being raised. And of course, it has been. Once again, I ran into prejudices which are the larger realities in political inter-course. This time it had to do with the question of internal subversion.

Premise: There *is* a problem of internal subversion. That is to say, there *do* exist Communists whose motivations are extrinsic to the stated purposes of the activities they engage in. The Communist who involves himself in the peace movement, for instance, is not interested in peace, but in something very different. The Communist who works for the government is not interested in the welfare of the government, but in something very different; indeed, he is opposed to the welfare of the government as understood by other people. The Communist who is involved in the civil rights movement or in the poverty move-ment is not interested in civil rights or in poverty in the sense that, let us say, Martin Luther King or Michael Harrington is.

Premise: A crypto-Communist is in a position to work mischief of several kinds. Working in government, he may be in a position to snitch documents and communicate vital United States secrets to the enemy. Working in the peace movement, or the civil rights or poverty programs, he is in a position to interfere with the idealistic purposes of such movements, to increase individual and corporate anxieties, to exacerbate the relations between the races, to traduce the integrity of a drive to reduce the misery of poverty.

Premise: The Communists therefore want watching—in order, by vigilance and exposure, to neutralize their influence.

Premise: There are those public figures who accept the foregoing premises, as witness (a) their public declarations on the subject and (b) their *de facto* support of those programs and agencies delegated to perform the job of Communist-watching; those who don't acknowl-edge the premises or support the programs; and those who do (a), but not (b).

Early in the campaign, Lindsay supporters gleefully announced to the press that "Buckley supporters" had accused Lindsay of being "some sort of a Communist."

God knows, God knows I knew the ambush I was being propelled toward. The only thing more damaging in New York City than to sug-gest that someone is pro-Communist, is to suggest that he is a McCarthyite.[3]

3. Replying to a complaint by Abraham Beame that the Presbyterian Church of New York had in effect endorsed John Lindsay, a spokesman for the Presbytery's governing body wrote that it had not in fact endorsed Lindsay. "However," it

The matter had come up as follows. A supporter of the Conservative Party, having consulted no one, dictated a message into a tape recorder and announced the availability of his message to anyone who would dial YE 9-2995. The message was leaped upon by the Lindsay people as suggesting that Lindsay was a "radical, or a Communist"—as Lindsay himself put it.

I studied the text of the telephone message carefully, and made the decision—obviously inept—that I would refuse to disavow the tape. Here, in its entirety, is what it said:

[Stenographic Transcript of Taped Telephone Message upon Dialing YE 9-2995]: John Lindsay continues to move leftward in his campaign for Mayor of New York [true]. The Republican Congressman this week called a press conference to assure liberals he would tolerate no anti-communist witchhunts in his administration [true]. Lindsay was sharply critical of the investigation of Mobilization for Youth, a multi-million dollar anti-poverty program, financed jointly by the city and federal governments [true]. The probe was prompted by news that MFY was honeycombed with radical leftists who have used its facilities to foment rent strikes and racial disorders [true]. An FBI investigation revealed that 37 members of the MFY staff had records of pro-Communist activity [true]. A committee of the New York State Senate singled out by name MFY staffers who had been identified as members of the Communist Party and other subversive groups [true]. When Lindsay last week denounced the MFY witchhunt, he asserted that the charges of Communist infiltration were overblown, untrue and unfair [true]. But the facts as uncovered by State and City investigations are clear [untrue—they weren't clear]. Testifying before a legislative committee, undercover agents for the FBI revealed that the Communist Party had made the infiltration of MFY a prime goal [true]. Whose judgment do you trust, the FBI's or John Lindsay's? [unfair—the FBI passes no judgments]. We urge you to vote for the Conservative ticket of Buckley, Gunning and Markey on November the 2nd. Let us elect people to office who have the ability to recognize problems and who have not sold their souls for a bowl of political porridge [hear, hear]. Call YE 9-2995 again next week for another conservative message. Thank you.

I arrived at the press conference and made a brief statement.

Mr. John Lindsay has complained that agents of the Conservative

---

went on, "Presbyterians reserve the right [to intervene] in extraordinary circumstances—for example the candidacy of a John Birch member [or such] racist political activity [as] in Nazi Germany or in the Deep South." One would have thought that, reaching for illustrations, the Presbytery might have added "or a Communist. . . ." But the fear of McCarthyism is the Number One fear.

Party have implied that he is, as he put it, a "radical, or a Communist." I have investigated the cause of Mr. Lindsay's complaint —which is a taped telephone message available to anyone who dials the number YE 9-2995—and have arrived at several conclusions.

1. There is nothing in the taped message to suggest that Mr. Lindsay is a radical or a Communist. The message criticizes Mr. Lindsay for pooh-poohing the investigation last year of Mobilization for Youth, and for promising that his Administration would not tolerate such witchhunts.

2. Mr. Lindsay has thus made a second attempt to broadcast his charge that the Conservative Party is launching irresponsible attacks upon him, the idea being to stimulate New York into pitying him, and drawing him to her womb for protection. I should like to point out to Mr. Lindsay, and to everyone concerned, that there are two kinds of smears, one of them of a much higher order of sophistication than the other. (a) It is a smear if you call a man who isn't one a Communist. (b) It is a smear if he says you called him a Communist, if in fact you didn't. The Conservative Party has not committed the smear of the first category. Mr. Lindsay, I regret to conclude, has committed the smear of the second category.

3. Since it now appears likely that Mr. Lindsay will return again and again to the suggestion that agents of the Conservative Party are calling him a Communist, I take the opportunity to state very clearly what exactly is the Conservative Party's position concerning Mr. Lindsay and the question of internal security. It is that Mr. Lindsay is insufficiently aware of the problems of internal security, and that, by his record, he shows that if he were Mayor, not only would there be no witchhunting, there would be no Communist-hunting. Mr. Lindsay co-sponsored resolutions with Mr. James Roosevelt in 1963 whose effect would have been to abolish the House Committee on Un-American Activities. This Committee, which has done valuable work, is the symbol of Congressional concern over the problem of Communist infiltration and Communist subversion. Not everybody who desires to abolish the House Committee on Un-American Activities is a Communist. But everybody who desires to abolish it is ignorant of the Communist problem, and anybody who desires to abolish it and is also a public official, is dangerously ignorant.

It was not therefore a surprise that Mr. Lindsay should have opposed the investigation of the Mobilization for Youth—even after the Federal Bureau of Investigation reported that it had become infiltrated. Accordingly, I endorse the charge that Mr. Lindsay is recklessly negligent of the problem of internal security, and I commend to his attention a scholarly analysis of the work of the House Committee on Un-American Activities to which twelve distinguished authors contributed chapters, and which I had the honor to edit. The book was published two years ago, and is generally available.

"Are you," Mr. Gabe Pressman of NBC, microphone in hand, the television camera whirring, "saying that Mr. Lindsay is 'soft on Communism?'" "No, Mr. Pressman," I answered, "I am precisely not saying that: I am saying that he does not have any apparent appreciation of the problem of internal subversion, which is different."

"William F. Buckley," wrote *Tribune* columnist Dick Schaap the next day, "is saying that John Lindsay is soft on Communism. . . . He has picked up the most tired and meaningless phrase of all. . . ."

And from nationally syndicated columnist Andrew Tully: "The trouble with the Conservative Party is that every time it comes up with a spokesman who seems intelligent and articulate—and even good-humored—he succumbs to the temptation to talk a lot of twaddle lest his more frenetic supporters suspect him of romancing Mao Tze-tung."

It isn't that the columnist bore me any grudge:

I like Bill Buckley, who is running for Mayor on the Conservative ticket. He has a brain and he does some of his thinking in depth, and he is not afraid to talk unpleasant turkey to the voters. In the tedious field of politics, his sense of humor is very nearly unique: he often laughs at himself, a crime Adlai Stevenson discovered is punishable by the rack and which even John Kennedy indulged in furtively.

But even Bill Buckley apparently is intimidated by the corseted screech owls and the wild-eyed vigilantes mobilized to save the country from imminent takeover by the communists. He has endorsed, in language straight out of Joe McCarthy's sleazier utterances, a telephone smear campaign against one of his opponents, the determinedly cleancut Rep. John Lindsay.

The smear is contained in a taped telephone message that can be heard by dialing a New York City number. It implies that Lindsay is "soft on communism" because he criticized the investigation of communist infiltration of an anti-poverty outfit called Mobilization for Youth, and urges listeners to vote for Buckley.

Buckley has okayed this sordid appeal to the idiot mentality. He says Lindsay's record, which includes co-sponsorship of a resolution to abolish the House Committee on Un-American Activities, shows that "there would be no Communist hunting" if Lindsay were elected.

This is the kind of arrant and vicious nonsense which causes instant nausea among those of the American electorate capable of deciphering a simple declarative sentence. It is nonsense which, happily, will prevent the Conservative Party from winning any significant elections even unto the Last Trump, because it is not only tired but stupid.

Buckley, of course, is not stupid, which makes his endorsement of such vapid imbecilities all the more pathetic and tragic. By lending his name to a smear of this kind, Buckley acknowledges what he hitherto has gone to considerable pains to refute, that the Conservative Party as now constituted is dominated by dangerous fools whom a candidate running in their name offends at his peril."[4]

I wrote to Mr. Tully:

. . . I am taking the trouble gently to inform you that you don't know what you are talking about when you suggest that my interest in internal security is the product of my summer madness. I don't know whether you ever saw the text of the telephone communication which you characterize as done "in language straight out of Joe McCarthy's sleazier utterances . . . a smear campaign."

(1) Here is the text of the telephone message.

(2) Here is my covering statement concerning it; and most important,

(3) Here is my own contribution to a book on the House Committee on Un-American Activities which seeks, I hope, to give you successfully the perspective from which I spoke.

He replied:

. . . I have read all your enclosures dealing with the telephone campaign waged against Lindsay ("soft on Communism"), and I hold to my views expressed in the column to which you refer.

The language in the telephone message was "sleazy" because it implied in the most unctuous tones that Lindsay could not be depended upon to take Communist subversion seriously. Surely, *you* know this is stale twaddle [I didn't and don't]. But such messages are very effective, as you must know [they aren't, as he ought to know]. Your opponents are always making points by accusing

---

4. For the prurient, a few additional quotations. From the New York *Post*, James Wechsler, October 5, 1965: "Moreover, Buckley, with diminishing subtlety, has addressed his appeal to the city's McCarthyite residue [as when] he suggests that John Lindsay is soft on communism." *The New York Times*, October 26, 1965, caught Lindsay's campaign manager in *flagrante*. "Mr. [Robert] Price then listed five [only two were mentioned] instances in which, he said, Mr. Buckley had accused the Republican-Liberal candidate of being pro-Communist. One of the instances attributed to Mr. Buckley a sentence that actually appeared in a New York *Post* editorial denouncing Mr. Buckley. Another instance quoted Mr. Buckley as saying, 'I don't doubt that there are Communists supporting Mr. Lindsay . . .' However, Mr. Price did not quote the rest of the passage, which was: 'The point is, is it correct to infer from the existence, let us say, of a Communist voting for Mr. Lindsay, that Mr. Lindsay is a Communist? Obviously not. That is the way of the demagogue, and I'm trying to resist demagoguery, and I wish that Mr. Lindsay would succeed half so well.' " From Irving Howe, *Dissent*, Winter, 1966: "[Buckley] learned how stirring it can be to excite the McCarthyite hooligans. . . ."

you of a plot to make the wheel illegal. Polite language is a far more powerful weapon than Billingsgate. I enjoy you because your language is polite and your utterances thoughtful. I almost don't blame you when you use whatever gimmick is lying around. But not this "soft on Communism" bit, please, Mr. Buckley. It makes you sound silly, and you're not. Come on back and let me enjoy you again.

A few weeks after the internal-security exchange, the Democrats-for-Lindsay-Mollen-Costello issued a flyer (see also below) headlined, "Will the Real Liberal Please Stand Up?": ". . . Beame is *not* carrying the liberal banner in this campaign [the text began]. John Lindsay is. . . . As a crusading Congressman, John Lindsay . . . with Democratic Congressman William F. Ryan, fought to abolish the House Un-American Activities Committee. . . ."

Now if the fight to abolish the House Committee on Un-American Activities is worth stressing in a pamphlet arguing the *liberal* credentials of a candidate, then by logical deduction the fight to abolish the House Committee on Un-American Activities is worth stressing in a statement arguing the non-Conservative credentials of the same candidate. If, as regards a controversial matter, one side says that X is good, may not the other side maintain X is bad? *I.e.,* if it was significant to liberals that Lindsay opposed HUAC, surely it was significant to conservatives that he opposed it? But any mention of his opposing it, or of his collateral positions respecting the investigation of the Mobilization For Youth—becomes sleazy twaddle.

Another approach: When public commentators—as for instance, on several occasions during the past few years, Joseph Alsop, Rowland Evans, and Robert Novak—warn of the problem of Communist infiltration of organizations involved in the civil rights movement, their observations either are, or aren't, significant. If their criticisms are *not* significant, they ought to be criticized as witch-talk; which however the record does not show was done. Why not? If, on the other hand, the alleged infiltration by Communists of the civil rights movement is a matter of public concern—then, surely, an aspirant mayor of the largest city in the United States should acknowledge that the problem is one which he should concern himself with, New York being the center of the civil rights movement?

Enough. The distinctions are obviously there to be made, and demagogy consists not in raising the problem, but in refusing to consider the distinctions. Shades of Mrs. Liuzzo, about whom it could not be said with impunity that because she defied the warnings not to travel at night between Selma and Montgomery, she had courted danger: that distinction simply could not, in the current mood, be entered. No more, in the current mood, the distinction concerning the question of Communist subversion. Politics simply isn't the place to make distinctions, it is frequently enough said. Hopelessly, one wonders why those transcendent spirits professionally concerned with distinction-making cannot bring themselves to ponder distinctions when they are made in political situations. I have a horrible suspicion that what matters to most of them is not the distinction, but its provenance. *Quod licet Jovi, non licet bovi.*

4. General Pulaski

October 1. A phone call from Neal Freeman at headquarters at 9 a.m. Chaos, absolute chaos. Press Secretary Kieran O'Doherty melodramatically announced to the entire office that the story in the morning's *Tribune* will cost us one hundred thousand votes. I replied that that is probably more votes than we were going to get in the first place, and Freeman remarked that, if I didn't mind, he would *not* convey this remark back to O'Doherty.

The trouble (headline): "PULASKI PARADE: 'NO' BY BUCKLEY"

. . . One of the ripest vote-gathering fields each autumn is the Pulaski Day Parade, but one mayoral candidate won't be on hand at harvest time this year. William Buckley Jr., the Conservative Party candidate, has rejected an invitation from the Pulaski Day Committee to review the parade this Sunday on the ground that he wants to avoid "ethnic appeals." Democratic Abraham Beame and Republican-Liberal John Lindsay were quick to accept the invitation and will be in the reviewing stand . . . between 1 and 6 p.m.

In replying to the invitation from parade committee chairman Frank Wazeter, Neal B. Freeman, assistant campaign manager for Mr. Buckley, wrote: "I am sorry to report that Mr. Buckley will be unable to attend the annual Pulaski Day Parade primarily because he has pledged himself to make no specifically ethnic or nationalist appeals. I hope you will understand his policy: it is to treat the voters of New York as responsible adult-individuals and not as members of monolithic voting blocs. Thank you so much for your interest."

Of the three candidates, Mr. Buckley was clearly the favorite among some 300 members of the parade committee—that is, until his letter was read. The group—leaders of Polish communities throughout the Metropolitan area—met Wednesday night. They were relatively silent at the mention of Mr. Beame's and Mr. Lindsay's names, but applauded Mr. Buckley's, then groaned when they heard the letter.

I had not heard either of the invitation, or of Freeman's refusal of it,[5] and it went through my mind that I wouldn't myself have handled the invitation quite that way—although I understood, and valued, Freeman's attempt to honor the no-bloc insignia of the campaign. It comes down to a question of elementary diplomacy: it is one thing, on your own initiative, to go into Italian or Jewish areas in order to eat pizzas or blintzes, another to decline an invitation to join in paying friendly tribute to a people who, once a year, parade their history-laden pride before the people of their adopted city. Add the special consideration, that the Poles have been a subjugated people for so much of so many centuries, and compassion figures, along with the formal requirements of courtesy. How, then, to maneuver, so as (a) not to look *too* foolish; (b) to affirm confidence in one's staff; and (c) to minimize the bleeding.

Freeman raced up and accompanied me to Fordham University where I was to speak at 11 a.m. in the huge gymnasium where, a few days later, Costello was to denounce my anti-Catholicism, and we discussed the problem. He stoutly maintained that the letter would help, not hurt, the campaign. But in deference to contrary opinion, he volunteered to resign (ridiculous), or to accept the humiliation of a public reprimand (unthinkable). I decided to write a second letter to the head of the Pulaski Day Committee, give copies to the press at the meeting that afternoon, and ride out the storm.

Dear Mr. Wazeter:

I was not aware of Mr. Freeman's letter to you until I read it in the newspaper this morning. I endorse the main point Mr. Freeman has made, which is that too many politicians believe they can manipulate nationality groups by attending their parades. For that reason, I regretfully declined the invitation to attend the Steuben Day Parade, as I shall, also regretfully, decline the invitation to the Columbus Day Parade. If I had written the letter myself, I'd have added that I wish you every success with your parade, that if you invite me next year to attend, when my presence would not be construed as politically motivated, I shall accept with pride and pleasure. And I might have added, as a longstanding supporter of the American Friends of the Captive Nations, that my sympathy for the ordeal of your people is more than ritualistic.

Yours faithfully,
[WFB]

I got many letters, the burden of which was that my stand had been

---

5. I wonder how often Lindsay and Beame—and political candidates in general— read in the morning papers about decisions they have taken, which decisions they were never consulted about.

just plain stuffy. I tend to agree. Later, an official of the Conservative Party begged me to ride in a motorcade through Brooklyn, with my wife and son—"just to let the voters see your face." I hated to say no, because he appealed to me personally: but I did, reasoning that to do so now would fly in the face of my harangues against Lindsay for his walking tours—which I criticized as unrelated to analyzing the problems of the city. It was another example, I now think, of a doctrinaire extension of an otherwise sound principle. It isn't demagogic to expose yourself to your constituents, though if that is *all* you do the imbalance is patronizing in effect, as though the Beatles spent *all* their time reviewing their fans, and none at all in making music. Perhaps my dogmatic stand is excusable only in the sense that paradigmatic campaigns may every now and then be excusable— bending over backward in order to try to dramatize a point. At any rate, the Pulaski episode did force me to take a stiffer position—in application of the no-bloc rule—than in my heart of hearts I found reasonable, or easily defensible—politics, complexities thereof, lesson X, in the long textbook I never mastered.

5. The Other Buckley

October 5. A surprising number of people were writing and telephoning to HQ to ask (suspiciously) what exactly was my relationship to Charles Buckley, the failing Democratic boss of the Bronx, against whom JVL had been directing broadsides for lo these many weeks, alleging that Buckley is not only boss of the Bronx, but boss of Beame (whence "Buckley, Buckley and Beame"). The easiest thing would have been to drive home the dissociation by a routine blast against Charles Buckley, easy enough since he is an orthodox Democratic politician. That would be not only ill-advised, but unnecessary, I was told. The old curmudgeon is affectionately regarded by many people in the Bronx who admire if not the techniques by which over the years he has maintained himself in power (the same techniques that sustained his predecessor Ed Flynn, FDR's principal agent in New York) at least Buckley's treatment of the doctrinaire reformers. Many of them have been concerned less with the fact of boss rule than with unexploited opportunities to accelerate the city's march toward socialism, and toward them, Buckley's patience has been obscenely and endearingly short. Don't, was the word, go out of the way to knock him. Accordingly I made the following statement; which put a stop to the phone calls.

Many New Yorkers have called this office to ask (a) am I the same Mr. Buckley who is said to preside over the Bronx; or (b) am I related to the said Mr. Buckley; or (c) am I a stooge of the said Mr. Buckley?

I wish to record that I am not related to Mr. Charles Buckley, either politically or biologically. To quote Mr. Gerosa: I have, in fact, never met the gentleman.

I herewith request Mr. Charles Buckley to do me, and the voters of New York, the favor of ending the confusion by the simple expedient of changing his name. I would volunteer to do as much for him under reversed circumstances, but considering that I am running for political office and he is not, I think it natural, *noblesse oblige*, that he should take the initiative.

The whole "boss" issue, I thought, incidentally, was largely an evasion. In political lingo, one's own bosses are "leaders," the other fellow's, "bosses." Powell, though a boss, was nevertheless steadfastly uncriticized by Lindsay. The Republican Vincent Albano of Manhattan is a boss—who of course backed Lindsay. Stanley Steingut of Brooklyn, much attacked by Lindsay, is undisputedly a boss in the sense that he controls the Democratic machinery in Brooklyn—yet he was democratically elected by district leaders, themselves democratically elected. Not so Charles Buckley, it being the (undemocratic) custom in the Bronx for the district leaders to be chosen. On the other hand, Steingut and Raymond Jones were chosen in the same way, but nothing is heard about "Boss" Jones of Manhattan, whereas it is always "Boss" Steingut.

I said in a release on the subject:

> What matters is less the system—there are several systems by which the people can express themselves—than the results. Mr. Adam Clayton Powell, Jr., for instance, would be objectionable as a leader whether he became leader following a city-wide putsch, or whether he became leader having got one hundred per cent of the vote of his constituency. I join Mr. Lindsay in deploring the reliance of any governor on the acquiescence of powerful men. But it is no worse that Mr. Beame should be indebted to Mr. Steingut, than that Mr. Lindsay should be indebted to Mr. Dubinsky. Tinkering with the election laws won't substantially improve government in New York. What will substantially improve government in New York is the residual independence of its governing officials.

JVL, who made so heavy a point about the necessity that New York be ruled only by officials directly elected by the people, designated— as his first appointment on being elected—Timothy Costello for the post of Deputy Mayor. Costello was disavowed by said people, rather emphatically, on Election Day. He ran over four hundred thousand votes behind the winning candidate. JVL's other Deputy Mayor was his campaign manager, Robert Price. Who could defend the proposition that two agents of Mr. Charles Buckley would have fared worse at the polls than Mr. Costello, who was pulverized, and Mr. Price, whom even I could probably have beaten?

6. Epicene Demonstrators?

October 21. I arrived at headquarters ten minutes before the scheduled press conference at which I was to release my position paper on air and water pollution. Kieran O'Doherty, my brother Jim, and Neal Freeman collared me to say that the press, already assembled, wanted above all commentary on the noisy anti-Vietnam demonstration that took place over the weekend. I was reluctant to extemporize an extended analysis of the demonstration and recalled that I had written a newspaper column for syndication the previous April commenting on the anti-Vietnam demonstration outside the White House on Easter Saturday. From a file at headquarters, I pulled out the column that had been published in New York City (and in 150-odd) newspapers on April 22, read it over quickly to remove a couple of anachronisms, ran a copy through the Xerox machine from which to read to the press, and handed over the original for stenciling and mimeographing.

I felt like an awful fraud, handing out a six-month-old analysis of another (though not significantly different) demonstration as though it were freshly minted, but I rationalized that such were the exigencies of a political campaign. And anyway, I reasoned, the press would probably (a) give it little space anyway; or (b) perhaps recognize it as having already been published and toss it away as second-hand.

But the next morning, page 1, *The New York Times*: "BUCKLEY ASSAILS VIETNAM PROTEST/Condemns Marchers Here as 'Young Slobs' Strutting 'Epicene Resentment.'" There followed a very long, carefully written digest of my six-month-old newspaper column—and, hundreds upon hundreds of words down the length of the story, a two-paragraph reference to my air- and water-pollution paper, on which I had lavished so many hours of work.

The *Times* appeared especially interested in my use of the word "epicene" . . . "Mr. Buckley said: 'I wonder how these self-conscious *boulevardiers* of protest would have fared if a platoon of American soldiers who have seen the gore in South Vietnam had parachuted down into their mincing ranks?' Noting that they would not die for Vietnam, he snapped (*sic*): 'What *would* that group of young slobs die for? Their idealism?'" (I had gone on to say: "What *are* the

idealisms of the young protestors? Freer education? More free speech
at the University of California? Idealism is a hierarchy, if it is any
idealism at all.")

The *Times* went on: " 'It may be idealistic,' he said, 'to lay one's
body across the street in order to protest the neighborhood slum
where the tenants pay $50 for a $10 room.' But he asked how seriously
could one take the gesture of that idealist who then protests against
contributing his tax payment of $20 a year to save women and chil-
dren in South Vietnam from murder by the Vietcong. 'Why did not a
single one of the demonstrators denounce the Vietcong imperialists?'
he asked." (I had added: "What goes on in the minds, always sup-
posing that is the word for it, of the youth who fret and fuss and moan
over a minimum wage of only a dollar and a quarter an hour, and
strut their epicene resentment over a gallant national effort to keep
an entire section of the globe from sinking into the subhuman wretch-
edness of Asiatic Communism?")

" 'Why,' (the *Times* account continued) 'do they demand that the
United States withdraw, but fail to demand that the Communists
withdraw?' he asked. 'These were no mere pacifists,' he declared.
Rather, he said, they would 'have lit bonfires of jubilation' if the
President had sent marines into Alabama to wipe out the Southern
resistance. In summary he said the marchers were 'the kind of people
who would have deserted little Anne Frank, if her tormentors had
been Communists rather than Nazis.' " (I had added: "Their failing
is intellectual above all; but intellectual in the sense that all true
intellection is moral, because, disembodied from moral precepts,
thought is misleading, empty, ugly.")

I am fascinated by the kind of attention that can be attracted to
one's thought by the mere act of running for public office. My general
position on Vietnam and on anti-Vietnam demonstrations was (a)
widely known; and (b) hardly relevant to the campaign for the mayoralty of New York. What induced *The New York Times*, I wondered,
all of a sudden to give it that kind of coverage? The editors would not
have situated on its front page the views on Vietnam of any member
of the Foreign Relations Committee of the Senate (excepting Senator
Fulbright, its chairman)—unless they were dramatically heterodox.
Why mine? Had I done or said anything so unusual as to invite man-
bites-dog attention? But my general position was predictable and
consistent. Could it possibly be that by using the word "epicene" I
had given scandal? Surely, surely nothing so square. Yet the *Times*
had carefully defined the word it selected to use in the headline.
"Webster's New International Dictionary," the reporter had dutifully

recorded, "defines epicene as sexless, 'neither one thing nor the other' and 'effeminate.' " Was that the operative communication in the entire story? I found it hard to believe.

But sure enough, incredibly, the very next day—"LINDSAY MEN TALK OF A 100,000 EDGE." And on down the story:

> Mr. Lindsay's associates said the candidate believed that part of his gain between now and the election would come from conservative Republicans who were becoming disenchanted with William F. Buckley Jr., the Conservative party candidate. The move away from Mr. Buckley, the Republican-Liberal has told friends, began with the Conservative's comments . . . in which he described Vietnam protest marchers as displaying their "epicene resentment" against the country's involvement in the Asian war. Mr. Lindsay is said to think that intellectual Republicans [hardly numerous enough to affect an election—WFB] who oppose him because of his refusal to endorse Barry Goldwater last year, would be repelled by suggestions that anti-war marchers were homosexuals or effeminate.[6]

So help me, I could not believe my eyes. The sheer, utter, hopeless, humorless, philistine fatuity! Their resentment is epicene, therefore *they* are. Lindsay's befuddlement approximates Eleanor Roosevelt's, therefore he is a woman. To be so helpless amid the minor eddies and downdrafts of a language system as to be blown from the abstract noun ("resentment") that a metaphor ("epicene") characterizes, clear back to the class of people generating said resentment, and thus to suppose that the metaphor characterizes them. . . . By Lindsay's Rule, "Jones uttered a feline snarl" would give Jones four paws; and if "Jones penned a heavenly ode to his mistress," that would make him—divine.[7]

The Vietnam business did, as it happened, develop into a williwaw. Democratic City Councilman Matthew Troy, together with the New

---

6. Contrast: "The revolt against masculinity is not limited . . . to simple matters of coiffure and costume . . .; or to the adaptation of certain campy styles and modes to new uses. There is also a sense in which two large social movements that have set the young in motion and furnished images of action for their books . . . are connected analogically to the abdication from traditional maleness. The first of these is non-violent or passive resistance, so oddly come back to the land of its inventor, that icy Thoreau who dreamed a love which '. . . has not much human blood in it, but consists with a certain disregard for men and their erections. . . .' "

—Leslie A. Fiedler, *Partisan Review*, Fall 1965

7. I raised the point at the time, in a reply to a letter from Norman Mailer which he has refused me permission to print, perhaps because he is reluctant to record the effusiveness of his endorsement of Lindsay, perhaps because he regrets a pleasantry directed toward myself. At any rate, he referred to Lindsay as the "hope" of the GOP, and he said of me that he regretted that in foreign policy I was such a . . . burro. ". . . JVL, the hope of the Republican Party!" [I replied] "My dear Norman, go back and play fair for Cuba. . . . I note your hero this morning

York *Journal-American,* decided to sponsor an opposing demonstration the following Saturday, three days before Election Day. I was
invited, as were the other candidates, to march in the front rank to
the reviewing stand, and from there to witness the parade. I showed
up—Lindsay and Beame did not. I filed into place between Louis
Lefkowitz, the State Attorney General, and Senator Jacob Javits, who
was on temporary furlough from his campaign to warn the voters
that I was planning concentration camps for them. He greeted me
most affably; and I him. At the reviewing stand, the front file was
crowded, and I stood back. But as it happened, wave after wave of
the marchers shouted my name. Javits took me by the elbow and
propelled me forward, dispossessing a Congressional Medal of Honor
winner who had been situated there: "Come on, Bill, you're running
for office, you *belong* in the front row." Like getting your six-month-
old column on the front page of the *Times*—because you're running
for office, you *belong* in the front row! On and on the marchers came,
and it surely seemed as if I would be getting, the next Tuesday, somewhere between ninety-eight and ninety-nine per cent of the vote.
"Yellow Buckley buttons," the *Tribune* commented glumly, "were
abundant on the lapels of the marchers and at times the parade
seemed to turn into a Buckley rally as passing units chanted his name
and cheered. Mr. Buckley stood with hands jammed into his coat
pockets and was visibly pleased." Mr. Buckley may have been visibly
pleased, but he was not actually pleased, because the affair was embarrassing—a patriotic rally was in fact beginning to look like a factional pro-Buckley rally. What to do about it? I proposed slipping
away, but the publisher of the *Journal-American* would not hear of it.
Message after message had been coming in from the crowd just behind the cordon to the left of the reviewing stand—would I come
down and shake a few hands and sign an autograph or two? I resisted,
then finally reasoned that here was an excuse to absent myself from
the reviewing stand and give some surcease to the embarrassed sponsors, who didn't quite know what to do about the Republican and
Democratic dignitaries who were being roundly ignored by the
paraders as they marched by shouting my name and waving at me
(I had several times softly brought my finger to my lips pleading with
them to be silent as they marched by). I went down to the crowd and
there was a minor uproar as they surged toward me. I disengaged
myself with difficulty after a few minutes and scurried back to the
reviewing stand, where an angry official met me. "Do that kind of

---

avers that I will lose the 'conservative intellectual Republican vote' because I
described the 'epicene resentment' of the Vietnam marchers, and so implied they
were all fags! In your better moments you wouldn't have forgiven even Harry
Truman that one."

thing one more time," he threatened—by which he meant change the focus of attention from the reviewing stand to somewhere else— "and you'll *lose* votes." I may have lost votes later; there and then I lost my temper—the only time during the campaign, I think—and told him in words of four letters that I had not been trying to draw attention to myself, but *away* from myself, and if he thought I was here to win votes, he could . . . , whereupon I quickly shook hands with a few of the officials at the stand and left, before the parade was half done.

It is the final curse of politics that nothing, but nothing, is permitted to be spontaneous. *Everything* one does is supposed to have been done with reference to votes. And the pressure sets up a counter-pressure: no one will treat you other than on the assumption that that is what you are up to. The sponsors of the parade, for instance, are friends of mine (and clients—they publish my column). Even so— but once again I quote Kempton (November 2):

> . . . What was curious about the *Journal*'s account of this triumph was the omission of its central figure. William F. Buckley was by all accounts, master of the revels and object of all the enthusiasm the marchers directed to the reviewing stand. . . .
>
> And Buckley is a *Journal* columnist; even so, the *Journal* omitted every reference to his special command of its assemblage.
>
> The reason has to be that the *Journal* is supporting Abraham Beame for mayor. Buckley, a rival candidate, is therefore to be treated as a non-person. . . .
>
> Now what is about to be said embarrasses me a little, because I am a partisan in this election myself, and the *Journal* is not my paper—and thus no special kidney is required to criticize it. . . .
>
> I refuse to think Buckley deserves his supporters; but, as children of God, they certainly deserve him. And he gets a fairer shake in every paper in town than he does in this, the temple of his true faithful. We are all sinners working for sinners; but, by heaven, that management makes even me feel virtuous.[8]

7. The Problem of Principle

October 11.

TO: WFB
FROM: Neal Freeman
RE: Staten Island Speech
DATE: October 11, 1965

Very seriously for a moment . . . if you even suggest that the

8. Richard Pollak also wrote on the parade in the *Columbia Journalism Review*, Winter 1966, and remarked the anomaly.

fare be raised for the Staten Island ferry, our support there will evaporate. It is, literally, sacred.

NBF : ags

The above memorandum was the sum total of my briefing for my single appearance at Staten Island.

Staten Island is a rather unlikely borough of New York City, green, removed, pacific, for generations connected to Manhattan only by the five-cent ferry, though now there is a great bridge—the Verrazano Bridge—to Brooklyn. (Goldwater quipped after the campaign that things were looking so bad for the Democrats in New York that Bobby Kennedy had put Staten Island in his wife's name.)

The memo gave me a wild delight. Needless to say, I could not bring myself to withhold it from the audience at the Staten Island Rally, a packed house,[9] which roared with (nervous?) laughter.

On getting the memo I was, as the saying goes, torn between principle and political expediency. Staten Island is, so to speak, my *querencia*; a relatively neurosis-free, ethnically reposed enclave in Greater New York, unsundered by ideology, tension, urban jitters. Here is where Hugh Markey is from, candidate for Comptroller on the Conservative ticket, a bachelor businessman of retiring disposition, who runs now for public office because of his seignorial convictions about the requirements of peace and amity and order, a man about whom it could honestly be said that Norman Mailer would find him no stranger than he would find Norman Mailer. Must I now disappoint him, and his followers on Staten Island?

I didn't. Would I have, if I hadn't actually discerned an intellectually irrefutable defense of the five-cent ferry? I don't know. I can report that I did find it, in the nick of time; and Neal is pleased with me. It is this simple. Staten Island pays taxes to New York City levied by New York City assessors; *i.e.*, no special dispensations are made on account of its geographical remove from New York. The city charges the same rate for public transit riders who come into midtown Manhattan from whatever point, whether from Pelham Bay, ten miles away, or from Wall Street, twenty blocks away. A resident of Staten Island, although paying the same taxes, has not available to him the same public transit facilities at the same price. To travel to midtown Manhattan from mid–Staten Island, he must pay fifteen cents for the bus to the ferry, then five cents for the ferry, then another fifteen

9. Addressed also by the affable, witty, intelligent Robert Connor, the only candidate running for the presidency of a New York borough who had been tendered, and accepted, Conservative Party support—greatly offending JVL, who had forbidden, to the extent his authority permits the use of the word, his Republican running-mates to accept Conservative Party backing. Connor was, ironically, the only Republican candidate for borough president who was elected.

cents for the bus or subway to his destination: for a total of thirty-five cents. Considerations of equity—for so long as Staten Island remains a borough of New York City—therefore easily justify the five-cent fare; indeed, would justify a free ferry-transfer token. Whew!

I felt, understandably I think, a very special obligation to hew closely to principle—beyond the point to which I would have expected the most honorable man to go who had actually set his sights on election. Mine was conceived as what I have called a paradigmatic campaign—of what use would it otherwise have been? An additional one, or two, or three hundred thousand votes would not, I figured, have meant very much if I lost the only caste I had, as the scrupulous —sometimes, I thought, perhaps even perverse—adherent to principle—the kind of adherence that caused the Chicago *Tribune*, for instance, to comment (October 26) from afar, "[He] breaks all the established rules of political campaigning. He refuses to kowtow to any racial, religious, or nationality group. He does not pussyfoot on any issue, even the touchy ones. . . ."

It is on account of this resolution, which required no heroism at all under the circumstances, that I was especially dismayed every time (I remember three occasions) commentators concluded that the bug had caught me. A *Newsweek* reporter in September observed what was almost unanimously unobserved by anyone else. ("Last week, when [Buckley] was told that high Lindsay aides predicted the Conservative candidate would get 10 per cent of the vote, there were no witticisms, only a look of pleased anticipation, like a small boy anticipating 10 per cent of a very large cherry pie. . . .") Kempton, at one point, accused me of actually believing—and, worse, tailoring my statements to the incredible assumption—that I might *actually* be elected. (". . . he is beginning, ever so remotely, to entertain the illusion that he might win. He has thus given head to those impulses which are essential to politicians and dangerous to philosophers.") And several commentators speculated that my statement (see above) on the internal security problem derived, for some reason, not from the gist of two published volumes on the subject that bear my name— but from a desire to court votes even at the expense of my own views.

The high resolution I speak of, I restress, is not of the kind that required any special kidney; if you do not expect to win an election, it takes minimal courage to defend unpopular points of view in public. Such courage as *is shown* is in the occasional encounters with your own associates, each one of whom is likely to feel—and, often, for the most plausible of reasons—about at least one unpopular position one appears consigned by one's philosophical fates to defend, that the rationale actually exists for modifying it. It is much, much easier to disappoint a hundred thousand anonymous people than one colleague who sits next to you at a staff meeting and earnestly pleads, say, the case for supporting a subsidy for the subways; or for letting the city absorb the cost of installing water meters.

And then, too, nothing is more futile—or, for that matter, more anticonservative—than to indulge the heresy of extreme apriorism. "Prudence is," I remarked to the Third Anniversary Dinner of the Conservative Party, "as the catechism teaches, a virtue. And you have exercised prudence most prudently. Prudence doesn't happen to be the virtue I am myself best at. But I do greatly honor it, and do believe that prudence plays, or ought to play, an important role even in the development of paradigmatic political platforms, such as ours have sought to be." On a dozen occasions, I admitted into the position papers I had drafted modifications, accommodations, emulsifiers, which, I thought, subtly, intelligently, humanely, bent the doctrine to the reality: but each one of them, I happily believe, stopped short of the (admittedly impalpable) line between prudence and expediency.

The exception clings to mind. At a policy meeting to discuss the education paper, I proposed that we should come out four-square for the proliferation of private schools—by advocating such tax rebates as are often spoken of in theoretical literature and, in Canada, are widely given to parents who desire to send their children to private schools. I know of no single educational reform that appeals to me more than this one, which might do so much, as far as I can see, to shield the student from the intellectual and moral monoliths of the central political orthodoxy. But Mrs. Gunning was dismayed, pleading a point of personal privilege to which she was eminently entitled, namely that as chief organizer of the Parents and Taxpayers Association she had been widely denounced, that being the cant objurgation, as an Enemy of the Public Schools—which in point of fact she was not, is not. To endorse the growth of private schools while she was on the ticket would appear to vindicate her critics, and would disappoint her friends. The proposal was dropped.

8. Did You Know Lindsay at Yale?

October 11. I had the usual call at 10:30 a.m., after Lindsay's morning press conference. Incredibly, the *crise du jour* was: did Lindsay and I actually know each other at Yale? "Seriously," my monitor told me from the paybooth, "that's *all* they seem to want to talk about. Lindsay says you're having delusions of grandeur."

It was true, I learned on arriving at HQ for my own press conference, for which I had prepared statements on bossism, the newspaper strike, and the ADA's endorsement of Lindsay. That *was* all they wanted to talk about.

The issue arose from a chance remark I had made on ABC television the day before. A reporter asked whether I had met John Lindsay while at Yale. Yes, I said, "As a matter of fact we did a little witch-hunting together."

The next day: (from a transcript of the press conference):

REPORTER: John Lindsay says that you had illusions, that the two of you didn't even know each other at Yale and that you never went witch-hunting [together].

WFB: Illusions about what?

REP.: I gather, about knowing him at Yale.

WFB: I'm told he said I'm having "delusions of grandeur." Grandeur was not defined, while I was at Yale, as having the knowledge of John Lindsay. On the other hand, he hadn't yet announced himself as a big historical moment. But I'm surprised that Mr. Lindsay, who has gone to such pains to establish his reputation as a friendly fellow, going around shaking the hands of everybody in New York, should at this [late] point suggest that he didn't [do as much] at Yale University, which is much smaller than New York.

[In point of fact, I did know him.]

REP.: Mr. Buckley, Mr. Lindsay denies that he went witch-hunting with you at Yale.

WFB: Well, it's too bad to have somebody deny the highest glory of his career. I'm beginning to think he peaked too early.

REP.: *How* did you go witch-hunting together?

WFB: We heckled a fellow-traveling demonstration in New Haven. He and a guy called Bob Lounsbury, a guy called Hank Healy, and a guy called—me—the four of us.

REP.: You don't think Lindsay could have forgotten you, do you?

WFB: Well, he's supposed not to forget any potential voter.

REP.: Was that the only incident where you were together?

WFB: No, on another occasion he gave me some libel advice— when the fellow travelers threatened to sue us.

REP.: Was it good advice?

WFB: I didn't get sued. I never said he was a bad *lawyer*.

REP.: But Mr. Lindsay said today that he never knew you at Yale at *all*—

WFB: Well, I'm surprised he said that because it's not true. If he is suffering from some sort of dysphasia, that would make a whole lot of his recent behavior understandable—Can I ask *you* a question? I wonder if people *care* about it [the subject under discussion].

REP.: I'll explain it very simply. In the course of a long, tedious campaign, everyone gets bored with everything that happens day in and day out, that's all there is to it.

WFB: Look, this is off the record now. Over there [*I pointed*] is my brother and campaign manager, whom you all know. He and John and David Lindsay were classmates at Yale. He [my brother] is the godfather of one of David's children. We overlapped at Yale for two years—the Lindsays and my brother at law school, I in the undergraduate school. *You* decide whether the probability was that I should have known my own brother's friends. I really wonder why John wants to press this.

REPS.: [*in unison*]: Why off the record?

JAMES BUCKLEY: Because I don't want to trade on my friendship with Dave Lindsay, that's all.

The subject was finally dropped. ("Why spoil a good story with the facts," said Gabe Pressman.) *The New York Times* published the names of the two men I cited as having been present at the heckling session. They were both Lindsay supporters. They were nowhere quoted as denying my allegation.

Lindsay's foray into Yale was not, to judge from the papers the next morning, merely a twitch of exasperation. The *Times'* front page headline was, as we have seen in another connection: "LINDSAY AND BUCKLEY DUEL/Attack shifts to Buckley." And the lead: "John V. Lindsay, the Republican-Liberal candidate for Mayor, dropped his seeming unconcern about William F. Buckley Jr. yesterday by delivering a stinging denunciation of the Conservative candidate. Mr. Buckley answered in kind . . ." And the *Tribune's*: "LINDSAY FIRES AT A NEW TARGET—BILL BUCKLEY." Lead: "As though he's become suddenly, almost startlingly aware of the magnitude of the threat, John V. Lindsay dropped the cudgel he's been using against the larger Democratic menace and picked up the scalpel yesterday to amputate a smaller but more irritating thing called William Buckley before it grew too big. But it wouldn't go away. . . ."

The second article of Lindsay's indictment concerned my alleged forensic skill. "Mr. Lindsay [the *Times* began] angrily attacked one of Mr. Buckley's greatest strengths—his skill as a public speaker.

" 'The great debater has become a limp balloon,' Mr. Lindsay said caustically. 'He keeps dribbling off into irrelevancies all the time, which are rather pathetic.' "

REPORTER: Mr. Lindsay said today that he was disappointed in you as a debater. Mr. Lindsay also said that your prowess in this field left him pretty cold, because you were in his words 'a limp balloon.'

WFB: Yes, that sounds like him. There is that distinct facility of expression, what Doris Fleeson of the New York *Post* has identified as his "Stevensonian wit."[10] I never said I was a particularly adept debater, but I should think I would leave Mr. Lindsay extremely confused. I do have some sort of addiction to logical, propositional thought. I'm not surprised he doesn't understand me. . . .

The old *tu quoque.* I don't blame Lindsay. I had heard he was greatly roiled when, at the Conservative Convention a couple of weeks earlier, I had analyzed a couple of sentences from Lindsay's keynote speech about which his supporter Murray Kempton observed that it made the campaign speeches of Johnson read like a collection of the parliamentary addresses of Charles James Fox.

Mr. Lindsay [I had written], says of Mr. Beame that he "promises not progress but procrastination, not ideas but indifference, not energy but evasiveness, not advancement but apathy."

What is wrong with that sentence—other than its suicidal search for alliteration? What is wrong with it is that it is unintelligible. How can an orderly mind maintain that Mr. Beame "*promises* procrastination"? And in what sense is "evasiveness" the opposite of "energy"?

As for your servant, Mr. Lindsay accused me of seeking "to downgrade and vitiate, to divide, to negate, and to prey upon the tensions and fears among our people." Now (a) I would be very happy, indeed, to "vitiate" the tensions and fears of our people— that, in fact, is why I am running for office. So why should Mr. Lindsay (unless he favors *validating* the fears of the people), criticize this? And, (b) How on earth does one "divide" a "*tension,*" let alone a "*fear*"? And how can one *simultaneously* "vitiate a tension," and "prey upon it?" Is Mr. Lindsay seriously concerned about the educational standards of New York City? How would he know if they were inadequate? Mr. Lindsay is constantly criticizing me as the candidate from Connecticut. I don't know why he is so hostile to Connecticut. Perhaps he went there to be educated and, for manifest reasons, is displeased with the results.

It was as I put it at the press conference: "The feline phase of the campaign has started."

10. So help me God. 10/3/65.

9. On Reporters

October 29.[11] It gets hectic during a campaign, even for a "non-serious" candidate. Requests come in every day from correspondents for influential newspapers and magazines for individual interviews. After a while the sheer lack of time requires grouping a few of them together. On Thursday three of them, whose by-lines are recognizable throughout the country, piled into my station wagon, agreeing to do their interviewing while I chased about from one to another appointment, and we chatted back and forth with a candor which appears a little reckless in the light of the foreknowledge that the chances are better than even that, if it is a conservative who is involved, the interviewer is honing his ax, the interviewee baring his neck. The whole business of the tendentious journalist has been greatly explored, and, I think, insufficiently understood. Richard Nixon's blast against the press after his defeat in California in 1962 was set down as neurotic, and worse. Charles Mohr of *The New York Times* wrote a devastating article against Barry Goldwater for *Esquire* in August 1965, intending to demonstrate that, in fact, and as a matter of charity, the press had rather mothered Goldwater, than abused him. The trouble, of course, as I noted in connection with the talk to the New York police, is that *ex post facto* demonstrations of tendentiousness are terribly boring; and that weighted reporting is psychologically explicable with reference to the community's passions, fears, taboos, and myths. Just as Goldwater probably should not have speculated publicly on other people's speculations about the possible use of an atom bomb for the purposes of defoliation, so (the argument might run), the use of the word "wallow" in connection with the disposal of garbage by Negroes outside their windows as justified by James Baldwin, should never have been used—however fastidiously, in the first instance, the distinctions were drawn so as not to permit, let alone encourage, the least overtone of racial invidiousness. It isn't only the press that might misunderstand, or distort. There are, inevitably, Paul O'Dwyers in the room. One always hopes that a serious reporter will seriously listen; and one is often disappointed. The only alternative—not to grant interviews at all—is pretty nearly impossible, though such refusals can, and recently have been, justified.[12]

11. The date is arbitrary.
12. *E.g.*, by Dwight Macdonald, the erratic but always interesting critic, who rushed to defend *The New Yorker* (*New York Review of Books*, February 3, 1966) against attacks on it by the *Tribune*'s Tom Wolfe. Macdonald defended the refusal of William Shawn, *The New Yorker*'s editor, even to talk with Wolfe: "Given Wolfe's scholastic habit of deducing his facts from his assumptions . . .—given this method, the practical result of any cooperation by Shawn would have been

I came to appreciate, in the course of the campaign, the difference between truly competent reporters, and those others who are simply untrained at listening to, and then conveying, rigorous analysis. The latter are usually the most biased, probably because bias slurps over a lot of details it is unwilling, or unable, to confront intellectually; and in any case, biased interviews are easier to sensationalize. The truly fine reporters—for instance, of the quality of most of those who write for *The New York Times*—can very well manipulate a bias (indeed, some of them at the *Times* must have majored in the art at the Columbia School of Journalism), but they give evidence of their capacity to follow an argument. A reporter of quality, unless he is totally dazed by ideology, or by personal animosity, will *listen;* will ask the deft question; will try to understand; and I enjoyed talking with them. Many are themselves wonderfully candid, altogether capable of relaxing, and levelling with you.[13] It was from them, for instance, that my impression was confirmed that John Lindsay's press conferences were wooden affairs—an objective theatrical datum that had of course no bearing on their strategic appreciation of Mr. Lindsay, or their hopes for his election. An assistant editor of *National Review* attended John Lindsay's press conferences every morning at the Roosevelt Hotel at 9:30, and he would telephone to my apartment at 10:30, from a pay booth, to brief me on what had gone on, in time for my own press conferences at 11 (mine were far less frequent than JVL's, though toward the end they were, as a matter of necessity, held almost daily). I gathered, from my own representative, that JVL's tended to be prosaic affairs, repetitious, formalistic, called not so much for the purpose of continuing a dialogue with the other candidates, or with the voters, as for purely personal exposure. This was not necessarily an act of vanity by Mr. Lindsay or his managers; it was strategy. His jejune position papers were merely props. What was wanted was the redemptive omnipresence; but that is hard, after a while, on working reporters of intellectual curiosity, who *themselves* desire to be interested.

The routine of a press conference, by the way, is as follows. The candidate arrives (decorously late[14]) with a statement, or two, or

---

to strengthen the articles by eliminating the more glaring factual errors without necessarily, or probably, changing their general line."

13. A free-lance writer related something I have never checked back on, for fear it might prove apocryphal, namely that at a party, toward the end of the campaign, a senior editor of *The New York Times* confessed to him that he had taken to dispatching different reporters to my press conferences, because "everyone who came back after a couple of them said he was going to vote for the son of a bitch."

14. I arrived exactly on time for a taping early in the campaign and found no one, but literally not a living soul, in the studio. I was to learn that punctuality is yet another sign of the non-serious candidate.

three or four, to make. He reads them. Copies are handed out to the roomful of reporters, and they ask questions for about twenty minutes or a half-hour. Then the television crews take their turn. The candidate repeats his statements or, if they are too long for TV, salient excerpts from them. The television reporters ask their own questions. And always the questioners gravitate to the most salacious issues of the day, preferably personal ("Mr. Lindsay: Mr. Beame said yesterday that your statement that he could not wait for the death of Mrs. Roosevelt and Senator Lehman so as to be able to re-embrace the bosses, was 'vicious' and 'inexcusable.' What is your comment on that, sir?" "Mr. Lindsay: Mr. Buckley said yesterday that while at Yale you did a little witch-hunting together . . . ?"). Lindsay, the record shows, almost never took off ad libitum. On the one or two occasions when he did, it became especially clear why he hewed most of the time to his resolution not to do so. He husbanded his impromptu performances for carefully selected newsmen whose sympathies he had every reason to be confident of, and he was seldom disappointed. It did appear, at one point in September immediately after the first televised debate and the reappearance of the *Tribune* (the newspaper strike was on, but the *Tribune* abruptly abandoned the Publishers' Association) with its dismaying poll showing Abraham Beame leading Lindsay by ten per cent, as though at least the national press was about to desert Lindsay as a lost cause.[15] Many of the reporters would arrive at my own headquarters hungry for the human satisfactions they knew they could take only from a "non-serious" candidate licensed to say the unsayable. This was the peculiar advantage I had in the campaign. Although it was out of the question that I might win, what I said became, from about mid-September on, objectively newsworthy because the polls showed that my own exiguous vote was climbing, that Beame and Lindsay were beginning to show a concern over it. Indeed, they would (see above) end up vying with one another to arrest the little landslide toward the Conservative Party, each one fearing that the movement was at his own net expense. Toward the end it became a rabid contest to determine which of the two, Beame or Lindsay, was the more greatly offended by me and my supporters, and which of the two could strike a more authentic note of indignation as regards the Far Right, and the threat therefrom. Lindsay had taken the early initiative and was away and running on this issue well before Beame, belatedly, got into

15. *Time* and *Newsweek* had both scheduled cover stories on Lindsay for about that time but postponed them on account of the general boredom with Lindsay in September and the prevailing opinion that he had lost the election. When he won, they instantly retooled the cover stories, comparing him with the rising sun and the aurora borealis.

the act. There are those who say that this was what won the election for Lindsay: the specially designed appeal to the important Jewish vote. It was that special appeal, as we bounced around in the station wagon, that the three reporters—one from the *Times*, one from the *Tribune*, and one from the Washington *Post*—had, with complete candor, been discussing with me as we pulled up to the curb and stopped outside the CBS Building for the fourth and final live three-man debate of the campaign, on October 28. I came close, in the heat of that debate (see above), to revealing their identity.

10. "Fifty Bucks from Buckley"

October 14. The *Tribune* had a big story this morning by Evans and Novak; headline, "50 BUCKS FROM BUCKLEY." The scoop: that during the 1964 Congressional campaign one William F. Buckley, Jr., of Stamford, Connecticut sent a check for fifty dollars to Donald J. Irwin, a liberal Democrat running against the "moderate Republican incumbent, Ab Sibal" from Fairfield County, for Congress.

"Why," E & N asked, ". . . would Conservative Buckley make a contribution to a liberal Democrat running for Congress?" And quickly they provided—"The answer—calculated sabotage of the Republican center—[which] goes far beyond that congressional race in suburban Connecticut. It explains why Buckley is working so hard today to prevent the election of a Republican moderate as mayor of New York. This political cannibalism is the real tip-off that conventional unity is impossible in the Republican Party today.

"Even more ironic [they continued] is the fact that Sibal was no leftist son of the wild jackass during his four years in Congress. The liberal Americans for Democratic Action (ADA) credits him with 20 'correct' votes out of 42 for a 47 per cent liberal rating. In contrast, the ADA gave Democratic Irwin 16 'correct' votes out of 18 for an 88 per cent liberal rating during an earlier stint in Congress."

And the closing ". . . in a recent conversation with newspaper reporters, Nixon described the Buckleyites as a threat to the Republican Party even more menacing than the Birchers. Considering the fact that Buckleyism helped topple Sibal in Connecticut and now undermines Lindsay in New York, Nixon has a point."[16]

All in all quite a column, especially the last part; though I doubt the press will play it up because, without a context supplied, the

16. In March 1966, Nixon more or less disengaged himself from the quotation. He meant, he said, that Buckley, having attacked the John Birch Society, would get more votes than otherwise, and hence become "more dangerous" to Lindsay.

"danger" of the "Buckleyites" to the GOP simply isn't manifest (though I don't doubt it *is* a latent danger if the GOP is going to fashion itself after John Lindsay).

An interesting internal contradiction in the column. E & N refer (1) to "liberal Democratic candidate Donald J. Irwin"—whom all Connecticut Republicans should have opposed. Then they refer (2), to the *"Republican moderate"* Lindsay—whom all New York City Republicans should be backing. Then, (3), by way of proving that Sibal, Irwin's opponent in Fairfield County, is *"no leftist son of the wild jackass,"* they turn to the ADA scorecard. The ADA gave Sibal a 47 per cent rating. By contrast, the ADA gave Irwin an 88 per cent rating. That certainly establishes that Irwin is a left-liberal, doesn't it?

The datum *not* supplied by E & N: the ADA gave the "Republican moderate" Lindsay, this last time around, a rating of 87 *per cent*. Why should all Connecticut Republicans band together to oppose a Connecticut legislator (Irwin) with an 88 ADA record, and all New York Republicans band together to elect a New York legislator (Lindsay) with an 87 ADA record? Should I write to them and point out the contradiction?

When I reached headquarters, there was a lot of buzz about the column, specifically about the gift I had made to Irwin. I vaguely remembered that I had sent a letter to Irwin accompanying my contribution. By great good luck I found I had kept a copy. It was quickly mimeoed and distributed at the press conference already called that afternoon for the purpose of issuing the position paper on a single value-added tax. The letter read:

August 17, 1960

The Hon. Donald J. Irwin
House Office Building
Washington, D.C.

Dear Don:

Alas, we are in one of those piquant situations which can make life quite miserable. I would like so much to support your political career simply because you are yourself, and an old friend. But to do so would make a mockery out of my life. By the standards of the Americans for Democratic Action, you voted satisfactorily eight out of nine times on "critical issues" during the last session. By the standards of the Americans for Constitutional Action, you voted only 15 per cent of the time in behalf of sound money *vs.* inflation; 10 per cent of the time in favor of economy *vs.* waste; 27 per cent of the time in favor of private enterprise *vs.* government interference; 20 per cent of the time in favor of private ownership against government ownership; not once in favor of individual freedom versus increased coercion. *Qué hay que hacer?* If you will promise me that you will use a tiny little contribution from me for a good dinner and a bottle of champagne for you and your wife, and not on anything connected with your politics, I should be most happy to send the check along.

Siempre, tu amigo—[17]
William F. Buckley, Jr.

11. The Debates

October 22. Lindsay, in answer to a question, said at his press conference this morning that it is untrue that he had declined a television debate with me for the Sunday before Election Day. Strange, because he *did* decline the debate, pure and simple. NBC had wired both Lindsay and me on October 8 that Beame had declined an invitation to a three-man debate, but that the invitation was nevertheless open "contingent on acceptance by both you and Mr. Lindsay." On October 20, NBC wired me: "This is to advise that WNBC-TV is withdrawing its invitation for a debate as outlined in wire of October 8 between you and Mr. Lindsay. The withdrawal is necessitated by the fact that Mr. Lindsay has declined on the basis that he would only be interested in a Lindsay-Beame-Buckley debate, which was the original proposal."

Flat Lie Department?

Or is there no such thing as a flat lie in politics? We dutifully handed out photostats of the NBC telegrams to the press. No ripple. Who cared?

There was much suspense in anticipation of the debates. It was widely speculated that, at that particular form, I had the advantage, having in pursuit of unpopular ideas been frequently required over the years to face the opposition. I suspect—an admission against personal interest—that those points I have scored are primarily on account of their own cogency, rather than on account of any personal adeptness at formulating them. And in dealing with politicians running for office there is, of course, a preternatural advantage. How

17. The sign-off was in Spanish because Irwin and I had been Spanish instructors while we were contemporaries at Yale. I received a note from Congressman Irwin the same day the Evans-Novak column appeared: "Bob Novak called today to check on your generous contribution to me in 1964. . . . I'm delighted to reciprocate your generosity . . ." and he enclosed a check for fifty dollars. Irwinism is clearly more dangerous to the Democrats than Communism?

can you lose, in a public debate with aspirants for the mayoralty in New York, by asking, nay, pleading with your opponents to join with you in, say, denouncing Adam Clayton Powell, Jr., as a demagogue? I mean, it's almost unfair. They are not going to say: No, he isn't a demagogue—because to do so would be to fly in the face of a fact of New York as conspicuous as its skyline. On the other hand, they won't agree with you that that is what he is, because Adam's boys (approximately 90,000) are first and last Adam's boys, and they will not like that, not at all. I first tried it on Paul O'Dwyer, in our *mano a mano* in August when he was contending for the Democratic nomination. It was very difficult for him, since we were able to speak back and forth to each other, to ignore the question; but ignore it he did, time after time after time. I tried it with Beame and Lindsay. Beame ignored the challenge, Lindsay did too a half-dozen times, and finally—rather shrewdly—replied to it by saying: "I don't know why you ask *me* to renounce Adam Clayton Powell, Jr., since Powell has come out for Mr. Beame." A classical example of what the logicians call *ignoratio elenchi*—I hadn't asked him whom Powell had come out for, but what he *thought* of Powell as a leading figure in New York politics and sociology. But it took him off the hook, I expect, in the eyes of many listeners—as *ignoratio elenchi* frequently does, which is precisely why it was identified millenniums ago in the first category of evasions.

I found the debates greatly constricting. The formula was always the same: round and round we went, whether posing our own questions or commenting on the moderator's: one candidate, the second candidate, the third candidate. The opportunity for evasion is enormous. Jones: How, Brown, are you going to raise the money to pay for that housing scheme you proposed? Brown: I want to answer Smith's ridiculous suggestion that I voted against the poverty bill. . . . Smith: Jones has yet to make an original suggestion concerning traffic. . . .

It was always so, the third man serving the second as a means of getting away from the first, while still leaving the impression that somehow he had been responsive. The moderators took pains to stay out of the way, except to clock the time-period exactly. None was ever heard to say to Jones: Honorable Jones, before you get off on that tangent, why don't you answer Smith's question about X? A three-man debate is not properly a debate but a forum. And unless its participants are permitted to colloquize, there is little engagement, infrequent resolution.

My associates kept urging on me a single point to stress, above all others[18]; they urged, particularly in my opening and closing statements, that, instead of tangling with Beame and Lindsay, I should speak over their heads (as they were continually doing over mine and each other's), directly to the voters, giving them reasons why they should vote the Conservative ticket. I tried to do that, as often as it occurred to me; but often it didn't occur to me, my ungovernable instinct being to fasten on a weakness in the opponent's reasoning and dive in; or on a weakness in my own, and apply sutures—on the (Platonic?) assumption that voters will be influenced by the residual condition of the argument. A good debater is not necessarily an effective vote-getter: you can find a hole in your opponent's argument through which you can drive a coach and four ringing jingle bells all the way, and thrill at the crystallization of a truth wrung out from a bloody dialogue—which, however, may warm only you and your muse, while the smiling paralogist has in the meantime made votes by the tens of thousands.

Lindsay throughout the campaign was accusing me of collusion with Abraham Beame—"Buckley [me] Buckley [Chas.] and Beame" was his anti-doxology during the last few weeks. I sheepishly admit that there *was* one instance of such collusion. A very close friend of Beame begged me, in October, to denounce Beame during one of the debates as the logical candidate of "Roosevelt, Kennedy and Johnson" —the triptych of the overwhelming majority of New York voters. I thought about it, and decided, Why the hell not? I had, after all, never said anything to suggest that the three gentlemen were my muses, and a whole lot to suggest otherwise. So, at the last debate, I dutifully suggested, while staring Beame in the face, that he was the logical candidate of Roosevelt, Kennedy, and Johnson. I wondered whether I would get a flicker of appreciation, a shaft of love. Nothing. Mr. Beame had probably never been told by his representative about our great collusion.

I had working for me, I repeat, an invaluable advantage, namely that I did not expect to win the election, and so could afford to

18. I was also urged to ask one or two specific questions. I remember, for instance, repeatedly being urged to ask Lindsay: "Mr. Lindsay, if Nixon is nominated by the Republican Party for the Presidency in 1968, would you support him?" The thinking was that he would have the devil's own time answering. If on the one hand he said, "Yes"—he would gravel the Nixon-haters in New York's liberal camp, roughly speaking one hundred per cent of the population. If he said, "No" —he would alienate his Republicans. I never did get around to asking the question, in part unintentionally, in part, I think, because I figured that Lindsay would have an easy enough time bunting it away by some such statement as, "Mr. Buckley is always trying to punish me for irregularity, his whole campaign is pitched around my failure to vote for Goldwater"—or any of a dozen other debater's ways of shuffling off the mortal coil. Nothing makes you look foolisher in debate than to ask a pregnant question which your target can successfully dispose of.

violate the taboos. Lindsay and Beame had taboos' mother to observe:
Beame could not afford to criticize Boss Powell or Boss Steingut;
Lindsay could not afford to criticize Boss Rose or Boss Dubinsky.
Neither would breathe a word of criticism against John Kennedy, or
Mrs. Roosevelt, or Herbert Lehman, or Lyndon Johnson, the welfare
state, the press, the voting population, labor unions, universal suf-
frage, or the Statue of Liberty. That left them precious little to
criticize except inexperience (Lindsay's), fatigue (Beame's), crypto-
Republicanism (Lindsay's), the bosses (Beame's)—and of course,
(all together, boys), me, Goldwater, and the nineteenth century. They
joined in deploring the existing situation in housing, schooling, water,
transit, slums, hospitals, air pollution, whatever, with slightly different accents. (We must be doing *something* right, Beame would plead,
citing the dozen hundred million dollars that had been spent on—
housing, schooling, water . . . ; while Lindsay would say that not
enough had been done, and that under his stewardship much more
would be done to improve—housing, schooling, water. . . .)

Lindsay would arrive at the studios very tense, and instantly he
would cover the desk area in front of him with a half-acre of three-
by-five cards on which were graven in Magic Marker the salient
points or statistics he intended to make and cite in the course of the
fracas. (I had a mad impulse, one time when he went off for a moment to pose for a picture, to scramble the cards around, or maybe
doctor the statistics, just a little, horrible bit.)

Always, when the camera first focused on the candidates, during
the few seconds when they are being identified by the moderator,
they would manage a warming half-smile. Perfectly proper, utterly
professional—there isn't anyone in the business who doesn't do it,
whether Elvis Presley, Eric Sevareid, Lyndon Johnson, or U Thant.
Twelve years earlier I had signed up for what turned out to be a
a half-hundred consecutive weekly television episodes, and I noticed
the other members of the panel regularly producing the half smile—
I remarked it not with contempt but, increasingly, with envy—because I simply could not, and cannot to this day, manage it. At one
point my wife, playfully, tried to make me practice, as if it were a
calisthenic; but there is no practicing it, because, inevitably, you roar
with laughter at yourself (try it). I have developed a sort of anti-tic
at such moments—my lips will simply not move, unless I am moved
by an elfin provocation, in which case I completely spoil the intended
effect of a sort of half-smiled reserved benevolence by breaking out
in a disconcerting sea of teeth.

Beame, so nervous that his hand shook when he reached for a piece
of paper, had several notebooks, and several brilliantly memorized

passages of rhetoric, one of which he never changed (see above)—
he always closed with it. "New York has done a great deal for me.
It sent me through school. I love this city. I owe a lot to this city. . . ."
I commented about the third time around that if he really desired to
requite his obligation to New York, perhaps he should consider withdrawing from public office in favor of me. He managed a wan smile.
Lindsay's perorations changed verbally, but not in substance. Their
thesis was that New York greatly needed a change, and that here
was New York's historical opportunity to effect that change. He used
on more than one occasion a figure of speech which I found biologically disconcerting. It was what we came to call at HQ "the
three-handed pitch"—"I ask all New Yorkers to join me, to roll up
their sleeves, to care, to adopt the view that there must be from now
on *one* hand for the self, *one* hand for the family and *one* hand for
the city." He had clearly outbid all mortal men.

12. How to Get to LBJ

October 31. Beame was thunderstruck last Tuesday, one week before Election Day, by the astonishing failure of Hubert Humphrey,
here to preside at a $100-a-plate fund-raising dinner for Beame, to
communicate formally Lyndon Johnson's endorsement of him. The
Democrats, already piqued by Johnson's bewildering procrastination,
had expected, finally, a robust endorsement; and were paralyzed with
mortification when it failed to come. The very next day George Meany,
of the AFL-CIO, and Edwin Weisl, Democratic National Committee-
man from New York, went industriously to work, telephoning to
Washington and to Austin, Texas (where LBJ was staying); to friends
of Johnson; and to friends of friends of Johnson. But it looked bad:
if Johnson had declined to back Beame on the last of the opportune
occasions, it was hardly likely that he would do so now, particularly
since LBJ doesn't like to appear to have bent under pressure.

Republicans-for-Buckley,[19] of all unlikely agencies, came to the
rescue. Acting on his own initiative, Chairman Peter W. Hoguet
called the press and read a statement which, to judge from the heated
treatment of it by White House Press Secretary Bill Moyers two days
later, may very well have provoked the President into taking the
step he had heretofore been so greatly reluctant to take. "The absence
of a formal endorsement of Comptroller Beame by President Johnson,"
Hoguet said, "may have put the President in Congressman Lindsay's

19. Whose members included Clare Boothe Luce, Earl E. T. Smith, and Frederic
Coudert, Lindsay's predecessor in Congress.

corner—in recognition of Lindsay's liberal Congressional voting record. President Johnson," Hoguet added, "may have wanted to temper the activities of certain local Democratic leaders [read: Sen. Bobby Kennedy]. The failure of LBJ to endorse Democrat Abe Beame certainly gives rise to a hidden ball-play—Johnson to Lindsay—leaving Beame in left field without a glove or endorsement."

This was of course pure speculation. On the other hand, speculation was clearly in order. Why *hadn't* Johnson backed Beame? No one put any stock in the official explanation that the President did not wish to intervene in mere municipal elections. Did he in fact wish to deflate Bobby Kennedy, who was energetically campaigning for Beame? Was he afraid Beame was going to lose,[20] and therefore that he would dissipate some presidential prestige? Was there anything to Hoguet's speculation that Johnson was secretly for Lindsay? (Earlier in the year, Johnson had complimented Lindsay, on the ironic grounds that he was "so much like Wagner.")

At any rate, Moyers conferred the belated endorsement on Beame in answer to a spicy question from a reporter asking whether President Johnson had indeed arrived at a tacit understanding with Lindsay. Such a charge, Moyers fumed, was "absolutely untrue, ridiculous." "A lot of lies were being spread, a lot of innuendoes made and voices were crying in the wilderness and the truth needed to be made clear," he added, evidently quite carried away—whereupon the so hungrily sought-after benediction: Mr. Beame knows the President is strongly and enthusiastically behind him. Mr. Beame knows that if the President voted in New York he would cast his vote for Mr. Beame and his ticket." Mr. Beame, of course, had known no such thing until this moment, which is why he was instantly reported as "jubilant."

"Pressures kept building up"—the UPI looked back on the election (November 3)—"for the President to issue a statement of support for Abraham D. Beame, the Democratic candidate for mayor in New York City. Johnson resisted these pressures for a long time. . . . But the President's ire was aroused—according to the best information available—when supporters of Conservative Party candidate William F. Buckley Jr. said Johnson wasn't endorsing Beame because of a deal with . . . Lindsay. Johnson sprang back not only with an endorsement of Beame but with his most partisan utterance since he ran against Barry Goldwater for President in 1964."

Actually, it proved too late to corral the straying sheep. Coming

20. A plausible argument for LBJ's behavior at this point, perhaps, with Lindsay and Beame running neck and neck in the polls; but hardly so three weeks or a month before, when Beame was way ahead.

that late, and quite possibly provoked by causes extrinsic to the President's appreciation of Abraham Beame, the endorsement rang hollow. Insiders argued that it would have hurt Beame even more if it hadn't come at all, but that coming now, at this late moment, it failed to accomplish what might otherwise have been accomplished. Still, lawyer Hoguet came as close as he is likely to come to a judgeship.

13. A Goldwater Operation?

October 9. At 11:45 A.M. I was still at home, working on a talk for Queens College that night, and wondering whether, at the televised debate that afternoon, Lindsay or Beame would say anything unusual.[21] The telephone rang. It was Barry Goldwater. How was I, how was he, how was my wife, how was his wife, etc., etc. I asked if he could join me for lunch, which I had already scheduled with my brother Jim, and my brother-in-law Brent Bozell, formerly associated with Senator Goldwater; and two members of the staff. He said he could join us for a drink, but would probably have to go off before lunch, to accommodate a crowded schedule. A few minutes later we met at Voisin on 65th Street, and in short order the six of us were greatly enjoying ourselves—and G. stayed right through. He was in fine form, relaxed, sharp, detached. I had not seen him since the Convention in San Francisco (and there only fleetingly). We had exchanged a number of letters, usually about matters tangential to our principal concerns. I had spoken to him over the telephone before announcing my candidacy. In the remoter past, I had visited with him more frequently, and I was glad to refresh my memory of him as among the world's most engaging men. To say nothing of the most candid.

He was to be in New York for only a few hours, en route to Bermuda to some meeting or other of airplane enthusiasts. I asked him whether he was aware that Lindsay was to an increasing extent orienting his campaign on an anti-Goldwater basis, and he replied that of course he was, that they have newspapers in Arizona too, perhaps not as few as absolutely desirable. Did he, I asked, feel the tug of organizational loyalty to Lindsay? His answer was gloriously unambiguous: No. It wasn't, he said, merely Lindsay's refusal to support Goldwater as the choice of the National Republican Party the year before, though that was a technical delinquency of heavy bearing on Lindsay's current claims to organized Republican support. Lindsay,

21. No.

he felt, by his voting record and his public announcements, had identified himself as belonging outside the plausible limits of Republicanism as currently understood; and, he reasoned, Lindsay had under the two circumstances—organizational infidelity and infidelity to the most lenient expressions of Republican principle—disqualified himself from any call to loyalty from Republicans *qua* Republicans.

And on we went to other matters—he talked most amusingly, I remember, about how Lyndon Johnson manages to upstage every meeting of the Republican National Committee in Washington, and how he had pleaded with Dwight Eisenhower to resist, on the occasions of National Committee meetings, invitations from Johnson to the White House, which inevitably overshadow news of the GOP gatherings.

I began to notice a rather distracting *sotto voce* conversation on my left between my brother and brother-in-law—less than absolutely courteous, I thought. Now Jim was scribbling something on a yellow legal pad. He suddenly interrupted Goldwater, in mid-sentence. "Senator," he said, "Brent tells me that since we're in politics, we've got to be terribly businesslike. I've written out a three-sentence statement. Do you mind if I read it to you?"

"Go ahead," Goldwater said.

"Throughout my public career," Jim began, "I have worked for unity within the Republican Party, regardless of shades of opinion, within the broad principles which characterize our Party. Today, in New York, there is only one candidate for Mayor who is running on Republican principles, and who is proud to identify himself with those principles. In my opinion, Bill Buckley is the only true Republican running for Mayor of New York, and I urge all good Republicans to support him this November."

"Would you sign that?" Jim asked.

Quick as a shot—"Sure," Goldwater said, reaching in his pocket for a pen with one hand, with the other for Jim's notebook—and signed: "B.M.G."; and resumed his reminiscences.

We drove to the television station elated, a piece of front-page news in Jim's pocket. The newspapers were still on strike, but before the broadcast was over we were informed by the moderator that a settlement had just been reached, that the strikebound papers would resume publication the following Monday. That would be the moment to release the news!

Over that weekend, cooling down, we decided not to publish the endorsement at all.

Our reasoning: that if we directly involved Goldwater in the campaign, post-election analyses would begin at the figure 800,000, the number of votes Goldwater himself had got in New York City in the 1964 Presidential election. The difference between *that* figure, and the inevitably lower figure the Conservative Party would score would prompt the refrain from the analysts that thus further had conservative fortunes fallen in the twelve-month interval between 1964 and 1965. They would, predictably, not heed, as we, of course, did, the intervening factors. (1) Goldwater had run on the established Republican ticket and could count on automatic Republican votes, which would now go to Lindsay. (2) Goldwater was a candidate for President, and as such received immense publicity which reached and influenced voters who would not be influenced merely by an endorsement from Goldwater. And (3)—beginning at the other end of the scale—whatever progress the Conservative Party stood to make over its previous showing would inevitably be attributed exclusively to Goldwater's nonrecurrable endorsement. In short, we calculated, neither the conservative movement, nor Goldwater, nor the Conservative Party, stood to profit strategically from the publication of the endorsement.

I wrote Goldwater and informed him that such was our reasoning and our decision. He replied that he perfectly well understood. He must, as a politician of superior skill, have well understood what took us the whole weekend to fathom; undoubtedly he intuited it all in the moment it took him to reach casually for his pen and initial the endorsement. He initialed it anyway, because he is a valiant man and a faithful friend: and he was moved by our eagerness.

Neither Lindsay nor the pro-Lindsay press ever learned about the proffered endorsement; though it hardly mattered to them in formulating their own public strategy, which was that I was the Goldwater candidate, on which theme improvisations were rendered reaching even, as already mentioned, to the suggestion that my candidacy was an intricate Arizona plot. The accusations that Goldwater was a vindictive underworlder, managing my campaign for the purpose of evening a score with Lindsay, grew so frequent that I finally acknowledged them at a press conference:

"The charge that Mr. Goldwater is running my campaign," I said on October 25, "seems to me quaint. I don't know who is running Mr. Lindsay's campaign, but I certainly don't blame him for guarding anonymity. I have talked with Mr. Lindsay more frequently during Calendar 1965 than I have with Senator Goldwater, who in fact, as titular head of my party, the Republican Party, and as a personal friend, I have shamefully neglected, and to whom, wherever he is, I take this opportunity, through the public media, to transmit my affectionate greetings."

X.

The Campaign

On September 25 the *Tribune* announced, to the infinite relief of the Lindsay camp, its resignation from the New York Publishers' Association, and its decision to resume daily publication beginning September 27. Lindsay had especially missed his daily tribute, and had been generally shaken by the sudden cessation, when the newspapers closed down on September 17,[1] of the copious publicity that had been fueling his campaign. Shortly before the strike, Abraham Beame had won his unexpected victory in the Democratic primary, sorely disconcerting the carefully-wrought strategy of the Lindsay forces, which had been based on the assumption that the front-runner Paul Screvane would win. Screvane had, from Lindsay's point of view, the double disadvantage of being (a) unrepentantly tied to Wagner, and (b) non-Jewish—Lindsay strategists now feared that the temptation would be marginal among too many New Yorkers to vote for the man who might become the first Jewish Mayor of New York. Still another interruption in Lindsay's plans was myself. "Strategists for John Lindsay," the *Daily News* commented[2] the day it resumed publishing, "devised a simple defense tactic for their man against acid-tongued[3] Conservative Wm. F. Buckley Jr. at the start of the present campaign. The defense gimmick? Ignore him. Now, however, they're

1. Excepting the New York *Post.*
2. Edward O'Neill, October 11, 1965.
3. I have fretted, particularly in this chapter, over the problem of how to handle adjectives and comments concerning myself which might be construed as complimentary. I considered the expedient of simply suppressing them altogether, and finally rejected it—to do so would be not only antihistorical and inartistic, but stilted—*e.g.*, as when faced with the above, "Strategists for John Lindsay devised a simple defense tactic for their man against . . . Conservative Wm. F. Buckley Jr." There will be more than enough quoted material of an invidious sort to wilt the posies.

asking themselves in shocked whispers: 'How do you ignore a man who appears well on his way to picking up [several] hundred thousand votes on Election Day?' "

On top of these difficulties, Lindsay was simply not fleshing out his own narcissistically projected image. His position papers had not galvanized, the initial debates had not inspired, his rhetoric had not transported. On these points and others, the testimony from national columnists who supported Lindsay, and who stuck with him to the end, was abundant and—variously—disappointed, melancholy, exasperated, hortatory.

Lindsay had lost his poise? Mary McGrory wrote on November 1: "The chief cause of the frayed nerves of the principals, the Tory Buckley, had long since glided away from the scene [of the final debate]. He is the only man who is now enjoying the election. He has brought his silken baritone and well-bred sneer to every reunion of Lindsay and Beame, sitting between them with a glittering expression of haughty amusement and detachment doodling elegantly while they frantically scribble and glare at each other."

Lindsay's humorlessness was showing? Charles Bartlett of the Washington *Star* wrote on October 14: "Buckley has a cruel grip on Lindsay's Achilles Heel, which is an unreadiness to laugh at himself. Television is a medium on which Lindsay would normally flourish, but his impact in the confrontations to date has been dented by Buckley's agile needle. The Conservative's jibes pinion Lindsay into an unbecoming stiffness."

Maybe he was a little mean? On October 29 New York *Post* columnist Joseph Kraft wrote: "Buckley has pierced the Lindsay mask . . . [revealing] to the public two Lindsay traits that project the Sheriff of Nottingham more than Robin Hood. For a starter, it became clear that Lindsay was not good in the cut and thrust of debate. That, in turn, he was neither funny nor clever. Worse still, it became clear that he had a nasty temper. Far from emerging as a cool, distant, Olympian figure, a fit object for incense, Lindsay was made to look just like everybody else—perplexed and harassed."

Was he a little superficial? *Newsday*'s Marquis Childs wrote on October 12: "[Lindsay] is discovering . . . that the city's problems do not respond to campaign rhetoric." The *Journal-American*'s Marianne Means added: "The people [interviewed by a pollster] tend to dismiss Beame as a dull bookkeeper and Lindsay as a rich lightweight." And Ralph McGill: "Mr. Lindsay seems to have been revealed by television as a handsome, attractive man, but also a somewhat superficial one."

Not really up to the challenge? Eric Sevareid, on October 31, hinted at it: "A city that can discover noble leadership in an Abraham Beame can with equal ease find clay inside the shoes of John Lindsay, the earnest Jimmy Stewart of this script, the wasp that seemed to lose both its color and its sting as soon as it was exposed to the political fumes of the New York streets." And *Newsweek*'s Raymond Moley on October 4: "John Lindsay, who seeks the support which elected the late Fiorello La Guardia three times, has had the La Guardia words but not the tune—the passionate righteousness in the Little Flower's campaigns which was the promise of indefatigable activity as mayor. . . . His campaign promises are lamentable, and would shackle him to minority interests if elected Mayor." And even the *Tribune*'s Joseph Alsop: "Lindsay has hardly proven that he is a man with the toughness, ingenuity, and vision to start a giant, near-bankrupt city on a wholly new course" (October 27).

And, perhaps worst of all from the point of view of a political campaign—just plain dull? Scripps-Howard columnist Bruce Biossat sighed: "Lindsay is *not* an exciting campaigner" (November 2).

Everyone sat chewing his nails, waiting for the first, widely trumpeted voters poll organized by the *Tribune* for publication on October 7. The results were worse for Lindsay than he had anticipated. Lindsay 35.6 per cent, Beame 45.7, Buckley 10.2. After spending over a million and one-half dollars, basking in national publicity for five months, organizing an *omnium gatherum* fusion ticket, excreting every semblance of Republicanism, Lindsay now ranked in popularity (after distributing the undecided vote) a mere three points above the Republican sacrificial lamb (Louis Lefkowitz) sent out to slaughter in the preceding mayoralty election.

I am not a confident political diagnostician, and cannot therefore describe with any personal assurance what exactly it was that finally determined the outcome of the campaign. Several things are, however, conspicuously a matter of record, and in the absence of transcendent intuitions, one might as well suppose that they proved crucial.

In such a narrative as this it might seem natural to follow the egotist's course and stress the bearing of the author's candidacy. I proceed to do so with easier conscience only because it happens also to have been stressed by, if not dispassionate commentators (I don't think there were any), at least by the preponderant number of commentators on the campaign. They bore down on two points: (1) New York City was in a fearful jam, from which it was unlikely that Mr. Beame, of limited imagination and mobility, could deliver it. And (2) if the Conservative Party contrived the defeat of Lindsay, the result would be not only to deprive New York of a glittering historical opportunity, but to strengthen the hand of those dark elements within the Republican Party that had nominated Senator Goldwater for the Presidency and so grievously embarrassed the republic. The election, it was subsequently acknowledged, turned as much on the second, as on the first, of these propositions.

During October, which was the month during which the election turned, very little attention was given to the position papers issued either by Mr. Lindsay or by Mr. Beame. And for reasons perfectly understandable, namely that by *The New York Times'* own headlined reckoning on Election Eve—"[MAJOR] CANDIDATES FLOOD THE VOTERS WITH POSITION PAPERS BUT REVEAL FEW DIFFERENCES"—there was little to choose between them, whether concerning housing, or schools, or transit, or air or water pollution, or crime, or whatever. The attention was, rather, on the candidates.

Beame's personal integrity was unimpeachable. But "personal integrity," as applied to a politician, can mean merely that he is not of the breed of politicians who line their own pocket (as, for instance, was regularly done in New York during the age of Jimmy Walker). Beame was so clearly above that kind of suspicion that an insinuation to that effect was never even raised, not even in a campaign desperate for issues and gluttonous for *ad hominem* argument. On the other hand, Beame did not emerge as a man whose integrity was such as would permit him—say—to ignore Charles Buckley, Boss of the Bronx, or Stanley Steingut, Boss of Brooklyn, in handing out patronage. At this level Lindsay was held to be relatively, though by no means completely, unobligated. It was generally known, among those people who know about that kind of thing, that Lindsay's manager, Robert Price, had promised patronage to the Liberal Party, in return for its endorsement. And, indeed, Lindsay's instantaneous post-election appointment of his running-mate Timothy Costello as Deputy Mayor would soon ratify that obligation. Not because Costello wasn't technically qualified to serve as Deputy Mayor, but because the designation of Costello under the embarrassing circumstances of his enthusiastic rejection by the voters on Election Day clearly suggested that here was a duty-appointment—done in brazen defiance of the democratic canons about which, during the campaign, Lindsay had spoken so love-sickly. Apart from his separate organizational obligations to the Liberal Party, Lindsay's obligations, highly visible to the voters, were not at all different in character from Beame's. Those obligations, as columnist Raymond Moley put it, were "to minority groups": to those who desired preferential treatment, whether through subsidized subway fares, subsidized rents, subsidized higher education, a civilian review board, immunities for the labor unions; whatever.

Even so, Lindsay was regarded by many voters as *relatively* independent, if only because his genealogy did not go back to Tammany Hall; and Tammany Hall, whether directly as during the recent epoch of Carmine De Sapio, or most recently as a chastened but influential bystander after the reformist purge of Robert Wagner, had produced the New York City which, by everybody's standard was, indeed, a city in crisis. However elusive the differences between the programs of Beame and those of Lindsay, the one came out of a different political tradition from the other. And in a city where hope, after all, is all that one can hope for, Lindsay was the unknown. Yet, most important, the safely unknown, *i.e.*, he would not likely disturb the cozy ideological accommodations—and for that reason emerged, for many voters, as the preferable candidate.

It was undeniably to the disadvantage of John Lindsay that he was formally attached to the Republican Party. Here the Liberal endorsement proved crucial. Without it, Lindsay would beyond question have lost the election. Slight though the Liberal showing was (281,796 votes), it was sufficient to make the difference between a narrow victory and a showing not much better than poor Lefkowitz's. Beyond the actual vote, deliverable by the Liberal Party, the implicit certification of Lindsay's liberalism unquestionably prompted a substantial number of Democrats who would not otherwise have done so, to vote for Lindsay-the-Republican.

Beame, on the other hand, had working for him, it was generally supposed, the fact of his Jewishness. Mr. Beame himself greatly stressed this attribute, for instance by an ultramontane observance of every discoverable orthodox Jewish prohibition against activity on Jewish feast days, rather as if a Christian had declined to appear on *Meet the Press* on Sunday, in literal observance of the Third Commandment. During the campaign, his staff distributed two mailings to Jewish voters. The first, signed by a rabbi, was aimed primarily at orthodox Jews and explicitly stressed Beame's Jewishness. It was characterized by *New York*, the Sunday magazine of the *Tribune*, as saying in effect "Vote for Abe Beame because he is Jewish and will bring distinction to our people." The second mailing, also directed to Jewish voters, "cited Beame's long association with some 40 Jewish charities and social organizations."[4]

4. These and the following references are to an extensive wrap-up on the campaign that appeared in *New York* on January 2, 1966. The article was by Nick

Apparently these appeals backfired. "The net effect," summarizes *New York*, "was simply to make more people furious, lose more votes." And then the unhappiest single encounter of Mr. Beame—with the irrepressible Adam Clayton Powell, Jr., who was unexpectedly present (it had been Beame's distinct understanding that he would not be there) at Powell's own Abyssinian Church one Sunday, to which Beame was drawn for reasons, I am glad to confess, I cannot conceivably divine. Not only was Powell there, but Powell proceeded to embrace poor Mr. Beame and to utter perhaps the greatest of all ineptitudes: "Now we will elect a Jew as Mayor of New York City! If I don't get these Southerners, these Jews, these Catholics into office, how can I ever expect to be President of the United States?" That it should be Adam Clayton Powell, Jr., who should rally the diaspora! It is recorded that even Mr. Beame was alarmed at the implications of Powell's statement. "I know I should have jumped up and said I didn't want votes on that kind of basis," he is recorded as saying, later, "but it happened so fast. I didn't know what to do." "The upshot," the authors of the election summary state, "was that the Jewish voters, who had been slipping away from him anyhow, now fled in wholesale lots."

Concerning his Jewishness, something else, by general though unpublished testimony, apparently worked against Mr. Beame— snobbishness. "Could you imagine," one voter addressed me, of all people, "Mrs. Beame greeting the Queen of England at Kennedy Airport?"[5] Within the bounds of semi-decency, the point was constantly driven home, that Beame was—ordinary. (I once contributed to that impression, or rather leeched on it, at a speech at the Overseas Press Club where I remarked that Mr. Beame constantly stressed that he was educated by the City of New York, "which fact should be obvious"; and I am ashamed of it.) In due course it became as routine for newspapermen and columnists to describe Beame as "lackluster" as it was for them to describe Lindsay as "tall," or "handsome," or "glamorous"; and the point, I think, drove deep into the womb of racial and religious pride. So much so that, unquestionably, many Jewish voters reacted against Beame precisely because of his Jewishness, on the theme of "we can do better than Beame"—

Thimmesch (of *Time*) and Peter Maas (of Curtis Publishing). The article should be approached skeptically, as I have previously indicated, since it is an account of the campaign which might have been written by Lindsay's godmothers. But the hero-worship apart, there is a great deal of useful and illuminating material in the 10,000-word piece.

5. I have not met the Queen of England, but I have met Mrs. Beame, whose natural dignity and unmanicured grace I'd have proudly proffered Her Majesty, at Kennedy Airport or Buckingham Palace.

the same kind of thing that caused some Catholics to vote against Al Smith in 1928. The *Journal-American* columnist William S. White alone isolated the deft appeal to snobbery: "There is no end to the irony," he wrote (October 29). "Against Beame's good if not exciting record of municipal service no one has lodged a responsible indictment. So, his very virtues—adult conduct and wise fiscal management —have become vices. He has no 'style.' He is 'dull!' He is short and lacking glamour. He is—though this point is only carefully used— not 'aristocratic' to a curious group of Democratic snobs which is forever screeching against 'discrimination' when practiced by others."

The pay-off is said to have been Beame's attitude toward me— which, until the moment of his blurted demagogy three days before Election Day (see above), was held to be unforgivably undemagogic.

A major policy decision on William Buckley wound up costing Beame . . . votes. The orthodox theory about the Buckley candidacy was that it would hurt Lindsay more than Beame. So Beame steadfastly ignored Buckley. Even when it became clear that Buckley's strength was at the point where he *had* to be drawing conservative Democrats from Beame, the official line was why stir things up. As Buckley stepped up his attacks on Lindsay [I never stepped them up. They were stepped up as far as they would step on the day I announced my candidacy] outraged Liberals who wanted to vote against Buckley had no place to go except to Lindsay. Shouldn't something be done about this? When some Beame staffmen made the suggestion three weeks before the election, two members of Beame's inner circle . . . turned the idea down.

Finally, there worked against Beame, and in favor of Lindsay, as concentrated a barrage of editorial exhortation as history records in New York City. Not even in the sacred cause of Johnson *vs.* Goldwater was it exceeded. I am bound, ruefully, to concede, on looking over the material, that it was I who apparently inserted the ginger in the columnists' tail. There is no doubting that the case for Lindsay against Beame would have been more difficult to make if it had had to depend exclusively on Lindsay's own relative virtues and promise. I do not know whether Mr. Beame had this in mind when, at 2:00 in the morning, conceding defeat, he said in answer to the question "Why did you lose?" "On account of Buckley." Maybe he meant that I had, in total, drained away from him more votes than I had drained away from Lindsay; in which case he was wrong. If he meant that I had served as the *corpus vile*, firing the efficacious indignation of the press and causing a last-minute landslide to Lindsay, then, *mea culpa*, I think he was probably correct.

Lindsay's darkest days were rung in with the publication of the *Tribune* poll, which seemed to emblazon the general disappointment with him, the failure of his great crusade. The gloom was palpable. His headquarters were demoralized. The press, for the first time, began openly to acknowledge his personal shortcomings (as we have seen). Financial contributions to his campaign sharply contracted. The voters turned their attention to the World Series, and the closing days of the World's Fair. But Lindsay was not by any means deserted. The opinion-makers quickly, and spontaneously, banded together to give his campaign the old heave-ho. And, in any case, the gloom was of short duration, because it was less than a fortnight until the New York *Daily News* first published the results of its own poll, whose reputation for accuracy is legendary.[6] It flatly contradicted the *Tribune* by listing Lindsay as running *ahead* of Beame in a hair-raiser: 42 per cent to 41.8 (and an astonishing 16.2 for me).

During the critical weeks in October, Lindsay emphasized certain themes he had touched on before, foremost among them (explicitly), his own liberalism; and (implicitly), his aloofness from the Republican Party. He developed a complementary theme, namely the necessity of saving New York City from the curse of reaction. By early October it had become clear to Lindsay's manager, Robert Price, that even assuming Lindsay had done himself damage with Republican voters by overemphasizing his detachment from the Republican Party, it was just plain too late to alter Lindsay's anti-Republican image. On the contrary, better bravely to underscore the anti- Republicanism and hope to flush loose from their habits ideologically motivated Democrats than fear the loss of disaffected Republicans who (a) were less numerous than prospective converts; and in any case (b) were, if already disaffected, probably irretrievably so.

The most ostentatious symbol of Lindsay's dissociation from the GOP was his absence from a great clan-gathering of Republicans on October 2, at which every major Republican ever heard of was present. Rockefeller, of course, was there; and Richard Nixon, and Herbert Brownell, and Jacob Javits. But not Lindsay, who pleaded an uneaten blintz in a remote corner of Brooklyn, or whatever, leaving the quite clear impression that he was absenting himself because he desired to absent himself, period. Even Governor Rockefeller was visibly disconcerted. Lindsay apologists pleaded in self-defense (when accosted by indignant Republicans), that the embarrassment had after

6. It has never erred on a New York Mayor since it began in 1933. It has predicted state-wide elections twenty-two out of twenty-five times. In 1964, the *News* was accurate within .5 per cent on Robert Kennedy *vs.* Kenneth Keating, only 1½ per cent off on Johnson *vs.* Goldwater.

all been Rockefeller's fault in the first place for scheduling the Republican jamboree in New York City over Lindsay's protests (why didn't Rockefeller convene the goddamn Republicans in Niagara Falls or someplace?). In any event, Rockefeller, piqued, began his oration at the conference by saying sententiously, "I'm a Republican and proud of it." ("This," Marquis Childs, the columnist, divined, "was a rebuke to Lindsay.") But the boycott by Lindsay nevertheless continued. Nor would Lindsay go out of his way even for fellow Republican office-seekers. "Local Republican candidates," wrote *Journal-American* columnist Harold Harris (October 18), "are openly voicing their displeasure with John Lindsay over his refusal to campaign with them or to appear at GOP clubhouses. Several GOPers early in the campaign turned down [proffered] endorsement from the Conservative Party because Mr. Lindsay requested them to do so. And, now they find that the expected Conservative vote to be cast for mayoralty candidate William F. Buckley Jr. could've given them a fighting chance in several close district contests for legislative posts. . . ."

Many political observers openly acknowledged the meaning of Lindsay's tactical gamble. The columnist Marianne Means, for instance:

> Boyish, blond, John V. Lindsay is proposing to live in sin with the Republican Party until the time he can make an honest woman out of her. . . . If Lindsay is elected . . . it will be because he has convinced hundreds of thousands of voters he has only an illicit relationship with the national GOP leadership. . . . If Lindsay had his way, nobody would utter the word "Republican" in his hearing. He bills himself as an "independent-non-partisan" and he displays pictures of himself with Lyndon Johnson. . . . Lindsay is for everything the Democrats are for, only he says he will do it better. He has begged national GOP figures to stay away. When a campaign strategist was asked whether Richard Nixon had been in touch lately, the fellow responded with a grin: "Who?" (*Journal-American*, October 29)

Other observers went so far as to conjecture that Lindsay's dissociation from the Republican Party was not only tactical but organic. Lyle Wilson, syndicated columnist, wrote: "Republican candidate . . . John V. Lindsay's claim to the GOP label is weak if not absolutely bogus. . . . Lindsay's effort to mix the political principles of the Liberal and Republican Parties is as outrageously unnatural as a mix of oil and water" (October 29).

William S. White, former political reporter for *The New York Times* and now a political syndicated columnist, gave way to progressive

manifestations of indignation at Lindsay's imposture (October 19):
"[Lindsay's] Republicanism is a joke. But it is a joke which most of
the regular Republicans still swallow sourly, on the theory that at
least he isn't a Democrat, either, and that anyhow perhaps a vic-
torious Lindsay, even as a so-called Republican, would give the
Democrats nationally something to think about in 1968. . . ." And
again (October 22): "Mr. Lindsay is a pseudo-Republican: a far-out
liberal whose purpose is to out-liberal even the quite liberal Democratic nominee, Abraham Beame. . . ." And one more time (October
29): "Lindsay is demonstrably a most un-Republican Republican in
alliance with a third force of demonstrable ultraliberalism, the
splinter Liberal Party. But"—a truly forbidden observation—"while
his flight from the GOP via the door on the left side is fine and up-
standing, the flight from the right-hand GOP door of his ultraconservative fourth party opponent, William F. Buckley, Jr., is the act
of an all but unconstitutional renegade."

Finally, to dissolve any lingering doubts on the matter, Lindsay's
staff heightened the campaign to situate Lindsay to the left of Abraham Beame. Lindsay's literature had long stressed his association
with the domestic programs of Presidents Kennedy and Johnson:
("For seven years he has represented New York in Congress where
he has supported the programs of Presidents John F. Kennedy and
Lyndon B. Johnson.") Harry Golden of the New York *Post* disconcerted
the liberal community by coming out against Lindsay on the grounds
that he was a Republican and "I do Lindsay no injustice when I say
he is definitely aiming for higher things. He may conceivably be on
the Republican national ticket in '68 if he wins this municipal election." But Golden largely made up for it by conceding (October 10)
about Lindsay what his liberal backers mostly desired to stress: "Now
it is true that Lindsay is somewhat to the left of Beame." It was all
very obvious to socialist Michael Harrington: ". . . as a sophisticated
conservative,[7] [Lindsay] is to the left of the Comptroller and his old-
fashioned economics" (October 24).

And in the final days of the campaign, Democrats-for-Lindsay
published a flyer to which they gave enormous distribution:

Will the Real Liberal Please Stand Up

. . . Why are the reactionary forces of Conservatism determined
to destroy John Lindsay's candidacy for Mayor of New York?

---

7. Michael Harrington (*Tribune* columnist), uses political labels playfully. In
Cavalier magazine (January 1966), he called for the emergence in America of a
"true Conservative" leader. No one I could think of would have fitted Harrington's definition since the death of Trotsky.

Beame lays claim to the proud banner of liberalism. Why doesn't Wm. Buckley concentrate his fire on Comptroller Beame? The answer is simple, Beame is not carrying the liberal banner in this campaign. John Lindsay is. . . . Says who?

The Citizens Union says so.

Americans for Democratic Action says so.

The New York *Post* says so.

The Liberal Party says so.

The New York Times and the *Herald Tribune* say so . . .

And finally, to cope with the Golden argument that a Lindsay victory would play into the hands of the Republican Party, David Dubinsky published a letter from Golden to himself and his own answer to it in full-page ads. Dubinsky's clincher: "Suppose we elect Lindsay as Mayor of New York City. What lesson does this teach to the other Republicans elsewhere who also would like to be elected? They must conclude that the way for a Republican to get elected is to act like Lindsay."

Dubinsky had skewered the great dilemma of the New York mayoralty campaign. If dilemmas were the kinds of things that greatly inconvenienced contemporary political moralizers, one might suppose this one would have stopped them cold. The *Tribune*, on the day I announced my candidacy, triumphantly deduced that the salient venality of my candidacy was that I was hauling into the New York mayoralty election altogether extraneous considerations of national politics.

> . . . The principal political business before the City of New York this year is electing a mayor, not staging esoteric [*sic*] debates. . . . Buckley may well, of course, have decided that John Lindsay, as a potential national Republican leader, poses so serious a threat to Buckley-style "conservatism" that Lindsay's ambitions have to be checked, and that reconsigning New York to the Tammany maw is simply the price that has to be paid. If so, it's not an approach likely to appeal to the average New Yorker, who, we imagine, would like to consider the mayoralty an office not thus to be trifled with.

The *Tribune* never went on to register a complementary dismay with Dubinsky for proclaiming that a victory for Lindsay would mean a rebirth of the Republican Party on a liberal image. The dilemma tore at other opinion-makers, but the affront on logic dismayed them not at all. By October, no self-respecting commentator could pretend that New York's election was a parochial affair, that Lindsay was merely a fusion candidate anointed to storm the gates of Tammany Hall. They came in waves, affirming the contrary. "[Lindsay is] potentially a valuable Republican property," said Doris Fleeson, columnist for the New York *Post* (October 21). And, again, Miss Fleeson: ". . . Lindsay is a shining symbol of Republican youth and hope" (October 3). "In the very nature of the struggle," wrote Robert Spivack, *Journal-American* columnist (October 14), "that's the way it has to be. For if Lindsay should win, with aid of the traditional 'good government' elements in New York and dissident Democrats, it would mark the obliteration of the Goldwater movement on the East Coast." "All American citizens have a fat stake in next month's election," said Lyle Wilson (October 20), underlining the national political implications of a Lindsay victory on the Republican Party: "[Lindsay], this non-Republican, would automatically upon his election be projected onto the national scene as a potential presidential candidate of that party as it stands today . . . the scenario, as it looks now, reads re-election for mayor in 1969; election as governor, 1970; the presidential nomination, 1972. All of this, of course, is based upon some highly optimistic 'ifs' " (October 29). And William S. White: "Though Lindsay is the spokesman for an un-Republican and basically no-party coalition, his apostles see him, at one and the same time, as the highest hope nationally of the Republican Party and also as the matchless symbol of pure, non-partisan, 'fusion' politics" (October 29).

Drew Pearson in the New York *Post*: "Some Republicans figure that if Lindsay is elected mayor, he could be the next GOP candidate for President . . ." (October 31). *The New York Times'* James Reston: "The GOP is already in desperate trouble in the cities. . . . There is no way to make a Republican comeback without Republican unity, and without the kind of success Lindsay is trying to achieve in New York" (October 31). And Dick Schaap, columnist for the *Tribune*: ". . . John V. Lindsay actually wants to be President of the United States. It is indicative of the silly state of politics that this ambition, which is a totally reasonable one, cannot even be mentioned in the campaign. Lindsay, instead, must pretend that all through his life he has dreamed of being Mayor of New York. I would imagine that his nightmares are brighter than that. The truth, of course, is that Lindsay got into this race for one main reason: If he wins, he automatically becomes a major national figure, a contender for a place on the Republican national ticket in 1968, or, more likely, 1972" (November 1).

Even so, conservative New York voters concerned with the future of the Republican Party as a vehicle for opposition to the Democratic way, were expected to ignore the national ramifications of a Lindsay victory. And to do so, moreover, even though they were convinced that a victory for Lindsay would not mean the substantial emancipation of the City of New York, but pretty much more of the same. The exhortations to drop everything and join the Lindsay bandwagon were for that reason almost uniformly evasive, and infuriatingly so when read alongside political analyses calmly predicting that a Lindsay victory would be parlayed into a national defeat for traditional Republican principles. The pro-Lindsay injunctions tended to ignore the national implications of the race, for the duration of their delivery, and on the matter of Lindsay's desirability over Beame, to be primarily asservative: Lindsay *will* help New York while Beame *will* hurt it. A resident of New York might well have argued, with his honor intact, that *even* if he were convinced that Lindsay would be a better mayor of New York than Beame, a Lindsay victory would result in national complications (damage to the two-party system) whose gravity outweighs the relative improvement Lindsay might bring to the administration of New York City. (Hardly a hypothetical fantasy. The analysis was used frequently in postwar Europe, to argue against electing leftist municipal officials, however civic-minded and efficient, on the grounds that their election would strengthen leftist influence nationally).

Neither reservation was acknowledged in the blasts of the opinion-makers: who regularly wrote as though the Conservatives *acknowledged* that Lindsay would make a better mayor. Michael Harrington, for instance: "Since his only political aim is to wreck the candidacy of John V. Lindsay, Buckley can afford to camp it up. On television, he has been arch, condescending, droll and very 'U', *i.e.*, all the things that a serious politician would not be. As a protest candidate, he can afford to be whimsical about a contest which will affect the destiny of eight million people [note the planted axiom], most of them without country estates in Connecticut where they can take refuge from incompetent mayors" (October 3). (And again the other relevant axiom ignored: Country estates in Connecticut are not immune from the results of the disappearance of the two-party system.)

And Inez Robb of the New York *World-Telegram:* "He [me] is the little fox trying to spoil the grapes for eight million New Yorkers— trying to spoil the grapes out of spite, to avenge Goldwater . . . and to continue the political degradation of New Yorkers who would have a chance for something better if Buckley could, for a moment, forget his arrogance and his mean revenge" (October 29). Or Richard Wilson on November 2: "The choice is so easy that it is hard to see how a serious-minded New Yorker could miss it. [Note the necessity, in the course of making the point, to convert Beame-supporters Robert Kennedy, James Farley, Averell Harriman, Franklin Delano Roosevelt,

Jr., and the editors of the New York *Daily News* and *Journal-American* into non-serious-minded New Yorkers] . . . Beame is not qualified to be mayor under existing conditions. What New York needs is a drastic change in its political system. [What I had been saying all along.] The only hope at all lies in Lindsay [a *non sequitur*]."

And Murray Kempton: *"The point about Lindsay is that he represents our last chance for civility"*[8] (October 12).

It all became, in the last couple of weeks, rather ferocious. Mr. Lindsay had for some time now been spending his most noticeable moments describing the horrors that would visit New York if I succeeded in beating him; and Mr. Beame, belatedly, joined him in competing for the honor of principal target of the forces of reaction. ("Deep down in your heart," Beame said at Lindsay in their two-way debate on the Saturday before election, "you *know* that Mr. Buckley is hurting me more than you.") The *Times* summarized the turn of affairs in a headline (October 29): "LIBERAL MANTLE HOTLY CONTESTED/BUCKLEY HAS BECOME ISSUE AS WELL AS CANDIDATE." Joseph Kraft, New York *Post* columnist (October 29) summarized: ". . . each of the leading candidates is pressing for recognition as Buckley's chief victim. And as a matter of fact, both have a claim to be the injured party." I had hurt, argued Kraft, Lindsay's image as an Olympian figure, heavily reducing his pretensions (see above): while hurting Beame by drawing away from him the fiscal conservatives among Italians and Irish who resented "the [costly] welfare projects that benefit the Negroes."

Lindsay opened up against me formally on October 12, in the celebrated conference about not knowing me at Yale and not appreciating me as a public speaker. On October 14, Senator Javits renewed his attacks on me as "the candidate of the ultra-right."

On October 15, Lindsay's candidate for President of the City Council proclaimed that I was anti-Catholic. On October 16, Lindsay charged (I quote the *Times)* that " 'on the streets' Mr. Buckley's campaign has become a racist campaign. 'I don't say that Buckley is a racist, but that is the effect of it on the streets. . . . The city's a powder keg and Buckley's doing his best to light the fuse.' "

8. Murray Kempton, March 15, 1966: "It occurs to me that this [the Lindsay Administration] is the first group of public officials ever elected with my endorsement. It's too early to confess myself wrong; but it's late enough to admit that, if I was right, it was for the wrong reasons. It was my notion that, as mayor, John Lindsay would restore civility to this city. He may restore honesty and dedication to this city, but civility never. It is impossible to pick up a paper without seeing the mayor's face; and he always looks like the leading man in Slattery's People the day the ratings come in. His habitual public expression is that of outraged victim. The one sort of mayor I never thought he'd be was the kind who never for one minute is free of assurance that we're lucky to have him or the opinion that he's unlucky to have us."

On October 19, Javits (I quote the *Times*) "accused Mr. Buckley of advocating 'sending people on welfare to concentration camps.' " On October 25, the *Times* reported that Lindsay would formally file charges with the Fair Campaign Practices Committee (he never did) charging Buckley with "subtle appeals to racial prejudices," and with making "religion an issue by noting that he and his two running mates are Catholics and by mentioning, to a predominantly Catholic audience . . . that Lindsay is a Protestant." On October 27, *Tribune* columnists Evans and Novak revealed that Lindsay has been distributing endorsements of me by Kent Courtney, a white supremacist. On October 27, Buckley "supporters" were reported as "jeering Lindsay at Wall Street." Marvelous!⁹

The chorus responded full-throatedly, as though Toscanini had rapped his baton. Some were intensely personal (". . . the case against Buckley is that he is an exhibitionist and a snob, an *arriviste* trying to take on respectability by the contemptible tactic of swanking it over unfortunate people."—Joseph Kraft, New York *Post*, October 29). Some presented highly original psychoanalytical speculation (". . . The fact is that the Goldwaters and the Buckleys of this world . . . are united in a desperate attempt to prove that self-government will not work. They do not oppose Lindsay because he might not be a good mayor, but simply because they are terrified at the thought he might be a good one. . . . Buckley . . . is a philosophical anarchist dedicated in the present instance to proving that the people of New York are doltish swine who are incapable of ruling themselves."—Richard Starnes, columnist for the *World-Telegram*, on October 29).¹⁰

Walter Lippmann weighed in with a novel contribution to American history (October 28): ". . . Because there is in Buckley a strong streak

---

9. Copyright, Tom Wolfe.
10. An argument of wonderfully versatile usefulness. Murray Kempton plugging for Lindsay: "Or is it true that most of the people who live here have lost all hope that there is any promise of government or hope of civilization any larger than this? There doesn't seem to be. They have treated us as slobs for 20 years. Now they have won. We *are* slobs." Or, Doris Fleeson (October 21) doing the same: "[If the voters] embrace Beame, this would amount to a cynical conclusion that the City is probably ungovernable anyway, so it might as well bear the ills it has." Or, in the High Poetry Department, Norman Mailer's rich chocolate prose, again to the same effect: "A man like that [me] cannot be kept from getting an enormous minority vote. The aged put rouge on their cheeks, and in a dying city, theatre is life, Camp is all. Camp is going to defeat John Lindsay, for Camp is the iridescence of the malignant and cancer cells are bizarre but beautiful under a microscope . . . if Lindsay loses, Camp will have defeated him—a secret admiration for Buckley's high Camp has been cutting into the righteous wrath of all us Wagner-aged citizens—we are finally apathetic about the great dump in which we live, we laugh at Buckley, we laugh with him, we say let the city burn, let it burn, and Lindsay goes wrong, a little solemn, a little empty, too earnest, much." (*The Village Voice.*) I don't even remember going quite as far in desperation about the voters as some of the critics who charged me with holding them in contempt.

of fanaticism he would rather rule the wreckage than try to win an election. There is no real precedent in American politics for the kind of wrecking operation that Buckley is conducting." (No precedent, at least, since way back in 1964 when Lindsay contributed to the wreckage of the Republican Party in New York City by exhibiting what was widely hailed, by among others Lippmann, as political independence. One man's political independence is another man's wrecking operation.) Another count against me by Lippmann: "There is in [Buckley's] performance not a scintilla of interest in the good government of the City of New York." (Mr. Lippmann had access to all ten position papers.)

It was also charged that I was wholly ignorant of New York City: ". . . Buckley who does not live in New York and probably couldn't tell you who is Borough President of Staten Island without looking it up in the Green Book. . . ." (Mr. Maniscalo *was* Borough President of Staten Island. He was beaten by Robert Connor, who ran on the Republican and the Conservative lines.) That it was all, somehow, too, too macabre, *e.g.*, Eric Sevareid: ". . . His is a wrecking operation with Lindsay the wreckee presumptive, but this is a town that loves a wit if it be caustically anti-hero, and Buckley's is that. . . . The laughter echoes as in a burial vault" (October 31). And an elegant variation from Emmett Hughes of *Newsweek*: "There is William Buckley. A vehement performer, he has revived the apache. This well becomes his encounter with John Lindsay. For the wild choreography here demands a partner to be a victim first to be taunted, then demeaned, finally knifed" (November 1).

And of course, again and again, the meat and potatoes: "An Aristocratic Racist Casts Shadow on the City," headlined *The Worker* (October 3). And from Joseph Alsop on October 27 a shiver of disgust: "He is one of the people who have been trying for years to impose a new and thoroughly nasty pattern on American politics. . . . By all sorts of hints, and very shrewdly, Buckley has appealed to these people's prejudices, already inflamed by the problem of de facto neighborhood school segregation. . . . A big Buckley vote, therefore, such as the wiseacres now expect, could set back the cause of sanity and decency in the Northern urban school systems in a really frightening degree. . . ."

And the strategist Max Lerner pleading with those who might just be bemused: "Buckley . . . has grittily taken every position that a right-wing Republican could take on the issues of New York City. The fact that he has done it with quips, and often with a disdainful use of words that sent the reporters to the dictionaries, should not obscure the seriousness of his intent . . ." (October 27). And James Wechsler

(New York *Post*), suddenly rejoicing that after all, in this best of all possible worlds, all New Yorkers had an equal opportunity to vote against me: "Buckley could inadvertently become Lindsay's secret weapon if he transforms this contest into a test of the city's bi-partisan better instincts."

In the final days before the campaign, no fewer than twenty columns and as many editorials appearing in New York City pounded away on these themes. My guess is the whole business must have had some effect. On reading it over, I am reminded of Senator Goldwater's opening sentence to the press in Paris a few months after his defeat. "I've been going around town talking to a lot of people," he said. "I've learned a lot. I had no idea what a son of a bitch I was."[11]

In any case, that is apparently how it happened. I leave the pre-election summary to two political analysts, Messrs. Evans and Novak, and to my faithful epiloguist, Murray Kempton.

Evans and Novak, October 27:

> Having failed to crystallize one paramount issue in his campaign for Mayor, Republican John V. Lindsay has now been handed his issue on a silver tray by William F. Buckley, Jr. The issue is the latent threat of Buckleyism—the application of a militantly conservative doctrine to the ills of the nation's biggest city. Buckley's roguish wit and flashy idiom are made for television and this is a television campaign. As a result, New York's liberal voters are being exposed to a larger dose of Right-wing ideology than they've ever had before from a mayoral candidate and it's beginning to create a sense of unease among the large minority voting blocs that control New York City politics. . . . Lindsay badly underestimated Buckley, only belatedly recognized Buckley not as a mischievous dilettante, but as a deadly threat both to Lindsay's chance next Tuesday and to the future of the Republican party in New York. And now, ironically, it is Buckley's very success and the uneasiness it is spreading among New York's liberal voters that becomes Lindsay's possible salvation.

And, in another mode, Murray Kempton:

> Mr. Buckley has said, on occasion, how surprised he is that John Lindsay has no sense of humor. But he is thinking about the aesthetics of a different game. A debate between him and say, Norman Mailer, is really a contest to see who can save the other's soul. But the great candidates do not think about souls; to them, the other man is simply an object. So John Lindsay did not listen to

11. It would be distorted and ungrateful to suggest that I received no encouragement, personal or political, at all from the press during the campaign. Some excerpts are therefore quoted in Appendix F.

Mr. Buckley and he did not talk to him; he merely waited until the time was proper and then he picked him up and held him aloft and scared the liberals to death. It does not occur to the great candidates in the last week that the other man is a fellow creature. And so it is Mr. Buckley who is John Lindsay's tool, and it is Lindsay who's the hard and cold one, because that's not his mask but his job.

XI.

Election Night

The suspense on Election Day was very great, the final polls registering negligible differences between Beame and Lindsay, as if to symbolize the differences between their platforms. There was something in the air, though, and it suggested that Lindsay was marching and Beame faltering. The *News* poll, first published on October 19, had launched Lindsay at 42 per cent, Beame at 41.8; myself at 16.2. In the ensuing fortnight the poll varied very little. Lindsay, according to its findings, peaked between October 23 and October 27, rising to a high of 42.4, a barely perceptible change from the first day of the poll. He had slid back to 42.0 on Election Eve. Beame meanwhile dropped steadily, a fraction of a percentage point at a time, diminishing from his original 41.8 to 40.0 on Election Eve. My own vote, as a percentage of the whole, moved more substantially than either of theirs, beginning at 16.2 and edging up, on November 1, to 18.0. During the same period, the *Tribune* moved Lindsay up from 36.6 to 41.5; Beame down from 43.8 to 42.3; and me up from 12 to 16.

The crucial question, as generally posed, was whether traditional Democratic loyalties would once again deliver the city to the party of its fathers. Or would the mighty exhortations of the city's and the nation's most galvanizing moralizers combine with the legendary organizational skill of Robert Price, and with my own dislocative presence in the race, to elect John Lindsay?

I had no hunch on the matter. I would not have been surprised with either result. Nor, apparently, would Lindsay have been, who, with that infuriating efficiency which makes less organized men like myself helpless with envy, arrived at his headquarters, it is duly recorded, with two prepared statements, the one to be used if he won, the other if he lost. It takes an iron control to do that kind of thing, it had occurred to me many times while observing over the years candidates in close elections deliver finished valedictories, or polished victory statements, seconds after Univac had announced the verdict. How can one know exactly what one's emotions or thoughts will be if one loses? Or if one wins? How can one capture them authentically ahead of time? I suppose the answer is that in the big league, anyway, they usually aren't authentic. They are, to use the exactly appropriate word, programed. Safer, one supposes.

The Conservative Party laid on a dozen kegs of beer and took a huge ballroom at the New Yorker Hotel, which by 9:30 p.m. was teeming with excited people. A large anteroom was available for VIPs, party workers, and friends, with lots of television sets, and bar service. On an upper floor two dozen of us sat viewing the returns in a small suite. They came in slowly—the polls, though officially closed at 9 p.m., having stayed open to handle the tens of thousands of voters who were still lined up to vote.

For over two hours the results were ambiguous. Beame and Lindsay seesawed. It was only clear that whichever of them ended up winning would do so by a very narrow margin, the narrowest in the memory of the average New Yorker. (La Guardia very narrowly beat O'Dwyer in 1941.) Each candidate's vote was periodically projected by the television cameras as a percentage of the whole that had been tabulated as of that moment. My own vote went up, almost instantly, to about twelve per cent, and started to climb, but very slowly; and I soon reckoned that it would probably reach thirteen per cent, or go a little over. Nothing like the eighteen per cent projected by the *Daily News* in its final report the day before. I was not particularly surprised. A week before I had placed the only bet (sealed) I made during the entire campaign—with my brother, the campaign manager; and with Marvin Liebman, who ran the headquarters staff. Liebman guessed I would poll 280,000 votes. My brother guessed 400,000. I guessed (literally guessed—none of us had attempted any scientific homework before depositing our estimates in envelopes and sealing them) 340,000. I polled, finally, 341,226. Sheer luck; but, on election night, I reflected that the results had confirmed my own rough expectations of the week before; they were more than double my original expectations, and so I could not reasonably be disappointed. The very sharp drop (about 150,000 votes less than expected) from the pollsters' estimates was no doubt mainly due to two factors. One was the final, impacting barrage in the press, and on radio and TV, which the Lindsay forces used to such great effect during the preceding four or five days. The other was the final crystallization of the datum (always clear to me) that I had no hope in the world of winning; the result of which was that at the moment of truth many voters decided to affect the result of the campaign more directly than they could hope to do by voting for me. Assuming that either one—or both—of the polls was accurate, the final results (Lindsay 45.3, Beame 41.3, Buckley 13.4) indicate that for every four voters who had registered their preference for me but finally decided *not* to vote for me, three went on to vote for Lindsay, one for Beame. Their motivations are not difficult to deduce. The largest group were finally persuaded that above all New York needed a change, and that therefore no matter what they thought of Lindsay, they would leave me and vote for him in order to effect that change. The others (one out of four) went at the last minute to Beame. Most of them feared, I think, an augmentation of Lindsay's influence on the national Republican Party, feared just such elated reactions to the outcome as were duly forthcoming the very next day, *e.g.*, in *The New York Times*: "[Lindsay's election] catapulted Mr. Lindsay into a position of national leadership in the [Republican] Party. He is almost certain to be considered a Presidential or Vice-Presidential possibility in 1968 or 1972. . . ."

I sat making small talk with my friends and family, but mostly watching the returns, a portable typewriter on the table in front of me with sheets of yellow paper on which I found it impossible to put down anything particularly interesting, though I knew I would be expected very soon to go down to the ballroom, and say something, anything. I reflected that the whole arduous business had projected three theoretical goals. The first was utterly unrealizable. Even so— inevitably—there were those Conservatives who predicted the miracle —the election of their candidate, notwithstanding my own obdurate pessimism, or rather, realism; notwithstanding the polls' unflinching objectivity. The second objective of the Conservatives was by contrast thoughtful, and practical: the goal of outpolling the enormously influential Liberal Party, whose votes (see chapter III) have had such a critical leverage on New York's, and hence the nation's, affairs.

The third objective, let's face it, was to beat Lindsay.

It has been frequently asserted by commentators that this was *the* goal of the Conservatives—asserted usually after an introductory stretch of psychoanalysis (". . . although they have never formally admitted it, the spoiler campaign of the Conservative Party is motivated by the desire to take vengeance on John Lindsay for his refusal to support Senator Goldwater in the campaign of 1964 . . ."). Actually, the words necessary to confirm that the defeat of Lindsay was one of the Conservative Party's objectives were available from my own mouth, so that those who wished to make the point not by psychological but by logical deduction could easily have done so by quoting me directly. I had said to the National Press Club on August 5, in the question-and-answer sequence reproduced as the prologue to this book, exactly that—in almost but not quite as many words: namely, that from the point of view of conservative New Yorkers, the election of Beame would in fact be preferable to the election of Lindsay. For some reason—notwithstanding their eagerness to document precisely that ambition—the political commentators never assimilated, nor drew the indicated conclusions from, the relevant passages of an address that had been widely publicized. They seemed to prefer divining the ulterior meaning of the Conservative campaign—as though it had never been made semi-explicit. I quote from the National Press Club appearance (italics added):

> Q. Are you [WFB] saying it makes no difference whether Lindsay or a Democrat wins in New York?
> A. I am saying it makes no difference to *New Yorkers*. It makes a lot of difference to John Lindsay, and his entourage, and to . . . Mr. Beame . . . and [his]. And it makes a lot of difference to people outside New York, both Democrats and Republicans.
> Q. Oh?
> A. . . . As far as Republicans are concerned, out over the country, they may very well not care at all *what* kind of government New York gets. But they should care very much if a Republican running in New York, who refused to support the Republican presidential candidate, now gladly supports New York socialists and is supported by them, hoping to graduate into eminence in the national Republican Party. There was weeping and gnashing of teeth only a year ago among the Democrats when George Wallace piled up huge votes in Democratic primaries in Wisconsin, Indiana, and Maryland. Shouldn't Republicans also worry about interlopers?

Reduced to the relevant propositions, the above says: (a) a conservative New Yorker has no reason to believe that the election of Lindsay, given his platform, will cause any significant change in the government of New York City. Under the circumstances, (b) the secondary consequences of Lindsay's election become the primary consideration. If Beame wins, he will not in any noticeable way affect the trend of Democratic national politics. If Lindsay wins, he is very likely to affect the trend of national Republican politics, in a way conservatives oppose. The explicitly undistributed yet incandescent middle in this series of propositions, eminently suppliable, one would think, by working pundits, is of course: (c) conservative New Yorkers are also conservative Americans—concerned with the future of the national GOP, through which they hope to serve their nation.

From which it follows, according to my analysis, (d) that conservative New Yorkers were logically bound to prefer the election of Beame
to the election of Lindsay.

I remember, the evening before composing the speech for the
National Press Club, suggesting at dinner to Dan Mahoney, the
Chairman of the Conservative Party, that I make the soritical leap and
announce quite frankly, giving the reasons why, the defeat of Lindsay
was *an* objective of the Conservative Party. He demurred, insisting
that in politics such things are better left to others to deduce, that
they should *never* be spoken; that I could walk all around the subject,
but must not, ever, on any account, come out and *state* it. I blurted
out that he was asking me to perform an act of *coitus interruptus,*
and he replied, laughing, that I would have to do worse than that in
politics; and so it was left. He was of course quite right. You may, in
politics, come out for (a), and come out for (b); but apparently you
must not automatically acknowledge the consequences of (a) plus
(b). It is as if Lindsay had described the tax consequences of his
proposals (a) and (b). Shocking.

It was 10:30 p.m. A reporter from *The New York Times* sent up
word that he would like to talk to me, to record my impressions as
the television returns began to show a slight edge for Lindsay and
the spirits began to sag in the ballroom. I put the reporter off—*The
New York Times!* I thought back on a luncheon conversation I had
had with, *mirabile dictu,* the editors of *The New York Times,* just
four days earlier. It was the very day in which they had published
(see above) their most relentless editorial, denouncing me for inciting
the brutish instincts latent in the breasts of people who disagree with
The New York Times. I fondled, as the television recorded the steady
rise in Lindsay's plurality, the memory of the acutest pleasure of any
I had experienced during the grueling weeks—arriving to keep my
luncheon appointment and walking through the corridor of the *Times*
building, past the information center, up the elevator to the august
quarters of my hosts—and having to pause every step or two to
shake gratefully the outstretched hands of porters, clerks, secretaries,
elevator men, who, spotting me, wanted to wish me well, several of
them whispering to me their subversive resolve to vote for me the
following Tuesday. The irony elated me, that the maintenance force
of this august newspaper, or at least those members of it who happened at that moment to stand between the street and the *sanctum
sanctorum* had, so many of them, been more greatly persuaded by the
positions of the Conservative Party than by the thunder-machine of
their employers. I met with the editors and publishers, a disappoint-
ingly civil and charming assembly—who however got down almost

instantly to brass tacks as we dove into the first course of a superb meal. We touched on a number of things—on brutish instincts, of course; on racism; on political courage; on New York's problems. And then toward the end of the meal, one of my hosts said to me gravely: "Do you *realize* that as a *practical* matter, your candidacy—which let us concede is idealistic from *your* point of view—is likely to result in a grave setback to the fortunes of New York City by depriving the city of a Lindsay Administration?" "I have thought of that aspect of the business," I said. "And six weeks ago I went to someone whose judgment I profoundly trust—because his record of civic responsibility and of a shrewd devotion to New York's interests, is, I think, unimpeachable. And I asked him point-blank: would New York fare better under Lindsay or under Beame? He answered, without a moment's hesitation: 'under Beame.' "

The editors, tense, nevertheless spilled out traces of a smile, which they discreetly communicated to each other. "Who?"—one of them finally asked, after a few seconds of silence—Who possibly could have come to such a conclusion. Robert Welch? General Walker? Mrs. Joe McCarthy? "Is this lunch off the record?" I asked. In unison they said: "Yes—absolutely—completely." And I gave the name. The effect was as if they had sat down comfortably at breakfast to read the morning editorial page of their paper to find it had come out for Goldwater for President. The dismay was paralytic.

I wondered, still do, how, as practical men, they had succeeded in convincing themselves that the watershed of civic virtue drained only to Lindsay. James Farley, Peter Strauss, Robert Kennedy, are not, by their lights, evil men; but they were for Beame. All right, they are regular Democrats. But the editors of the New York *Daily News* also were for Beame. So were the editors of the New York *Journal-American*. They too would have to continue to do business in New York, to live in New York; and they weren't professional Democrats, on the contrary their record was predominantly Republican—why should *they* have come out for Beame, unless they reasoned that Beame would be a better Mayor? And yet, somehow, the Conservatives, going only so far as to conclude that New York would fare about equally under Beame or Lindsay, were, in the eyes of my egregious hosts, motivated by a prejudice, by a desire for vengeance, by the gravitational pull of dark and brutish instincts. . . .

On leaving the *Times* building I found a television crew waiting outside to question me for comment on LBJ's sudden endorsement of Beame, which had just come in over the wire. We disposed of that subject, and Gabe Pressman of NBC, the cameras still rolling, asked me jocularly how I felt on emerging from the *Times* building and I said—the kind of thing, I fear, that makes some people gray with anger—that it was as though I had just passed through the Berlin Wall. "What is the first thing you would do if elected?" he pressed. "Hang a net outside the window of the editor." If I had been more conservative, less impulsive—more civic-minded?—I suppose I would have recommended a commission to investigate the desirability of suspending such a net.

It was 11:45. The swing to Lindsay was marked, though not yet conclusive. I decided to go down to the ballroom and acknowledge that Lindsay was the apparent winner of the election, and to thank, from a very full heart, my friends. For the first time, and I expect the last, I knew what it was to be totally the prisoner of the police, who formed the traditional flying wedge to get me through to the platform, where the crowd, young, uproarious, cheered by the technical victory it seemed clear they had won over the Liberal Party, but obviously disappointed by Lindsay's emergence as the victor, waited for confirmation of the bad news. I hadn't prepared a statement. It flashed through my mind to repeat a story I had recently heard. About a young Jewish man who fell in love with a Catholic girl whose parents would not consent to the marriage unless the suitor took instructions in the Catholic faith. He agreed to do so and the marriage day was set. But, at the ceremony, he did not appear, sending word that he had been so captivated by the Catholic faith that he had decided, instead, to become a priest.

But I couldn't, somehow, rouse the old heave-ho. So I didn't say very much, except to compliment the Conservatives for working so very hard and for accomplishing so very much. The crowd and I made love to each other and I returned upstairs. An hour or so later, I came down again, after the results had been more or less certified, to say that Lindsay had indeed been elected, and that we could only hope that he would succeed in helping New York City by touching his magic wand upon it; and again I thanked the crowd, greatly diminished at this late and unfruitful hour; and went back upstairs, and waited a few more moments there, with my family and friends. And then returned to my apartment, to help, ineffectually, my valiant wife to prepare for our trip to Vancouver the next day, to attend the funeral of her father, who had died the day before, during the final event of the campaign, a broadcast at 11 p.m. on the Barry Gray Show. Still later I watched Mr. Beame on television, brave and dejected; a loser surrounded by winners—his Democratic candidate for President of the City Council, the invincible Frank O'Connor, who ran almost three hundred thousand votes ahead of John Lindsay; and his Comptroller,

Mario Proccacino, who endeared himself to me early in October, when he introduced his running-mate O'Connor to a large crowd, arm over his shoulder, with the resonant endorsement, "He grows on you like cancer!" Beame said his words, and then was asked by a reporter whether he knew why he had lost. "Do you think Mr. Buckley was a major factor in your defeat?" "I don't think so, I know so," Beame answered flatly. Mrs. Beame wept quietly in the gloom. I was, perhaps, the proximate cause of the defeat of her husband. But—I wished I might have communicated my analysis to her at that moment—*if* I had not run at all, Mr. Beame would have been beaten, and even more so; because, as the pollster Samuel Lubell had repeatedly pointed out, and would later confirm, of the first 200,000 votes I took, most of them would otherwise have gone to Lindsay. It was only toward the end that I began to hurt her husband more than his opponent. At 2:30 in the morning John Lindsay appeared, wonderfully in control of himself, sober, reflective, incredibly and admirably preserved even though he had campaigned until three o'clock that morning and all during the day and would rise a few hours later to make the traditional appearance at the Fulton Fish Market. He professed his pride in the city, suggested that the city had been vindicated, and promised that, together, he and the city would march forward; that "we will work together to make our great city civil again, the Empire City of the world."

A Brief Afterword

I prefer that whatever I have written in this long book which might
be of use to others should be gleaned by them without the aid or interference of summary exhortations. But I do wish, in concluding, to
touch briefly on just two subjects.

1. One of them has to do with the purpose of the detailed recounting of what I said to the Ladies Pancake League, what the press said
I said, which wasn't what I actually said, what exactly were the misrepresentations, etc., etc. The purpose is primarily to capture the
realities of the polemical situation in our time, rather than to try to
do something to alter them. I haven't meant to suggest that only
conservatives are misrepresented, though it should be clear that liberals tend to be freer to behave with abandon; that they can as a matter
of fact go out and make politics without spending their lifetimes,
undressed, before the grand jury of public morals. (Test: Who said
[a.] "[It] is my firm belief that Dwight Eisenhower is a dedicated,
conscious agent of the Communist conspiracy . . ."? Who said [b.]
"Goldwater Republicanism is the closest thing in American politics
to an equivalent of Russian Stalinism"? Everyone knows the answer
to [a.]. Who knows—or will care, particularly—that the answer to [b.]
is William Fulbright?) It all has to do with the *Zeitgeist* which, because its path, like a tornado's, is set, has perforce to be accommo-
dated by practical men—it isn't very useful to stand in front of it and
blow; though it is useful to chart its course, to discover how to get out
of its way. I am talking, of course, about what politicians need to know
—the philosopher must be prepared to stand in the way of the furies,
to oppose the spirit of the age even if his shirt is ripped off his back.
The politicians and the favor-seekers need to know that this is the
age when a Linus Pauling can sign a statement charging that Harry

Truman and Thomas Dewey have brought the nation to "the brink of war and fascism" and get away with it—by which I mean, proceed with his career and his avocations relatively unreproached by the community's standard-keepers. Whereas the equally irrepressible and equally irrational right-crackpot who advances a complementary inanity—say, that "Eisenhower and Kennedy have brought us to the brink of surrender"—is instantly identified by the relevant forces as what he is, and the forces of opprobrium, social and intellectual, quickly maneuver to consign him to Coventry. My own view—quite by the way—is that our society has recently tended not to over-censoriousness toward outlandish positions but rather to a permissiveness that belies a self-doubt sometimes bordering on self-hate. I merely record that that permissiveness tends to indulge only such views as are in line, however remotely, with the vector of historical prejudices. There has been more angry copy in *The New Republic* in recent years about Trujillo than about Tito.

This book isn't an optimistic contribution to the balancing of the scales of judgment. To attempt such a thing at this point is rather like attempting a raid on the National Bureau of Standards in order to change the avoirdupois ounces that go into the making of the official pound. There are, to be sure, those who, in the quiet of their monastic cells, may wish passively to meditate on these data, if only because they· are devoted to the study of realities. But they are not legion—to begin with; and, temperamentally, they are not given to sit-in demonstrations against the double standard. The lesson for them is—that that is the way things are, and are likely to be, for quite a while. The lesson for practical men is to maneuver within an area of possibilities more meticulously charted.

2. Conservatism in America is rather a force than a political movement. The Republican Party, which has been its political vehicle, on and off, faces a dilemma that is quite probably, though not necessarily, insuperable. The GOP is at the moment without a doctrine: for the very good reason that conservative doctrine, with which (however inadequately) the GOP has identified itself in the past, seems to lack, for the time being, the mass appeal without which a major party is unviable.

I think the probabilities are against the survival of the Republican Party as a major party, defined as a party that offers effective opposition and, from time to time, exercises power. Even under the moderate Eisenhower—the Republican exemplar, according to the rules of prevailing opinion—the registration figures continued to polarize, as they had during the preceding two decades. Two years before the good general came into office, the national registration figures were 45 per cent to 33 per cent in favor of the Democrats, according to Dr. Gallup. When he left the pulpit, eight years later, the infidels had in fact increased, the figures having separated to 47 per cent Democrats and 30 per cent Republicans.

What did emerge in the post-Eisenhower years among Republicans was a considerable hunger for orthodoxy, for an intellectual discipline in the formulation of policy. It was fueled in part by the long diet of blandness that had produced a body lacking in tone and coordination; but also by telling critiques of the liberal ideology, effected by scholars and teachers and journalists. The Goldwater phenomenon was not, in the experienced judgment of Mr. Theodore White, a freak geological tremor, unlikely to recur in another thousand years. Something was stirring and would continue to stir; something that cried out for political representation.

The New York campaign *proved* nothing, or—perhaps better— proved only the obvious. "I do not know what else Mr. Lindsay's victory established," I said the day following the election, "than that people do scare easily and that New York is a very 'liberal' community. Mr. Lindsay's energetic and costly effort to confirm these sociological and psychological truisms was a venture in redundancy." And I ventured a prediction: "What *is* significant . . . is the crystallization of a vote of responsible protest. The Conservative Party of New York greatly improved on the showing of the Liberal Party during recent years, and intends to exercise its influence in state politics. The Conservative Party, which with meager resources and total organiza- tional inexperience drew more than fifty per cent as many votes as there are registered Republicans in New York City, will, if it should continue to grow at the current rate, emerge either as the second major party in New York State or—preferably—will use its influence to rejuvenate the Republican Party."

I leave it to professional scholars—I happen to know of two who are currently engaged in sociological and political analyses of the New York campaign—to project, if they can, its meaning nationally. I pause to remark only that the flavor of real solutions to real problems does in fact excite a community beset by real worries. Goldwater's showing in New York, in 1964, of 800,000 votes was considered dismal. Yet Lindsay conquered the city with 1,150,000 votes. Gold- water had the organizational support of a major party, but he had, also, extraordinary disadvantages extrinsic to his basic positions—an awkward historical moment (the long political wake that followed the assassination of John Kennedy); the apostasy of the four principal Republican luminaries in the state—the Republican governor; the two Republican senators; the most prominent New York City Republican, Mr. Lindsay—and a lack of political electricity which was the result of his candidacy's apparent unrelatedness to municipal issues. Even so, the bad loser did three-quarters as well as his triumphant successor, Mr. Lindsay. Is it inconceivable that Republicanism plus electricity could equal conservatism? It is interesting to note, in anticipation of the objection that such are the private hallucinations only of reactionary Republicans, the comment of the superliberal Professor Martin Dworkis, who ran unsuccessfully against Lindsay in 1962: "I don't think Lindsay is beatable from the left, so to speak. I think that it may be possible for a strong Democratic Party candidate with a rightist inclination to make serious inroads into Lindsay. But not a strong Democrat with a liberal background."

The Republican leadership has, in my judgment, a great disillusion in store for it if it attempts a major comeback in 1968 on a Goo-gooist program—waste in the administration of the poverty program, bottlenecks in the flow of matériel to Saigon—that kind of thing. If it follows the lead of its John Lindsays, it is going to lose the vital support of a very considerable minority who yearn for the recovery of a set of presumptions highly dissipated over the years by the tinsel-attractions of contemporary liberalism. The Republican leadership cannot hope to go much further in the direction of social statism and of a surrender to bloc-interests than, say, its counterpart in England has gone; and has no reason to expect, at the polls, to go any further, on such a program, than the Conservative Party went in the last British election (42 per cent of the vote).

I greatly regret the prospective decline of the GOP, because the alternative is likely to be a congeries of third parties, adamantly doctrinaire, inadequately led, insufficiently thoughtful, improvidently angry, self-defeatingly sectarian. If they materialize, the Republican leadership will have done much to midwife them; because of the high tactical impatience manifest in the orgy of self-disgust Republicans indulged in after the defeat of Goldwater, whose campaign might better have been absorbed as a necessary convulsion, a prelude to the crystallization of strong new programs distinctively Republican—bracing, realistic, courageous, strategically adventurous. Such programs at a national level should be delineated; and, if they aren't soon, by more experienced men, I suppose I shall have to threaten another book, if not another campaign.

Appendix / Index

Appendix A

Remarks to the New York Police Department
Holy Name Society, April 4, 1965

Gentlemen:

In appearing before you today, in the general atmosphere of hostility towards the police force, I feel a little like the man in Madrid a few years ago who was asked at a sidewalk cafe, "What do you think of Franco?" "Come with me," he spoke mysteriously. The questioner got up and followed his quarry, who led him silent through the streets, past the park, to the shore of a lake. Wordlessly he drew up a rowboat, beckoned the man in and rowed silently to the middle of the lake, looked suspiciously about him, and whispered: "I like him." [*laughter*]

We live—as all men have ever lived—in two worlds. Roughly speaking, it is the world that makes the newspapers, and the world that doesn't. The world of the unusual and the world of the usual. In the journalistic world they define a news story as man bites dog, that is, the reverse of what is normal. In the plain and ordinary world, dogs bite men. In the newsworthy world, the man bites the dog. A world structured on common sense recognizes the difference between the two acts, ignores the one as commonplace, remarks the other as an occasion worth commenting on. Something special is happening in our world that blurs the old distinctions between the commonplace and the unusual. We are departing from realism, so much so that one wonders whether we are not entering an age of surrealism. An age when it is considered far more remarkable that a dog should bite a man than vice versa. An age, here in New York, where it is considered far less extraordinary that a criminal should break a law, than that a criminal should be apprehended for doing so. [*laughter*]

The moment a criminal is apprehended, the noisiest forces of modern society seem to go into a co-ordinated act of resentment and suspicion. The doctrine that a man is innocent until proved guilty seems to have been stretched to mean that the apprehending officials are guilty unless proved innocent. [*laughter*] The members of the community who control the news—and I speak here, not only of the news that makes the newspapers, but of the news that gets into the thought, and forms the opinion, of the intellectuals, those whose reactions dominate the thought of society —the members of the community who control the news in this broader sense seem to be, in respect of crime and punishment, infinitely more concerned to do away with the latter, than with the former. [*laughter*] They justify that concern on any number of grounds: all of them, needless to say, of impeccable moral breeding. [*laughter*] They care greatly that injustice be not committed. They care greatly that brutality be avoided. They care infinitely that a man's right to dissent be not curtailed. I care too about these things. So do you. But I care as a citizen, and you care as those who devote your lives to guarding the rights of citizens, for the corresponding rights of the party of the first part; the party of the first part being, in a civilized society, those who abide by the law, and succeed, without external pressure, to discipline their lawless impulses sufficiently to

311

respect the rights of others. Those men and women who are killed, mauled, and molested on our streets are, unlike those who are arraigned and charged with having committed the offenses, victims of injustice beyond a reasonable doubt. The man on whom brutality has been inflicted, in a subway car, in a silent street, in the darkness of the park, is a man condemned to brutality beyond the powers of any of us to set right. The republic whose vital secrets are stolen by the dissenter, or whose good faith is broken by him, is weaker on that account beyond the capacity of any judge or jury to redress.

Here is where one sees, with an alarm that borders on panic, how the concern of the most outspoken members of our society, the concern over the privileges of the suspected malefactor, rather than over the violated privileges of the law-abiding citizen, makes us wonder whether we are not living now in a dream world, where the news is made by the dog biting the man rather than the other way round. We all admire a thirst for the protection of the innocent. But nowadays in the eyes of many, the only way to qualify as an object for whose justice it is proper to thirst, is to kill or maul someone, stage a sit-in at City Hall, [laughter] or, most preferably, to strike a policeman. Nobody is more sacrosanct these days than the man who strikes a policeman. No man more guilty than the policeman who strikes a defensive blow; or for that matter who enforces the law, or who uses his ingenuity to apprehend a law-breaker.

Policemen, they say, should be human. But when they act human, it is deeply resented that they are not inhuman. [laughter, applause] Outside the window of my office on 35th Street I saw a mob gather outside the quarters of the 17th precinct last spring to protest a policeman so human as to have disarmed and incarcerated a young gentleman who in pursuit of his ideals had landed his fist on said policeman's jaw [laughter] in the course of a routine demonstration outside the United Nations Building protesting, as I remember, American attempts to bring law and order to South Vietnam. Great was their indignation. They howled out their protests in song and verse, knowing that from coast to coast there were men and women willing to serve as their echo chambers. Four weeks ago at Selma, Alabama, the conscience of the world was aroused at the sight of policemen swinging their sticks with considerable purpose on the bodies of demonstrators who had set out to march to Montgomery, Alabama. The television cameras did not show—how indeed could they have done so?—the most dramatic part of the sequence. Dr. King and the demonstrators had crossed the bridge and there the policemen, acting under orders—whether ill-advised or not is most precisely not the business of policemen, who are not lawmakers or governors but agents of the lawmakers and governors—informed them that they might not proceed. The next thing the American viewer saw was a flurry of night sticks and the pursuit of the screaming demonstrators back across the bridge into the streets of Selma. What the viewer did not see was a period of time, twenty long minutes, 1200 seconds, freighted with tension, when the two camps stood facing each other, between the moment the sheriff told the demonstrators to return, which order the demonstrators refused by standing there in defiance of it, until the moment when the human cordite was touched—who threw the lighted match? we do not know—and the policemen moved, excitedly, humanly, forward: *excessively* yes, and their excesses on that day have been rightly criticized, but were ever the excesses criticized of those who provoked them beyond the endurance that we tend to think of as human? The television viewer, as I say, saw nothing of the policeman's restraint in the face of an order defied: nothing of the twenty long minutes. They saw only the order to turn back, instantly followed by buzz-saw police tactics.

Ten days later the whole world stopped to mourn, and properly so, the death of the lady from Detroit who went down to register her solidarity with the marchers. Two days later the 58th page of *The New York Times* noticed in a two-inch story the unprovoked killing of a policeman in Hattiesburg, Mississippi, by a twenty-year-old in his car. The policeman's name was Humphrey, no relation of the Vice-President [*laughter*], who did not appear at his funeral, nor even offer, so far as we know, his condolences. [*applause*] Dead policemen, unlike dead criminals, are an undramatic event in a world that is unconcerned when man bites dog.

Mrs. Liuzzo of Detroit went down to Alabama to protest conditions there, conditions of injustice to Negroes and a general lawless disregard of their rights and honor. It was generally conceded—most specifically conceded by the governor of Alabama—that anyone arriving in Alabama to protest the existing order under the glare of national klieg lights, precisely needed protection against the almost certain recourse to violence of the unrestrained members of almost every society who are disposed to go to criminal lengths to express their resentment. That, after all, is why the President mobilized the National Guard of Alabama—at the Governor's urging. So the lady drove down a stretch of lonely road in the dead of night, sharing the front seat with a young Negro identified with the protesting movement; and got killed. Why, one wonders, was this a story that occupied the front pages from one end to another, if newspapers are concerned with the unusual, the unexpected? Didn't the killing merely confirm precisely what everyone has been saying about the South? About the intensity of its feelings? About the disposition of some of its members to resort to violence to maintain the status quo? Who could have been surprised by this ghastly episode? Not Governor Wallace—who had precisely called on the federal government to provide protection for the demonstrators. Not, surely, *The New York Times*, which has told us for years that in the South lawlessness is practiced. So why was a dog-bites-man story so heavily accented? If the grand wizard of the Ku Klux Klan were to announce that he and a band of his fellow cretins were coming up to Harlem to demonstrate against the voting rights bill [*laughter*], would we not warn them of the dangers of any such affront, and would we be surprised if fewer Ku Kluxers left Harlem, than arrived there? Who knows, his honor the Mayor might even refuse them the right to demonstrate; as, in my judgment quite properly, he refused to George Lincoln Rockwell and his Nazi maniacs the right to demonstrate in Washington Square four years ago: [*applause*] pleading the demands of law and order. And so, one asks, why in Alabama was a dog-bites-man story so heavily accented? And since it is not in any sense to be expected that a young Negro in Hattiesburg, Mississippi, driving in company with two others, should shoot down a policeman who stopped the car to ask a question, wouldn't one think that here was an act surprising enough, outrageous enough, to occupy greater space in the daily newspaper?

What goes on here? My friends, we live in a world in which order and values are disintegrating. In which sometimes in order to view reality, to hope to understand, one needs to take the printed page and read it backwards, as off a mirror. Every age in which values are distorted, an age like our own—in which truths are thought either not to exist, or to exist only as quaint curios from the dead past—the wrath of the unruly falls with special focus on the symbols of authority, of continuity, of tradition. It is no accident at all that the police should be despised in an age infatuated with revolution and ideology. It is no surprise at all that the Catholic Church should in our time have been singled out for the brunt of the organized hatred of the principal agents of revolution—the Church with its unyielding devotion to eternal truths which resist the plastic manipulations of the willful revolutionaries. Who are the enemy? The agencies of order and tradition. The truths of Christianity. The guiding lights of our tradition. The loyalty to our country and to our traditions. The laws that were bequeathed to us, given to us as what T. S. Eliot called the democracy of the dead: these are the enemies of the class whose restlessness of soul is ultimately a sign of a spiritual anemia, of a rootlessness which expressed itself in a resentment of the old values. It is absurd to contend that everyone who is critical of the police is a revolutionary, just as it is absurd to maintain that every Southerner who opposed the civil rights bill is an accomplice in the killing of Mrs. Liuzzo. But the men who rail against the policemen, who side instinctively with the accused, who care less for the rights of the peaceful than for the rights of those who break the peace: they tend to have a relationship with the revolutionaries, however attenuated, which can be compared with the relationship, however attenuated, between the lackadaisical Southerner who does not trouble himself about injustice to Negroes, and the Southerner who killed the lady from Detroit. Your lot, in the heat of this injustice to yourselves, is especially galling. You cannot, protesting the enormities of your critics, join together, arm in arm, to picket the pickets, singing hymns to the virtue of your own cause, and insisting that you too will overcome the pressure of those who dishonor you. [applause] You must stand mutely, and suffer the slights ungladly, but silently. You must know that you will be hated for doing your duty, and be reviled by those who misrepresent you. But bear this in mind, that there are the two worlds I speak of, and that though the voices of the one seem sometimes so very much noisier than the voices of the other, that other world, the world of sensible men and women, looks on you with pride and gratitude. Sustained by the implicit gratitude of the people, you are also sustained no doubt during this holy season by the knowledge of the silence with which the author of all values walked during his own days on earth. [applause]

Appendix B

On John Lindsay's Voting Record

During the years between 1960 and 1964 Presidents Kennedy and Johnson required the votes of Republican members of the House of Representatives on many occasions in order to achieve passage of a piece of legislation. Following is a selection of key votes in which John Lindsay joined with a few other Republicans to give the Democratic administration a legislative victory they could not otherwise have achieved.

Eighty-Seventh Congress: First Session—1961:
R.C. 5 (Roll Call 5)—H.R. 127 (House of Representatives 127). A resolution providing that during the Eighty-Seventh Congress the Committee on Rules shall be composed of fifteen members. So-called "rules packing." On agreeing to resolution. January 31, 1961. Passed 217–212. "Present" 1. Dem. 195–64 Rep. 22–148. Hailed as major Kennedy-Rayburn victory.
R.C. 28—H.R. 3935. A bill to amend the Fair Labor Standards Act of 1938, as amended, to provide coverage for employees of large enterprises engaged in retail trade or service and of other employers engaged in commerce or in the production of goods for commerce, to increase the minimum wage under the Act to $1.25 an hour, and for other purposes. On motion to recommit. March 24, 1961. Failed 196–224. Dem. 172–79 Rep. 24–145.
R.C. 46—H.R. 3935. A bill to amend the Fair Labor Standards Act of 1938. Conference report on adoption. May 3, 1961. Passed 230–196. Dem. 197–58 Rep. 33–138. Key administration vote.
R.C. 75—H.R. 7446. A bill to provide a one year extension of the existing corporate normal-tax rate and of certain excise-tax rates. On motion to recommit with instructions to repeal the 10 per cent tax on railroad, air, water, and bus travel. June 8, 1961. Failed 189–196. Dem. 43–189 Rep. 146–7. President opposed to motion.
R.C. 179—H.R. 8028. Juvenile Delinquency Act providing $10 million annually for three years. On Griffin amendment to limit pilot project to the District of Columbia. August 30, 1961. Failed 187–217. Dem. 55–188 Rep. 132–29.

Eighty-Seventh Congress: Second Session—1962:
R.C. 111—H.R. 11990. A bill to increase the debt ceiling to $305 billion. On passage. June 14, 1962. Passed 211–92. "Present" 1 Dem. 202–39 Rep. 9–153. Major victory for President.
R.C. 186—H.R. 10904. A bill making appropriations for the Departments of Labor and Health, Education, and Welfare, and related agencies for the fiscal year ending June 30, 1963, and for other purposes. Conference report, on motion to recommit to delete $100 million more for NIH that the Senate added. August 1, 1962. Failed 173–214. Dem. 40–188 Rep. 133–26. A victory for the Administration.
R.C. 215—S. 2768. An act to authorize the President to purchase $100 million worth of UN bonds and the appropriation of funds therefore. On motion to recommit with instructions to bar loans until UN Assembly

adopted the World Court opinions on financial obligations of members. September 14, 1962. Failed 171–219. Dem. 44–193 Rep. 127–26.

R.C. 241—H.R. 13175. A Foreign Aid Appropriation Act for the fiscal 1963. On motion to recommit with instructions to reduce economic aid appropriation by $100 million. September 20, 1962. Failed 190–203. Dem. 65–169 Rep. 125–34. Nay vote was in support of President.

Eighty-Eighth Congress: First Session—1963:

R.C. 4—H.R.5. A bill permanently to enlarge ("pack") the House Rules Committee from 12 to 15 members. On agreeing to resolution. January 9, 1963. Passed 235–196. Dem. 207–48 Rep. 28–148. Administration and liberal victory.

R.C. 174—H.R. 6237. A bill to authorize appropriation of $500,000 annually for 5 years for collection, reproduction and publication of documentary source material significant to the history of the United States and for other purposes. On passage. October 15, 1963. Passed 158–154. Dem. 148–30 Rep. 10–124. President favored.

R.C. 219—H.R. 6196. A bill to pay a cotton subsidy to domestic textile mills and for other purposes. On motion to recommit. December 4, 1963. Failed 179–224. "Present" 2. Dem. 43–191 Rep. 136–33. Key Administration vote.

R.C. 220—H.R. 6196. A bill to pay a cotton subsidy to domestic textile mills and for other purposes. On passage. December 4, 1963. Passed 216-182. "Present" 7. Dem. 182–48 Rep. 34–134. Key Administration vote.

R.C. 237—H.R. 4955. A bill to expand Vocational Education program and extend NDEA Act at cost of $921 million over four year period. Conference report on motion to recommit with instructions to delete $150 million. December 12, 1963. Failed 180–193. Dem. 42–173 Rep. 138–20. Administration victory.

Eighty-Eighth Congress: Second Session—1964:

R.C. 131—H.R. 11202. A $5.1 billion Agricultural Appropriation bill for 1965. Bow motion to recommit the bill with instruction to amend it to prohibit the use of funds for export payments or export subsidies on agricultural products shipped to Communist nations. May 20, 1964. Failed 186–187. Dem. 30–182 Rep. 156–5. Five Republicans saved the day for the President.

R.C. 152—H.R. 11380. The Foreign Assistance Act of 1964. Adair motion to recommit the bill with instructions to reduce the fiscal 1965 authorization for development loans by $750 million and the President's contingency fund by $50 million. June 10, 1964. Failed 193–211. Dem. 45–189 Rep. 148–22. Major foreign aid victory for the President.

R.C. 169—H.R. 3881. Urban Mass Transportation Act of 1964. Bolton motion to recommit the bill to the House Banking and Currency Committee with instructions to deter action until the House and Senate Banking and Currency Committees had studied the results of current federal mass transportation demonstration programs and the status of metropolitan transportation planning being carried out pursuant to a requirement of the 1962 Highway Act. June 25, 1964. Failed 190–214. Dem. 56–180 Rep. 134–33. A "nay" was a vote supporting the President's position.

R.C. 173—H.R. 11812. The $3.7 billion Foreign Aid appropriation for fiscal 1965. Adoption of a resolution (H.R. 793) waiving all points of order against the bill. June 30, 1964. Passed 222–162. Dem. 187–34 Rep. 35–128.

R.C. 176—H.R. 11812. Foreign Aid bill. Rhodes motion to recommit the bill to the Appropriations Committee with instructions to reduce economic aid funds by $247.8 million as recommended by Rep. Passman, Chairman of the Foreign Operations Subcommittee. July 1, 1964. Failed 198–208. Dem. 55–185 Rep. 143–23. A "nay" was a vote supporting the President's position.

R.C. 213—H.R. 11377. Poverty bill. On adoption of Landrum substitute. August 7, 1964. Passed 228–190. Dem. 208–20 Rep. 20–170. Key vote on issue.

R.C. 216—H.R. 11377. Final passage of Poverty bill. August 8, 1964. Passed 226–184. Dem. 204–40 Rep. 22–144. Hailed by President Johnson as a great victory for his Administration.

Appendix C

The Welfare Mess
New York City—Soaring Costs

I. *Total Cost:* 30 years

    1935: $10,650,815   Up over 4500 %
    1965: $629,969,572*

II. *Total Cost:* This Decade

    1960: $318,886,326   Up 97.5 %
    1965: $629,969,572*

III. *Total Cost:* Yearly Increase

			Cost of ADC (Aid to Dependent Children)
1960:	$318,886,326		*1960:* $71,985,373
1961:	363,242,064	Up 13.9%	*1961:* 92,137,719** Up 28%
1962:	410,592,695	Up 13.1%	*1962:* 108,335,692** Up 17.6%
1963:	475,476,795	Up 15.8%	*1963:* 140,823,240** Up 30%
1964:	549,690,072	Up 13.5%	*1964:* 172,588,717** Up 44.4%
1965:	629,969,572*	Up 13.4%	*1965:* Not yet available

IV. Numbers of ADC Recipients:

    1960: 200,127
    1961: 235,807** Up 13.3%
    1962: 251,632** Up 17.8%
    1963: 301,553** Up 6.7%
    1964: 345,449** Up 19.8%

ADC increased 140% from 1960 to 1964 (All data on this page are from Annual Reports published by Dep't of Welfare. Figures on numbers of persons in each assistance category are given only for *December* of that year. Figures at left are thus not for entire year, only 1 month.)

*All figures shown as total costs are called Grand Totals in Dep't of Welfare Annual Reports. They are not the same as Dep't of Welfare budget. Thus, in 1964, total department budget was $414,047,484. But Dep't also disbursed $82,547,778 for Public and Private Hospital Care, etc., and $53,094,710 for Institutional and Foster Care of Children, although these appropriations are made to the City Comptroller. This makes a Grand Total of $549,690,072. The 1965 Dep't of Welfare budget is $494,327,092. As the $82 million for Hospital Care and the $53 million for Care of Children seem to remain fairly constant, they have been added on to the 1965 budget figure to arrive at an estimated Grand Total as shown for 1965.

**Dep't of Welfare ADC and TADC (Temporary Aid . . .) figures have been combined into one figure.

318

Appendix D

New York City Business Tax

Quarterly Return Filed_____ 196___

For Calendar Quarter

ending_____ 196___

1. Business Name and Address_____

_____

_____

2. How operated? _____
   (Corporation, Partnership, Sole Proprietorship)
   Kind of enterprise? _____
   (Line of business, product or service offered)

3. Credit, if any, carried over from Line 9
   of last Quarterly Return.........................$_____

4. Receipts from goods and services sold...........$_____

5. Payments to others for goods and services
   purchased ....$_____

6. Enter sum of Lines 3 and 5 here................$_____

7. If Line 4 is greater than Line 6
   enter net added value balance here..............$_____

8. Multiply Line 7 by   % (fill in tax rate)
   and enter tax being paid with this return
   opposite appropriate Quarter:

	First Quarter Tax due April 15	$_____
	Second " " " July 15	$_____
	Third " " " October 15	$_____
	Fourth " " " January 15	$_____

9. If Line 6 is greater than Line 4
   enter net payments-to-others balance here and
   carry over to Line 3 on next Quarterly Return......$_____

Official signature _____

Title of person signing_____

319

Appendix E

Population of New York City
and Its Various Boroughs

Borough	1940	1950	1960	1940–1960 Population Increase or Loss
Manhattan	1,889,924	1,960,101	1,698,281	−191,643 Loss
Bronx	1,394,711	1,451,277	1,424,815	30,104 Gain
Brooklyn	2,698,285	2,738,175	2,627,310	−70,966 Loss
Queens	1,297,634	1,550,849	1,809,578	511,944 Gain
Richmond	174,441	191,555	221,991	47,550 Gain
Total	7,454,995	7,891,957	7,781,984	326,989 Gain

Combined Populations of Manhattan, Bronx and Brooklyn

1940	1950	1960	1940 to 1960
5,982,020	6,149,555	5,750,415	−232,505 (Loss)

Increase in Number of Housing Units 1941–1961

Manhattan	18,085	(at 3 persons per unit—	54,255 people)
Bronx	70,605	(at 3 persons per unit—	211,815 people)
Brooklyn	99,234	(at 3 persons per unit—	297,702 people)
Queens	208,199	(at 3 persons per unit—	624,597 people)
Richmond	16,076	(at 3 persons per unit—	48,228 people)
Total	412,199	(at 3 persons per unit—	1,236,597 people)

Increase in Number of Housing Units
1941–1961
Manhattan, Brooklyn and Bronx
187,924   (at 3 persons per unit—   563,772 people)

Appendix F

"The only one in the group I would dare call collect long distance for a loan is William F. Buckley Jr. He also made a splendid speech on the New York problem to the National Press Club in Washington, a choice of location indicative of his commendable refusal to tramp our streets until they are cleaned fit for the shoes of a gentleman. There are occasions when Buckley tempts you to remember Macaulay's grudging compliment to Burke, which was that he generally chose his side like a fanatic and defended it like a philosopher."

—MURRAY KEMPTON, New York *World-Telegram,* August 26, 1965

"Love him or hate him, TV fans found it difficult to turn off a master political showman. His rolling eyes, deft handling of the English language and razor-sharp debating techniques were exciting to watch. Even tall, handsome and personable Lindsay found himself being upstaged time and time again. . . ."

—EDWARD O'NEILL, New York *Daily News,* October 11, 1965

"Buckley is making up some new rules for the game. He is a good Catholic, but he has foresworn ritualistic truckling for the Catholic vote. He is talking Yale English, and, most astonishing, he is talking sense. To borrow a phrase from the late Joe McCarthy, it is, for New Yorkers, the most unheard of thing they ever heard of. . . .

"On all these propositions, and a great many others, Buckley has pronounced his views with candor, conviction, and elegance. . . ."

—JAMES J. KILPATRICK, *Newsday,* October 14, 1965

"Mr. Buckley has come as far as he has in the race not only because of his appeal to conservatives but because he has wowed New York on television. He is more fun to listen to than most professional comedians. And he has a way of disdaining Rep. Lindsay and Mr. Beame that has diminished both of them in the eyes of many voters.

"Mr. Buckley could make a fortune on Broadway. He is . . . charming, witty, gay, intelligent, provocative and wonderfully articulate.

"Though he has a political philosophy that his critics [say] went out-of-date with McKinley, he knows how to make merry use of it. . . ."

—ROBERT J. DONOVAN, New York *Journal-American,* October 21, 1965

"While Republican John V. Lindsay and Democrat Abraham D. Beame grimly pursue a majority among the city's 2.5 million voters, Bill Buckley light-heartedly violates all the political rules. He outrages many racial and social groups by his recommendations for tough solutions to New York's problems. He treats his opponents as twin simpletons unworthy of serious consideration. And he cheerfully concedes he hasn't the slightest chance to win." . . .

"Still, Mr. Buckley remains a refreshing change from the men who have asked New Yorkers for their support in the past. Many of his admirers are grim zealots, but he masks his own unbending conservative convictions with an engagingly humorous manner. His worst political enemies find him, to their consternation, entertaining and stimulating—as well as a disconcertingly quick-witted antagonist.

"Mr. Buckley is therefore a favorite with reporters covering an other-wise dull campaign. Even when they feel that his views are preposterous, they give him attention that normally a minor third-party (Conservative) candidate would never rate. And the same qualities that endear him to newsmen make Mr. Buckley a formidable threat to the Lindsay hopes.

" 'Lindsay is running as a bright young man,' a member of the Democratic camp explains, 'but Buckley is brighter and younger. And he can make people laugh, which is something Lindsay just can't seem to do.' . . .

"Whatever his intentions, Mr. Buckley's technique has been to do what many a frustrated idealist has daydreamed about: Saying exactly what he thinks about the issues, without the slightest regard for the political consequences. His critics charge this requires no great courage on Mr. Buckley's part: 'he knows he'll never have to make good on anything,' one complains. But it unquestionably holds a secret appeal for many voters. . . ."
                              —DAN CORDTZ, Wall Street Journal, October 25, 1965

"The biggest issue in the mayoral campaign has turned out to be—not bossism, not time for a change, not crime in the streets—but the role of a third-party candidate who, with his flair for arch phrase-making, has sparked much of the controversy and almost all the humor of the contest. William F. Buckley Jr., the Conservative Party nominee, has generated so much interest with his provocative exposition of a right-wing philosophy that his potential vote next Tuesday is widely put at well over 300,000. . . ."
                              —RICHARD WITKIN, The New York Times, October 26, 1965

". . . To be fair it must also be said that no one could have been more majestically suited for spoiling Lindsay's campaign. Buckley's personality is the highest Camp we are ever going to find in a Mayoralty. No other actor on earth can project simultaneous hints that he is in the act of playing Commodore of the Yacht Club, Joseph Goebbels, Robert Mitchum, Maverick, Savonarola, the nice prep-school kid next door, and the snows of yesteryear. If he didn't talk about politics—if he was just the most Camp gun ever to walk into Gunsmoke I'd give up Saturday nights to watch him. But he does talk about politics time to time, and his program for New York is to drop an atom bomb posthaste on the atom bomb of the Chinese. . . ."
                              —NORMAN MAILER, The Village Voice, October 28, 1965

"Mr. Buckley (no relation to the Democratic boss) is, like Mr. Lindsay, New York-born and Yale-educated. He is the most sparkling philosophical mischief-maker ever to stoop to a mayoralty race. His candidacy for mayor is nonsense in any practical sense—yet he is anything but frivolous. His purpose is not to govern the city but to reshape the Republican Party in city, state and nation by destroying John Lindsay.

". . . On TV Buckley is a star. His haughty face, its puckering and hesitation as he lets loose a shaft of wit, would have made him Oscar Wilde's favorite candidate for anything. In television debate Lindsay is normally flanked by Beame, who wants to talk about budget figures. But when Lindsay can free himself from Beame's figures to loose any of the visions of his task forces, there, on his other flank, is Buckley, puncturing the dream or hope with a witch's shaft of rhetoric."

—THEODORE H. WHITE, *Life*, October 29, 1965

"Buckley is a technician with words—his typewriter pours out ornate, intricate pages of polished prose; his voice produces multisyllable, mellifluous streams of oratory—and he has the technician's trait of standing off a bit and dispassionately observing his own handiwork."

—MAURICE CARROLL, New York *Post*, October 31, 1965

"Buckley walked into a pedestrian, lackluster political campaign and gave it verve. . . ."

—DREW PEARSON, New York *Post*, October 31, 1965

"The Buckley phenomenon must, it seems to us, have some connection with what he is saying. Agree with him or not, he has the honesty to actually propose fundamental remedies for the problems of the crime-ridden, traffic-snarled industry-losing metropolis. . . .

"Mr. Buckley, on the other hand, definitely promises something different. Like a little imp, he shatters the shibboleths about public welfare, the policing problem, school busing, taxes and just about everything else, including trash removal. He thus sounds outrageous, or at least naïve, to those accustomed to the miasma of big city politics.

"But a lot of people, perhaps to their own consternation, find themselves grudgingly conceding that he's saying a lot of commonsensical things. The result is very nearly total confusion in New York City politics. . . ."

"Commentators like to explain the Buckley showing by his refreshing personality and candor on the issues. For our part, we are convinced that is only a part of it. The indisputable fact is that he not only listed the fundamental ills of the City, but offered concrete remedies, which the other candidates, in the fashion of politicking, shied away from doing."

—*Wall Street Journal*, October 22, October 29, and November 4, 1965

"Set aside for a moment Mr. Buckley the object—whether as the undreamed-of ornament for his partisans or as the instrument so suddenly, so coolly, so almost brutally employed by John Lindsay for his necessities. Observe simply the work of art.

"The process which coarsens every other man who enters it has only refined Mr. Buckley. To attempt to convey the tone of his press conferences by quotation would be to pretend to play a Mozart glass harp concerto by printing the notes.

"The theme of Buckley's morning hour yesterday was his traffic program. 'Just think, only three more months of traffic problems.' One of its elements is an overhead bikeway down Second Ave. 'You could get from 125th St. to First St., if anyone should want to get there, in 20 minutes.'

" 'Shall we,' a visitor asked, 'call this the Buckley Bikeway?'

" 'Yes,' Buckley answered. 'My finest hour.' The smile was wild shared delight. 'I did have trouble getting it through the Conservative party bureaucracy.'

"We almost forget, in these moments, how serious a man Buckley wants to be, and how exhausting must be the concentration essential to the production of any spontaneity so true. But a work of art is something we know then we'd rather see than be. This is enjoyment at a pitch which must almost be agony to produce and sustain. One thinks of Mozart at 8 playing these simple impulses of delight, driven, of course, by his father. The Conservative party is Mr. Buckley's Leopold Mozart; and, although he cherishes the parent, there are moments when he very much dislikes the piano.

"He seems to have tried, first from being conscientious and then from real interest, to find solutions to some of the problems of the city. The results do not seem terribly useful, running, as they do, rather too often to solving insoluable people by shipping them out of town. But, in the end, oddly and rather sadly, he seems to have settled, as so many others of us equally confused already have, on the notion that it might help if New York had a Mayor who is a gentleman.

"That is a sentimental idea; but Mr. Buckley is an unexpectedly sentimental man; one begins quite soon to suspect, when he pronounces Lindsay's name with a face that cannot otherwise have been seen in public since the Marquess of Queensbury called Oscar Wilde out from his club, that we are watching the heroic contrivance of armor against sentiment. And John Lindsay is, after all, the only gentleman with a chance to be Mayor; and one has to think that there is a part of Mr. Buckley whose candidate is Congressman Lindsay.

"He was saying the other day that he found the crowds rather an ordeal. He wondered, Yale wondering about Yale, how John Lindsay felt about his crowds. But Yale cannot answer Yale in this case; this is Lindsay's life; and, when a professional is fighting for his life, he looks at a crowd only to count it.

"Mr. Buckley has said, on occasion, how surprised he is that John Lindsay has no sense of humor. But he is thinking about the aesthetics of a different game. A debate between him and say, Norman Mailer, is really a contest to see who can save the other's soul. But the great candidates do not think about souls; to them, the other man is simply an object. . . ."
                                          —MURRAY KEMPTON, October 28, 1965

"Bill Buckley is giving TV a smarter, fresher, slyer, slicker, more articulate series of socio-political eye-swats than all of TV's so-called topical comedians harassing viewers; certainly he's more effective as the TV conscience of both Republicans and Democrats, and especially of John Lindsay, than 'That Was The Week That Was' attempted in its distended TV inanities. . . . Mostly spokesmen for either the left or right tend to be solemn asses; Buckley's sin is to be entertaining, with a wild serio-comic instinct for the jugular, doing his most glorious dirty work with a smile.

"Last night's supposedly three-sided Ch. 5 debate, 'The Run for Mayor,' in which Buckley won all honors in his customary 'Devastation Can Be Fun' thwack—at Lindsay, for the most part—was typical of what has become almost a new Marx Brothers comedy act, poor Lindsay winding up more like Zeppo, the brother who looked nice but never did anything; and with Abe Beame as a professional politician stating his cases straightforwardly, in attractively spunky style.

"Lindsay, who once seemed an up-and-smiling politician with good looks,

seems to have left all his best forensic tools at the studio make-up table. . . .
He was a cathedral of inattention to Beame's and Buckley's pertinent and
impertinent questions; his psychology, if we might bend a word and call
his aggressive blandness that, leads him to ignore Buckley as if he weren't
there, to fling generalities at Abe Beame, and to erupt occasionally in
hyper-thyroid threnodies patently polished in what Lindsay believes is a
Jack Kennedy Image; too bad of course that Bob Kennedy is a Beame man."
                —JACK O'BRIEN, New York *Journal-American,* October 11, 1965

Appendix G

Some Statistical Tables

(The figures and commentary are by David P. Stuhr)

1. Summary, Results of 1965 New York Mayoralty Elections

TOTAL VOTES CAST

COUNTY	JVL (GOP)	JVL (Lib.)*	JVL (Total)	ADB (Dem.)
Queens	258,932	72,230	331,162	235,478
Kings	231,309	77,089	308,398	343,108
Richmond	33,625	3,523	37,148	22,239
New York	211,192	80,134	291,326	181,183
Bronx	132,252	48,820	181,072	201,101
City-wide	867,310	281,796	1,149,106	983,109

Percentage of the Total, Three Major Candidates

Queens	36.8	10.3	47.1	33.5
Kings	30.0	10.0	40.0	44.5
Richmond	41.5	4.3	45.8	27.4
New York	40.4	15.3	55.8	34.7
Bronx	28.8	10.6	39.5	43.8
City-wide	34.2	11.1	45.3	38.8

* Includes Independent Citizens vote.
** Civil Service Fusion.
*** Percentage of total (all candidates) received by the three major candidates

326

ADB (C.S.F.)**	ADB (Total)	WFB (Cons.)	TOTAL (3 major candidates)	TOTAL (all candidates)
15,184	250,662	121,544	703,368	731,775
23,252	365,360	97,679	771,437	809,359
1,228	23,467	20,451	81,066	84,505
12,047	193,230	37,694	522,250	545,754
12,879	213,980	63,858	458,910	481,058
63,590	1,046,699	341,226	2,537,031	2,652,451

				Percentage Of Total***
2.2	35.6	17.3	100.0	96.1
2.9	47.4	12.7	100.0	95.3
1.5	28.9	25.2	100.0	95.9
2.3	37.0	7.2	100.0	95.7
2.8	46.4	13.9	100.0	95.4
2.5	41.3	13.4	100.0	95.6

2. Registration by Party

COUNTY	GOP	Democratic	Liberal	Conservative	TOTAL (4 major parties)	TOTAL (all parties)
Queens	220,076	591,753	13,469	5,108	830,406	893,266
Kings	179,816	767,751	20,935	4,311	972,813	1,029,791
Richmond	29,134	64,612	574	1,013	95,333	99,867
New York	139,229	464,820	14,424	2,393	620,866	682,731
Bronx	93,891	429,542	12,468	2,740	538,641	576,034
City-wide	662,146	2,318,478	61,870	15,565	3,058,059	3,281,689

Percentage of the Total, Four Major Parties

Queens	26.5	71.3	1.6	.6	100.0	93.0
Kings	18.5	78.9	2.2	.4	100.0	94.5
Richmond	30.6	67.8	.6	1.1	100.0	95.5
New York	22.4	74.9	2.3	.4	100.0	90.9
Bronx	17.4	79.7	2.3	.5	100.0	93.5
City-wide	21.7	75.8	2.0	.5	100.0	93.2

3. Religious and Ethnic Distribution of Population

Percentage Based on 1960 Census

COUNTY	Protestant	R. Catholic	Jewish	Italian	Other Central Eur.*
Queens	22.8	55.3	19.7	11.2	13.5
Kings	20.6	43.3	33.9	14.2	18.6
Richmond	24.3	68.3	5.2	14.9	4.5
New York	32.7	47.5	17.6	5.2	10.9
Bronx	15.2	47.4	35.2	11.4	17.3
City-wide	23.0	48.4	26.5	11.0	15.1

	German	Irish	U.K.	Non-White	Puerto Rican
Queens	7.4	4.5	2.8	8.5	.9
Kings	2.1	2.7	1.8	14.3	6.8
Richmond	9.1	4.1	3.2	4.5	1.4
New York	4.5	3.9	2.3	24.4	10.6
Bronx	3.5	5.9	2.1	11.4	13.1
City-wide	4.2	4.0	2.2	14.3	7.9

* Russian, Austrian, Polish.

4. The New York Daily News Poll and the Vote

In the table below a comparison is made between the final New York *Daily News* poll results and the actual vote. Figures are shown for each county and for the city-wide vote. A third column records the number of percentage points which the candidate gained or lost over the final *News* poll results. A minus sign indicates the candidate lost strength between the last poll and Election Day.

It is apparent that Buckley lost strength in every county between the last poll and Election Day. The attrition of voters can probably be attributed to the voter's desire, in the final analysis, to have his vote count for one or the other of the two major candidates and thus exercise a direct influence in the selection of the next mayor.

It is interesting to note that Buckley's lost votes did not all go to Lindsay.

5. Eleventh-Hour Changes in the Vote
(based on final New York Daily News Poll)

COUNTY	LINDSAY Actual	LINDSAY News Poll	LINDSAY Diff.	BEAME Actual	BEAME News Poll	BEAME Diff.
Queens	47.1%	43.3%	+3.8%	35.6%	34.5%	+1.1%
Kings	40.0	38.3	+1.2	47.4	43.7	+3.7
Richmond	45.8	38.1	+7.7	28.9	30.7	−1.8
New York	55.8	48.8	+7.0	37.0	40.3	−3.3
Bronx	39.5	38.9	+0.6	46.6	42.9	+3.7
Total (Avg.)	45.3%	42.0%	+3.3%	41.3%	40.0%	+1.3%

6. Selected Assembly Districts

Listed below are seven Assembly Districts in which Buckley lost a very substantial part of his support between the last polls and the election:

A.D.	BUCKLEY Trib. Poll	BUCKLEY News Poll	BUCKLEY Actual	LINDSAY News Poll	LINDSAY Actual
Queens 30	18.4%	13.9%	7.0%	50.4%	53.2%
Kings 44	23.4	21.8	13.0	32.9	34.1
Kings 53	16.5	25.5	10.4	45.1	43.8
Richmond 64	40.0	35.7	27.8	36.2	45.2
Richmond 65	31.8	31.0	23.2	39.5	46.7
Manhattan 72	16.6	12.9	7.8	66.5	77.6
Bronx 88	24.3	23.7	16.4	28.4	36.6

In both the Bronx and Brooklyn (Kings), Beame picked up more of the Buckley defectors than did Lindsay (6 to 1 and 3.5 to 1 respectively). In Queens, Lindsay took 3.5 of Buckley's votes to every one Beame took. In Richmond (Staten Island) and New York (Manhattan), Lindsay picked up votes from both Beame and Buckley.

The over-all (city-wide) defection from Buckley to the other candidates was about 2.5 to 1 in favor of Lindsay. This suggests that more of the voters who left Buckley were drawn to the position that Lindsay was the "last best hope," rather than to the position that Lindsay was a threat to the two-party system. It is probable that a very large percentage of these last-minute vote switchers were Republicans who preferred Buckley but wanted to make their vote count, hence switched to Lindsay.

| BUCKLEY | | |
Actual	News Poll	Diff.
17.3%	22.2%	−4.9%
12.7	17.5	−4.8
25.2	31.2	−6.0
7.2	10.9	−3.7
13.9	18.2	−4.3
13.4%	18.2%	−4.8%

| BEAME | |
News Poll	Actual
35.7%	39.8%
45.5	52.9
29.4	45.7
28.1	27.0
29.5	30.1
20.6	14.5
47.9	47.0

6. Selected Assembly Districts—Notes

Only in the Queens A.D. did both candidates split the Buckley vote; in the two Kings A.D.s Beame took the Buckley vote; in the Richmond and Bronx A.D.s Lindsay took the Buckley vote; and in the Manhattan A.D. Lindsay took the Buckley vote and the Beame vote. The Manhattan district in question is Lindsay's own Congressional District, which explains Lindsay's good showing. In general Lindsay picked up Buckley's votes in the more Republican districts, while Beame picked up Buckley's votes in the more Democratic districts. The conclusion to be drawn from these data is that there was not a one-way movement of the Buckley vote to one or the other candidate, but that the movement was significantly correlated to the party registration figures.

Since Lindsay acquired WFB defectors at a rate of 2.5 to 1 on a city-wide basis, and since the more heavily Republican Assembly Districts showed the greatest switch from WFB to Lindsay, it is clear that WFB lost many more Republicans at the last minute than he did Democrats. In this sense WFB "helped" Beame. If he had kept these votes, Lindsay would have been in a much tighter race. (The total WFB loss represented about 125,000 votes of which 35,000 went to Beame, 90,000 to Lindsay.) If WFB had held all his votes, Lindsay would still have won the election—but by only 47,000, instead of 102,000, votes.

7. Actual Results Compared with WCBS-TV–Louis Harris Vote Profile Analysis

(A total of 40 Election Districts were polled by WCBS-TV; 11 in Queens County, 13 in Kings, 1 in Richmond, 8 in Manhattan, and 7 in the Bronx.)

COUNTY	LINDSAY Actual	V.P.A.	Diff.	BEAME Actual	V.P.A.	Diff.
Queens	47.1%	45.1%	+2.0%	35.6%	35.4%	+0.2%
Kings	40.0	41.6	−1.6	47.4	44.9	+2.5
Richmond	45.8	*	*	28.9	*	*
New York	55.8	49.5	+6.3	37.0	44.2	−7.2
Bronx	39.5	39.5	0.0	46.6	45.5	+1.1
City-wide	45.3%	43.8%	+1.5%	41.3%	42.3%	−1.0%

	BUCKLEY Actual	V.P.A.	Diff.
Queens	17.3%	19.0%	−1.7%
Kings	12.7	12.4	+0.3
Richmond	25.2	*	*
New York	7.2	5.6	+1.6
Bronx	13.9	13.6	+0.3
City-wide	13.4%	12.9%	+0.5%

*VPA polled only one election district in Richmond and included the results in their figures for Kings County.

The accuracy of Vote Profile Analysis depends on the proper interpretation of the results of intensive surveying of representative Election Districts of the city's population. The above results indicate that the WCBS-TV survey was reasonably accurate except in Manhattan, where more voters voted for Lindsay (and a few more for Buckley). This does not necessarily mean that voters switched from Beame to Lindsay; instead it indicates that the experts who analyzed the survey results misjudged the meaning of their sample results and weighed them improperly.

Bearing in mind the limitation of VPA the following ethnic vote estimates
have been made by WCBS-TV:

8. Religious and Ethnic Distribution (according to VPA—see above):

Ethnic Group	No. of E.D.s polled by VPA:	Lindsay	Beame	Buckley
Jewish (Manhattan)	7	49.3%	47.1%	3.4%
Jewish (Kings-Bronx)	5	34.8	61.1	3.6
Italian	7	40.7	40.1	17.8
Irish	4	40.4	37.5	21.9
Other Catholic (Central European)	4	33.5	39.5	26.2
German (Lutheran)	2	50.4	22.5	26.3
"WASP"	5	60.9	15.9	22.6
Negro	5	42.4	54.9	1.1
Puerto Rican	1	24.5	72.4	2.9

9. Twelve Assembly Districts in Which Buckley Attracted His Highest Percentage of the Vote:

A.D. No.	County	WFB percentage	Percent G.O.P. Registration	Description
94	Bronx	27.1	29.5	Parkchester-City Island-Pelham Bay
23	Queens	26.8	37.9	Ridgewood-Glendale
60	Kings	26.7	36.5	Bay Ridge
64	Richmond	26.7	30.3	Fox Hills-Richmond-Tottenville
25	Queens	24.7	31.0	Woodhaven-Ozone Park
29	Queens	24.1	38.3	Hollis-Queens Village-Bellerose
31	Queens	23.8	35.5	Richmond Hill-Jamaica
27	Queens	23.1	34.5	Bayside-Douglaston-Little Neck
65	Richmond	22.2	28.2	West Brighton Pt.-Richmond-Travis
93	Bronx	21.6	28.3	Woodlawn-Baychester-Morris Park
61	Kings	21.5	31.5	Brooklyn Heights-Prospect Park
59	Kings	21.4	32.8	Bay Ridge-Bath Beach

The Buckley vote was mostly Republican. If this listing is compared with the most heavily registered Republican Assembly Districts we find that all twelve of them are among the fifteen Assembly Districts with the highest percentage of Republican registration. The other three "high GOP Registration districts" are all in the Manhattan Silk Stocking District, the home of John Lindsay. The correlation is exact between the most Republican and the highest WFB vote Assembly Districts (ignoring Lindsay's home Congressional District), and therefore it is virtually certain that the Buckley vote came to a very large degree from Republicans and not from Democrats as has so often been suggested. (Apply the same test to Gerosa's vote of 1961; only half of his best districts are among the highest Republican registration districts.)

10. Miscellaneous Data:

Lawrence Gerosa, the conservative Democrat whose showing in 1961 as an independent candidate for mayor (321,604 votes) is often compared to Buckley's, out-polled Mayor Wagner when he was running for re-election in 1957, when he (Gerosa) was running for Comptroller, by 17,056 votes.

Lindsay spent $2.24 per voter.

Beame spent $2.08 per voter.

Buckley spent $.72 per voter.

Buckley's vote was 51.1 per cent as large as the total number of registered Republicans in New York City.

The New York World's Fair conducted a mayoralty poll in which only New Yorkers were (theoretically) permitted to participate. The (cumulative) results on the closing day of the poll were: Lindsay 41.5 per cent, Beame 23.8 per cent, Buckley 34.7 per cent.

Index